JOHN HUSTON:

COURAGE AND ART

BOOKS BY JEFFREY MEYERS

BIOGRAPHY

A Fever at the Core: The Idealist in Politics
Married to Genius
Katherine Mansfield
The Enemy: A Biography of Wyndham Lewis
Hemingway
Manic Power: Robert Lowell and His Circle
D. H. Lawrence
Joseph Conrad
Edgar Allan Poe: His Life and Legacy
Scott Fitzgerald
Edmund Wilson
Robert Frost
Bogart: A Life in Hollywood
Gary Cooper: American Hero
Privileged Moments: Encounters with Writers
Wintry Conscience: A Biography of George Orwell
Inherited Risk: Errol and Sean Flynn in Hollywood and Vietnam
Somerset Maugham
*Impressionist Quartet: The Intimate Genius of
Manet and Morisot, Degas and Cassatt*
Modigliani
Samuel Johnson: The Struggle
The Genius and the Goddess: Arthur Miller and Marilyn Monroe

CRITICISM

Fiction and the Colonial Experience
The Wounded Spirit: T. E. Lawrence's Seven Pillars of Wisdom

A Reader's Guide to George Orwell
Painting and the Novel
Homosexuality and Literature
D. H. Lawrence and the Experience of Italy
Disease and the Novel
The Spirit of Biography
Hemingway: Life into Art
Orwell: Life and Art

BIBLIOGRAPHY

T. E. Lawrence: A Bibliography
Catalogue of the Library of the Late Siegfried Sassoon
George Orwell: An Annotated Bibliography of Criticism

EDITED COLLECTIONS

George Orwell: The Critical Heritage
Hemingway: The Critical Heritage
Robert Lowell: Interviews and Memoirs
The Sir Arthur Conan Doyle Reader
The W. Somerset Maugham Reader

EDITED ORIGINAL ESSAYS

Wyndham Lewis: A Revaluation
Wyndham Lewis by Roy Campbell
D. H. Lawrence and Tradition
The Legacy of D. H. Lawrence
The Craft of Literary Biography
The Biographer's Art
T. E. Lawrence: Soldier, Writer, Legend
Graham Greene: A Revaluation

JOHN HUSTON:

COURAGE AND ART

JEFFREY MEYERS

CROWN
ARCHETYPE
NEW YORK

Published in the United States by Crown Archetype,
an imprint of the Crown Publishing Group,
a division of Random House, Inc., New York.
www.crownpublishing.com

Crown Archetype with colophon is a trademark of
Random House, Inc.

Library of Congress Cataloging-in-Publication Data
Meyers, Jeffrey.
    John Huston: courage and art / Jeffrey Meyers.—1st ed.
        p. cm.
    Includes bibliographical references and index.
    1. Huston, John, 1906–1987. 2. Motion picture producers
and directors—United States—Biography. I. Title.
PN1998.3H87M49   2011
791.4302'33092—dc22
    [B]   2010047642

ISBN 978-0-307-59067-1
eISBN 978-0-307-59069-5

Printed in the United States of America

JACKET DESIGN BY WHITNEY COOKMAN
JACKET PHOTOGRAPHY: (front, spine) *Chinatown* © Photofest,
The Treasure of the Sierra Madre © The Everett Collection,
The African Queen and *The Maltese Falcon* © Photofest;
(back) © Maureen Lambray

10 9 8 7 6 5 4 3 2 1

First Edition

CONTENTS

viii   *Contents*

ILLUSTRATIONS

ACKNOWLEDGMENTS

John Huston would be worth a biography even if he'd never made a film. I am pleased to acknowledge the generous and always illuminating help I received from many people who knew him. For interviews I would like to thank Jacqueline Bisset, Seamus Byrne, Barnaby Conrad, Carter De Haven III, Charles Elliott, Hampton Fancher III, Frances FitzGerald, Michael Fitzgerald, Guy Gallo, Leonard Gardner, William Gardner, Eloise Hardt, Patrick Hemingway, John Hurt, Allegra Huston, Celeste Huston, Danny Huston, Stacy Keach, Pancho Kohner, Susan Kohner, Jan Lavender, Joseph McBride, Walter Mirisch, Michael Parks, Tim Pigott-Smith, Janet Roach, Zoe Sallis, Wieland Schulz-Keil, Roberto Silvi, Thom Steinbeck, Curtice Taylor, Penelope Tree, Anna van der Heide, Bayard Veiller, Christine Viertel and Susannah York. Charles Elliott, Guy Gallo, Celeste Huston, Zoe Sallis and Anna van der Heide—a newly discovered lover—also sent valuable material.

I previously interviewed (many of them now gone) Lesley Black, Jack Cardiff, Sir Patrick Leigh Fermor, Afdera Fonda, Evelyn Keyes, Ring Lardner, Jr., Joseph Losey, Arthur Miller, Ivan Moffat, Inge Morath, Oswald Morris, Vincent Sherman, Peter Viertel and Sir John Woolf. For letters I am grateful to Angela Allen, Albert Finney, Robert Gottlieb, Julie Harris, Anjelica Huston, Tony Huston and Edna O'Brien.

Many friends and colleagues made useful introductions; provided new medical, legal and cinematic information; and sent films, books, articles and unpublished papers: Dr. Ellen Alkon, Paul Alkon, Rudy Behlmer, Mary Berg, Lesley Brill, William Chace, Allen Cohen, Lisa Coletta, Denis Donoghue, Rory Flynn, Robert Freeman, Kevin

Froggatt, Andrew Gordon, Valerie Hemingway, Norman Holland, Annette Insdorf, Darin Jensen, Francis King, Thomas Kuhnke, Harry Lawton, Patrick McGilligan, Mario Menocal, Rachel Meyers, David Peoples, Claude Potts, Loren Rothschild, Caroline Seebohm, Paul Sidey, Paul Tiessen and Tony Tracy.

I did my most extensive research in the Huston papers at the Herrick Library of the Academy of Motion Picture Arts and Sciences in Beverly Hills, California (Jenny Romero and Stacey Behlmer). These papers span the years 1932–81, encompass sixty-three linear feet and reveal what problems Huston encountered and how his films were made. The archive consists of production files, including script material and research, correspondence and subject files. They contain material related to both produced and unrealized projects, including budgets, employment agreements, casting information, shooting schedules, interoffice memos, cutting notes, censorship correspondence, publicity clippings and reviews. I also received important material from the Bibliothèque Nationale, Paris (Clélia Guillemot); *Bien Public,* Dijon (Jean Viansson Ponte); Carson McCullers Center for Writers, Columbus, Georgia; Department of the Army; FBI, for Huston's once-secret files; *Film Comment;* German Film Institute, Berlin; J. Paul Getty Museum; *GQ: Gentlemen's Quarterly;* Harry Ransom Humanities Research Center, Austin, Texas; Hemingway Collection, John F. Kennedy Library, Boston (Samuel Smallidge); *Interview* magazine; Legion of Honor Museum, San Francisco; Los Angeles Superior Court; National Personnel Records Center, St. Louis; Nevada, Missouri, Public Library; Pacific Film Archive, Berkeley; Schlesinger Library, Radcliffe Institute, Harvard University; Sotheby's, New York; St. Clerans Hotel, Craughwell, County Galway, Ireland; UCLA Library; Warner Bros. Archive, University of Southern California Library (Ned Comstock); Vernon County Historical Society, Nevada, Missouri (Patrick Brophy); *Vogue Paris* (Stéphane Durand); and Wisconsin Historical Society. The library of the University of California, Berkeley, has been a lifelong resource. The translations from Latin, French, Italian and Spanish are my own.

My agent, Ellen Levine of Trident Media, secured the contract. My wife, Valerie Meyers, provided vital help with the archival research and personal interviews. With sound judgment and critical perception she also scrutinized and improved each chapter, and compiled the index.

Rather than moralizing about Huston's conduct, I would urge readers to take pleasure in his impressive achievements.

To

PAUL THEROUX

I am tormented with an everlasting itch
for things remote. I love to sail forbidden
seas, and land on barbarous coasts.

—MELVILLE, "Loomings," *Moby-Dick*

JOHN HUSTON:

Courage and Art

HUSTON AND HEMINGWAY

Andrew Sarris called Huston "a Hemingway character lost in a Dostoyevsky novel." Norman Mailer—who portrayed Huston as Charles Eitel in *The Deer Park* (1955)—observed that he is "the only celebrated film artist to bear comparison with Hemingway. His life celebrates a style more important to him than film." In an interview Huston said of Hemingway, "I was very influenced by his writing and by his thinking . . . his values, his reassessment of the things that make life go."[1] These suggestive statements merely hint at the striking parallels between the two men. Both sought to live a life filled with the action, adventure and romance they created in their work. Keen sportsmen who courted danger and took risks, they enjoyed early success, cultivated a Byronic persona, and knew the satisfactions of celebrity and the perils of fame. Hemingway's character, virile ethos and code of honor strongly influenced Huston, whose best films can be thematically defined by Hemingway's titles: *Men Without Women* and *Winner Take Nothing*.

· I ·

Both Hemingway and Huston had grandfathers who fought with the Union Army in the Civil War, and both self-educated men were born in the Midwest at the turn of the century: Hemingway in 1899, Huston in 1906. Their mothers had dominant personalities and professional careers. Both men refused to attend college, set out to learn from direct experience in the world, lived in Paris in their twenties and began their writing careers as journalists. Both were enthusiastic about Latin culture: Hemingway about Spain and tropical Cuba, Huston about tropical Mexico, where he made four movies and spent the last years of his life. In *The Night of the Iguana* the Mexican hotel, which the tourists led by Richard Burton choose to bypass, is named for the Ambos Mundos—Hemingway's hangout in Havana.

Both were powerful boxers in their youth and later life, and were always eager to get into a punch-up about an insulting remark. Hemingway's opponents included Ezra Pound, William Carlos Williams and the Canadian novelist Morley Callaghan, with Scott Fitzgerald as incompetent timekeeper. The young Huston won twenty-three out of twenty-five amateur bouts, breaking his nose in one of them, and became a ranking California lightweight before abandoning the sport. Both were heavy drinkers, but did not let alcohol interfere with their work.

Huston shared with Hemingway a fascination with cruelty, wounds and death. Hemingway witnessed these things as a Red Cross volunteer on the Italian front in World War I; Huston rode with Mexican cavalry in his early twenties. Both participated in fierce fighting in World War II in Europe, Hemingway as a war correspondent, Huston as a documentary filmmaker. They enjoyed testing their own courage in difficult situations and liked to subject their friends to danger to see how they'd react. Their overpowering personalities dominated everyone around them. Hemingway constantly challenged competitors; Huston took great risks with the health and lives of his actors and crew. On separate occasions both men intimidated Tennessee Williams with their aggressive machismo.

Hemingway and Huston felt compelled to demonstrate their toughness and strength. Huston followed Hemingway, made his own way through the Master's tumultuous wake and practiced the same dangerous masculine pursuits: bicycle racing, horseback riding (and betting on horses), marlin fishing, bullfighting and hunting elephants and big cats. In December 1954 a friend wrote that the forty-eight-year-old Huston had actually "fought a bull in Madrid, made quite a few good passes and has the photos to prove it."

The Maharajah of Cooch Behar, a bullfight aficionado and friend of Hemingway, organized a tiger hunt in Assam, in the foothills of the Himalayas, for Huston. On August 25, 1955, Huston sent an enthusiastic cable to Clark Gable, a keen hunter, urging him to join their expedition: "Am seizing opportunity and joining Maharajah of Cooch Behar hunt on 18th. This last of great hunts sixty elephants all the trimmings. Only be four guns. One gun still open. Would you like me to make res for you." Gable, confined by a movie contract, was forced to refuse.

After Huston had climbed the ladder to the shooting platform on his elephant, the huge beast (he wrote) "suddenly began to trumpet . . . and out came [the tiger], fast as a flaring bird. . . . As I pulled the trigger, my elephant swayed wildly, throwing me to one side. I fired again, knowing I'd miss, as the yellow-and-black devil darted away into the brush. . . . He'd covered 200 yards in under 10 seconds." Though Huston missed his first shot, he got his second and bagged a tiger that was eight and a half feet long. In Peter Viertel's novel *White Hunter, Black Heart* (1953), the character based on Huston says that Hemingway's "Francis Macomber experiences the greatest sensation of his life after he has killed his first buffalo. He has overcome fear. We're after those same sensations."[2]

Both men, for all their obsession with courage, danger and the elemental struggles of mankind, had romantic natures and domestic inclinations. Hemingway had four wives, Huston had five (and all his marriages ended badly). Hemingway shot a lion; his fourth wife ate lion; Huston's fifth wife boldly *rode* a lion—and has the photos to prove it. Each married increasingly younger women and, while married, fell in love with a series of women even younger than their wives. Huston, however, was unashamedly promiscuous, while Hemingway was a guilt-ridden serial monogamist. Both had three children and were difficult, demanding and frequently absent fathers. Both owned large houses, retreats from the world, to display their trophy wives and hunting trophies, and both had fine collections of modern paintings. Hemingway had a grand house in Key West, and then the Finca Vigía near Havana, and owned works by Klee, Gris, Braque, Miró, Masson and several valuable bullfight posters. Huston owned St. Clerans, his

Georgian mansion in Ireland, where he displayed works by Klee, Gris, Monet, Modigliani, Chaim Soutine and several nightlife posters by Lautrec.

The novelist and screenwriter Peter Viertel, their mutual friend, introduced the eccentric and ebullient Huston to Hemingway in May 1948, when Huston was in Havana to make *We Were Strangers* (1949), a movie about Cuban revolutionaries. At the time Viertel was more worried about Huston's response than Hemingway's. "I was never quite sure how [Huston] would react in any given situation," Viertel recalled. "I knew he could be violent if provoked." But Huston loved trials, hardships and disasters, and was soon given the chance to test his strength and courage. At first Hemingway challenged him to a boxing match and threatened to "cool" the gangling lightweight. Anticipating Huston's tactics, he said, "With those long arms you might just stand off and keep jabbing me in the nose, mightn't you? Maybe cut me up?" Huston chivalrously replied, "I wouldn't dream of doing that, Papa." But the match did not come off. Mary Hemingway told Huston that Papa was ill and begged him not to fight.

Inevitably the two, so similar in character, engaged in a competitive test. Hemingway invited Huston and Viertel on his boat, the *Pilar*, where they discussed Havana and war, writing and potential movie deals. Huston shot an iguana from the boat, and Hemingway insisted he retrieve it. Huston and Viertel searched for it in the crevices of the rocks and saw some spots of blood, but gave up after forty minutes and swam back to the boat. Though dissatisfied with their inept performance, Hemingway did not send them back. Instead, he himself searched for two more hours, among the rocks and under the blazing sun, found the wounded iguana, put a bullet through its head and brought back the hideous trophy.

It may have seemed pointless, even foolish, to search through burning rocks for a dying iguana instead of enjoying the tropical breeze, cool shade and icy drinks on his boat. But the arduous quest was an important example of Hemingway's personal courage, showy endurance, sense of duty and moral lesson to his younger disciples. In this Day of the Iguana episode, Hemingway also meant to humiliate

Huston by showing that he was (though seven years older) a tougher man who lived by his own virile code. In *Green Hills of Africa* (1935), Hemingway—wounded in the Great War—justified his passion for hunting when he identified with his wounded prey. He remarked, "I did nothing that had not been done to me. I had been shot and I had been crippled and gotten away."[3]

Huston liked the challenge of shooting his films in distant and difficult locales, and his reading of Hemingway had drawn him to Africa. The burning of the missionary outpost in *The African Queen* (1951) was filmed in Butiaba, near Lake Albert and Murchison Falls in Uganda, where Hemingway had two plane crashes (and was reported dead) in January 1954. Hemingway's pilot, Roy Marsh, was the same former RAF officer who'd flown Huston around central Africa. And the *Murchison*, the boat that rescued Hemingway after a plane crash, was the same one that Huston had rented while making *The African Queen*.

Huston always tried to keep in touch. In 1954, amid his hectic film schedule, he reminded himself: "11:00. Call Papa—Palace Hotel, Madrid." Later that year, on November 21, he congratulated Hemingway on winning the Nobel Prize and mentioned the overwhelming problems on his current picture: "*Moby Dick* is a tough one to make. I have been at the actual shooting four months now and don't see daylight even yet. Misfortunes multiply as we go along; the only thing that hasn't happened yet is for somebody to get killed"—though there were a few close calls. In 1956, when *Moby Dick* was released, an English journalist, sensing the parallels between Hemingway's work and Huston's films, parodied the style of *The Old Man and the Sea* when describing his adaptation of Melville's novel: "He was an old Huston who filmed alone, and he had gone many days now without making a film. . . . 'I fear the Dick of Moby,' the boy said, 'It is difficult to make and will cost many dollars.' 'I do not fear,' said the old Huston, 'I know many tricks and I have faith.' "

Huston had suggested a meeting before he read the Pulitzer Prize–winning *Old Man and the Sea* (actually, one of Hemingway's worst books). On the last day of 1956, he apologetically wrote: "It seemed to me, before starting one of your finest books, I should talk or anyway have a drink with you. I even imagined that you would consider my not coming to see you a rudeness. . . . In any case, there was no thought in my mind of asking for your help on the screenplay. I mean, I only wanted to come in and get warm."[4] (He didn't want to seem as rude as David O. Selznick, who had infuriated Hemingway by failing to stand up when his wife Mary came into the room. But Hemingway did not know that Selznick, in his underwear, had good reason to stay seated.) Huston was one of the best screenwriters in the business; Hemingway had never written a screenplay (and was proud of it). But Huston—who deferred to no one but his actor-father, Walter Huston—felt obliged to assume an extremely deferential tone with the hypersensitive novelist and assure him that he was *not* seeking help with a script. Aware of Hemingway's touchiness and competitiveness, and admiring his writing, Huston had a unique relationship with him.

Though they met only a few times and corresponded rarely, Huston (with some exaggeration) claimed that Hemingway "was a very close personal friend of mine." He then nailed down Hemingway's impact: his values, ideals and courage. "I've enormous admiration for Hemingway," he said, "and to my generation he was a great influence. . . . Hemingway laid down a certain set of standards for my time, standards of behavior. He made some effort to describe tastes and the good things of life and put them down on record, evaluating their importance. . . . It was important for a man to be brave and have valor. . . . They influenced my generation to the point of being . . . almost a new religion."

When Hemingway committed suicide, Huston "approved completely." He felt that if Hemingway could not live a heroic life, it was better not to live at all. Better, Huston felt, to die while sane than exist while crazy: "He knew he was on the way out; his mind was gone. Papa had been having persecution complexes, phobias, and life was dreadful for him. He had a moment or two of sanity and killed himself in one of those moments."[5]

· II ·

Both Hemingway and Huston admired Kipling, a major influence on their work. His example encouraged them to develop a sceptical and stoical, colloquial and belligerently masculine style, with speech and gestures cut down to a minimum. Their best work, *The Sun Also Rises* and *The Maltese Falcon,* remains as fresh and alive as the day it first appeared. Huston, director of Kipling's *The Man Who Would Be King,* was repeatedly drawn to a group of intensely masculine writers—Melville, Crane, Kipling and Hemingway—whose adventurous heroes stood at a slight angle to the universe. Huston's own early fiction portrayed this type of character, who often reappeared in his films, embodied certain American values and changed the way Americans saw themselves.

Huston's two boxing stories—"Fool" (March 1929) and "Figures of Fighting Men" (May 1931)—published in H. L. Mencken's prestigious *American Mercury,* were strongly influenced by Hemingway's prose style, bitter stoicism and theme of victory in defeat. In the second story Huston wrote that "a second-rater dipped his gloves in rosin and rubbed them in the old-timer's eyes during a clinch. His sight was ruined, but his fighting days were not over. Now he showed them he could take it. He became a punching bag in the small clubs. His pretty-boy face was knocked lop-sided. In a few months he was one of the old men of the ring."

The blasphemy at the end of the first story—the idea that Christ and Judas were in cahoots and the Crucifixion was fixed—recalls the blasphemy in Hemingway's playlet "Today Is Friday" (1926), in which three Roman soldiers callously discuss the Crucifixion in a modern idiom. Huston later made an excellent picture about washed-up boxers, *Fat City* (1972), whose final scene was influenced by "A Clean, Well-Lighted Place." James Agee, Huston's most perceptive critic, alluded to Hemingway's famous phrase "grace under pressure" and seemed to be talking about the novelist when describing Huston's films: "His movies have centered on men under pressure, have usually involved violence and have occasionally verged on a kind of romanticism about danger."

Most of Huston's films were adaptations of serious novels. As a reader, writer and director with a powerful connection to literature, Huston liked to quote Hemingway's views on writing. "There was no greater feeling in the world," Hemingway said, "than anchoring your words firmly on paper . . . when the words took wing."[6] Comparing

Hemingway to his leading contemporary, Huston told the screenwriter of *Under the Volcano* (1984) that Hemingway's work was essential to his own filmmaking: "Scott Fitzgerald is not as visceral as Hemingway, who gets you into the scenes, not just into the words." He later added that Hemingway had an uncanny ability to bring scenes and characters to life: "Certain American writers have . . . a peculiar ability to re-create, to make you feel that you are actually present in something. If Hemingway had anything, he had that."[7] This was the great goal of twentieth-century moviemaking: to give the audience an even more intimate and immediate connection with the characters and action on the screen than readers could have with a novel.

Huston specialized in movies about male comradeship during violent conflict: *The Treasure of the Sierra Madre* (1948), *The Red Badge of Courage* (1951), *Moby Dick* (1956), *The Man Who Would Be King* (1975) and *Victory* (1981). Hemingway was also a great admirer of Stephen Crane's work and of the coarse-grained texture and white sky of the Mathew Brady photographs that inspired both the novel and Huston's film. In his introduction to *Men at War* Hemingway observed: "Crane wrote [*The Red Badge of Courage*] before he had ever seen any war. But he had read the contemporary accounts, he had heard the old soldiers, they were not so old then, talk, and above all he had seen Mathew Brady's wonderful photographs. Creating his story out of this material he wrote that great boy's dream of war that was to be truer to how war is than any war the boy who wrote it would ever live to see. It is one of the finest books of our literature."

The Killers (1946), directed by Robert Siodmak, could have been an ordinary film noir. But, elevated by the screenplay written by Huston with his friend and longtime collaborator Anthony Veiller, it became an important picture. It was the only film based on his work that Hemingway actually liked. In Hemingway's story (which reads like a screenplay) the killers, awaiting the arrival of their victim, taunt and intimidate the workers in a diner with a series of challenging insults that require immediate assent. One of the killers—imitating gangster movies like *Little Caesar* (1930) and *The Public Enemy* (1931)—tells the counterman

George, "Ever go to the movies? . . . You ought to go to the movies more. The movies are fine for a bright boy like you."

In the film version Huston re-created Hemingway's hardened hero, torn between ironic fatalism and despairing courage, who seeks authentic values and adheres to a strict code of honor. *The Killers* opens as the gangsters enter a diner that recalls a classic Edward Hopper painting. They are not smartly dressed, as in the story, but make a lot of menacing wisecracks. The workers, who are frightened and don't understand what's going on, are ironically called "bright boys." The haunted victim, played by Burt Lancaster, is about to be murdered for stealing the gang's money after a successful robbery (rather than for failing to throw a fight and betraying the gamblers, as in the story). Just before his death Lancaster, with stoic resignation, says, "There's nothing I can do about it. . . . Once I did something wrong. . . . I'm through with all that runnin' around." After he's killed, the insurance investigator, played by Edmond O'Brien, discovers through a series of flashbacks the reason for his death.

Huston planned to make another movie based on three Hemingway stories, to be directed by himself and two Europeans: his mentor William Wyler and his friend Billy Wilder—a strange choice for a work by Hemingway. On July 5, 1954 Huston wrote to his longtime agent, Paul Kohner, "I would be delighted to do either 'Fifty Grand' or 'The Undefeated.' Now it's up to them to make their choices." These stories of courageous losers had a strong appeal to many readers. In "Fifty Grand" (1927) an aging boxer bets $50,000 against himself in a hopeless match. He almost wins when he's fouled by a painful low blow, but survives to lose the fight and win his bet. In "The Undefeated" (1925, also in *Men Without Women*) an old wounded bullfighter attempts a comeback in a Madrid night fight. Though tossed twice and gored, he kills the bull on the sixth try and is rushed to the hospital. " 'I was going good,' Manuel said weakly. 'I was going great. . . . I didn't have any luck. That was all.' "[8] Though the subject, style and theme of these stories were a perfect match for Huston, the movie—because of complications with the other directors—was never made.

In 1954 Huston tried to coax Hemingway, who staunchly resisted all temptations from Hollywood (and condemned Faulkner for swallowing the bait and selling out), to take part in another film based on the greatest bullfighter of the time: "I think the idea of you and Peter [Viertel] and me doing the one with [Luis Miguel] Dominguín is great and an absolute must." Huston, a keen aficionado, had also been considering Barnaby Conrad's bestselling *Matador* (1952), based on his career as an American bullfighter. But Huston told Kohner that he preferred the Hemingway project: "I don't think [*Matador*] would have the immediate and widespread appeal as *Death in the Afternoon by Ernest Hemingway*. And I believe Papa could be coaxed into doing the script himself or perhaps himself with Peter. If the three [Hemingway] stories idea falls by the wayside, I would like to aim for that. I couldn't guarantee it would come off, but, if it did, it would certainly be big medicine." The producer Harold Mirisch was keen on this idea and cabled Huston: "Everyone here terrifically enthusiastic over Hemingway idea. You have our blessings. Investigate possibilities of subject."[9] But Hemingway, who hated Hollywood, could not be coaxed and the project was dropped.

Huston was asked to direct *The Old Man and the Sea*, with a screenplay by Peter Viertel, "but couldn't see the old Cuban fisherman played by a [professional] actor, and the studio couldn't risk doing it without one." In 1958 the movie, leadenly directed by John Sturges, starred the rotund, red-faced and absurdly miscast Irish-American, Spencer Tracy, who owned the rights and was co-producer.

Despite these setbacks, Huston was still determined to direct a Hemingway film. The producer David Selznick, a kind-hearted companion and long-standing friend, wanted to remake *A Farewell to Arms* (the 1932 movie had starred Gary Cooper and Helen Hayes) with Rock Hudson and his own adored wife Jennifer Jones. The budget was $4.2 million, and Huston's unusually high fee was $250,000. On October 25, 1956, Selznick cabled Huston: "Could you concentrate wholly on *Farewell* [*to Arms*] until completion photography, after which believe you would feel safe leaving post-production, including editing, entirely in my hands?"

Far from feeling safe with Selznick, who wanted complete control and appropriated the power that traditionally belonged to the director, Huston sensed the danger and felt uneasy. Selznick, hand over heart, falsely claimed "there have been few books ever transcribed to the screen with the studied and loving care that [Ben] Hecht and I gave this one through many weary months." But Huston realized at the outset that their debased version had turned one of Hemingway's greatest novels into a banal and cliché-ridden romance. In his autobiography, *An Open Book,* Huston recalled, "From the moment I saw the script, David and I were in conflict. Through David's influence on Hecht, the Hemingway story had simply become a vehicle for the female lead— Jennifer Jones."[10] Well aware of the challenge, the strong-willed Huston pretended to agree with Selznick while plunging ahead and making the movie his own way.

Selznick's biographer remarked that Huston criticized all the material that was not in the novel and that Selznick and Hecht had put into their ninth draft. Following his habitual method, he insisted that "they should stay as close as possible to Hemingway's original scenes." In typical Hollywood fashion, which Huston strenuously opposed, Selznick had paid a fortune for a brilliant novel and then ruined it with his own inept additions. Selznick's biographer also explained the irreconcilable differences between the two powerful egos: "Huston liked to keep himself open to any new ideas he might have until just before shooting a scene, which meant that camera set-ups could be—and usually were—changed, lines of dialogue altered, blocking and other staging details revamped, thus giving his scenes an edgy, almost improvised spontaneity. Selznick, on the other hand, wanted as much control as possible." After spending an entire day working with three different secretaries, Selznick sent Huston a tedious and offensive sixteen-page memo that criticized Huston's careful planning and accused him of procrastination. His secretaries warned Selznick that the memo would have a disastrous effect, but he preferred to risk a showdown and sent the ultimatum:

> I should be less than candid with you [Selznick wrote] if I
> didn't tell you that I am most desperately unhappy about the

way things are going. It is an experience completely unique in my very long career. It is an experience that I feel is going to lead us, not to a better picture . . . but to a worse one.

Fervently as I want you to direct the picture, I would rather face the awful consequence of your not directing it than to go through what I am presently going through.

Though Selznick emphatically maintained, "I have learned that *nothing matters but the final picture,*" the only thing that really mattered to him was Jennifer Jones.

Before he'd finished reading the memo, Huston—generous, extravagant and always short of cash but unwilling to bend the knee—packed his bags, left the film and gave up the money. Unable to protect the integrity of the novel, he was immensely relieved to abandon the project, which he knew Hemingway would hate and would destroy their precious friendship. Huston was replaced by the plodding Charles Vidor. Released in 1957, the picture was a critical and commercial failure, and Hemingway never got the additional $100,000 that Selznick had promised to give him. In his response to this debacle, Huston quoted Hemingway's story about a picador's comments after his matador's disastrous performance: "There was a division of opinion. Some wanted to shit on his father, some wanted to shit on his mother."[11]

Though Huston had failed to direct a film by Hemingway, he did play him on the screen. In the early 1970s Huston took on the role of James Hannaford, a movie director modeled on himself and Hemingway in Orson Welles' *The Other Side of the Wind*. Welles had observed Hemingway and his followers at bullfights in Spain. But Welles, who had more unfinished projects than Leonardo da Vinci, never completed this picture.

Hemingway had been writing his Venetian novel, *Across the River and Into the Trees* (1950), his first book since the tremendously successful *For Whom the Bell Tolls* (1940), when he first met Huston, and they had discussed the possibility of making a film of the book. In 1975–76 Huston and his longtime mistress, secretary and collaborator, Gladys Hill, worked on a script of *Across the River,* which he planned to direct. He knew the difficulties—the book has no real action and a lot of repetitive scenes and boring dialogue—and explained that Hemingway "was trying something that didn't come off—it's an experiment, a kind of indulgence." He also told the *New York Times* that "the book, which was largely a disaster, is a dialogue between a colonel who is dying and a very young Italian girl. Papa was very dejected by the reception of the book and I've got correspondence from him [now lost] which was written when he was so down about it. I know the background, a lot of personal things. He really exposes himself in the book and it is hard to draw the line between Hemingway and the old colonel." Armed with inside knowledge, Huston cut to the essence of the novel. The film would show "the compassionate and sensitive side" of Hemingway and define "what it means to be a soldier."[12]

Even with all their considerable skill, Huston and Hill failed to animate the characters or dramatize these dead words and lifeless scenes. (I've tried to write the script myself; it can't be done.) Huston (awed by Hemingway) followed the novel too faithfully instead of inventing new scenes (as he had done in *The Killers*) to flesh out and vitalize the story. The 117-page typescript in the Herrick Library begins with Colonel Richard Cantwell driving in a jeep with Sergeant Jackson and remembering his past. There are flashbacks to battles in World War II; an allusion to duck shooting in the Venetian marshes; and a reference to the always obliging porter and bartender in the luxurious Hotel Gritti on the Grand Canal. There's a good deal of arch conversation, and scenes in the streets of Venice and in Harry's Bar. Cantwell talks to his friend Alvarito, meets the beautiful young aristocrat Renata (his rebirth) and asks her, "Would you ever like to run for Queen of Heaven?"

After another flashback to the war, Cantwell says, "I don't care about our losses—because the moon is our mother and our father." (Imitation bad Hemingway is even worse than real bad Hemingway.) Renata keeps asking him to recount his tedious war exploits. Thus encouraged, Cantwell disparages the generals who destroyed his career. When they dock at St. Mark's Square, Cantwell, despite his weak heart, gallantly punches two American sailors whom he thinks have made insulting remarks about his true love. He and Renata admire her portrait, which he has commissioned; and he ungallantly tells her younger sister Vittoria (Huston's invention), "You are so god-damned beautiful it's heart-breaking. Also, you are jail bait."

Well aware of his physical decline, Cantwell tells himself, "You are half a hundred years old, you beat up old bastard you." Hemingway revealed in this autobiographical novel that he regarded himself as old and finished at fifty, his age when he wrote the book. Cantwell makes plans for the future in America. He talks to the headwaiter at the Gritti, whom he elevates to Gran Maestro, and discusses their fanciful award, the Ordine Militar. He bitterly and obsessively recalls the hopeless attack whose failure demoted him from general to colonel. The duck hunt, the best scene in the book, is shifted to the end of the film, and the boatman, who suggests Charon, the oarsman of the underworld, foreshadows the colonel's death. The script returns to the opening scene, and Cantwell dies in the jeep, leaving written orders to give the portrait to Renata and his guns to Alvarito. As the jeep drives off, the screenplay ends. A second version, dated April 2, 1976, is revised but essentially the same. Huston could not solve the intractable, impossible problem: that nothing much, and nothing interesting, ever happens in the novel or the film. Huston confessed in an interview that, with all his strenuous efforts, "I never got a proper script. I worked on it myself, but I never got it. . . . I did use flashbacks [which he disliked], but the script never came off."[13]

Huston used the climactic shootout of *To Have and Have Not* (1937) in his *Key Largo* (1948). But it was terribly sad, despite the perfect match of novelist and director, and for all Huston's admiration and passionate commitment to Hemingway, that he never directed a film based on his friend's work.

Hemingway and Huston lived egoistic, adventurous and dangerous lives. They nurtured in themselves and their friends a cult of masculinity and often reckless courage, which inspired some of their finest artistic achievements. They were lionized in the 1940s, but by the 1950s they were also satirized, as in Lillian Ross' *New Yorker* portrait of Hemingway. Both men, toward the end of their lives, had some failures, and both had an entourage of courtiers and camp followers, flatterers and parasites. But after being written off, they made a strong finish: Hemingway with the posthumous *A Moveable Feast* (1964) and Huston with several superb films and a final cinematic masterpiece, *The Dead* (1987).

ONE

BRAVING THE WATERFALL,
1906–1923

· I ·

John Huston's earliest memory went back to his infancy in Weatherford, Texas, just west of Fort Worth. He vividly recalled riding at night with his mother, an expert equestrian who had once crossed the Mississippi on horseback. He sat in front of her in the saddle and was mesmerized by the sound of the horse's hooves striking the rough cobblestones. This primal memory—distant, nocturnal, tactile and auditory, riding through the streets in town—had a dreamlike quality. As the horse gently rocked them, his mother held him tight and bound him firmly to her.

Horses would play a vital part in Huston's life. As a young man, he spent a year in the Mexican cavalry and in later life went foxhunting in Ireland; he owned racehorses and bet heavily on and off the track. He had friendships, love affairs and marriages with those who shared his passion. Horses also played an important role in many of his films: from the wounded gangster seeking refuge on his Kentucky horse farm at the end of *The Asphalt Jungle* to the terrified heroine being trampled to death by a horse at the end of *Under the Volcano*. He particularly liked *Gulliver's Travels* because Swift gave the horses the power of speech and made them far superior to the humans.

His young parents first met in a romantic theatrical setting during the 1904 World's Fair in St. Louis. His twenty-three-year-old mother, Rhea, was a local reporter. His father, Walter, three years younger, had a small part with a touring company in a popular historical tragedy, *The Sign of the Cross,* where Christian martyrs were thrown to the lions. She recalled that "I watched the show and when I went backstage to interview the star, I ran into this handsome young man. . . . We went to an ice cream parlor. I told him I wanted to write plays and he was very encouraging. After that, while the show was in town, we saw each other almost every day. We went to the World's Fair, we roller-skated, bicycled, visited penny arcades, and had our fortunes told." One was a writer, the other an actor, and both parents had creative lives connected to performance. Even during their courtship, they were always on the move.

Rhea's grandfather, Colonel William Pitt Richardson, had had a distinguished career. He attended Washington College in Pennsylvania, fought against Mexico in the war of 1846–48 and became a lawyer. On May 2, 1863, when the Union forces were defeated at Chancellorsville, Virginia, Richardson was severely wounded in the shoulder and lost the use of his right arm. In 1864 he became attorney general of Ohio and later that year was brevetted brigadier general. Ten days before he was wounded, the men of the 25th Regiment of the Ohio Volunteer Infantry presented their colonel with a silver-sheathed sword. Huston inherited this sword and proudly used it in his Civil War film, *The Red Badge of Courage,* based on the battle at Chancellorsville.

Huston was named after his maternal grandfather, John Marcellus Gore, himself named after a Roman military commander in the Gallic War. Gore "was a genius at riding the crest of a wave and a raise-the-pot gambler. . . . Extravagance was typical of him. When things were going his way, the sky was the limit—and even when they were going against him, the best was none too good." Huston resembled him in his wild gambling, reckless spending and love of luxury.

Rhea (pronounced REE-ah) was named for the mother of Zeus. She was born in New Castle, Indiana, about forty miles east of Indianapolis, in 1881. An only child, adored by her father, she was only five feet four inches tall, but was ambitious, critical, willful and domineering. A youthful photo shows her, slightly horse-faced, in a cloche hat, a long string of pearls and a velvet dress. John Weld, Walter's friend and future biographer, later met her in Paris and found her "rather plain-looking, nobody of any charm or attractiveness. She wasn't pretty and she wasn't dressed particularly smartly, but she *was* very talkative." Like the American novelist Theodore Dreiser, born in Indiana ten years before, Rhea became a roving reporter. Whether unable or unwilling to hold a steady job, or restless and eager to advance by moving around in the profession, she worked on the *St. Louis Star, Cincinnati Enquirer, Niagara Falls Gazette* and *Minneapolis Tribune*. A rather masculine woman by the standards of the time, dowdy and opinionated, fiercely independent and aggressive, she smoked and rode horses, had a career and competed against men in their profession. Huston later recalled that his mother sometimes played the helpless female. Rhea could burst into tears whenever she wished and her reason for crying was as false as her tears. Pausing for emphasis, he described her as "nervous . . . very active . . . smoked. When I say nervous, I mean tending toward the neurotic. She was better with animals than with people. She liked excitement. Still, I was closer to her than to my father."[1] Like Rhea, John was energetic, a heavy smoker, thrived on excitement and knew how to handle animals.

John's father, Walter Huston, was born in Toronto in 1884. Walter's mother was Scottish, his father an Irish carpenter. The youngest of four children, the restless Walter attended five different schools. But he left school early, against the wishes of his father, who warned him that he'd have to start working immediately. The writer James Agee noted that John inherited Walter's height and good looks: "John is a leathery, ski-nosed man, with hard, arresting eyes, who suggests a hammered-out version of his father." Like Walter, John was incorrigibly restless and wandering, refusing to settle down to anything that resembled a stable existence. Walter's parents thought their twenty-year-old son was too young to marry and disliked Rhea, who seemed to be trying to trap him. But the Hustons' disapproval made no difference. Despite their brief acquaintance, the couple married in St. Louis—secretly and privately—on December 31, 1904. After their wedding, Walter returned to acting, and they set off with a theatrical road company that went as far west as Arizona.

· II ·

By the summer of 1906 Rhea and Walter had run out of money and were living near her parents. John Marcellus Huston was born on August 5, 1906, in their brick house at 404 S. Adams in Nevada, Missouri—in the same year as the film directors Billy Wilder and Otto Preminger. The town, with a population of 7,400, was located about a hundred miles from Kansas City, in the southwest corner of the state. It was named by a county clerk who'd visited Nevada City, California, after the Gold Rush of 1848. A local historian noted that "agriculture was the major business, though the railroads were big for a time. Also in 1906 there were two huge employers: a lead-zinc smelting industry (two or three firms) with five hundred employees; and the State Hospital for the Insane (originally the Lunatic Asylum)." Assuming a huckster's tone in a rapturous but ironic letter, the Missouri-born Mark Twain portrayed the state as a place of fair promises and false hopes: "Come right along to Missouri! Don't wait and worry about a good price but sell out for whatever you can get, and come along, or you might be too late. . . . It's the grandest country—the loveliest land—the purest atmosphere. . . . I've got the biggest scheme on earth. . . . Mum's the word—don't whisper—keep it to yourself."

Huston's grandfather John Gore, like Twain's father, had run out of luck and come to grief after being lured to Missouri. Ever optimistic, he had "purchased the public utilities after they had been thrown into the hands of the receiver by the St. Louis Trust Company. . . . He started to build a new power house in the railway yards directly east of Union Station and had much machinery purchased and delivered, but was financially unable to complete his plans and later sold out."[2] Gore placed these valuable properties in the unreliable hands of his son-in-law Walter, who had some slight training as an engineer.

According to one version of the story, soon after John's birth a fire broke out that tested Walter's grasp of the valves and gauges. As the far end of town blazed out of control, the fire chief kept screaming for more water pressure. Walter warned him of the danger, but followed the frantic orders and kept raising the pressure until the pistons of the pump exploded with a horrific bang. The water main burst, the street was flooded and the raging fire destroyed a considerable part of the town. The town council wisely refused to extend Gore's franchise and he was driven into bankruptcy. John, heightening the story of his father's epic incompetence and hasty departure, later transformed it into one of his star turns. In *An Open Book* he wrote that his parents "were living in Nevada, Missouri, because John Gore had won the light-power-and-water company of that town in a poker game. When Mother and Dad arrived, Grandpa made Dad the chief engineer of the company. . . . When a fire broke out in town, the fire chief called for more water pressure and Dad gave it to him. Apparently he shouldn't have, or perhaps he turned the wrong valve, because the water main broke. The entire town on one side of the tracks burned down. We left precipitously in the middle of the night by buckboard—and headed for the state line." These biblical portents seemed to mark the birth of an extraordinary child, but this amusing, oft-repeated story was not true. In a 1950 telegram to *Life* magazine, which was running an article on Huston, the editor of the local newspaper reported the actual facts: "Local files show two fires in year after Huston was born. Water pressure good at both conflagrations. No record of ruined machinery at water plant. Town didn't burn down. No record of Hustons fleeing community."

The family left Missouri, and Gore, supreme manipulator and con artist, managed to acquire the electric light and power plant in Weatherford, Texas. He once again hired good old Walter to run them. Realizing that he was out of his depth, the impulsive, sometimes irresponsible Walter told Rhea that he wanted to return to the theater. During one of their frequent arguments Walter, aware that itinerant acting and family life were incompatible, exclaimed that "he would have left long ago had it not been for the baby." She angrily replied: "Don't detain yourself on his account!" Realizing that they were hopelessly mismatched, she packed her things, took all their money and left him forever. They parted company in 1909, when John was three years old, and divorced three years later. Emphasizing her youthful innocence, though she was actually twenty-three at the time of her marriage, Rhea later described her feelings in an unpublished memoir. She had a "blind passionate eagerness that swept her off her feet when she met and married Walter, before her hair was up and her skirts down. She had just walked out on Wally because eventually her whole nature revolted at his petty cowardices."[3] She felt he was inhibited, weak and feckless, and was furious at his refusal to settle down and take responsibility for his family.

Walter drifted out of his son's life, and they would not be reunited until John moved to New York in 1924. After joining a stock company in Topeka, Kansas, Walter formed a vaudeville team with an oddly named woman, Bayonne Whipple, which lasted from 1910 until 1923. They led a precarious wandering life, often broke and hungry, sitting up all night in rocking trains between brief stops in cheap boardinghouses, dreary hotels and run-down theaters on the muddy streets of provincial towns. Bayonne, seven years older than Walter, married him in 1915; they separated in 1924 and divorced in 1931. John, who had no regrets about his father's divorce from Rhea, wondered why Walter had ever married Bayonne: "I remember thinking: My God, how could my father bear to have this tagging along? She was just dull, narrow. A vaudevillian trying to be a lady. She was full of pretenses. But I must say, the Hustons were extraordinary with her. They treated her as though she was possible. And she wasn't."

After many years of struggle, Walter's stage career finally took off in 1924 when he left Bayonne and appeared as Ephraim Cabot in Eugene O'Neill's *Desire Under the Elms*. Ten years later he acted in the stage version of Sinclair Lewis' *Dodsworth*, and he became friends with O'Neill and Lewis, both Nobel Prize winners. Walter went to Hollywood in 1929, soon after talkies began. He made his first film at the age of forty-five, and then played the villain, opposite Gary Cooper, in *The Virginian* (1929). His effective, understated acting got him plenty of work; his other notable appearances included the title role in *Abraham Lincoln* (1930) and the sex-obsessed missionary in Somerset Maugham's *Rain* (1932). He worked both in Hollywood and on Broadway and often returned to the stage. He enjoyed a memorable success when he sang the poignant "September Song" in Maxwell Anderson's *Knickerbocker Holiday* (1938), and his performance became a classic recording.

Walter's eventual success as an actor would later give John enormous benefits, but his parents' separation and financial struggles made for a difficult childhood. He recalled his own precocious stage debut at the age of three, when the family had moved to Texas, in George M. Cohan's patriotic play *Little Johnny Jones* (1904). In a photograph he wears a red, white and blue satin Uncle Sam costume, with wide-striped trousers, cutaway jacket speckled with four large stars, high stiff collar and black string tie. He looks like an angry midget, with wild curly hair, a scowling expression and his right hand raised in a defiant gesture.

John never experienced a normal family life and had no stability as a child. As Rhea tried to support herself and her son, they wandered—in a curious parallel to Walter's life—from Missouri and Texas to Indiana (where her sister lived), St. Paul, Los Angeles and Phoenix. "When I was a kid I never had a home," John said. "I was always on the [move], living out of dressing rooms and hotels." Though it was difficult to attend new schools and make new friends, he found the constant movement adventurous and exciting: "I never tired of traveling from town to town with Mother. I've always loved trains. I remember so well the smell, look, taste of soot, the sounds of passing over trestles and bridges, walking through the cars, feet braced and struggling for balance"—as in a boxing match. "There was the thrill of sleeping in upper berths and the splendor of the dining cars." Later on, when John tried to put down roots in Ireland and Mexico, he continued to travel for most of the year while making movies all over the world.

A third early memory completed the suite that would dominate John's life: horses, acting and sex. He remembered lying in bed with the nursemaid who'd been hired to take care of him: "Her skirt was up and her behind was bare. I patted it and stroked it and laid my cheek against it."[4] He looked forward to further explorations, cheek to cheek, but was keenly disappointed when his mother, suspecting the worst, fired the seductive nursemaid.

Though spoiled, John also felt stifled by the oppressively close connection to his neurotic mother. Rhea, who'd lost her first baby in a miscarriage and had left her husband, clung to her sickly only child. She sometimes coddled him, but sometimes, when absorbed in her work, offloaded and ignored him. "I thought she was suffocating," John later said. "She would adhere too closely." Then, as if speaking of himself, he added, "She was a mass of contradictions. There was an element of desperation. She had extraordinary physical courage. Liked excitement. I admired her on the one hand, couldn't stand her on the other. She was alternately very true and very false." His mother was "dominating, demeaning, hysterical, overbearing, proud, protective. She was an adventuress, a gambler, a horsewoman, hardened by convent training, embittered by an alcoholic father, unlucky in love, frustrated in her dream of being more than a sob-sister feature writer for newspapers." Like many parents, she thought the sun rose and set on her brilliant child and counted on him to fulfill her own ambitions.

Rhea met her second husband, a prosperous businessman, Harold Stevens, while working on the *Minneapolis Tribune* and married him in about 1915. Stevens, vice president of the Northern Pacific Railroad, was a colleague of the fabulous multimillionaire, James J. Hill, who had made St. Paul the headquarters of his prosperous railway and fulfilled the American pioneer's dream by driving it across the western wilderness to the Pacific coast. Stevens was a leading citizen of the twin city, St. Paul, where belonging to the upper class depended on background, good manners, the appearance of morality—and money. Most of the wealthy people lived on Summit Avenue, an elegant boulevard on a bluff overlooking the commercial town and a bend of the Mississippi River. A widower, Stevens wanted a mother for his two small children as well as a wife for himself. The two hard-up Hustons had no trouble fitting into this new world. Stevens taught the nine-year-old John to play billiards, and gave him his first and lasting taste for luxurious life. While Walter was sitting up all night in seedy third-class compartments, John was allowed to indulge his taste for trains by taking long trips in Stevens' private railroad car, handsomely equipped with its own servants and splendid dining room. As an adult he could still remember most of the stops on the Santa Fe and Northern Pacific railroads.

In her memoir, an exercise in rewriting history, Rhea said that when she married Stevens, in contrast to Walter, "it was with maturity's full realization of what she was doing. . . . With her decision to marry again came the determination to make a go of it and to remain with him till death did them part."[5] In fact, she left him two years later, though they were not legally divorced until 1928. By doing so, she followed the scandalous family tradition: her mother had divorced John Gore; both Rhea and Walter were divorced twice; and John would trump them with no less than four divorces.

· III ·

In his novel *Tarr* (1918), Wyndham Lewis noted how the artist-hero benefitted from the kind of close connection that John had with his mother: "An enervating childhood of mollycoddling . . . has its advantages. He was an only child of a selfish vigorous little mother. The long foundation of delicate trustfulness and irresponsibility makes for a store of illusion to prolong youth."

The first major crisis in John's youth, which would have a tremendous impact on his character and later life, took place in 1917 when he was eleven years old. A doctor, summoned to the Stevens house to attend a sick maid, was worried by the dark circles under John's eyes and asked if he could examine him. The best doctor in St. Paul mistakenly diagnosed an enlarged heart and chronic nephritis, and cast a shadow of death over him. He prescribed a bland diet, with no meat or eggs, and complete bedrest, with absolutely no exercise, for two years. This virtual prison sentence forced John to leave the harsh winters of Minnesota for the warm desert air of Arizona. Rhea, perhaps bored by now with her marriage, never questioned the diagnosis, abandoned her husband and stepchildren, and took John to Phoenix. The doctors there saw that John was actually suffering from malnutrition and changed his meager diet, but they confirmed the St. Paul doctor's view of the case.

John's so-called illness lasted, through puberty, for the next two years. The doctors warned him that though he was doomed to die at an early age, violent exercise would surely kill him at once. The boy burned with frustration, felt he had nothing to lose and was determined to earn his wet badge of courage. One night he rose from his bed, sneaked out of the house and bravely went for a swim in a nearby canal. The floodgates were open and the canal turned into a crashing water-fall. "I got caught in the current," John wrote, "and suddenly found myself being sucked under the water. I thought I was drowned for sure, but then I found myself being ejected on the other side and I was perfectly all right!" This death-defying experience shocked his mother, but his newfound confidence in his body and strength set him free from invalidism and once again allowed him to live a normal boy's life. He gorged himself with food, went swimming, took walks and attended school. He lived the rest of his long life untroubled by either cardiac or kidney disease but retained the psychic wound.

In adult life Huston always made certain that the loneliness and boredom he'd suffered as an invalid would never recur. He kept constantly busy, often moved around from place to place, and surrounded himself with a wide circle of colleagues and friends, lovers and wives. His early risk-taking began his obsessive confrontations with danger and death. He was always eager to gamble and take dangerous chances (often putting others at risk), feeling he was invulnerable and could always beat the odds. His third wife, Evelyn Keyes, shrewdly observed that his delicate childhood seemed to have humiliated and "offended him deeply and he was bent on exorcising it even if it meant killing himself in the process."[6] The science fiction writer Ray Bradbury, who worked with him on the script of *Moby Dick*, thought Huston so reveled in risk that he was "not comfortable in any situation unless death was near."

This extraordinary experience, in which he took the initiative and defied authority, set up a recurrent pattern of escape in Huston's life. He refused to be restricted to one wife or one lover, and was determined to live as intensely as possible in case his life should come to a sudden and unexpected end. Yet his two years of illness engendered one of the most appealing aspects of his sometimes-abrasive character: his sympathy for weak, sick and vulnerable people. He felt compassion for the wounded American soldiers he filmed in the World War II documentary *The Battle of San Pietro* (1945) and for the psychologically traumatized patients in *Let There Be Light* (1946). He adopted the homeless Mexican orphan Pablo Albarran; gave his name to and supported the four-year-old Allegra when her mother was killed and her father rejected her; revived the paralyzed and moribund writer Carson McCullers by inviting her to visit his estate in Ireland; cared deeply about his disturbed and disabled stepson, Collin Green; and agreed to help the dying William Wyler end his life.

After John and Rhea moved to Los Angeles while he was in his teens, he took up boxing to test his courage and recover his strength. He admired this gladiatorial sport, which required physical toughness, cunning technique and a dancer's agility. He'd come out of the corner with his fists hugging his sides, then bring them up to fly around his face like butterflies. The tall, angular fighter said, "I didn't swing, I didn't telegraph my punches." He described his unusual technique in his boxing story "Fool": "I was naturally a straight hitter, right from the start when I had my fights at grammar school. I developed a short jab in my left that was almost automatic. It would work without my thinking of it. The blow was not hard, you understand, but it was stinging and cutting, and it used to make them first mad and then disheartened." Overcoming his sickly youth and able to take punishment, he won all but two of his fights and became an amateur lightweight champion in California.

To toughen him up and instill some discipline, Rhea sent John to the San Diego Army and Navy School for a year and to St. Thomas Military Academy for two years. But he had, in fact, the same level of formal education, in the Los Angeles public schools, as his future protégée Marilyn Monroe. A voracious reader who was one of the most intelligent writer-directors in Hollywood, Huston was highly respected as a cultured, literary man, yet he left high school at fifteen and was mainly self-taught.

The would-be painter learned his most valuable lessons at the Smith School of Art and the Art Students League in Los Angeles, which he described as "just a group of painters who fell together, hired a model and a little room down on Main Street, which was a slum area of Los Angeles."[7] The first *Self-Portrait*, completed in 1923 when he was seventeen, was modeled on the defiant self-portraits of Gauguin and Van Gogh. He portrayed himself as an artist, holding a brush and sitting before an easel. In a three-quarter view, his head tilted slightly to the left, he wears an open-necked, high-collared tunic and gazes straight out at the spectator. He has a wide white cloth, or bandage, wrapped around his dark hair, with stray locks toppling over it, thick eyebrows, deep-set eyes, protruding left ear, strong nose, turned-down lips, small goatee and scowling, pugnacious expression. In the 1920s he did a caricature of George Gershwin that the composer considered good enough to use on his Christmas cards.[8] Huston believed he had talent and wanted to become a professional artist, but he married young and needed to support his first wife. He was forced to give up his art career, but continued to draw and paint throughout his life, and the fine arts had a profound influence on his films.

Huston's parents formed his character and defined the course of his life. Like Rhea, he loved horses and gambling, and spent money freely, wanted to write, had a sense of adventure and was eager to take risks. Like Walter, whom he physically resembled, he became an actor and a remote but always generous father. Like both parents, he led an unstable and restless existence, and went in for impulsive marriages and multiple divorces.

TWO

RESTLESS YOUTH,

1924–1935

· I ·

In a late-life interview Huston contrasted Los Angeles, where he'd reached the peak of his profession, with New York, where he'd begun his career and taken part in the theatrical, literary, artistic and sporting life. He came to believe that Los Angeles—with its boring parties, pointless conferences, and endless talk of money and success—degraded talent and culture: "I never liked it. All the values dissipate there along with the people, and I mean people you can see anywhere else who fascinate you, they are cheapened by the place." New York, however, was alive with artistic potential and athletic pleasures: "What a life one could have there when I was a kid. During Prohibition, after midnight, you went to Harlem as a matter of course. Then the bicycle races at [Madison Square] Garden and a workout at Stillman's [gym] during the day. And all your friends played poker. It was a sporting scene all right. And the writers—Sherwood Anderson, Dreiser, O'Neill." He actually appeared in a play by Anderson in O'Neill's Provincetown Playhouse.

John was reunited with his father when he was eighteen. He had rarely seen the wandering Walter since his parents' divorce; his mother had told him only that Walter was an actor, which made him seem a glamorous and idealized figure. In one of his recurrent youthful dreams, John felt weak, dissolute and shiftless because he was penniless and had to ask his father for assistance. But in New York and later in Hollywood, the generous and now-prosperous Walter was always willing to help. Though Walter had had very little to do with John when he was growing up, he did everything possible for him when he was an adult. In a similar fashion, John would have very little to do with raising his own children, but when they grew up, he would do all he could to advance their film careers.

Walter thought it was high time to give John some manly authority to balance, even counteract, the long years of Rhea's maternal influence. In 1924 he invited John to New York, where the son immediately began to benefit from his father's experience. Huston recalled that watching his father at work was an education and showed him what he wanted to do with his life: "I would attend rehearsals of plays he was doing and I'd see what he would do with a scene. It was mostly his creation of a role, to see how he went at it, that was a lead into direction." Both Rhea and Walter thought their son was a genius—and they were right. His father had often told the producer Walter Wanger, "You want to watch my son. He has great talent and imagination, and some day he's going to make a great mark for himself in this business." John remarked that "fortunate accidents played an enormous role in my life," but Walter paved the way. A rare example of a talented son who surpassed his successful father, John would follow in Walter's slipstream and shoot to the top in Hollywood. He later acknowledged, "I didn't find my father's reputation difficult to deal with. I rode on it, for all it was worth."[1]

John rented an apartment at 434 Lafayette Street in Greenwich Village, in the same building as Sam Jaffe, who had an extraordinary career and became a lifelong friend. The short, skinny, toothy, crinkly-haired actor was born in 1891 on the Lower East Side of New York. Educated at City College and the Graduate School of Engineering at Columbia, he began as a high school math teacher. In 1915 he made his stage debut with his actress-mother in the vibrant Yiddish theater. He would make his first screen appearance in 1934 and play the Tibetan lama in *Lost Horizon* (1937) and the title role in *Gunga Din* (1939). He would appear in two of Huston's films, playing the criminal mastermind in *The Asphalt Jungle* (1950) and the translator of Japanese in *The Barbarian and the Geisha* (1958). Huston, well aware of his own limited education, admired Jaffe's culture and intellect. He wrote that Jaffe "knew about painters and painting; he was a fine pianist and composer; he'd studied philosophy at the New School for Social Research; he had done original work in mathematics; and he was a good boxer."[2]

Jaffe introduced Huston to the illustrious Provincetown Playhouse, which had been founded in 1915 on a wharf at the end of Cape Cod. O'Neill was their leading playwright; and Robert Edmond Jones, their set designer, was married to Walter's sister, Margaret Huston, a well-known concert singer. The playhouse added a small theater in Greenwich Village in 1917, which began with one-act plays and moved to full-length works, becoming a laboratory as well as a theater. It developed new playwrights, encouraged innovative designers and took risks with experimental works. In 1925 Huston made his stage debut at the Provincetown Playhouse in *The Triumph of the Egg*, an unpromising one-act play that dramatized Sherwood Anderson's short story about a failed chicken farmer and soon closed. Later that year Huston appeared with Jaffe in *Ruint* by Hatcher (a better name for a play about eggs) Hughes. He played a rich young liberal who stops in a backwoods southern town on his way to Palm Beach, witnesses the superstitions and wretched poverty, and seduces the local beauty.

The following year, after John suffered from an ear infection and had to have an operation for an inflammation of the jawbone, Walter gave him $500 to recuperate in the mild climate of Mexico. John sailed from New York to Vera Cruz, on the east coast, took a slow train ride to Mexico City and spent about a year there. He took riding lessons and indulged his passion for horses. When he ran out of money, his teacher suggested he accept an honorary commission as a member of the equestrian team in the Mexican army, where he could use the officers' mess and his expenses would be covered. Huston wrote, "There would be no pay, of course, but I could have meals at the barracks, a place to sleep if I wanted, and the best horses in Mexico to ride. I jumped at the offer and was given the temporary rank of lieutenant."

Though Huston enjoyed a hedonistic life in Mexico, the country was a dangerous place in 1926. D. H. Lawrence had visited Mexico three times between 1923 and 1925. His personal reaction to ten years of revolutionary violence was fear, tempered by a fascination with primitive power, reflected in his letters as well as in his novel *The Plumed Serpent* (1926). In a letter of April 1923, just after he arrived in Mexico City, Lawrence wrote with alarm and anger: "In these states almost every *hacienda* (farm) is smashed, and you can't live even one mile outside the village or town: you will probably be robbed or murdered by roving bandits and scoundrels who still call themselves revolutionaries." In the novel Ramón tells Kate, "I think of all the Mexican revolutions, and I see a skeleton walking ahead of a great number of people, waving a black banner with *Viva la Muerte!*"[3] Lawrence was frightened by the vibrations of this rather malevolent place, this dark, threatening Mexico.

Huston, who ignored revolutionary politics and associated with young men from the colorful and dissolute ruling class, was attracted to the violence and excited by the danger. "It was a perilous city then, after nightfall," he wrote. "There was a 10:30 P.M. curfew and, after it sounded, you walked the streets in double jeopardy: stickup men and cops. It was simply a question of who got you first. Getting robbed or being fined, it was for all you had on you. Outside Mexico City, you only traveled by day. Bandidos still ranged the countryside—leftovers from the Revolution."

One of his wild Mexican friends became secretary of the treasury and printed his mistress' pretty face (why not?) on the volatile currency. Another high government official saved young Huston from making a trip to the local bordello: "He had an outdoor swimming pool—and he had it full of whores, without any clothes on. He had brought them out for our visit. We dived right in. Life was a constant revel." When other American boys were scarcely out of high school, the twenty-year-old Huston thrived in that congenial masculine society and led an even livelier existence than he had in New York: "What a time that was! Always going places in Packards. You'd go the rounds of the cafés. Then you'd go to somebody's *finca*. Then you'd play the next thing to Russian roulette. You'd cock a pistol and throw it up and hit the ceiling with it. It was great. Just great. I was their top jumping rider. God, those were wonderful days!"[4] Huston told his fantastic stories and established his legendary image long before he published them in his autobiography. But if his Mexican friends had continued to throw their cocked pistols against the ceiling, the whole troop would have been wiped out by ricocheting bullets in a few weeks and there would have been considerably more room in the packed Packards.

It's odd, considering his love of Mexico and year in the Mexican cavalry, that Huston never bothered to learn the language. Like Bogart, the only two Spanish words he picked up were *Dos Equis,* or Double X, the name of a popular beer. He would never learn French during his time in Paris in the 1930s; and he was mightily impressed, later on, to find that the Puerto Rico–born, Princeton-educated actor José Ferrer spoke Spanish, French and Italian. Despite his lack of Spanish, Mexico had a powerful impact on his life. He learned that he could get away with almost anything there, no matter how outrageous. Later in life he would make four movies in that highly charged country; he collected pre-Columbian art, both real and fake, and often smuggled it into America; he built his last home near Puerto Vallarta, where, at the end of his life, he was cared for by a devoted Mexican servant.

· II ·

When Huston returned from Mexico to Los Angeles, his wild oats sown but not reaped, he impulsively married his high school sweetheart Dorothy Harvey. He said "she was beautiful, with a heart-shaped face and wide-set gray eyes with that heavy fringe around them the Irish sometimes have. She was a gifted student in college, majoring in philosophy, and meant to become a poet. She was the first girl to whom I had ever made love that I had any feeling for other than carnal." In a reprise of the Walter-Rhea wedding, in 1926 John and Dorothy, without telling anybody and to avoid parental disapproval, had a private ceremony with a justice of the peace. They soon moved to Greenwich Village, where Huston painted and boxed, and Dorothy wrote poetry. In 1929, when their money and Walter's subsidy ran out, John worked briefly on the *New York Evening Graphic,* where Rhea was currently employed.

This mendacious and exploitative tabloid, published from 1924 to 1932, had the well-earned name of "pornoGraphic." Huston called it "the worst possible scandal sheet, a model for all bad newspapers."

The *Graphic*, at least, exposed him to low life and got him writing. He did not, strangely enough, write about his fabulous experiences in Mexico, but wrote two boxing stories, influenced by Hemingway's subject matter and style. He showed them to Walter, who was appearing in a play by the sportswriter Ring Lardner. Ring showed the stories to H. L. Mencken, who published them in the prestigious *American Mercury* in March 1929 and May 1931. In "Fool," the naïve narrator describes how his friend Victor allowed the narrator to beat him in a boxing match, though Victor could easily have knocked him out: "I never knew a guy like this Victor. He stood up there and let me break his nose like the shameful fool I was when he could have stretched me unconscious with either hand in less time than it takes to tell it here. That's what I call a man of mercy."[5] The narrator wins the fight, but feels foolish and ashamed for betraying a friend.

The more episodic "Figures of Fighting Men" contains brief sketches of boxers from champs to badly beaten has-beens. Most of the writing is taut and sharp: "The Irish boy has a half-frightened look on his face. His body is tense, the muscles flexed in his big rigid arms, and his movements are short and jerky." But Huston sometimes got carried away with attempts at fine writing: "From a shivering, sick child the champion is transfigured into a flashing wraith, elusive and beautiful as a flame, who bewilders his victim, lashes him into position for the knockout, and drops him with a blow."

Capitalizing, perhaps, on the "Frankie and Johnny" story that formed the centerpiece of *HIM* (1927) by his Greenwich Village neighbor E. E. Cummings, Huston got a substantial $500 advance from the small but innovative publishers Albert Boni & Charles Liveright for his marionette play *Frankie and Johnny* (1930). He may have been drawn to this unusual art form for the same reasons that Heinrich von Kleist stated in his famous essay "On the Marionette Theater" (1806): "The marionette combines naturalness with lightness and with the unawareness that saves it from affectation [and displays] the charm of innocence." Huston dedicated the book to Dorothy, and it was illustrated by the Mexican-born artist Miguel Covarrubias, who was popular in the 1920s and whose work often appeared in *Vanity Fair*. The crime that had inspired the popular song "Frankie and Johnny" took place in St. Louis, in his native Missouri, in October 1899. In Huston's play Johnny has "died from knife wounds inflicted by Frankie Baker, an ebony-hued cake-walker." The prologue opens with his lover Frankie on the scaffold with a noose around her neck and the sheriff asking if the condemned prisoner has anything to say "afore we take in the slack." Frankie then tells her story in three short scenes—"Let them hear my tale how I loved an' done wrong"—and is hanged in the epilogue. Twenty variants of her story are printed at the back to pad out this short book.

There's a lot of black dialect ("I get a-scairt") in the story, which Huston picked up from *Huckleberry Finn* and his musician friends in Harlem as well as from earlier versions of the song. When Johnny threatens to leave her, he says:

J: I can see now ye've been schemin' an' connivin' from the
     day we first met. . . .
F: Ye ain't ditchin' me, Johnny?
J: Aye, I'm a-lightin' out for good.

(Huck "lights out" for the Territory at the end of the novel.) After Johnny begs for mercy and Frankie kills him, the Madam poetically says: "She's drilled him clean. Ye can see the starlight through him."[6]

Huston belonged to the social circle of George Gershwin, who promoted talented young men. In his diary entry for December 15, 1929, the syndicated columnist Franklin Pierce Adams recorded that at Gershwin's house he saw "a marionette show, written and directed by young John Huston. It was a dramatization of *Frankie and Johnny*, and it was not the way I thought it would be at all. . . . The characters were vocal and the play was done in prose for the most part. It was as beautiful a thing as I ever saw, and written with a skill and lyrical sense that I thought exceptional."

Huston may have been drawn to this piece of folklore by the colorful characters: the gamblers, dandified men and diamond-laden women, the sad lost souls fighting for their identity as well as for their lives. Similarly, condemned criminals would be paraded through the town square at the beginning of *Beat the Devil* (1953), and the motif of death by hanging would recur in two films. Bogart and Hepburn narrowly escape hanging at the end of *The African Queen* (1951), and there are many ruthless and indiscriminate hangings in *The Life and Times of Judge Roy Bean* (1972).

· III ·

When Walter first went to Hollywood and made *The Virginian* in 1929, John sent the old pro a joking telegram, with a friendly sting, that chided him for abandoning the serious theater on Broadway: "Understand you've signed contract to appear in twelve pictures annually for ten years stop When are you going to get time to practice acting?" The year after *Frankie and Johnny* was published, John followed Walter to Hollywood, just as he had followed him to New York. Walter got him jobs writing additional dialogue on two films in which he was the star, with William Wyler the director and Paul Kohner as associate producer. In *A House Divided* (1931; its title echoes St. Mark and Abe Lincoln), a rough New England fisherman struggles to retain the love of his mail-order bride. In *Law and Order* (1932)—which foreshadowed *Judge Roy Bean*—Walter plays a marshal who brings peace to Tombstone, Arizona, by killing all the baddies in town.

Walter was well liked and extremely well connected. His sister, the concert singer, was married to a famous stage designer; his second and third wives were actresses. (Later on he would be invited to the White House by Franklin Roosevelt and would play golf with General George Marshall.) John followed closely in his footsteps and worked with many people who had once worked with his father. Wyler would become John's close friend and mentor, the pragmatic and effective Kohner his lifelong agent. John would collaborate on several screenplays with W. R. Burnett. Mary Astor, who costarred with Walter in *Dodsworth,* would appear in two of John's early films. John would work under the director Frank Capra when he made documentaries during the war. David Selznick would be a good friend until their angry clash over *A Farewell to Arms*. For good luck, Walter even played unbilled cameo roles in John's first two films: the wounded sea captain who carries the black bird in *The Maltese Falcon* (1941) and the talkative bartender in *In This Our Life* (1942).

William Wyler, four years older than John, was born in 1902 in Mülhausen, Alsace, then part of Germany. He was educated in Switzerland, studied the violin in Paris and in 1922 was invited by his cousin Carl Laemmle (who had a very large faemmele) to work at Universal. As a director, his painstaking Germanic perfectionism, the exact opposite of Huston's studied spontaneity, would earn him the nickname "Ninety-take Wyler." He later directed *The Best Years of Our Lives* (1946), *Detective Story* (1951) and *Roman Holiday* (1953). Like John Huston and Sam Jaffe, Wyler was a cultured all-rounder with many talents. John admiringly wrote that " 'Willy was certainly my best friend in the industry. . . . We seemed instantly to have many things in common. . . . Willy liked the things that I liked. We'd go down to Mexico. We'd go up in the mountains. And we'd gamble. He was a wonderful companion.' . . . [Wyler] was equally capable of playing Beethoven on his violin, speeding around town on his motorcycle, or schussing down steep virgin snow trails."

Three later episodes illuminate their intimate friendship. When John wanted to return to Hollywood after the war, he rewrote the treatment for *Three Strangers* (1946), made a collect call to Wyler (rather than to Walter) and asked him for money. Wyler sent him $500 (the same magical amount that Walter had given him to go to Mexico and that Boni gave him for his marionette play) and he stayed with Wyler in Hollywood. He also borrowed money from Wyler to buy racehorses and bet on them. In 1981, after an agonizing operation for lung cancer, Wyler turned to John for help and begged him to put an end to his suffering. He said, "Johnny, I don't want any more of this. They won't let me die, and I want to die." Huston urged him to try to get well, to stick with the treatment for another two weeks. Then, he promised, "if you still feel that way, Willy, I'll help you die." He assured his friend that he'd take the consequences. Wyler made a temporary recovery, and Huston didn't have to keep his promise. But he encouraged the dying man with his compassion, loyalty and willingness to risk prison for his sake.[7]

During Huston's early years in Hollywood, while he was working as a screenwriter for Goldwyn, Universal, Twentieth Century-Fox and Warners, his marriage to Dorothy Harvey began to deteriorate. He continued to behave as if he were still a bachelor, had many affairs with eager young actresses and was caught out by his increasingly suspicious wife. After he started earning good pay at the studios, he bought Dorothy a $2,000 wardrobe at Bullock's on Wilshire Boulevard and charged it to Walter, who good-naturedly paid the bill. But John's attempt to repair the marriage, bribe Dorothy and extinguish his guilt failed to work. She became withdrawn, resentful and hostile. Rhea, who noticed Dorothy's condition before the self-absorbed Huston did, told him that Dorothy was drinking heavily and had become an alcoholic. By the afternoon her vision was blurred, her step unsteady, her speech incoherent. One night while drunk and smoking in bed she burned herself badly. They divorced in 1933; he paid $50 a week alimony for three years. Later he admitted, "I was responsible for the breakup of my first marriage, which was followed by a series of failures."

Dorothy, who either temporarily recovered or was able to hide her grim condition, would marry Dr. George Hodel in 1940. But, their son Steven recalled, "During the war years my parents' marriage fell apart. Upset and unhappy, Mother began drinking heavily, and Father stayed away from the house most of the time. . . . She became an alcoholic, her life shipwrecked and wasted, its enormous potential cast away. . . . Her binges would sometimes last for days, and after the second or third day she could not work, cook, clean, iron our clothes for school, help with homework, or even stand up and walk." The boy came home one day to find a strange man in bed with his mother. The stranger, dissatisfied with her drunken performance, exclaimed, "You ain't nothing but a whore," and ungraciously added, "Just so you know, boy, your mother—she's a lousy fuck."[8] Alleging extreme cruelty, Dorothy divorced her husband in 1944. In the mid-1950s her desperate teenage sons, reading that Huston was staying at the Beverly Hills Hotel, sought him out and asked for help. Generous as always, he gave them the magic figure of $500 and taxi fare back to Pasadena.

In November 1931, while John's marriage to Dorothy was coming to an end, Walter married his third wife, Nan Sunderland. Born in Fresno, California, where her father was mayor, she had appeared in 1928 with Walter in Ring Lardner's play *Elmer the Great*. Nan was a tall, attractive woman, about five feet eight, with auburn hair and a charmingly freckled face. After Walter had become a well paid movie star, Bayonne was reluctant to divorce him and would have demanded even more money if she'd known that Walter was eager to marry Nan. While waiting in the wings, Nan amused herself by having a brief affair with Walter's all-too-friendly friend John Weld. But John Huston liked Nan, a welcome contrast to lowlife Bayonne. He often visited the ranch that Nan and Walter built at Running Springs, about a hundred miles east of Hollywood and 7,000 feet high in the San Bernardino Mountains. The sumptuous redwood mansion had a swimming pool and tennis court, nearby ski slopes and horses for hire, and a spectacular view across the wide valley.

The frequency of divorces in the unstable atmosphere of Hollywood, the practice of couch casting, the willingness of young actresses to sleep around to advance their careers, the brief flings that stars often had when making a movie and the retaliatory episodes to arouse jealousy ensured that many women were passed around from friend to friend. Weld slept with Nan before she married Walter. Zita Johann had been married to the director John Houseman (with whom John later worked) before becoming John's mistress. Both the director Anatole Litvak and Errol Flynn enjoyed the favors of Olivia de Havilland before she got involved with John. Doris Lilly moved on from John to Ronald Reagan. After their divorce, John's third wife, Evelyn Keyes, had brief affairs with Kirk Douglas, David Niven and other actors. All this caused more than a few awkward moments at drunken parties.

The breakup of John's first marriage cut him adrift from a safe anchor and he began to drink more heavily. Between February and

September 1933 he was involved in two drunken accidents and a fatal
car crash. The first time he banged into a parked car and spent the
night in jail. The second time he was with his current girlfriend, the
beautiful Hungarian-born actress Zita Johann, who had emigrated to
America at the age of seven in 1911. John Houseman called her "exciting
and vulnerable, with glowing dark eyes and a smile which . . . I found
irresistibly moving." On February 24, 1933, Huston crashed his car into
a palm tree in the Hollywood Hills. Zita hit the windshield and her
face was mutilated by flying glass. The accident got into the newspapers
because she was currently appearing in local theaters with Boris Karloff
in *The Mummy*.

Seven months later, on the night of September 25, 1933, Huston had
a far more serious accident. As he was driving along Sunset Boulevard,
a Brazilian dancer called Tosca Roulien suddenly stepped into the street
from between parked cars. Huston's car hit her, her body slammed into
his hood and windshield, and she was knocked thirty feet along the
street. He jammed on the brakes and just avoided running over her, but
her head was crushed and she was dead. Shocked and devastated, John
was locked in jail and bailed out by Walter. Fortunately, a grand jury
eventually exonerated him. The traffic light had been green, Roulien
had carelessly stepped into the oncoming traffic and Huston had not
been drinking or speeding.

Huston now had to endure an onslaught of attacks in the newspapers. His family and friends thought he should get out of Hollywood
till things cooled off, and in 1935 Walter, as always, came to the rescue.
He got John a screenwriter's job with Gaumont studios in London, at
$300 a week for three months, about three times the standard salary
for English writers. He wrote the screenplay for Carol Reed's first film,
It Happened in Paris (1935), about a wealthy American who studies painting in Paris and poses as a poor man. But three months were not long
enough for John to recover from an overwhelming sense of guilt and
failure. He was nearly thirty years old and felt he was getting nowhere.
When his contract ran out, he allowed himself to sink into destitution.
These were the three low points of his early life: his childhood illness,

the fatal accident in Hollywood and his period of abject poverty in London.

In *Down and Out in Paris and London,* published two years before Huston himself was down and out in those cities, George Orwell wrote that "the evil of poverty is not so much that it makes a man suffer as that it rots him physically and spiritually." Like Orwell, Huston could always escape from poverty by getting money from his father. But he was unwilling to beg, yet again, for Walter's help and chose to drift into the lower depths. In a letter to the novelist B. Traven, Huston recalled this period of homelessness and wrote, "I was only on the bum once in my life and that was in England where one is graded for politeness rather than for brevity" when begging. He claimed he was actually reduced to living in Hyde Park, sleeping on the Thames Embankment and earning a few coppers or sixpences by singing cowboy songs on the streets. "Hollywood had been a failure," he later wrote, "and England had been a dismal experience. Nothing discernible had been accomplished, and I remember thinking that perhaps I should have stayed with my painting—and starved."⁹ Huston finally saved himself by winning £100 in the Irish Sweepstakes and selling a screenplay for £500, but he did not go home right away. He decided to spend some time in Paris and seize his last chance to become a serious professional artist.

Huston's second, undated self-portrait seems to have been painted in a period of failure and depression, perhaps after he arrived in Paris. It was influenced by Picasso's *Old Guitarist,* completed during his Blue Period in 1903. Huston's naked, gaunt, bony figure, indented by sharp shadows, is seated on a black floor that is sharply divided from the cloudy gray background. He has blurred features, prominent collarbone, elongated limbs, large hands and feet. Tilted slightly to the left, he assumes a yogalike position, with his legs spread apart and one arm covering his genitals. The long spiky fingers of his right hand rest on the flat leg; his left hand, palm upward, is extended in a mendicant's gesture. This rather sad, ascetic figure, strikingly different from the aggressively self-confident youth in his earlier self-portrait, lacks Huston's characteristically commanding presence.

The art critic Robert Hughes wrote that Paris had always been "the essential finishing school, the great switchboard, storehouse, and information-exchange of ideas about art, architecture, and their possibilities." In the first sentence of *Tarr,* Wyndham Lewis had declared, "Paris hints of sacrifice"—of poverty and suffering. But Huston relished the artistic life, which had a lot of Baudelairean *volupté* but not much *luxe* or *calme.* Though the evidence is thin, Huston, following in the modernistic wake of Picasso and Matisse, seems to have lived the classic expatriate life that Hemingway had led in the 1920s. During the Depression and while his money held out, he tried to adopt a bohemian existence. He lived in an austere garret, drew nudes in ateliers, took mistresses from models and shopgirls, visited art galleries and studied masterpieces in the Louvre, strolled through the Luxembourg Gardens and browsed in the crowded bookstalls along the banks of the Seine, went to boxing matches and six-day bike races, talked endlessly to fellow exiles in the Left Bank cafés—the Dôme, Select and Rotonde—while reading about massive unemployment, the rise of fascism and rumors of war in the ever-depressing newspapers during that low, dishonest decade. He sold his drawings to the dwindling number of tourists, socialized with Americans and never bothered to learn French. He may also have visited the famous Museum of Ethnography and become interested in the West African tribal masks that had influenced the art of Picasso and his followers. But the most important lesson Huston learned during his time in Paris was that he was only a talented amateur and would never become a distinguished painter. When his money ran out, he sailed back to America.

In his early youth Huston had tried various roles: lightweight boxer, amateur artist, expert horseman, newspaper reporter, story writer, stage actor, marionette playwright, Hollywood screenwriter—and bum. Though these adventures gave him valuable experience, and he'd achieved a certain success in everything he did, he would not or could not commit himself to a single profession. Most mothers would have been mightily impressed by John's good looks, bold spirit and many talents, but Rhea was dissatisfied and critical. Despite her constant talk about her brilliant son, John rather bitterly said, "Nothing I ever did pleased my mother."[10] He not only refused to pursue a single goal, but also followed Walter's career, shot past her and left her in obscurity.

Walter worked in one of the few industries to thrive during the Depression. To compensate for his past neglect, he constantly offered his help and (unlike Rhea) always praised his son. He invited John to New York, gave him important theatrical experience, introduced him to leading writers, helped publish his stories, paid for his trip to Mexico, brought him out to Hollywood, got him writing jobs on two American films, arranged meetings with influential colleagues and with his future agent, protected him from scandal, sent him abroad after the accidents and secured work for him in London. He would play small parts in two of John's early pictures, narrate two of his war documentaries, and always be willing to fork out for his extravagance and send cash in a crisis.

THREE

Many Talents,

1936–1940

· I ·

Huston's second assault on Hollywood, after his return from Europe in 1935, was more successful than the first. He was now more experienced and mature, and his character, tastes and interests were fully developed. When he entered the army in 1942, he was (according to his military file) six feet, one inch tall. At 165 pounds, he was rather gangly for his height and had an unmilitary "slovenly walk." His eyes were brown, his hair black. He had a long, narrow head and wore glasses, soon to be replaced by contact lenses. In her *New Yorker* profile, Lillian Ross, with her journalist's eye, brought him to life and got his height almost correct: "Huston is a lean, rangy man, two inches over six feet tall, with long arms and long hands, long legs and long feet. He has thick black hair. . . . He has a deeply creased, leathery face, high cheekbones, and slanting reddish-brown eyes. His ears are flattened against the sides of his head, and the bridge of his nose is bashed in. His eyes looked watchful, and yet strangely empty of all feeling, in weird contrast to the heartiness of his manner." His ears, which once stuck out, had been flattened by punches or by surgery. He certainly cast a cold eye.

Huston's most distinctive physical characteristic was his resonant actor's voice, theatrically pitched in a deep register. It was rich, gentle and cultivated; somber, hypnotic and seductive; soothing, melodic and mannered. He prolonged the last syllable of his words and emphasized

the final vowel, as in *repaíir* and *understáhnd*. His deliberate, idiosyncratic voice, which his actors liked to imitate, drew listeners toward him
and made them more attentive. He was a great storyteller, especially
with a spellbound audience, and would (for example) describe how he'd
saved Katharine Hepburn's life in Africa by dispatching a wild boar
that was just about to gore her. He was always curious about people and
receptive to new ideas, and like a priest in the confessional, he listened
carefully—especially to women.

Huston's speech was marked by his favorite phrases. People, animals, performances, even commonplace hamburgers and French fries
were all "splendid, simply wonderful." You could never take him by surprise. Instead of engaging with what was said, he'd merely reply, "Ah!
Is that so?" He often said, "It'll be fine, just fine"—a reassuring way of
dealing with disastrous situations. He thought his movie *Sinful Davey*,
ruined by a producer, would be "just fine" and *The Last Run*, from
which he angrily withdrew, "will be just fine." When a female chimpanzee shat all over the house, he tried to calm his frantic wife with "she'll
be just fine." In *Beat the Devil* Robert Morley, who was supposed to be
inside the car before it accidentally veered off the road and crashed
down the cliff, barely escaped injury. When Morley complained that
he might have been killed, Huston coolly responded, "Yes, but you
weren't, were you kid? So now you're fine, just fine." Morley liked to
illustrate Huston's untroubled attitude toward catastrophes. He recalled
how John once came across a dead man on Fifth Avenue, "knelt down
beside the man and taking his limp and lifeless hand held it for a few
critical seconds, before replacing it carefully on the pavement. 'He'll
be just fine,' he told the waiting ambulance men, 'He'll be just fine.' "[1]

Ever the actor, Huston loved to dress up for special occasions and
display his increasingly cosmopolitan wardrobe: Irish flat cap and
tweeds; red jacket and high boots for foxhunting; handmade shirts
and suits; velvet dinner costume and broad bow tie (*à la* Oscar Wilde);
tailored safari jackets; long Madras robes; furry Afghan hats; and Mexican beachcomber's kit. His jokey jockey friend, Billy Pearson, emphasized his dandy tastes. He "sported small checked caps, fancy shoes;

liked colored vests . . . often carried a cane." A child noticed that he had his initials—JMH—elegantly embroidered on his left cuff rather than on his chest pocket.

His longtime secretary Gladys Hill listed his rather simple taste in food: "JH likes fennel, celery, radishes, olives and fruit, Ham and cheese with mustard, Hamburger (very well done), Wurstel, Egg salad, Tunny salad, NEVER CHICKEN OR LIVER." He told his fifth wife, rather unconvincingly, that he had eaten human flesh in Africa and that it tasted "much like chicken." Though he loved the taste of wild duck, he hated chicken. After he was forced to give up cigarettes, he smoked Monte Cristo cigars throughout the day, after dinner and into the night.

Huston had a mania for backgammon and played whenever he had a spare minute. He was also a passionate and skillful poker player, and gambled heavily in both. He was too individualistic for team sports, but excelled in swimming, fishing and shooting, tennis and boxing, foxhunting and even camel racing. At the age of fifty-four, in the intense summer heat of the Nevada desert, he "played set after set [of tennis] for some six hours, against a changing assortment of opponents, when persons twenty years younger would have collapsed."[2] His strenuous tennis matches with the alcoholic James Agee, who was winded, overweight and seriously out of shape, brought on Agee's heart attack.

Huston could connect to animals on a primitive, instinctual level. Unlike his wives, they were obedient and always devoted to him. His exotic menagerie included monkeys and chimpanzees, iguanas and boa constrictors, but he was most passionate about horses. Eloise "Cherokee" Hardt, who grew up riding bareback on an Oklahoma Indian reservation and cared for the horses on his ranch in Tarzana, said he loved horses; he liked to sit on them, look beautiful and show off his polished riding skills. When he lived in Ireland he relished the social cachet of being Master of the Galway Blazers, and loved the challenge of high fences and dangerous jumps. But Eloise felt he had little practical knowledge of horses. When the mare was in heat in Tarzana, Eloise told him that she should be moved away from the stallions, who'd go crazy at her smell. Ignoring her warning, Huston ordered her to bring out a stallion and show him to his guests. When he tried to mount, the frantic stallion reared up and knocked him over.

Whales, elephants and iguanas are living symbols in three of his movies. The high point in *The Bible* (1966) takes place when Huston, playing Noah, leads hundreds of wild animals onto the ark. Horses were absolutely essential in many of his pictures. Reviving the traditional rig of silent movie directors—jodhpurs, boots and whips—he tried to direct *The Red Badge of Courage* on horseback. Racing prints appear on the walls of Bogart's apartment in *The Maltese Falcon*, and the Bogart hero in *Key Largo* introduces himself, like an equine pedigree on a racing form, as "Frank McCloud, by Frank out of Helen." In addition to his dramatic use of horses in *The Asphalt Jungle* and *Under the Volcano*, there are risky roundups of wild mustangs at the core of *The Misfits*, vivid foxhunting scenes in *The List of Adrian Messenger* and *Sinful Davey*, and several symbolic riding scenes in *Reflections in a Golden Eye*.

· II ·

Huston's army file, based on interviews with his colleagues, describes his character, which fit in surprisingly well to military life. He was "easy to meet; forceful; capable; intelligent; self-centered; odd personality." Many friends agreed about his extraordinary character. Evelyn Keyes, his third wife, said, "For Huston, life was a big game and he played it to the fullest."[3] The producer Henry Blanke, like many others, emphasized his idiosyncrasy as well as his irrepressible charm: "You'd see him at every party, wearing bangs, with a monkey on his shoulder. Charming. Very talented, but without an ounce of discipline in his make-up." Robert Morley, who appeared in two Huston films, observed, "He had the courage, the gift of leadership, the confidence, the charm and the cheek." The producer Gottfried Reinhardt agreed: "John can charm anybody into anything." Another producer, Dore Schary, added, "When he wants something from you, he sits down next to you and his voice gets a little husky, and pretty soon you're a dead pigeon."[4] Though Huston was an effective manipulator, he could be manipulated himself—by attractive young women, by Billy Pearson about dubious pre-Columbian art, by his partner Sam Spiegel and by his own staff in Ireland.

Huston often referred to one of his most dominant traits: "The trouble with me is that I am forever and eternally bored.... If I'm threatened with boredom, why I'll run like a hare." He devised various stratagems to conquer, or at least alleviate boredom: violent sports, high-stakes gambling, constant work on multiple projects, restless travel, frequent change of places and people, relays of wives and mistresses, dangerous exploits—and (to the discomfiture of his friends) practical jokes. These jokes, and others more elaborate and cruel, attracted attention, got laughs, made things more exciting and asserted his own superiority at the expense of his victims. He would also play childish tricks, like putting ice cubes with flies frozen inside them into his guests' drinks and rubber peanuts in a serving dish. Paul Kohner, aware of his wiles, would pick up the peanuts, pocket them and keep talking. Huston and Kohner were an odd couple, and his agent often rubbed him the wrong way. At lunch Kohner always wanted Huston to try his food, sometimes using the same fork, and would also insist on sharing his dessert. He would even arrive with sweet food when Huston was in an intensive care ward. Huston had a phobia about Kohner's intrusive habits, which often disgusted him.

Huston had a zest for life that originated in his childhood escape from the dangerous waterfall, and developed the knack of seeing exciting possibilities in every new experience. "I never do anything that doesn't entertain me," he exclaimed. "[I like] highly seasoned things, both foods and people."[5] His character was complex, rebellious and fearsome, with a dangerous edge. Crazily self-confident, he constantly had to be *doing* something. Bogart, his closest friend, observed, "If you want to get him roused, tell him something that appeals to his sense of justice or courage." Another friend called him "a dangerous man. He always had to live, privately or publicly, on the verge of the limit. He always had to be thrilled all the time." James Agee, an influential critic who first defined Huston's character, wrote, "He is magnanimous, disinterested and fearless. . . . Risk, not to say recklessness, are virtual reflexes in him. Action, and the most vivid possible use of the immediate present, were his personal salvation."

The film critic Andrew Sarris suggested that Huston's dominant traits, his "aura of danger and recklessness and ruthlessness and irresponsibility," clashed in his pictures with "despair and defeatism."[6] Huston showed courage in many ways: he made war documentaries under fire, he had a savage fistfight with Errol Flynn, he hunted tigers in India and elephants in Africa. He took near-fatal risks—sometimes with the lives of others—while making *The African Queen, Moby Dick* and *The Roots of Heaven;* he completed *The Dead* when he was mortally ill. In contrast to the accident-prone and frequently injured Hemingway, Huston, for all his bravado, seemed invulnerable and rarely got hurt.

Huston was social and gregarious, yet private and self-enclosed. A novelist portrayed him as "one of the loneliest men on earth." The producer Gottfried Reinhardt, with an apt comparison, elaborated this idea: "John is like a race horse. You must keep him in a good mood all the time. John is a charmer, you know, but he is really very forlorn, a very lonely man. He is out of touch with human emotions." When asked to name Huston's best friend, his fifth wife exclaimed, "Himself!" Eloise Hardt said he was a sweet, sensitive man who never had the courage to show the gentle side of his character. Zoe Sallis, who had a son with Huston, agreed that he was afraid of seeming vulnerable, felt he had to protect himself and didn't want to get too close to people. In an apt phrase she called him "a noble soul hidden behind a dreadful bravado."[7]

Huston went in for extremes of behavior and was cavalier in both senses: gallant as well as indifferent to others. Though characteristically generous and kind, he was also quite capable of gratuitous cruelty. He frequently tested the endurance and loyalty of friends (as he tested himself) by subjecting them to punitive ordeals. Jeanie Sims, one of his devoted secretaries, said, "He had to be cruel to see whether you were going to come through that and still be fond of him." Ben Maddow, Huston's collaborator on two films, emphasized his cool indifference to the feelings of other people: "He would indulge himself in any possible way, whose consequences on other people's lives he observed with great interest, but no compassion." His wartime colleague Jules Buck, who quarreled irrevocably with Huston, portrayed him as a ravenous beast: "John gets bored easily. He needs new people to feed on all the time. The desert is littered with their bones."[8]

These bitter condemnations were not entirely true or just. Huston, like everyone else in the course of a long career, certainly made a few enemies. But he repeatedly worked with the same loyal cadre of secretaries, writers, actors and crews. Most of the actors who had worked with him adored him and felt honored to have known him. The many women in his life (with the notable exception of his last wife) remained devoted to him long after their marriages or affairs had ended. How then, despite his occasional cruelty, did Huston manage to inspire such devotion? Eloise Hardt explained that he put people on a pedestal, created a fabulous aura around them, and made them feel important and essential, glamorous and valued.

Despite his ruthlessness, Huston was sufficiently self-aware to feel twinges of guilt and remorse, and to worry about the punishment he might suffer for his own callous behavior. When he and Guy Gallo, who wrote the screenplay of *Under the Volcano,* were discussing the translation of the popular street play used in the film, Gallo recalled quoting Don Juan's justification of his wickedness:

> "A moment's contrition makes up for a lifetime of sin."
> "Good, good."
> "Do you believe that?" I ask.
> "Yes, of course," says John.
> "But the whole point of the story is that it isn't true."
> "I don't care about the story. I mean for me. It better be true."[9]

· III ·

In 1937, when he was appearing in a play in Chicago, Huston met his second wife, Lesley Black, an attractive and intelligent Irish woman in her early twenties. She was traveling around the world and making her first visit to America while recovering from a brief, unhappy marriage. Huston immediately fell in love with Lesley, impulsively proposed and secretly married her that year. But he was flat broke and confessed, "I had no more business marrying Lesley than I had had marrying Dorothy." He gave the idealized Lesley credit for helping him recover from the dark period of heavy drinking, car accidents, failure and destitution in London, and try to gain another foothold in Hollywood: "She was beautiful, not just physically, but a lovely woman. She set a standard." She helped him settle down and concentrate on his work. (Lesley, whom I met at a dinner party in the mid-1980s, was a charming, cultivated woman, clearly well off, who lived in London and then in France. A rather cool and distant personality, she had literary ambitions and was a close friend of the writer Sybille Bedford.)

Screenwriter Howard Koch, who stayed with Huston when he first came to Hollywood in 1939, described—with an easterner's sharp eye—the impressive house Huston shared with Lesley and the art Huston had already begun to collect: "The home, typically California-modern, reflected his success. On three walls of the living room were paintings of the French Impressionists. The fourth wall was glass. On a clear day you could see Catalina [Island]. Jutting out over the sloping desert terrain was a grass terrace and the inevitable swimming pool. Like the homes of many of the movie colony elite hacked out of the Hollywood Hills, its hold on the sandy cliff seemed precarious."

Huston had even grander ideas for the home that still stands, in a now-posh suburban neighborhood, at 4535 Vanalden Avenue in Tarzana. It was then out in the country, and there was enough land for him to keep horses and other animals. It had guest houses and plenty of room for boisterous parties. The place was built on a hill that rose suddenly from the flat, surrounding gardens. The round back balcony, which extended over the swimming pool, had a diving board that allowed him to jump from the house into the water. "When he was planning his attractive home in the San Fernando Valley," Koch wrote, "he wanted it built of materials that would crumble and return to the earth after he and Lesley were through with it. Permanence of any kind was anathema."[10] This innovative ecological idea was consistent with the behavior of the miners who restored the wounded mountain after digging out the gold in *The Treasure of the Sierra Madre,* and with Huston giving Mismaloya, the setting of his *Night of the Iguana,* back to the Mexican Indians who'd originally owned the land.

In August 1938 Huston's mother, Rhea, died in Los Angeles of a brain tumor. Walter's friend, the writer John Weld, recalled that "John just crumbled. He didn't *cry,* but he was extremely depressed. I never saw him feel so strongly about anybody as he felt about his mother. He was very, very down. Greatly moved." His grief was intensified by his guilt, for "he wasn't sentimental enough to have told his mother that he loved her."[11] Rhea had shaped his cold character and occasionally cruel nature, and he loved her in an ambivalent and complicated way.

Huston had had no children with Dorothy Harvey. In January 1939 (in an incident that recalled Rhea's miscarriage before John was born), Lesley gave birth to a premature and stillborn girl. She wanted to have another child, but couldn't get pregnant again. Her reaction to this tragedy was extreme and an atmosphere of gloom settled over their house. Lesley (like Dorothy) sank into a deep depression, exacerbated—as she withdrew from him—by Huston's affairs with two stars in his films. Eventually she had a nervous breakdown. His second marriage, like his first, was undermined by his infidelity and lasted for seven years. It ended while Huston was in the army, in 1944.

FOUR

RETURN TO HOLLYWOOD,
1936–1940

· I ·

Huston's career in Hollywood began to take off at Warner Bros. when he coauthored the screenplay for Wyler's *Jezebel* in 1938. He spent the next ten years at Warners, interrupted by his military service and ending with *Key Largo*. During that time he had to contend both with the imperious studio head Jack Warner and with the censors. Huston dealt with both shrewdly and effectively, and made some fine films in the process.

With a rebellious and dominating personality, Huston was unwilling to take orders from anyone, and from the start clashed with his producers and studio executives. He complained that the son-of-a-bitch Jack Warner yelled so loud he didn't need a phone. Warner called writers "*schmucks* with Underwoods," and expected those creative types to follow orders and keep regular office hours on the lot. When he criticized Huston for coming in late and asked, "What kind of racket do you think this is?," Huston assumed a high moral tone and defied the boss: "I didn't know I was in a racket! This information comes as a considerable surprise to me. I don't associate with racketeers, but if such is the case, I prefer to terminate my contract here and now." Warner backed down and apologized.

Warner's blowhard, bullying manner was balanced by the cultivated producer Henry Blanke, who saw Huston's potential, was keen on his work, and became his champion and mentor. Five years older than Huston, Blanke was born in Berlin, and had worked for Ernst Lubitsch and Fritz Lang before joining Warners in 1927. Howard Koch called Blanke "a bouncy man, very personable, with the capacity to muster tremendous enthusiasm for whatever film he was currently supervising."

The Production Code, in force from 1934 to 1966, was particularly onerous for writers and directors. It was essentially a set of socially acceptable guidelines for the content of movies, devised by the major studios to forestall moral censure from churches, politicians and other self-righteous leaders of public opinion. The industry's own censors continuously interfered with the process of moviemaking, from script to finished product, and tried to impose an unrealistic and often absurd standard of morality. Scripts had to rigorously uphold religion and the church as well as the sanctity of marriage and the home (even married couples could not be seen sleeping in the same bed). The code rigidly suppressed scenes of lustful kissing, exposed breasts and sexual relations. Movies could not show violence or cruelty, and had to punish wrongdoing, crime, evil and sin. Certain topics were taboo: profanity and blasphemy, illegal drugs, venereal disease, sexual perversion and miscegenation.

Discussing the heavy-handed censorship that often brought writers to their knees, Huston (in an apt comparison) noted, "Awful things were forced on us. They were harder with us than Moses.... [But] very often censorship led me to do things that were even better than I would have done" without it.[1] The censors taught Huston to create a style of reticence and evasion, obliqueness and indirection, ambiguity and allusion to express his covert themes. His pictures evaded the censors, while revealing to a more sophisticated audience what he actually meant to say.

Huston's most brilliant collaborator, on both stage and screen, was Howard Koch. Born in New York in 1901, Koch graduated from Bard College and Columbia Law School, and began to write plays while practicing as an attorney. In 1938 he collaborated with Orson Welles on the wildly successful radio drama, *The War of the Worlds,* based on H. G. Wells' novel. This realistic portrayal of the invasion of spaceships from Mars was taken literally by a vast audience and caused widespread panic along the East Coast. Four years later Koch won an Academy Award as coauthor of the superb film *Casablanca*.

Huston seemed to be describing himself when he called Koch "a tall, thin man, amiable, perceptive and extremely likeable." The producer John Houseman, who also worked with Koch, said he was a "spindly, hollow-eyed, earnest young man." In his introduction to Koch's autobiography, Houseman—ignoring the tragic aspects of his friend's career—emphasized his naïveté: "There is something of Candide in Howard; his experiences in Hollywood bring to mind the adventures of Voltaire's innocent in the land of Eldorado. Like Candide, Koch finds himself—sincere, trusting, optimistic—moving in continuous wonder from one crisis to another."[2]

Walter Huston had played Abe Lincoln in his early movie *Two Americans* (1929) about Lincoln and Grant. In 1937 (the year he met Lesley Black) John played Lincoln in Koch's play *The Lonely Man*, sponsored by the Federal Theater, which ran for five months in Chicago. The drama imagined the young Lincoln's reincarnation in the 1930s as a liberal professor and labor lawyer. John had profited from studying Walter's technique, and Koch was tremendously impressed by and grateful for his performance: "There have been many Lincolns on the stage and screen, some very good ones, but I believe John's characterization stands out as the most penetrating. He used none of the usual make-up—no beard, no stovepipe hat, no drawl. He *thought* Lincoln with a brooding intensity that came over the footlights with such conviction that the audiences were mesmerized into accepting the story's fantastic premise . . . the return of young Lincoln to our contemporary world to find that slavery still existed, but in other forms."

On Huston's recommendation, Warners brought Koch out to Hollywood. The friends successfully collaborated on the play *In Time to Come* (1941) and on the films *Sergeant York* (1941) and *Three Strangers* (1946), and Koch wrote the screenplay of *In This Our Life* (1942), directed by Huston. His friend and contemporary Billy Wilder, who had a coauthor for almost all of his screenplays, explained how he (like Huston) worked with another writer: "It's *nice* to have a collaborator—you're not writing into a vacuum, especially if he's sensitive and ambitious to create a product of some value. . . . Two collaborators who think exactly alike is a waste of time. Dialogue or whatever comes from: 'Not quite, but you are close to it. Let's find something that we both like. This is a little bit too cheap, this is too easy. This character is not developed.' . . . Unless there are sparks that fly, it is totally unnecessary to have a collaborator." Sparks certainly flew between Huston and Koch.

In 1943 Koch wrote the script of the pro-Soviet wartime picture *Mission to Moscow,* and Huston was worried about Koch's career during the McCarthy witch hunts in the late 1940s. Though not a Communist, Koch was blacklisted in 1951 and forced to leave Hollywood; he worked in England and had to write under a pseudonym. Huston had been concerned and sympathetic about the blow to Koch's career, yet at some point the two had a falling out and were never reconciled. In 1961, when discussing the possibility of a film based on Herman Melville's *Typee* the producers asked Huston whether he would accept Koch if they could not get the playwright Lillian Hellman (who'd betrayed her friends by naming names during the witch hunts). Huston responded with an emphatic "NO!"

In his memoir, Koch was bitter and fiercely critical of his former companion and artistic partner: "To his friends he was extravagantly generous, but if anyone displeased him, he could be withering and sadistic. . . . Enormously creative, John was also destructive, both of himself and of others. . . . All his life he would be using up people and places, sucking them dry of whatever interested him, and then moving on to the next and the next and the next."[3] Koch clearly felt that he had been one of Huston's victims and had been discarded when he most needed help. But neither man ever explained the reasons for their quarrel or revealed if it was personal or political.

· II ·

Between 1938 and 1941, before directing his first film, Huston collaborated with Koch and several other writers on six prestigious screenplays. *Jezebel* (1938) was an antebellum melodrama about a selfish and egoistic woman who atones for her sins and redeems herself by nursing victims when an epidemic of yellow fever strikes New Orleans. William Wyler, who was having an affair with his star Bette Davis, got Huston assigned to the picture and gave him "a crash course in filmmaking and in the politics of sex and power in Hollywood." A film historian wrote that Wyler "had fallen so far behind schedule that John Huston was pressed into service to direct a key scene that did not include Davis: a duel between one of Davis's suitors and the younger brother of her former fiancé. The sequence was shot 'on location' at the Warners' ranch, thus marking Huston's directorial debut some three years before *The Maltese Falcon*."

The Amazing Dr. Clitterhouse (1938), inevitably referred to on the set as *Dr. Clitoris*, had a strong cast (including the boxer Maxie Rosenbloom as one of the heavies) and an intriguing script by Huston. Dr. Clitterhouse (Edward G. Robinson), writing a book on criminal behavior, joins a gang of jewel thieves to find out how they operate. Claire Trevor is the hard-nosed fence who falls for Robinson. Bogart plays the head of the gang, Rocks Valentine, whose nickname pays tribute to his previous heists. He habitually polishes his diamond ring, has brilliantined hair and wears a derby hat—like the gangsters in Hemingway's "The Killers."

In *An Open Book* Huston recalled, "Henry Blanke asked if I would be interested in writing a screenplay about Benito Juárez, the 'father' of the Mexican Republic. I couldn't have asked for a more attractive assignment. It seemed almost providential, tying in with my knowledge of Mexico and my love for that country. . . . The story was of the conflict between the deposed Mexican President, Benito Juárez, and the French puppet, Emperor Maximilian." (This episode had also inspired Edouard Manet's great painting *The Execution of Maximilian*, in 1868.)

In a thematic passage of *Juárez* (1939), starring Paul Muni as the idealistic leader, Maximilian asks, "What is it that [Juárez] seeks?" and General Porfirio Díaz high-mindedly answers: "To put an end to the things that he himself has endured. To liberate, to educate, to uplift, *through democracy*." Graham Greene—who'd just attacked the persecution of the Catholic Church in Mexico in *The Lawless Roads*

(1939)—praised Huston for resisting the temptation to make the country picturesque, and noted a touch of verismo "in the dry savage countryside" as "a vulture pecks at a child's body in a ruined village."[4]

Dr. Ehrlich's Magic Bullet (1940) is the most leaden of Huston's early screenplays. It portrays the German doctor and Nobel laureate who developed the drug Salvarsan, the "magic bullet" that cured syphilis. After some of his patients die, Ehrlich is put on trial and vindicated, but the bitter fight takes its toll and he too dies at the end. Edward G. Robinson had become a star by playing a character based on Al Capone in *Little Caesar* (1930). He longed for cinematic respectability and was delighted to appear as the sacrificial idealist.

The decent, homespun piety of *Sergeant York* (1941) exemplified the nostalgic agrarian belief, held dearly by Hollywood, that life is simpler and more virtuous in the country than in the city. Alvin York's personality seemed a perfect match for the image Gary Cooper had created in his action movies—gentle, but dangerous when provoked—and capable of killing 28 Germans and capturing 128 more. Cooper called him "a pious, sincere man, a conscientious objector to war, who, when called, became a heroic fighter for his country." Less piously, Dickie Moore, the child star who played York's adoring younger brother, called Margaret Wycherly, York's mother in the movie, "a pain in the ass." The real mother of Huston's longtime collaborator Tony Veiller, she came from the New York theater, thought she was too good for the movies and condescended to Hollywood. In *White Heat* (1949) she abandoned her homespun image and played the possessive mother of the crazed and murderous James Cagney. Though these scripts were conventional or even preposterous, they taught Huston screenwriting. He learned how to work with other writers, develop ideas and master the various genres of the popular movie.

Huston admired W. R. Burnett's novel *High Sierra* and wrote the script, the best of his six screenplays, with him. In March 1940 he told the Warners producer Hal Wallis that he wanted the film to remain faithful to the book and transcend mediocre gangster melodramas: "It would be very easy for this to be made into the conventional gangster picture, which is exactly what it should not be. With the exception of

Little Caesar, all of Burnett has suffered sadly in screen translation." Another writer agreed that if the story were "emasculated," it would be just another mobster movie, with "Sierras instead of skyscrapers" in the background. Huston had the ability to articulate and dramatize the theme, and suggest the mood and power of the novel. He wanted the film to emphasize "the strange sense of inevitability that comes with our deepening understanding of his characters and the forces that motivate them."

Despite their different modes of operation, Huston and Burnett were kindred spirits. "I never had so much fun in my life, John and I working together," Burnett recalled. "We got along fine. But we didn't work well together, because I work fast on the typewriter and he dictates. He likes to sit down and completely talk out a scene, which would take a day and wear me out." Burnett was also extremely pleased, despite twenty-seven pages of objections from the Production Code censors, that they had managed to evade the moral restrictions by never actually showing their sexual relations: "We had a girl living with two guys and we got away with it—in 1940!"[5]

Huston made Bogart's character in *High Sierra* emotionally complex and credibly human. He has a feeling for nature, an unlucky attachment to his dog Pard, friendships with men and hopeless love for two women. Unlike Bogart's earlier, one-dimensional gangsters, Earle is a criminal with integrity. Though he comes from a poor background and bitterly unhappy family, he's "never let nobody down," helps unfortunate outcasts, is loyal to his friends and has a code of honor. Huston described how Bogart realized his role: "Bogie was a medium-sized man, not particularly impressive offscreen, but something happened when he was playing the right part. Those lights and shadows composed themselves into another, nobler personality: heroic, as in *High Sierra*." A single fugitive, pursued by an army of police, Bogart heads for the mountains. After a high-octane car chase he encounters a roadblock, abandons his car and, followed by swarms of motorcycles, takes to the hills on foot. He can never come down again and will never be free till he's dead. Exposed by his all-too-faithful dog, he calls out to his girl, who's followed him into the High Sierras. As a radio announcer narrates the fatal events, he's trapped and killed by a marksman with a telescopic rifle. His bitter epitaph is spoken by a sneering reporter: "Big shot Earle! Well . . . Look at him lying there. . . . Ain't much, is he?"

American reviewers, like Otis Ferguson in the *New Republic,* praised the innovative script. But one significant dissent came from George Orwell, reviewing films for *Time and Tide* in London. Repelled by the obsession with violence in American movies, he ignored the complexity that distinguished *High Sierra* from the black and white morality of Bogart's earlier crime films. For Orwell, the movie represented the extremes of sadism, bully worship and gunplay, repugnantly combined with sentimentality and perverse morality: "Humphrey Bogart is the Big Shot who smashes people in the face with the butt of his pistol and watches fellow gangsters burn to death with the casual comment, 'They were only small-town guys,' but is kind to dogs and is supposed to be deeply touching when he is smitten with a 'pure' affection for a crippled girl, who knows nothing of his past. In the end he is killed, but we are evidently expected to sympathise with him and even to admire him."[6]

· III ·

Just as Huston's literary success in New York had drawn him to Hollywood, so his screenwriting triumphs in Hollywood brought him back to New York, and he continued to work on both coasts. In 1940 Walter—giving his son another boost—agreed to star in Ellis St. Joseph's *A Passenger to Bali* if John could direct the play. John wrote of this tepid Conradian drama, "All the action takes place on a tramp steamer plying the China Seas. The captain is cursed with the presence of a lone passenger he can't get rid of . . . [who] sets about undermining the captain's authority with the native crew. The captain finds himself a prisoner on his own ship." When the ship hits the rocks, the obstructive passenger is left to perish. The simplistic moral question propounded by the play was "Should the captain have put the passenger adrift in an open boat some time beforehand and saved his ship, or was he right in having acted according to the law even at the cost of his ship?" Walter was not greatly in need of John's guidance. But when Walter went overboard, John would wryly yet respectfully say, "Dad, that was a little too much like Walter Huston."[7] Despite the considerable talents of both father and son, the ponderous play—which John called an honorable failure—closed after only four performances.

Huston and Howard Koch wrote another Broadway play, *In Time to Come* (1941), directed by Otto Preminger. The theme of his second presidential drama was the failure to achieve peace through the ill-fated League of Nations. As John Houseman wrote, "It dealt with the last tragic years of Woodrow Wilson's presidency—from his triumphal departure for the Paris Peace Conference to the dark months, after his stroke, when everything he had worked for was being destroyed. The parallel with the present world situation was inescapable and called for an immediate production." But the stuffy Wilson was not a charismatic leader (the actor who played him was also rather wooden) and Congress prevented the United States from joining the League. The play, more about Wilson's ideas than about his character, ends when the broken president, his dreams shattered, is about to leave the White House.

The reviews were enthusiastic. Brooks Atkinson, in the *New York Times* of December 29, 1941, called it "an honest high-minded drama about a great subject." Though the play was more didactic than dramatic, Richard Watts, in the *New York Herald Tribune*, agreed that it was "a dignified, arresting and remarkably convincing historical document." But as Koch explained, the well intentioned "document" was doomed, not enlivened, by contemporary events: "Everyone foresaw a long run but as it turned out, our timing of a peace play was somewhat off. Pearl Harbor intervened [on December 7], and the country's preoccupation was not on the prevention of war but on its prosecution; after six struggling weeks, the production closed" on January 31, 1942.[8] At a time when democracies were threatened by the rise of fascism and by war against Germany and Japan, Huston's pictures and plays about Presidents Lincoln and Wilson, Benito Juárez, Dr. Ehrlich and Sergeant York were intensely idealistic.

Huston's scripts on Juárez and Ehrlich were biographical and paved the way for *Moulin Rouge* (on Toulouse-Lautrec) and *Freud. Sergeant*

York, about the greatest American hero in World War I, foreshadowed his choice of Audie Murphy, the most decorated American hero in World War II, as the star of *The Red Badge of Courage*. Huston's acting experience on stage proved useful when he took cameo roles in his own films and major parts in the movies of other directors. His failures as a director and writer for the stage propelled him back to Hollywood, where his talents flourished. By 1941 he was ready to create his first masterpiece.

FIVE

BLACK BIRD,

1941

· I ·

H uston not only had a commanding knowledge of serious literature but also, even rarer in Hollywood, a respect and reverence
for it. He didn't consider movies a high art, like painting and writing,
and respected the author, not the director, as the *auteur*. Thirty-four
out of thirty-seven of his feature films were adaptations of novels, stories or plays. He worked with many major writers: James Agee, Truman Capote, Arthur Miller, Jean-Paul Sartre, Tennessee Williams and
Christopher Isherwood. And he transformed into cinematic images the
books of many important authors: Dashiell Hammett, B. Traven, Stephen Crane, Herman Melville, Carson McCullers, Rudyard Kipling,
Flannery O'Connor, Malcolm Lowry and James Joyce. Huston became
successful and powerful enough to make films of his favorite books.
"I choose material that appeals to me," he said. "I don't try to guess
what 100,000,000 people will like. It's hard enough to know what I
like. Then when I thoroughly like something, I try to put on the screen
the qualities that I think are important." His wild, freewheeling films
had more *hauteur* than *auteur*, and his great theme was the tremendous struggle to achieve the impossible and the loss of the goal at the
moment of triumph.

In *The Maltese Falcon* (1941) all of Huston's talents as writer, actor
and director were finally disciplined and came brilliantly together. He
wrote the script, chose the actors and guided them through the picture.
The cast included his lover Mary Astor, his best friend, Humphrey

Bogart, and the great character actor Sydney Greenstreet, all of whom would reappear the following year in *Across the Pacific*. Bogart would also make four more good films with Huston; Peter Lorre, after a debilitating drug addiction, would turn up again in *Beat the Devil*. Huston used his expert knowledge of art and film when composing and framing the scenes, and staged deft boxing maneuvers when Bogart (Sam Spade) disarms Lorre (Joel Cairo) and Elisha Cook, Jr. (Wilmer). Robert Warshow, in an influential essay on "The Gangster as Tragic Hero" (1948), defined the gangster in words that apply equally to the daring and versatile Sam Spade. He is "the man of the city, with the city's language and knowledge, with its queer dishonest skills and its terrible daring, carrying his life in his hands." Spade's idiosyncratic code of honor places the detective uneasily between the criminals and the police. Hammett called his hero "a hard and shifty fellow, able to take care of himself in any situation, able to get the best of anybody he comes in contact with, whether criminal, innocent by-stander or client." Hammett's novel, *The Maltese Falcon* (1930), opens like a Sherlock Holmes story. An attractive and apparently helpless woman client comes to Spade's office with her sad story and he's immediately prepared to take on her case. Each chapter, as if ready for adaptation, has one or two separate, fast-paced scenes and lively, colloquial dialogue, strongly influenced by the terse style of Hemingway's "The Killers" (1927). Spade resists entanglements, but not sex, with Brigid O'Shaughnessy (Mary Astor) and with Iva Archer, his partner's wife. But he's most at ease with his nonsexual secretary and devoted pal, Effie Perine.

The names of the characters are suggestive. *Spade* and *Archer* connote hard-boiled action; *Wonderly* (one of Brigid's pseudonyms) is amazing; *Kasper Gutman* (Sydney Greenstreet), who makes a dramatic entrance about halfway through both novel and film, is enormously fat; *Cairo* hints at Levantine decadence. All the parts are perfectly cast. The events, which take place during four days in early December 1928, raise two questions: will the criminals get the falcon, and will Spade or the police get Brigid?

Censorship forced Huston to eliminate two scenes from the film that were in the novel. In the book Spade makes Brigid strip naked to see if she's stolen and hidden the missing thousand-dollar bill. Hammett also makes clear that Cairo and Wilmer are lovers. Brigid refers to Cairo's trouble with a young boy in Istanbul, and Spade refers to Wilmer as a "gunsel," which sounds like *gunslinger,* or hitman. This obscure but crucial word, which very few people would know, actually derives from the German *Gänsel* or "gosling" and means a catamite or sodomite. Huston had to cut the scene in which Cairo seductively puts his arm around Wilmer's shoulder and is hit by the outraged young man.

The best dialogue in the movie comes straight from the book:

GUTMAN TO SPADE: "I'm a man who likes talking to a man that likes to talk."

WILMER TO SPADE: "Keep on riding me and you're going to be picking iron out of your navel."

GUTMAN [WHOSE ELABORATE DICTION CONTRASTS WITH SPADE'S ROUGH SLANG]: "Have you any conception of the extreme, the immeasurable, wealth of the Order [of St. John] at that time?"
SPADE: "If I remember, they were pretty well fixed."

GUTMAN: "I shouldn't think it would be necessary to remind you, Mr. Spade, that though you may have the falcon yet we certainly have you."[1]

Huston rather cryptically mentioned, "There was something in the *Falcon* that attracted me, that hadn't been done in the [two previous] versions," but didn't explain what he meant. Spade's juggling three women who are in love with him is like Huston deftly managing his various wives and lovers. More significantly, in the novel Gutman travels with a daughter who has the unusual name of Rhea, and the elimination of the daughter in the movie strengthens the bachelor's emotional ties to Cairo and Wilmer. Spade gets hold of the fierce-looking falcon from Captain Jacoby (played by Walter) of *La*

Paloma, whose ironic name means "the dove." Recalling his dramatic entrance, Walter said: "I wanted to make it good, so instead of falling dead with a dull and indecisive thump, I reeled around and broke a lamp on the way down." When Gutman cold-bloodedly says, "If you lose a son it's possible to get another. There's only one Maltese falcon"[2] and agrees to hand Wilmer over to the police, the camera prolongs the dramatic moment by moving slowly across the astonished and relieved faces of the four other characters. The psychological dynamics of *The Maltese Falcon* symbolically destroy an entire family. Huston gets rid of his mother (Rhea), kills his father (Walter is shot and dies after delivering the black bird) and has the paternal Gutman sacrifice his substitute son.

In contrast to the director Otto Preminger who insisted, "I have no obligation, nor do I try, to be 'faithful' to the book," and to the screenwriter of an earlier version of the film, *Satan Met a Lady* (1936), in which the falcon becomes, for no good reason, the horn Roland blew at Roncesvalles, Huston adopted a new and radical method: He remained extraordinarily faithful to the original. As Hemingway, disgusted by the distorted script of *For Whom the Bell Tolls,* observed, "When you have something wonderful, why do you have to change it for something silly just because you are paid to put the book into film?" The style, action and atmosphere, as well as the dialogue, came right out of Hammett's novel. As Huston told the novelist Jim Harrison, "You simply take apart two copies of the book, paste the pages, and cross out what you don't like."[3] He explained that the script "was done in a very short time, because it was based on a very fine book and there was very little for me to invent. It was a matter of sticking to the ideas of the book, of making a film out of a book. . . . I tried to transpose Dashiell Hammett's highly individual prose style into camera terms—i.e., sharp photography, geographically exact camera movements, striking, if not shocking, setups."[4]

Huston conceded that Jack Warner had given him a "sporting indulgence" by allowing him to direct. The script was entirely his own, and in contrast to some later disasters, he did not have to accept any changes made by a relay of writers or team of heavy-handed producers.

Howard Koch was impressed by Huston's meticulous planning as both writer and director: "When John Huston was preparing to direct *The Maltese Falcon,* he showed me his shooting script. Practically every element of the action, down to the smallest detail, was anticipated in that screen play. Without diminishing his directorial talents, it seemed self-evident that Huston, the writer, had accomplished the basic creative work before Huston, the director, took over."

The Maltese Falcon was a critical and financial success that enhanced Huston's prestige and power at Warner Bros. His planning paid off, and the film cost only $327,000 to make—just under budget. The picture was shot in thirty-four days (including a full day's rehearsal for the long scene in Gutman's apartment, when all the characters gather to get the falcon) from June 9 to July 18, 1941. After shooting the blaze aboard *La Paloma,* the studio kept two firemen on the boat in case sparks flared up in the night. To create the statue of the fabulous bird, the art department made a sketch, the plaster shop cast a mold and turned out six hollow reproductions, and the paint shop sprayed them with black enamel—at a cost of $114. In December 1994, at Christie's in New York, one of the original six falcon statues was sold for $398,500—$71,500 more than it cost to make the entire film in 1941.

· II ·

Huston and the leading actors were all good friends and morale on the set was extremely high. Lee Patrick, who played Effie, recalled that Huston created an unusually congenial mood and got the very best out of his actors: "You felt you were working in an atmosphere of love. You were with a director who loved every one of you and wanted everyone to be good in his own way. He made everything very intimate to you. What he had to say to you was very quiet, in your ear. He could illuminate just what he wanted with a few words. He made you feel somehow that you were so important to the picture. And it only led to good performances."[5]

Huston's friendship with Bogart—like his later bonds with Hemingway, Errol Flynn and Orson Welles—was one of his most complex and interesting connections with another man. Huston had written the script for *The Amazing Dr. Clitterhouse* but did not actually meet Bogart until the filming of *High Sierra*. He soon became Bogart's close friend and would direct six of his best films: *The Maltese Falcon, Across the Pacific, The Treasure of the Sierra Madre, Key Largo, The African Queen* and *Beat the Devil*.

The two men, though very different in character and way of life, had deep temperamental affinities and a great deal in common. They had troubled relations with their mothers, preferred the company of men, were heavy drinkers, liked practical jokes and defied authority—especially Jack Warner. Both were rebellious and iconoclastic, had caustic tongues and cruel, sometimes sadistic streaks. Consummate professionals in their work, both were restless and easily bored. Like Bogart, Huston was a good listener as well as a witty and stimulating conversationalist. They liked to stir things up and amused each other with a teasing rivalry. When a secretary praised Bogart's sex appeal, he told Huston: "I yield to no man in the animal magnetism field." They shared strong views about how a wife should behave, but often behaved outrageously themselves. Evelyn Keyes, Huston's third wife, recalled that both men indulged in childish pranks and acted like a couple of schoolboys. They often got drunk together and once played football with a precious Ming vase.

Though Huston was seven years younger than Bogart, he was the dominant personality and called Bogart, and everyone else, "kid." Bogart deferred to Huston and wanted to earn his respect. Yet, comfortable at home, careful with money and faithful to his wives, he also envied Huston's sublime egoism, effortless seductions and exciting way of life, his ability to behave exactly as he pleased and indulge in the reckless adventures that the more cautious Bogart didn't dare to do. Bogart admired Huston's creativity and his exciting, quixotic character, and observed: "Risk, action, and making the best use of what's around is what makes him tick. When he isn't actually on the set, he sees his surroundings as a forest of windmills, bottles, women, racehorses, elephants and oxen, noblemen and bums." He also praised him as "the only real genius in Hollywood, a real poet." But Bogart, who liked to see a job completed, was also aware of Huston's limitations and his reluctance, once he had realized his artistic vision, to finish his films: "He's always murder to work with during the last three weeks of shooting. Always restless, wanting to quit for some new idea."[6]

Bogart's previous gangster characters, like Duke Mantee in *The Petrified Forest* and Roy Earle in *High Sierra,* were criminals hunted down by the police. He was killed within ninety minutes in nearly every Warners film he appeared in before 1941. Huston was instrumental in turning Bogart into a fine actor. Bogart made an impressive advance not only from the gangster roles of the 1930s to *The Maltese Falcon,* but also to his great performances in *The Treasure of the Sierra Madre* and *The African Queen.* Huston said he did not choose him for personal reasons: "The only reason Bogart was in so many films of mine was not because of our association, not because I liked Bogart, but because that face and voice and figure fitted in with the kinds of stories that I liked to write and make."

Bogart's hard-boiled Sam Spade was a realistic relief from the debonair, thin-mustached, dog-owning, genteel detective played by William Powell in Dashiell Hammett's *Thin Man* series, which ran from 1934 to 1944. Like Huston himself, Spade was detached, cynical and bemused. Huston called everyone "honey" or *"amigo"*; Spade calls Effie "darling" or "angel." The movie, like the novel, is told completely from Spade's point of view and he appears in every scene except the early murder of Miles Archer. The audience knows no more than Spade knows, and discovers the truth about the falcon and about Brigid exactly when he does.

Most tough guys in movies are extremely laconic, but Bogart talks rapidly and constantly. The producer Hal Wallis told Huston, "Bogart must have his usual brisk, staccato manner and delivery." Huston confirmed that the film would move as fast as possible: "I am shrinking all the pauses and speeding all the action. . . . This picture should gain in velocity as it goes along." Huston's assistant recalled that Bogart was not very imaginative, that he neither discussed his part nor argued about it. Instead, he sought Huston's views and took his direction. Huston told him what to do and Bogart did it.[7]

In *The Maltese Falcon* Bogart plays an isolated individual, hounded by the police, who opposes a gang of elegant and sophisticated criminals. The Sam Spade character, the private detective who is more intelligent, imaginative and effective, more honorable and principled than the stolid, flat-footed police, originates in the stories of Edgar Poe and Conan Doyle. The part suited Bogart, who has a tough, credible seriousness, a perfect foil to the other characters. His cold, appraising glance contrasts with Astor's fluttering eyelids, Lorre's childish alarm and Greenstreet's genial villainy. Next to Elisha Cook's perverse nastiness, Bogart seems all the more capable and courageous.

Bogart's Spade—a shrewd, dapper figure—rolls his own cigarettes, lives in a modest one-room apartment and does not carry a gun, though he twice disarms both Cairo and Wilmer. He must at once help his client, find out who murdered his partner and maintain his idealistic code. Rebellious and misogynistic, he risks his life for $25 a day. In their hostile love scenes, as Brigid tells him, "You're absolutely the wildest, most unpredictable person I've ever known," he tugs at his ear and pulls his lips back into a grimace. Looking at her with sceptical disdain, he ironically says, "You're good. You're very good," and then calls her a liar. After their first ambiguous kiss, he pushes her face back with his fingers. Though he looks up expectantly as Brigid prepares to overpay him, he's contemptuous of the materialism that dominates the other characters and drives them to destruction. He's had an affair with Archer's wife, whose marriage makes their adulterous liaison more exciting but also prevents him from marrying her. He despises his partner, removes his name from the office window immediately after his death and dumps Iva as soon as Archer is killed.

Spade's defiant encounters with Cairo and Gutman are the high points of the film. Cairo is preceded into Spade's office by the penetrating odor of gardenias. The Levantine homosexual has brilliantined curly hair, wears a wing collar and outsize bow tie, carries white gloves and a white-topped cane, whose rounded tip he suggestively puts next to his mouth. Foppish, affected and exquisitely polite, Cairo usually speaks with elaborately formal diction. "Our private conversations," he informs Spade, "have not been such that I'm anxious to continue them." The two characters are contrasted in a terse exchange when Cairo complains, "This is the second time that you laid hands on me!" and Spade replies: "When you're slapped you'll take it and like it."[8]

Cairo's Greek passport (which Spade inspects) says he was born in 1903 in the port of Lepanto. In 1539 (according to the legend in the film) the Knights Templars of Malta sent this falcon to Charles V of Spain, but it was stolen by pirates en route and disappeared. At Lepanto, the site of an actual battle in October 1571, the Maltese Templars joined the combined Christian fleets under Don John of Austria. They defeated the Ottoman war galleys, took control of the Mediterranean and prevented the Turks from advancing into Europe. Cairo's birthplace connects him to the golden falcon, encrusted with precious jewels, that he's been pursuing from Hong Kong to Istanbul.

Mary Astor, the leading lady, had been a child star, and acted while still a teenager in movies with John Barrymore and Douglas Fairbanks. She had a colorful past and notorious public image. Following a stormy affair with Barrymore and the death in a plane crash of her first husband (the brother of Howard Hawks), she married a gynecologist, Dr. Franklyn Thorpe. When they were divorced in 1935, Astor brought suit to regain custody of their daughter. To counter this action, Dr. Thorpe contended that Astor was unfit to care for the child, stole her diary (written in purple ink) and entered it into evidence. When the court suppressed the diary, he leaked large portions of it to the tabloid press and created a spectacular scandal.

The diary revealed Astor's voracious sexual appetite and assessed the erotic capacity of her numerous lovers. She confided that the married playwright George S. Kaufman, a sexual superman, had given her in one night as many as twenty orgasmic moments of "thrilling ecstasy." She didn't quite know how he did it, but certainly liked what he did. The diary, as well as her messy divorces and nervous breakdowns, filled the Hollywood gossip columns and nearly ruined her career. But in 1935, while she was appearing in *Dodsworth* with Walter, Sam Goldwyn refused to invoke the morals clause in her contract and, with adroit public relations, transformed Astor from an indiscreet nymphomaniac into a devoted mother fighting for her child. Huston wanted, and got, a piece of the action. In the early 1940s in Tarzana, Astor "was among the guests, to the obvious discomfort of his beautiful Anglo-Irish wife Lesley." But Astor stopped writing her diary after the scandal and did not fill in his scorecard. After *The Maltese Falcon* she began to drink heavily and was hospitalized as an alcoholic. In 1959 her autobiography became a best seller.

All these lurid events made her perfect for the role of Brigid O'Shaughnessy, the elegant and sophisticated deceiver, the murderess who plays a weak and helpless woman. Huston brought out "her voice, hesitant, tremulous and pleading, her eyes full of candor." She was a charming, ladylike contrast to the deadbeat gun molls in the crime movies of the 1930s. Bogart, referring more to her private life than to her intelligence, tells her, "You're O.K., baby. So you're not very smart—but you know it and what the hell's the matter with that!"[9] For Bogart, being smart was not an especially desirable quality in a woman.

Sydney Greenstreet, born in England and twenty years older than Bogart, had been a tea planter in Ceylon and a stage actor in London and New York since 1902. Somewhat nervous during the shooting of his first film, he asked Astor, "Mary dear, hold my hand, tell me I won't make an ass of meself!" As Kasper Gutman, an urbane, sybaritic, attractive villain, he was particularly good in scenes with Bogart and with Peter Lorre. Greenstreet, who weighed as much as 360 pounds, wore an old-fashioned frock coat, striped trousers, spats and bowler hat. Hammett described Gutman as "flabbily fat with bulbous pink cheeks and lips and chins and neck, with a great soft egg of a belly that was all his torso, and pendant cones for arms and legs." Huston's low-angled shots turned Greenstreet into a looming, ominous figure, whose plentiful paunch seems to be another obstacle that must be overcome. The producer Hal Wallis said "he had a deep chuckling laugh, a fruity voice, and a manner that was alternately genial and menacing." Gutman tells Spade, while waiting for the drugged drink to knock him out, "You're the man for me, sir. No beating about the bush." But he himself constantly beats around the bush, and as the plot unfolds, there are endless delays in talking about the falcon as well as in actually acquiring it.

Meta Carpenter, William Faulkner's mistress and the script girl on

The Maltese Falcon, gave a detailed account of Huston's extraordinary skill, his technical innovations and his effective camera setups during Bogart's second encounter with Greenstreet:

> We rehearsed two days for the twenty-two uninterrupted moves that Huston and cinematographer Arthur Edeson devised. The camera followed Greenstreet and Bogart from one room into another, then down a long hallway, and finally into a living room; there the camera moved up and down in what is referred to as a boom-up and boom-down shot, then panned from left to right and back to Bogart's drunken face; the next pan shot was to Greenstreet's massive stomach from Bogart's point of view; Greenstreet slowly rose from his chair and moved to the fireplace to stand facing Bogart as our camera followed him. The choreography of it was exacting and exciting. One miss and we had to begin all over again. But there was the understanding that we were attempting something purely cinematic, never tried before, and everyone — stars, camera operators, and cablemen — worked industriously to bring it off. . . . A hushed silence fell over the company as Huston called for a take. After a nerve-wracking seven minutes or so, in which actors and camera crew were incredibly coordinated, Huston shouted "Cut!" and "PRINT IT!" A shout went up and crew members heartily applauded.[10]

Huston's perfect preparation enabled them to do several days' work in a few intense minutes.

The baby-faced Lorre, born in Hungary in 1904 (a year later than the birth date on Joel Cairo's Greek passport), had had a distinguished career in the German theater. After a painful gallbladder operation in the late 1920s, he became a morphine addict for the rest of his life. Lorre, who had a sinister aura and could launch into alarming spasms of fury and fear, achieved fame as the psychopathic child murderer in Fritz Lang's Expressionist film classic *M* (1931). He came to America in 1934 and still had a strong central European accent. He said "da" instead of "the," and "ken-oo-ine" for "genuine," and the studio urged him to enunciate more clearly so that he could be understood. Yet his strange accent and high nasal voice provide a wonderful contrast to Greenstreet's plummy tones. Huston considered him "one of the finest and most subtle actors I have ever worked with. Beneath that air of innocence he used to such effect, one sensed a Faustian worldliness." Lorre later attributed the success of *The Maltese Falcon* to the unusual quality of the acting: "*The Maltese Falcon* was one of my happiest memories, a very nostalgic one, because for a few years we had a sort of stock company, an ensemble there at Warner Bros. . . . In each one of those people . . . there is one quality in common, that is quite a hard quality to come by, it's something you can't teach, and that is to switch an audience from laughter to seriousness."

The Maltese Falcon has several suggestive symbols that reveal character: Wilmer's guns, Brigid's fluffy fox fur, Cairo's gardenia perfume and ivory-tipped walking stick, Gutman's heavy watch fob and satin dressing gown. But the main symbol, of course, is the ever-elusive falcon. Unlike the ancient alchemists who tried to use the philosopher's stone to transmute lead into gold, Gutman's confederates have changed the golden statue into lead. In the best scene of the movie, they finally unwrap the long-sought treasure, chip off the crusty coating of the bird and discover it's a fake. Cairo, subservient until now, grimaces and—in a comically vituperative outburst that equates obesity with low mentality—screams at Gutman: "You—You imbecile! You bloated idiot! You stupid fat-head, you!" Gutman, who's spent seventeen years searching for the precious statue, is not easily discouraged when he wants something. Realizing that the falcon is more of a curse than a treasure, he remains monomaniacally obsessed by the quest. He intends to devote his life to finding it and leaves Bogart with a courtly compliment: "Frankly, sir, I'd like to have you along, you're a man of nice judgment and many resources."

Spade must finally deal with Brigid. He tells her that he knows she killed Archer (no one else could have taken him by surprise with a gun) and, choking her with his hand on her throat, says: "I hope they don't hang you, precious, by that sweet neck. . . . If you're a good girl, you'll be out in twenty years. I'll be waiting for you. If they hang you, I'll always remember you." As the pathological liar appeals to him for protection against the police, he exclaims: "I don't care who loves who! I won't play the sap for you! I won't walk in Thursby's, and I don't know how many others' footsteps! You killed Miles and you're going over for it." (This speech is better than the awkward speech in the novel when Spade says, "I won't walk in Thursby's and who knows who else's footsteps.") He speculates, "Maybe you love me and maybe I love you," but is willing to sacrifice personal feelings to achieve justice. He's also concerned that Brigid, if let free after killing Archer, might someday kill *him*. As the police arrive to arrest her, Spade brushes past Brigid as if she doesn't exist. Spade sacrifices Brigid as Gutman sacrificed Wilmer, and in the last shot the elevator gate closes in front of her as if she's already behind bars. As Raymond Chandler, Hammett's contemporary and rival, observed, "The only effective kind of love interest is that which creates a personal hazard for the detective. . . . A really good detective never gets married."[11]

· III ·

The source of the last line of the film has inspired a good deal of discussion by professors, film critics, biographers and Huston himself. When Detective Polhaus asks what the statue is, Spade replies, "The stuff that dreams are made of." Lawrence Grobel, for example, preparing the reader for a real revelation, states: "For forty-eight years the line has been attributed to Huston." He then quotes Huston's misleading assertion that this phrase "was Bogie's idea. It's been quoted a number of times, but this is the first opportunity I've had to tell where the credit for it lies. Before we shot the scene Bogie said to me, 'John, don't you think it would be a good idea, this line? Be a good ending?' And it certainly was."[12]

Bogart may have supplied the line, but Shakespeare wrote it. Toward the end of *The Tempest* (1611), the magician Prospero breaks off the masque he has presented to the lovers, Ferdinand and Miranda, and declares it has all been an illusion: "Our revels now are ended. These our actors, / As I foretold you, were all spirits and / Are melted into air, into thin air." Human lives, he says, are just as frail as make-believe: "We are such stuff / As dreams are made on, and our little life / Is rounded with a sleep." The line is indeed a wonderfully appropriate conclusion. Spade's reference to the famous Shakespearean epilogue rounds out the film, parallels the formal prologue at the beginning, and emphasizes the illusory quest for a falcon that has melted into thin air. Many lives have certainly been rounded with a sleep: Archer (killed by Brigid), Thursby and Jacoby (killed by Wilmer) are dead. Brigid, Gutman, Cairo and Wilmer have been arrested and will be sent to jail. Spade remains alone in a hostile world. And the real falcon has once again disappeared. The Shakespearean idea that all the world's a stage, that life—like art—is based on illusion, strongly appealed to Huston.

The Maltese Falcon rejected the conventions of the traditional gangster film—usually set amid the mobs of Chicago and New York rather than in San Francisco—and created a new genre. Instead of crude and violent criminals—played in the 1930s by Edward G. Robinson, George Raft and James Cagney—Huston introduces the genial, unarmed Gutman, the easily disarmed Wilmer, the precious and degenerate Cairo, and the apparently defenseless and enchanting murderess Brigid. As Mary Astor wrote, "The picture was a completely new conception of the 'gangster movie'; it was the story not of hoodlums, but of a group of evil though intelligent people playing for very high stakes." The critics were ecstatic about the film. James Agee called it "the best private-eye drama ever made" and praised Huston as the coming man in Hollywood: "There is nobody under fifty at work in movies, here or abroad, who can excel Huston in talent, inventiveness, intransigence, achievement or promise."[13]

Huston was well pleased with his debut as writer and director. Though he was one of the first directors to leave the lighting and sets of Warner Bros. and shoot more realistically on authentic locations, he later praised the benefits of the studio system, which had disciplined his behavior and controlled his recklessness. He even claimed (with some exaggeration) that he'd done superior work on the back lot: "I'm not sure I wasn't better then. Some of the worst pictures I ever made, I've made since I've had complete freedom." He'd continue to rebel against the oppressive rule of Jack Warner, but felt the studio executives at least knew how to produce movies: "They were people who wanted to make pictures, and they knew how to make them. They weren't accountants and bookkeepers, tax consultants and efficiency experts who don't know how to make pictures."

Huston also explained why most screenplays were superior in the studio era, when writers had more time and incentive to improve them: "In the old days, writers were on salary, and they wanted to stay on the script as long as possible. So the script got better and better. Now writers want to finish one job and get paid for it, and get on to the next. In the old days, the hacks wanted to be good writers. Now the good writers are constantly being tempted by the next deal."[14]

THE HUSTON TOUCH,

1941–1942

· I ·

With Charlie Chaplin (who began in silent films) and Preston Sturges, Huston was one of the first screenwriters to become a director. In the 1950s James Agee, his fervent admirer, insisted that "Huston, next only to Chaplin, is the most . . . vigorous and germinal talent working in movies today." Asked, later on, whom *he* most admired, Huston named three directors and, pointing to the mix of class and skill that he thought a director needed, playfully added a thoroughbred and a boxer: "Ingmar Bergman, Chaplin, Jack Ford, Nijinsky—the horse, not the dancer—and Mohammed Ali." The intensely productive Huston probably made more great films than any other director. Of his contemporaries, only Billy Wilder, David Lean and Orson Welles were comparable (see Appendix). Ray Stark, who produced several of Huston's films, told him, "You have rather spoiled me and I think I am going to find it difficult working with other directors."[1]

Huston, in his mid-thirties, made a career of directing when the art of the film was still comparatively young. Working in the theater and movies at the same time, he was at once a writer, actor and director, and used his persuasive charm on studio executives, actors and crew. All his characteristics as a director derive from his creative re-imagining of the text. He preferred his scripts to follow their original literary source and, without flashbacks, to keep a linear story line. He broke with several current customs: instead of shooting in the studio, he insisted on realistic locations, often abroad; he filmed in sequence whenever possible; instead of giving up aspects of the production to specialist departments, he involved himself directly in all parts of the process and stamped the movie with his own strong personality. At its best, the result was a convincing and exciting narrative.

Perhaps his greatest gift as a director lay in his handling of actors. He was as faithful to their integrity as he was to the books that inspired his films. On the set the director has the same aura and authority, and commands the same absolute obedience, as the captain of a ship. Huston, a natural leader, was very firm indeed when his command was challenged. But in contrast to Teutonic martinets like Fritz Lang and Otto Preminger, who exercised rigid control over actors, he usually treated them with respect, maintained authority with a firm but gentle hand and won their loyalty. Instead of giving precise directions on the set, he liked to rehearse before shooting began, then allowed the actors to shape their own performances. Once the rehearsals were finished, he tended to remain aloof during the actual shooting. He looked for spontaneity and was open to the actors' interpretation of their roles. If something new came out of the interaction of the players, he was eager to use it. Inspired to play their parts in their own way, they worked hard to satisfy him.

Instead of creating a new set of professional and emotional relationships on every film, Huston frequently used the same people, and developed a familiar, revolving company of actors and crew, most of whom thought working with him was the high point of their career. The genial leader of an experienced team, he had subtle social skills. Throughout his forty-five years as a director, he attracted all the best actors of his time. In addition to Bogart, Welles appeared in four of Huston's films, Ava Gardner and Robert Morley in three. Mary Astor, Peter Lorre, Jennifer Jones, Sam Jaffe, Montgomery Clift, Max von Sydow, Stacy Keach, Paul Newman, Jacqueline Bisset, Michael Caine and Albert Finney each appeared in two of his pictures. Huston, who could be extremely patient, was one of the very few directors willing to risk a second movie with the volatile Marilyn Monroe.

For Huston, making a film, especially on location, was a prolonged social event, a collaboration in which he was the ringmaster. He was the only filmmaker who directed his father, his daughter, his son and himself. He often cast his lovers (but never his wives) in minor roles. Friends and cronies who'd never acted before—the jockey Billy Pearson, the Austrian count Friedrich von Ledebur, the Irish journalist Seamus Kelly, even the producer Wieland Schulz-Keil—did well in cameo roles. His favorite actors, Bogart, Robert Mitchum and Richard Burton, were heavy drinkers, but performed well under his guiding hand.

One of Huston's cardinal principles was that he cast the actors himself. He believed the actor gives a convincing performance because "he *is* that character. He's not made into that character by the director." He was very sure about what he wanted and clear about how it should be achieved. He chose wisely and, like a good teacher, expected actors to have their own ideas. He felt (with the notable exception of Montgomery Clift in *Freud*) that it was pointless to try to break down an actor's ego, which provided essential protection, because "an actor without an ego is like a virgin without a petticoat." He was proud of his good relations with actors and said, "I've never fired an actor. Never had to." The only exceptions to his normally smooth and tactful management of actors were Clift and, to a lesser extent, Burt Lancaster and George C. Scott. Though he used Scott twice, he hated him and publicly condemned him with surprising bluntness as "a fool . . . a shithead . . . a pain in the ass."

Huston's tactful, hands-off yet personal method was similar to that of Claude Chabrol. The French director said, "I work with actors I know, so I can feel when they're not happy. I talk to them before. . . . I only show the actors the general direction, I give them a pointer. Then occasionally I make small but precise suggestions."[2] Huston explained his own innovative technique by stating, "In the initial conversations, I may talk about the idea of the role, what its relation to the whole picture is, the background of the character. . . . I try to tell them as little as possible, because I want to see what they can give me. There's always time later to give them what I've thought about." Marlon Brando, who starred in *Reflections in a Golden Eye* and whom Huston also wanted for *Heaven Knows, Mr. Allison*, *Fat City* and the unrealized film version of

Shakespeare's *Richard III*, thought the director was somewhat distant and detached, but always calmly in control: "John Huston gives you about 25 feet. He's out in the background. He listens. . . . He's an auditory guy and he can tell by the tone of your voice whether you're cracking or not. But he leaves you alone pretty good."

Two novelists who portrayed Huston gave vivid accounts of his methods. In Charles Hamblett's *The Crazy Kill*, the character based on Huston acts out the scenes before shooting them. Then, as an actor explains: "Once or twice I've known him to edge into a discussion and drop a word here and there, but most of the time he leaves you to find your own interpretation and work it out in acting. If it's not right he'll talk round it till you see points you haven't before, or clear up any obscurities he may have felt about the way you were doing it." Peter Viertel's *White Hunter, Black Heart* (1954) describes Huston on location for *The African Queen*. Viertel condemned his egomania and compulsion to hunt elephants instead of making the movie. But he also made clear that Huston inspired intense loyalty, even devotion, in his colleagues: "The crews in Hollywood had always loved Wilson and had worked themselves half to death whenever he had asked them to do so. . . . He was nice to everyone and everyone who worked with him was eager to do so again. . . . He relegated authority and was usually correct in his estimate of the people in whom he put his trust."[3]

Lillian Ross emphasized his calm, clear mind, even when dealing with major crises: "Huston showed no sign of being under any pressure. He was able to turn from one thing to another with ease, good humor, and concentration." His manner was relaxed and unhurried. Unlike Jack Warner, he rarely raised his voice. When he wanted to instruct an actor, he would draw him aside and tactfully whisper his suggestions in private. His longtime art director Stephen Grimes said, "Huston was one of the very few people who actually *was* thinking when he looked like he was thinking."[4]

Huston could be beguiling when he wanted to coax a certain performance out of an actor, but he could also be ruthless in order to get exactly what he wanted. To obtain a daring shot, he often rejected stuntmen and risked injury to his leading actors, exerting his power, testing their toughness and challenging them to reach the heights. But he was able to push them to their physical and emotional limits—as he recklessly pushed himself—without actually hurting them. He thought he could get a better performance from the actor who took the character to the extreme demanded by the script, and by so doing he often achieved an impressive level of realism.

Huston's sharp eye focused on setting up the shots, and he talked more to the cinematographer than to the actors. He was an expert with the camera and shot close to the bone. He knew from instinct, experience and a visual sense of drama exactly where to place the camera and how to film the scene. He explained that after careful planning "you already know the way the scene will be cut together, so you shoot only what's required. That's called 'cutting with the camera.' " He disliked flashy, self-conscious camera movements and insisted, when stating another fundamental principle, "in the best-directed scenes, the audiences should not be aware of what the camera is doing." Like Paul Cézanne, he didn't want his art to say "Look at me" but "Here it is." Roberto Silvi, his longtime film editor, noted that Huston did not take part in the actual editing. After they finished the shoot, Silvi took about eight weeks to make the cut, Huston returned for a day's screening and they made extensive notes on what had to be done. Silvi then needed two more weeks to make these changes, Huston came back a second time and they decided together on a final cut.[5]

As a director, Huston had the quality of *sprezzatura* that Castiglione described in *The Book of the Courtier* (1528). He accomplished difficult things with careless ease and hid the conscious struggle he had made. Like a Renaissance courtier, Huston displayed "a certain nonchalance, so as to conceal all art and make whatever is done or said appear to be without effort and almost without any thought about it." At times he seemed to be directing without even paying attention to the actors. When things went badly wrong he might get angry, but instead of venting his anger with outbursts of rage, he responded with icy disdain and withering sarcasm.

Huston could not always remain engaged when making a poor movie. If his interest flagged or the story did not satisfy him, he tended to slack off. When his pursuit of spontaneity descended into sloppiness, he adopted an improvised, even chaotic approach, abandoning his careful planning and missing the chance to create a better film. He didn't use a storyboard after *The Maltese Falcon,* and (his assistant recalled) when he got bored and lost interest in a movie, he could turn up on the set without a list of shots or plan for the day. He was willing to delegate responsibility and always believed that "if you choose the right people, they'll do the job well." The actor Stacy Keach thought Huston "enjoyed the process of work more than the results. . . . While cutting one movie he started working on another."[6]

Like all directors, Huston sometimes made what he knew were inferior movies because he wanted to work and needed the money. These admittedly dud projects, he explained, required a fatalistic attitude and a different kind of skill: "[The films] that got you down were those where you were working with material that wasn't very good— and you were trying to hide from the audience the fact that what they were seeing was not all that good. . . . You come in and try to keep it from disgrace but it's awful, and you're sorry you've ever done it. What can you do? Surgeons operate when they know the patient is going to die."[7] But even Huston's failures were worth seeing for their adventurous spirit, sardonic humor and painter's eye.

Huston's attitude to his work varied from film to film. He moved from the meticulous storyboard and controlled shooting in the studio in *The Maltese Falcon* to the cultivation of African chaos and danger in *The African Queen* and *The Roots of Heaven;* from the last-minute improvisations in *Beat the Devil* and complete indifference in *The Unforgiven* to a return to meticulous and detailed planning (in case his precarious health broke down) in his last picture, *The Dead.* Once he became a sought-after director, he usually chose a project that could be filmed on location in a foreign country that he wanted to visit. Sometimes he wished to smuggle art out of Mexico, pursue big game in Africa, absorb Japanese culture or hunt foxes in Ireland. He himself thrived on extreme hardships, which showed his toughness and ability to overcome the most challenging obstacles. He didn't care if he made others miserable or put them at risk. Besides the two films he shot in Africa,

Huston made many difficult, even disastrous movies. There were car accidents in *Beat the Devil,* raging seas and lost rubber whales in *Moby Dick,* captured wild mustangs in *The Misfits,* intractable script problems with Jean-Paul Sartre and psychological crises with Clift in *Freud,* sexual entanglements and collapsing buildings in *The Night of the Iguana* and wild animals to be handled in *The Bible.* The way he rose to these challenges and even relished them was often as interesting as the movies themselves.

· II ·

Despite his hyperactive love life, Huston restrained his emotions and disliked public displays of affection. In his films, he preferred suggestive to explicit sex scenes. Bogart nearly strangling Mary Astor as he kisses her in *The Maltese Falcon* and Albert Finney's humiliating impotence with Jacqueline Bisset in *Under the Volcano* were more to his taste. His daughter Anjelica said there was a Victorian streak in him, and he admitted, "It embarrasses me somewhat when a kiss goes on too long on the screen. Why, I want to turn my face away. I shouldn't be there. That's something between them!"

In contrast to his deliberate restraint on screen, Huston made a number of provocative and exaggerated statements about his real-life relations with actresses. Asked why he became a director, he crudely replied, "Because the director gets to fuck the star." Casting aspersions on his stars and pretending that sexual hygiene was more important than physical pleasure, he insisted, "As long as I don't get the clap from one of my leading ladies I'm satisfied." His advice about how to treat actresses was equally blunt: "If the actress is beautiful, screw her. If she isn't, present her with a valuable painting she will not understand. If they insist on being boring, kick their asses or twist their noses."[8] These arrogant remarks were probably designed to shock the interviewer and express his resentment of those who pried into his private life. In his view, no actress, comely or homely, was really worth a precious painting. He'd never put up with anyone who was boring, and when irritated, he *did* twist Bogart's nose. But he was a romantic man who often fell in love.

Huston had affairs with several of his leading ladies: not only with Mary Astor, but also with Olivia de Havilland, with Suzanne Flon in *Moulin Rouge* and with Eiko Ando in *The Barbarian and the Geisha*. Only insurmountable obstacles prevented him from seducing other actresses, who were hors de combat. Lauren Bacall, in *Key Largo*, was married to his best friend; Katharine Hepburn, in *The African Queen*, was besotted with Spencer Tracy; Jennifer Jones, in *Beat the Devil*, was guarded by her fiercely protective husband David Selznick; Juliette Gréco, in *The Roots of Heaven*, was the mistress of the jealous producer Darryl Zanuck; Audrey Hepburn, in *The Unforgiven*, was married to Mel Ferrer and pregnant; Marilyn Monroe, in *The Misfits*, was (precariously) married to Arthur Miller, who wrote the screenplay; Susannah York, in *Freud*, aroused his hostility, and Susan Kohner, in the same film, was the daughter of his agent; the star of *Annie* was a child.

Most of these liaisons lasted only while the picture was in progress, but his affair with Olivia de Havilland, which began in 1942 when he directed her in *In This Our Life*, was an exceptional relationship that lasted, with many sharp peaks and deep depressions, for the next decade. Huston loved the euphonious sound of her multisyllable names, the harmonious mixture of *l*'s and *v*'s, of *i*'s and *a*'s in *Olivia de Havilland*. She was born in Tokyo in 1916, the daughter of an actress and a patent attorney. After her parents' divorce, her mother took the five-year-old Olivia and her younger sister (who became the actress Joan Fontaine) to California. While still a freshman at Mills College in Oakland, the moon-faced Olivia appeared at the Hollywood Bowl as Hermia in Max Reinhardt's lavish production of *A Midsummer Night's Dream* (1935). Still only nineteen when she got the leading role in *Captain Blood* (1935) with Errol Flynn, she went on to play Melanie in *Gone with the Wind* (1939), and to win Oscars for best actress in *To Each His Own* (1946) and *The Heiress* (1949).

The real Olivia was very different from her saccharine, goody-goody public image, based on her roles as handmaiden to the dashing Flynn in *The Adventures of Robin Hood* and many other movies. She had a feisty, combative side to her character that appealed to Huston. In 1943, when her seven-year contract expired at Warners, she wanted to become a free agent. The studio claimed she'd incurred a six-month penalty for refusing (inferior) roles. She fought them in court for two years and, in an important test case that helped many actors achieve freedom from the studios, emerged victorious.

Unlike so many publicity stunts cooked up by the studio, their relationship was warm and real. Home movies show Huston and Olivia frolicking affectionately next to her swimming pool while he plays a bull to her matador. In a charming photo of 1943, Huston—wearing a bathing suit, kneeling on an outdoor lounge chair, smoking a cigarette, looking down, with dangling hair, and absorbed in a newspaper—seems completely oblivious to Olivia. Barefoot and wearing a short sun dress, with open bodice and disheveled hair, she playfully sits on his thin shoulders. She rests her hand on his lowered head (as if subduing him) and, after failing to capture his attention, smiles seductively at the camera. In October 1942 the Warners producer Henry Blanke told army investigators that Huston "had been seen quite a bit with Olivia de Havilland and was believed by most observers to be very much in love with her." Olivia, in a rather fine distinction, allowed that "when he was making *Across the Pacific* [1942] I didn't live with him, but he was a guest in my house, off and on, for more than two years." Huston's affair with Olivia and tenancy in her house coincided with his military service and marked the end of his marriage to Lesley Black.

Though Huston was in love with Olivia, she was more passionate than he was and understood his emotional makeup. John Houseman, alluding to Coleridge's "Kubla Khan," described her as a woman wailing for her "demon lover": "And all should cry, Beware! Beware! / His flashing eyes, his floating hair!"[9] Olivia's intense nature inevitably came into conflict with John's moody defensiveness. As William Wyler's wife emphasized, "Olivia just always comes on very emotionally. It's typical of her character to come on at a very high pitch about almost everything." Later in life Olivia remembered that "John was a very great love of mine. . . . He's capable of tremendous love of a very intense order. . . . He's very sensitive . . . a man pressured by witches . . . and he broods about everything he's ever done wrong to anybody. . . . He was a man I wanted to marry, and knowing him was a powerful experience, one I thought I would never get over. I watched him bring great destruction into the lives of [Lesley and] other women. Maybe he was the great love of my life. Yes, he probably was."[10]

When Olivia begged Eloise Hardt (another of Huston's lovers), "You've got to help me make up with John," the disillusioned Eloise surprised her by asking, "What do you find so interesting and attractive about him?" Eloise suggested that Olivia's passion and possessiveness may have disenchanted Huston: "Olivia was always a very outgoing and aggressive and positive person, an 'I want' kind of dame. She had claimed John during their life together and could never understand why it wasn't the greatest love affair in history." In Eloise's view, "John was everybody's lover because he let you fulfill your fantasy. He gave nothing of himself and the girls gave everything, they wrote their own story and he helped them fill in the blanks. . . . The more you loved him, the less respect he had for you."

If John was troubled by Olivia's all-consuming intensity, she was upset by his jealousy and unfaithfulness, a lethal mixture that was probably related to his mother's self-absorption, remarriage and neglect of him as a child. "John couldn't take any kind of rejection," she said, "without desperately going off and comforting himself with some female conquest. He was always imagining rejection or infidelity on the part of the other person. And he certainly expected fidelity, it was very important to him. He was always nervous about the other person being attracted to somebody else or straying off." Huston's infidelity wounded Olivia and turned her against him, but her anger merely incited him to resume the chase. "I must say I felt hatred for John for a long time," she recalled. "He saw me at a party when I was about to do *To Each His Own* in 1946 and he began his pursuit again. But I had simply been through too much. I didn't really trust him anymore."[11] By the time Huston separated from Lesley in 1944, he'd fallen in love with someone else. Then, when he courted her once again, Olivia, torn between emotion and reason, was reluctant to marry him.

In This Our Life (1942), which allowed them to work together, was the melodramatic story of a decadent and dysfunctional southern family, with Olivia as the rather soppy younger sister of the bitchy Bette Davis. After stealing Olivia's husband, Davis unconvincingly exclaims: "You don't hate me. I never meant to hurt you. . . . I never meant it. I never meant anything." Huston so blatantly favored Olivia in the picture that he was reprimanded by the front office and forced to reshoot some of the scenes. Jack Warner recalled, "When I saw the first rushes I said to myself: 'Oh-oh, Bette has the lines, but Livvy is getting the best camera shots.' 'Look, John,' I said to Huston, 'Bette Davis gets top billing in this picture, but you're writing her out of the big scenes and giving them to de Havilland. Let's get back on the track.' " Though love affairs with stars were almost de rigueur, they were not allowed to interfere with the way the movies were actually made. Huston, forced to give in after Davis' complaints, said, "There is something elemental about Bette—a demon within her that threatens to break out and eat everybody." The novelist Ellen Glasgow, dissatisfied with the movie version of her work, told the hyperemotional Davis, "If I had chosen acting over writing, I wouldn't be the overacting ham you are."

The movie has plenty of southern clichés, including both wise and deferential blacks. But it is notable for portraying an intelligent and educated black character, what a reviewer in the Negro press called "the first decent part that has ever been given to a colored actor in any major motion picture."[12] Davis gets drunk, runs over a child and blames it on an innocent black man, who is studying to be a lawyer and truthfully asserts, "Police don't listen to no colored boy." After her crime is discovered, Davis pleads with her wealthy and powerful uncle, played by Charles Coburn, to save her from prison. When he tells her he has a fatal disease and is not concerned about what happens to her, she explodes with "Who cares if you're dying? I've got my whole life ahead of me." But of course, she doesn't. In the final car chase, a rerun of the end of *High Sierra*, the terrified Davis, pursued by the cops, crashes her car and is killed.

Though Olivia was careful to protect her chaste screen image and was always discreet about her love affairs, she later confessed that before she met Huston she had been deeply in love for three years with Errol Flynn. On April 29, 1945, at the house of the producer David Selznick, she was the subject of a violent quarrel between Huston and Flynn. She could not tame either Huston or Flynn and was actually afraid of them, which was part of their attraction. Speaking of Huston, she said, "There was a man, someone I felt very, very deeply about after my long-term crush on Errol Flynn. . . . But he brought such great pain to the three women he did marry."

Their mano a mano, a chivalric duel about a woman's honor, was provoked by Huston's jealousy and his unfair remarks about Flynn. Flynn's wife Nora thought Huston needled Flynn, who had tuberculosis, "about the fact that he wasn't in the service. And it went on from there. And Flynn, instead of explaining why he wasn't in the service, got into hot words and the next thing you know they were throwing punches."[13] Wounded by Huston's caustic remarks about his cowardly evasion of military service, Flynn retaliated by mentioning his own sexual relations with the fair Olivia. Portraying himself as a gentleman and Flynn as a cad, Huston recalled that Flynn had said "something wretched about someone—a woman in whom I'd once been very interested and still regarded with deep affection. I was furious at his remark, and I said, 'That's a lie! Even if it weren't a lie, only a sonofabitch would repeat it.' "

They went outside where Flynn, who was twenty-five pounds heavier and an expert amateur boxer, kept knocking Huston down. He cut his elbows in the gravel driveway but kept getting up. "By the time I finally began to get his range," Huston wrote, "he'd marked me up quite a bit. I was cut over the eye and my nose was broken again. But I paced myself, and I began to score on his body." They fought, in Huston's exaggerated account, for more than an hour. Flynn won, verbally and physically, and both men needed medical attention: "Errol went to a hospital that evening, and I stayed over at the Selznicks' and checked into a different hospital the next morning." When Flynn called to ask about Huston's condition and report that he had two broken ribs, Huston—whose teeth hurt for the next six months—said he'd "thoroughly enjoyed the fight and hoped we'd do it again sometime." After venting their anger, neither man held a grudge, but Hollywood hosts now realized that Huston and Flynn, after a few drinks, could be dangerous guests. They were both irascible and pugnacious, willing to batter their bodies and their reputations over a provocative remark.

In about 1954, when Huston was making *Moby Dick,* Flynn sent a telegram offering footage from his own documentary film, which opened with fine shots taken from a helicopter of romping whales: "Hallo Johnnie. Suggest you get Warners to show you *Cruise of the Zaca* for whale sequences. If any use, have extra footage which happy to give you for free because you can't fight worth a damn. . . . Errol." Later on they became buddies and worked together in *The Roots of Heaven.* Speaking of Errol (after his untimely death) but also alluding to himself, Huston defined his own credo by praising his friend's boldness and daring, his attraction to danger and willingness to take risks: "I think Errol was capable of practically anything. He liked living on the edge. Errol took chances . . . to be more aware of life. [People] aren't keen, their senses aren't quickened, when there isn't an element of danger. And they're only half-alive unless they're threatened."

Over the years the bond between Olivia and John remained strong. In Los Angeles in December 1952 they fired up their smoldering affair, though by this time he was (rather loosely) married to his fourth wife and deeply involved with a French actress. The screenwriter Nunnally Johnson reported the small-town gossip that flourished in the Hollywood fishbowl: "John Huston is back and I think Olivia's got him. After seeing *Moulin Rouge* she was quoted saying: 'At last John has come of age.' Unquote. This statement rang through the town. . . . Later in the evening John went to sleep sitting up on a sofa and snored at the ceiling while Olivia tried to force black coffee down him while she stroked his brow"[14]—a tender variant of the active Olivia and passive John in their poolside photo of 1942.

· III ·

Huston's next picture, *Across the Pacific* (1942), brought him into the completely different world of entertaining war propaganda. It takes place in November–December 1941 on a voyage along the *Atlantic* coast from Canada to Panama. The title refers to an attack on Hawaii in the original *Saturday Evening Post* story and has nothing to do with the characters in the film. Mary Astor explained, "The first version wasn't bad. It was all about thwarting a Japanese plot to attack Pearl Harbor. By the time we had commenced work on it late in December of 1941, Pearl Harbor *had* been attacked [the screenwriters foresaw the threat before the U.S. Navy], and the story was changed to thwarting a Japanese plot to blow up the Panama Canal. Bogart said, 'Let's hurry and get this thing over with before the Canal goes too.' " Like Huston's play *In Time to Come* (1941), the film's theme was swamped by America's sudden entry into World War II.

As in *The Maltese Falcon,* Huston gave Bogart a witty and sophisticated relationship with the duplicitous Mary Astor and the evil Sydney Greenstreet. In this wartime propaganda movie he also portrayed the slimiest Japanese villains who had ever appeared on the screen. Astor recalled, "The government started shipping out our Nisei cast [to internment camps]. A little indignation and some wire-pulling held them at least until the picture was finished." But her memory was unreliable. All the Asian roles were played by Chinese actors, made to look as ugly and sinister as possible and to reflect the current hatred of the Japanese enemy. The dangerous plague of Japanese spies in the picture tacitly justified the internment of the Nisei.

In *Across the Pacific* Bogart, apparently dismissed from the army, sails with Astor and Greenstreet on an eerie Japanese ship whose stateroom blinds cast shadows that suggest the striped pattern of the enemy flag. She is going to her father's plantation, which (Bogart discovers) is being used as a secret base by the Japanese. Quoting Byron's "Hebrew Melodies," he says she "walks in beauty." During Bogart's playful, even roguish flirtation with Mary Astor, he blinks with pleasure after first kissing her, runs his fingers along her neck after their second kiss and smiles at her discomfort by asking:

"Say, are you getting sick?"
"I don't know. How do girls usually act when you kiss them?"

"They don't turn green."

"Then I'm sick."

But referring to her seasickness and sunburn, she acutely observes, "Seeing me in pain gives you pleasure."

The large and luscious Greenstreet, an admirer of Japanese culture and enemy agent, tries to get strategic information from Bogart and enlist him in his plot. Called "the fat man," as Gutman was in *The Maltese Falcon*, he tells Bogart: "You're always furnishing surprises." Greenstreet wears a homburg, Bogart a fedora. Huston shows Bogart pushing the bribe money around on the table with his index finger, as if reluctant to take it, and staring at Greenstreet's extended hand before shaking it. Greenstreet claims that "Japanese make great servants," Bogart observes that "they all look alike." Greenstreet boasts: "My gun is bigger than your gun," Bogart retorts: "I told you—mine is bigger than yours." At the end, Greenstreet, about to be arrested and remaining true to his adopted country, tries but fails to commit hara-kiri. Bogart, guided by Huston, moves effortlessly from apparent disgrace through light comedy to wartime heroics. Combining toughness with moral commitment, Bogart preserves an ironic distance from the propagandistic aspects of the picture.

Huston completed most of the film from February to April 1942, before he was called in to military service to make documentaries for the Signal Corps. His departure contributed to the myths surrounding *Across the Pacific*. In *An Open Book* he portrayed himself as a cheeky rebel and hyperbolically wrote, "I proceeded to make things as difficult as possible for my successor. I had Bogie tied to a chair, and installed about three times as many Japanese soldiers as were needed to keep him prisoner. There were guards at every window brandishing machine guns. I made it so that there was no way in God's green world that Bogart could logically escape. I shot the scene, then called Jack Warner and said, 'Jack, I'm on my way. I'm in the Army. Bogie will know how to get out.' "[15] In fact, Warner Bros. production files reveal that Huston—more professional than prankster—was actually given a

week's notice and made all the arrangements for a smooth transition to his successor.

The scene in which Bogart was hopelessly trapped may have been planned or fantasized by Huston, but it was never shot by Vincent Sherman, who took over on April 23 for the last ten days. Jack Warner, fed up with all the delays, told Sherman to "get in there and finish the goddamn thing." Sherman arrived on the set to find actors still walking around with the script and learning new lines. The Japanese airplane and Bogart's machine gun were already in place for the final scene. But this melodramatic climax was much less interesting than the beginning of the movie, which had built up the suspense, and Huston didn't quite know how to end it. Alone at the climax of the film, and trapped by the menacing villains, Bogart enacts a James Bond fantasy, triumphs against overwhelming odds and proves (as he confidently tells the enemy), "You may start the war, but we'll finish it." After one of the enemy soldiers goes berserk, Bogart overpowers his guard, captures a machine gun and shoots down a Japanese plane as it takes off to bomb the Canal. When someone questioned the logic of the scene, Sherman exclaimed: "Listen, if you ask me, we were lucky to get the bastard out of there at all."[16] The army would surely have let Huston finish the picture while they conducted the war without him for a few more days, but he wanted to escape from the propagandistic movie, which did not interest him, and from his current entanglement with the possessive Olivia.

SEVEN

INTO BATTLE,

1942–1945

· I ·

Recalling the danger, excitement and the achievements of the war years, as well as the love affairs he enjoyed while on leave, Huston felt "my whole time in the Army was, I suppose, the most compelling experience of my life." He began as a lieutenant, making movies for the Signal Corps, and ended as a major, awarded the Legion of Merit. The glow lingered on. Using military titles in peacetime was traditional in the British Isles, and his domestic staff in Ireland addressed him as Major Huston long after the war was over.

His first post (September to late 1942) was in the Aleutians, the northernmost American battleground, a 1,200-mile chain of islands running southwest from the Alaskan coast. In June 1942 the Japanese had landed small forces on the western islands of Kiska and Attu, and bombed the American air base in Dutch Harbor in the central Aleutians. The Japanese hoped, and the Americans feared, that these islands might become a bridge to the mainland. But as the literary critic Irving Howe (also stationed in the Aleutians) noted, "The Japanese had penetrated a few islands and then, in battles made particularly horrible by rain and fog, been driven back."

Two other distinguished writers were posted to the Aleutians. The reclusive Dashiell Hammett reached Adak about nine months after Huston left. Hammett's biographer described that remote outpost as "a barren volcanic island about eight hundred miles from the Alaskan mainland. In the winter winds reach eighty miles per hour on the

289-square-mile island, and the temperature dips to forty degrees below zero. After the Japanese were routed in the fall of 1943, the Aleutians were peaceful, used primarily for air bases and communications centers." Moved by the austere beauty of the lakes and mountains that no other place could match, Hammett lyrically wrote, "The smoke came out [of the Pavlov volcano] in slow-spaced smallish dark puffs from a vent near one edge of the top and usually hung for awhile just atop the mountain before the wind blew it away."[1]

The future novelist Gore Vidal was first mate on a freight-supply ship sailing between the Unalaska and Umnak islands, a thousand miles west of Anchorage. Less enthusiastic than Hammett, he described the bleak Aleutians as "home to huge ravens and small foxes, with beaches strewn with moonstones and jasper. . . . The main street of Dutch Harbor [on Unalaska] curved parallel with the beach for half a mile. . . . Bars and restaurants and one theater, all wooden, lined the street. . . . Behind two bars and a former brothel was the old Russian Orthodox Church." In a rare description of the natural landscape, Huston agreed with Hammett: "There is a strange beauty about the Aleutians—undulating hills of spongy moss laced with salmon rivers, without a tree or anything like a tree for 1,500 miles. Most of the islands are mountainous, and a number of mountains are volcanic, topped with white cones and streamers of smoke."

The Aleutians were certainly not peaceful when he was there. As the Americans increased their B-24 Liberator bomber missions against the Japanese bases—flying two or three hours west from Adak to Kiska and Attu—Huston's cameramen flew with them and filmed the action. His main photographer, Jules Buck, was described by his daughter as "a short, plump, ordinary man" and striking contrast to Huston, a "blithe spirit who did what he damned well pleased, and got away with it. All the time."[2] Huston sometimes squeezed in with the pilot and flew into battle, enduring heavy antiaircraft fire, attacks by Japanese Zeros and crash landings.

His documentary film *Report from the Aleutians* (1943) showed the military importance of the Aleutians campaign and of the bomber attacks that eventually drove the enemy off the islands. On their daily missions many planes were crippled, their crews wounded and killed, by artillery flak. But the documentary emphasized the crews' teamwork and mutual responsibility as they flew through rough weather to destroy enemy shipping, kill the Japanese soldiers and wreck their installations. When the Americans made an amphibious landing on Kiska in August 1943, they found it deserted. In an expert evacuation, the 4,500-man Japanese garrison had disappeared into the darkness and fog.

In the fall of 1942, while Huston was risking his life in the Aleutians, the army was conducting an investigation (his file stated) "to determine the discretion, integrity and loyalty of Subject, who is suspected of being a Communist." Huston was never a Communist, and it's not clear who accused him or why the army thought he was subversive. But during World War II and the Cold War that followed, one could come under suspicion for being "reportedly affiliated with the League of American Writers, an alleged Communistic organization, and also listed as a sponsor of the National Fund Raising Campaign for Russian Relief" and the American Friends of Spanish Democracy. The so-called Army Intelligence officers did not care that Russia was America's wartime ally and that the Friends of Spanish Democracy was an antifascist organization, passionately opposed to American wartime enemies in Germany and Italy.

The investigators interviewed Huston's superior officers in the Signal Corps. They found that the great egoist was obsessed with his film work and "impressed Major Davis as one who cares for nothing else and talked of nothing else but the picture business. Described as one who was self-centered." Colonel Schlosberg gave him a categorical clearance: "His loyalty and integrity to the United States is unquestioned. . . . Lt. Huston has no Nazi, Fascist or Communistic ideas whatsoever and is proud to be wearing the uniform of the United States Army."

On October 29, 1942, the army sagely concluded: "It is the opinion of this office that evidence does not support positive charges of disloyalty, nor does it cast serious doubt as to the subject's integrity. . . . But it does recommend that subject be placed in a position where he does not have access to confidential or secret information, and that he be kept under observation at his present station."[3] Though Huston was cleared of suspicion, the suspicion remained. The army—taking no chances with the suspected, reported and alleged Red—kept him under surveillance. The investigation and file that remained in his record indicate the paranoid fear of Communism that gripped American institutions during the war. Though the army employed technicians, writers and directors to create their propaganda, it continued to question their loyalty.

· II ·

In October 1943 Huston was sent to the battleground in central Italy and remained there until April 1944. A month before his arrival, American troops had landed on the coast at Salerno and fought their way up the peninsula from Naples toward San Pietro Infine. This village, ten miles south of Cassino and eighty-five miles south of Rome, commanded the main road through the Liri River valley to the capital. But the rough mountain terrain, in constant rain or snow, was fiercely defended, ridge by ridge, by some of the best troops in Europe. Historians wrote that "Field Marshal Albert Kesselring, commander of all German forces in the Mediterranean . . . conducted one of the most brilliant defensive campaigns in military history. . . . The Germans were always on the high ground in well prepared positions, our men always in the open, climbing the heights and kicking them off." The biographer of the American commander, Mark Clark, described the difficulties the Americans faced. They had to capture "a village of stone houses that resembled a citadel on a steeply terraced hillside and dominated the approaches from the south. It was a critical objective and had to be taken. He wanted no frontal attack. Make an outflanking movement. Swing wide to the east and go at the village from the side, across the slope instead of up it. That meant delay, for the soldiers had to work their way carefully around to the flank, across gullies and draws, over razorback ridges, along precarious ledges, all the while trying to remain out of sight of German gunners."[4]

The battle took place from December 8 to 17, 1943. By the time San

Pietro was captured, twelve of the sixteen Sherman tanks in the assault had been destroyed, three hundred civilians had been killed and the 143rd Infantry Regiment had suffered 1,100 casualties. An American officer bitterly recalled: "It was a stupid operation. My battalion was used to attacking at night. For us to attack in daylight across a valley and up a hill where the Germans had been fortified for a long time was suicidal." Another historian noted the ghastly significance of the assault that Huston filmed in *The Battle of San Pietro* (1945): "It was a relatively small operation tucked between the bloody landings at Salerno and the muddy stalemate at Monte Cassino. . . . For the first time in the war [American troops] were becoming massively expendable in a dirty, costly, extremely frustrating infantry campaign. . . . They have been ordered to assault an impossible objective in miserable weather, and Huston brilliantly conveys their resignation and foreboding as they move to the attack."

Both Huston and his English companion-in-arms, Eric Ambler, gave firsthand accounts of how the film was made. In *An Open Book* Huston explained the background and his mission: "After Caserta, north of Naples, bad weather set in, the Germans dug in their heels and the Allied attack foundered. . . . We were to proceed to the front and make a picture that would explain to American audiences why the U.S. forces in Italy were no longer advancing. . . . Highway 6, the only major artery to Rome, ran through the Liri Valley. At the entrance to the valley stood the little village of San Pietro." Both frontal assaults "were repulsed with heavy losses. The Germans threw up a wall of automatic weapon, mortar and artillery fire." After the tanks failed, "we crept forward and photographed the disastrous results. . . . We were able to get on film Italian men, women and children, as they came down from the hillside caves where they had been living during the battle."

The war correspondent Ernie Pyle, repeating the dreary word *down*, wrote that dead men, as if on their own, "had been coming down the mountain all evening, lashed onto the back of mules. They came lying belly-down across the wooden pack-saddles, their heads hanging down on the left side of the mule, their stiffened legs sticking out awkwardly from the other side, bobbing up and down as the mule walked."[5] This moving passage recalls both Hemingway's description in *In Our Time* of the Greek retreat from Turkey in 1922 and André Malraux's great shots of villagers carrying bodies down from the mountain in his Spanish Civil War film *L'Espoir* (1938).

Eric Ambler, the mystery writer whose novel *A Coffin for Dimitrios* would be made into a Lorre-Greenstreet film in 1944, was seconded from the British army to Huston's film unit. He mentioned that their camera lens reflected light and drew fire, and gave a grim account of the aftermath of the battle: "A whole company had been caught on that patch of stubble and the bodies of the dead were dotted everywhere. . . . The shrapnel fragments had ripped through everything. . . . This was the place where the wounded had crawled and died. . . . Those who had not died of their wounds and the freezing cold had, in trying to find warmth [in the granaries], probably suffocated."

Though Huston executed a cunning sleight-of-hand by appearing to shoot his film in the midst of combat, Ambler revealed that they did not arrive in San Pietro until December 16, the next-to-last day of the fighting: "Our best plan would be to move into the small town immediately after the enemy had left, and then make a film of what happened next to its inhabitants." The battle was actually restaged, between late December and late February, using survivors from the 36th Division. Huston did not have to risk his life under fire in order to make an effective film about the capture of the town. Ambler recalled, "Most of it was re-enacted 'combat' footage of a fairly impressionistic kind. One sequence, however, came over very strongly. It showed a burial party at work after one of the frontal assaults that had been so costly. With notable lack of ceremony, the dead men were bundled into GI body bags and dumped into shallow graves."

The Battle of San Pietro begins with a clear statement of the formidable military obstacles and, illustrated by a map, with the plan of battle. It shows that the approach to the village in the valley was either through a narrow path, enclosed by mountains and blocked by a swollen river, or by an arduous climb over those steep mountains. Since American bombers and artillery barrages had not been able to dislodge the enemy from their well-fortified positions, the infantry (despite

Mark Clark's original plan) was forced to make a direct frontal assault through barbed wire, land mines, machine guns and mortar fire. The initial assault was repulsed after an advance of only six hundred yards and one soldier was killed for every yard gained. The regiment finally captured the strategically essential village, abandoned by the enemy before they arrived, but some companies lost all their officers, and the cost was punitive. The documentary shows the destruction of the Texas regiment in a Pyrrhic victory. The bloody battle of Cassino (January 1944) lay just ahead.

Working together, as they often did, Walter Huston narrated *Report from the Aleutians* and John's third documentary, *Let There Be Light;* John narrated *San Pietro.* James Agee, always keen to praise John's achievements, wrote, "Huston's narration is a slightly simplified technical prose, at once exact and beautifully toned and subtly parodistic; it is spoken with finely shaded irony. . . . *San Pietro,* his microcosm of the meaning of war in terms of a fight for one hill town, is generally conceded to be the finest of war documentaries."[6]

A historian pointed out the ironic contrast between Huston's original intention and final result: "The purpose behind the documentary was to give new soldiers a glimpse of what combat was like . . . or to reassure the American public that its soldiers were being judiciously employed by competent commanders. . . . [But] Huston and his camera crew of six produced a startling anti-war film." Huston used a bleak verismo style (perfected in postwar Italian films) and had many shots of the American dead. He had to delete several scenes in order to make the documentary more palatable. "In the original version of the film," he said, "I had their voices speaking about their hopes for the future over their dead faces. I guess that would have been too much for the families. So it was cut." He also had to cut a close-up of a boot ghoulishly attached to a fragment of a leg.

Despite Huston's cuts, the War Department saw that it was indeed a bitterly ironic antiwar film, which would terrify and demoralize young draftees, and refused to show it. Huston defiantly replied, "If I ever made a picture that was pro-war, I hope someone would take me out and shoot me." Walter, proud of his son's achievement, once again came to the rescue. A golfing, hunting and fishing companion of the chief of staff, General George Marshall, he showed Marshall the documentary and helped persuade him to reverse the ban. Marshall, who believed its intense realism was a virtue, finally proclaimed: "This picture should be seen by every American soldier in training. It will . . . prepare him for the initial shock of combat."[7] And the film was shown to all the new soldiers.

· III ·

Let There Be Light (1946) was made, Huston said, "to reassure industry that the men who were released from the army on a section eight [a psychological discharge] were reliable, that they were not lunatics." The film was shot during three months in 1945 at Mason General Hospital in Brentwood, now part of Islip, in central Long Island. The title comes from the creation of the world in the opening of Genesis, when "darkness was upon the face of the deep" before God said "Let there be light" (1:2–3), suggesting that damaged soldiers can move from despair to cure.

Report from the Aleutians and *The Battle of San Pietro* portrayed combat; *Let There Be Light* showed its traumatic effects on the mind and spirit. Walter, narrating John's words, says, "Here is human salvage, the final result of all that metal and fire could do to violate mortal flesh." The film reveals that every man has his breaking point. Before their treatment, the patients "have in common unceasing fear and apprehension, a sense of impending disaster, a feeling of hopelessness and utter isolation." They still fear their own death and mourn the death of others, and have returned home not as triumphant heroes but as ruined victims.

San Pietro, with its focus on casualties and death, is grim; *Let There Be Light,* with its emphasis on cures, is more upbeat, though it is still painful to watch. This third documentary gives a rather simplified explanation of psychological processes and the use of sodium amytal for hypnosis, during the short eight- to ten-week rehabilitation process. The doctors (all officers) are more gruff than gentle when treating the sick enlisted men, and it's pitiful to see the soldiers' agonizing physical symptoms, tears and suffering. The Lourdes-like cures seem too facile and too rapid to be convincing, and suggest the kind of miracle that Jesus performed when he raised Lazarus from the dead. Huston writes, "Men who couldn't walk were given back the use of their legs, and men who couldn't talk were given back their voices."[8] The brave new world created for these troubled survivors, who emerge from the shadows of illness, must have recalled for Huston the sudden restoration of his health after he'd survived the perilous swim in the waterfall. Doctors have called this documentary "the most impressive piece of psychiatric propaganda ever made." But this all-too-realistic film, though therapeutic, was considered even more shocking than *San Pietro*. It was suppressed by the army for thirty-five years, and was not shown in public until Vice President Walter Mondale personally intervened in the controversy in December 1980.

Despite his struggles with the censors, Huston became more self-confident and refined his art during the war. He had light discipline and considerable freedom, and worked on minor projects with congenial colleagues like William Wyler and the director Anatole Litvak. He saw the advantages of using amateur actors and shot realistic footage overseas in Alaska and Italy. "In those instances," he said, contrasting its spontaneity to the controlled conditions of the studio, "one shoots everything, not according to the script. The script is written according to what is shot."[9] He learned to film men in action—as he would later do in *The Red Badge of Courage* and *The Man Who Would Be King*—and most important, proved his courage under fire. He took risks and he survived.

EIGHT

WOMEN IN LOVE,

1946–1950

· I ·

Though Huston married several times, marriage made little difference to the way he conducted his life. He was not unfaithful to
his wives in the conventional way, keeping the wife and family at home
and furtively having a mistress on the side. On the contrary, he lived
quite openly as if he were still a bachelor, and played the pasha in
Hollywood, in New York and in the sultanate of St. Clerans (his Irish
estate) with an exotic and wide-ranging array of lovers. He depended on
women all his life and in a variety of ways: he wanted sexual partners
and social companions, and needed practical helpmates to organize
his complicated daily life. No one woman could fill all these roles,
so a small cadre was required. He deftly juggled wives and lovers in
his private life just as he managed, as a director, the numerous actors
and crews in his films. He took delight in mixing up lovers, wives
and ex-wives, seeing them in the same room and watching their reactions. All his sexual relationships with women were transient, but he
remained friends with many of his lovers and kept the loyalty of his
stalwart female staff.

Huston had catholic tastes. Any woman who came into his orbit
was fair game, and most were willing, indeed eager, to sleep with him:
leading ladies and bit players, secretaries and coauthors, household
help and Mexican servants, patrician Yankees and aristocratic Italians, American Indians and East Indians, French and Dutch, Slavs and
Magyars, Irish equestrians and Japanese strippers, Gentile, Moslem and

Jew. Always fascinated by *autres pays, autres moeurs,* he assumed that having sex was a quick way of assimilating a new culture. He was an equal opportunity employer. He had "every movie star you could think of," in the words of one of his mistresses. "No lines were ever drawn. Including people who worked for him—maids, cooks." His fifth wife, Celeste Shane, confirmed that he slept with unattractive dependents (like Betty O'Kelly in Ireland and Maricela Hernandez in Mexico) for power and control. In one of his swaggering statements, he told Peter Viertel, "It was never a bad idea to bed down with a secretary as that ensured a fierce loyalty that he believed was beneficial." If such veneration was not forthcoming, he could simply replace the woman.

Though Huston was beaten up and even shot at in disputes over women, he thought sex was evidence of his vitality. As Celeste rather acidly remarked, "John would screw anything that wasn't nailed down, just to notch up another triumph."[1] Sex would keep him going, even if it was dangerous. Huston believed, Agee wrote, that "he has the right, even the obligation, to write and to fuck as much as he can and in ways he prefers to, even if doing so shortens his life or kills him on the spot." Sex was part of the Huston repertoire, a pastime as compulsive as drinking, gambling, hunting, writing and filmmaking.

Apart from his power, wealth and fame, which made him attractive to a great many women, Huston had the reputation of being a womanizer and a great lover. He was attractive and had the gift of charm. Women loved him because he flattered them and told them what they wanted to hear. Always curious about people, he spoke in a gentle, interested voice, asked them about their lives and listened carefully to what they said. In the view of Eloise Hardt, a lover from time to time and part of his household for several years, "John loved to get girls to fuss over him, and he knew how to convince every woman that she was the greatest thing on earth."

Unfortunately, for both John and his women, he rarely fell in love and could not sustain it when he did. Eloise recalled that he was always the actor: "John was a professional lover, studied to be a lover, loved the idea of being a lover, but was not in love." As one woman noted after the unhappy conclusion of their affair, "He had a compulsion to make people—especially women—love him, and then, once having secured their love, an equal compulsion to spurn them." He enjoyed seduction and liked to exercise his charm and power, but he was easily bored, hated to be tied down and soon lost interest. He was well aware of his own faults: his selfishness, infidelity and occasional cruelty; his indifference to women's emotional needs and physical illness, to his wives' alcoholism and mental decline. But like a relay runner handing over the baton, another woman was always ready to take him over. Though he would not or could not change his habits, he had a bad conscience and later confessed, "I'm incapable of loving anyone. What I've done to my ex-wives, I'm ashamed."[2]

· II ·

When Huston returned from the Aleutians to New York to turn his combat footage into a film, he was estranged from Lesley Black and far from Olivia, in Los Angeles. He was ready for a new romance and in December 1942, at the "21" restaurant in New York, he met the great love of his life, Marietta FitzGerald (later Marietta Tree). Born Mary Endicott Peabody, with New England names resonant in the works of Nathaniel Hawthorne, she came from one of the oldest and most eminent families in America. She was born in Lawrence, north of Boston, and raised in Chestnut Hill, near Philadelphia. Her grandfather was the founder and longtime headmaster of Groton School, her father an Episcopalian bishop, her brother governor of Massachusetts. She attended the University of Pennsylvania, but dropped out in her junior year after marrying a young lawyer, Desmond FitzGerald. Her elder daughter, the journalist Frances FitzGerald, said that her Protestant family were liberal Republicans at a time when Irish-Catholics ran the Democratic Party in Massachusetts. Marietta (as she was called), originally a New England bluestocking, became increasingly political and engaged in public life. She rebelled against her puritanical background and, as the longtime lover of Adlai Stevenson, became active in the Democratic Party.

The tall, blond, athletic Marietta was admired by everyone who knew her. A biographer said she was "elegantly beautiful, well-informed and intelligent, and exuded the sophistication of a distinguished family." The Texas-born Evelyn Keyes, who'd once been a chorus girl, was rather awed by Marietta and called her "a willowy blonde, almost as tall as [Huston], smartly dressed, class oozing from every pore." The historian Arthur Schlesinger, Jr., Marietta's close friend, described her as "walking in beauty and radiating life and delight as she walked. . . . Underneath her kind and impeccable manners, she was very sharp and funny and never missed a trick. She once said that her ideal was to be a combination of Carole Lombard and Eleanor Roosevelt."[3]

When she began her love affair with Huston, her husband was serving overseas and she was working as a researcher for *Life* magazine. Huston helped free her from the narrow restrictions of her social class, and (she said) "he taught me one thing: I was not Miss Boston; I was, instead, Miss World." Recalling their first meetings, she described the dazzling impression Huston made on a sophisticated woman: "John's outlook was so arresting and exciting, everything he said was an astonishment and of intense interest. It was all seamless: his personality, character, point of view. I was enthralled by his way of looking at art, history, making films. . . . I was overwhelmed by his knowledge. . . . He surely was a genius." Huston was amazed and pleased that he'd managed to capture this rare prize and arouse the passions of this rather cool and self-possessed woman, whose eastern background and social ease impressed him. Exceptionally, Huston made a physical and intellectual connection with a woman he respected.

Like his love for Olivia, Huston's love for Marietta did not lead to marriage. When Desmond FitzGerald returned from the war, Marietta asked for a divorce, but he insisted that she first see an analyst. When she completed her analysis a year later and decided to divorce him, she said, "It was the most traumatic period of my life. For a bishop's daughter to get a divorce was sort of reducing everything he stood for. I felt like I was murdering my family." For both Olivia and Marietta, Huston was a disruptive force who changed their lives, even though they stepped back from the brink of marrying him.

Huston, now back in Hollywood, was collaborating on the

screenplay of *The Killers,* based on Hemingway's story and starring Ava Gardner. Olivia had married, Marietta remained undecided. Accustomed to getting whatever he wanted, he seized whatever opportunities came his way. Ava's biographer wrote that she "remembered Huston becoming active with desire for her and chasing her out of the [Tarzana] house and through the woods." He soon captured her, and Eloise (always on the scene) found him "in bed with Ava."[4] In August 1946, as distance cooled his passion for Marietta, he became irritated by her delays and unwillingness to commit to him. He was weary of waiting, felt she didn't really love him and would never marry him. Smarting from the pain of rejection, he impulsively married Evelyn Keyes. In one bold maneuver, he would show his emotional independence, arouse her jealousy and intensify her desire.

A year later, on holiday in Barbados, Marietta met the Anglo-American multimillionaire Ronald Tree, twenty years older and a grandson of the department store magnate Marshall Field. Roy Jenkins described him as a man "of discriminating tastes, high good manners and large fortune." She married the bisexual Tree—a Conservative MP and friend of Winston Churchill—in July 1947. After two years of high living on his grand estate, Ditchley in Oxfordshire, they returned permanently to New York. Their daughter, Penelope Tree, became a famous model in the 1960s. When Huston was walking with Marietta in Manhattan and passed a tall office building, she casually said, "My husband owns that," and he was impressed.

Marietta later explained why, despite her great love for Huston, she never became his wife. The main reason was instinctive self-protection: "I was never really seriously thinking that I would marry him. I was certainly in love with him, he was the most attractive man possible and he changed my whole world around. . . . We remained so close because one knew that it really wasn't possible. It didn't have anything to do with smartness on my part but survival." Her daughter Frances added that "Marietta was terribly in love with Huston and had a very thrilling sexual relationship with him. But she thought he would have made a poor husband and had no regrets about not marrying him. It was a fortunate decision, and they were able to remain friends for life." Marietta's biographer explained, "Whatever she felt for him, she knew that his wildness, his financial unreliability, and his sexual fickleness would have made him a disastrous husband. . . . When asked how she managed to refuse the irresistible John Huston, she replied: 'It was simple. I could never have told my parents.' "5

Though they never married, Huston and Marietta kept in close touch, and were friends and lovers, through many vicissitudes, for the next forty years. In January 1948, accompanied by Evelyn Keyes and making *The Treasure of the Sierra Madre* in Durango, Mexico, he sent Marietta a drawing of a Mexican *bandido* riding a horse near two tall cacti and wearing a huge sombrero, with a rifle slung over his back and a bandolier charged with bullets across his chest. In a seductive letter from Mexico City that month, he emphasized the wildness of the place, mentioned his sexual fantasies about her and promised— if he could lure her to Mexico—to be less self-centered: "Everyone I ever knew has reappeared—from aging *bandidos* & retired syphilitic generals to unextraditable U.S. absconders & ex-N.Y. mayors [William O'Dwyer]. . . . Durango is supposed to be hot in the daytime—freezing at night & flat & dull all the time—the armpit of Mexico. . . . Maybe it will be *so* hot that I'll need you to give comfort—I'll do my best to be less selfish. . . . I miss you dear & dream & dream. Ever, John."

In July 1960, when Huston was making *The Misfits*, the forty-three-year-old Marietta, then deeply involved with Adlai Stevenson, attended the Democratic presidential convention in Los Angeles. She then came to Reno, Nevada, as a sort of fling. Huston was looking for an actress to play the wealthy divorcée whom Clark Gable has slept with, and can't wait to see off in the train station, at the beginning of the film. Suddenly Huston turned to Marietta and asked, "Why don't you do it?" She did, wearing her own clothes, but was bored by the endless waiting between the set-ups. The rich woman's offer to turn the wild Nevada cowboy into a midwestern businessman by saying her family owned "the second largest laundry in St. Louis" was an ironic comment on Marietta's own aristocratic background. Gable's impatience to get rid of her was an amusing contrast to Huston's desire to possess her. Marietta found it exciting to be around Huston and be glamorized by him, to appear in the picture and hear the Hollywood gossip. The film's producer, Frank Taylor, on the scene during her two-day visit, was convinced that she and Huston were still lovers. Schlesinger reported that when Huston took her to the Reno airport, there was a western-style showdown between her two rival suitors: "When he found Stevenson waiting there, both men were furious and hardly spoke to each other. Marietta then went off with Stevenson [to Lake Tahoe]. The next day Huston called to tell her she had to come back to Reno for retakes on her performance in the film. (She went.)"

After seeing Huston at work in Nevada, Marietta felt a new respect for his talent and intelligence. She told him that she was tremendously impressed by the way he dealt with his people and directed the film: "I've always been aware of your genius, but to see you in action—at a story conference or working with actors and technicians, knitting a huge, disparate group together, your long blue denim back gliding in and out of cameras, every molecule alert to every detail. All this combined with your kindness and delicacy and appreciation of each individual was a revelation!"[6]

Huston's rapturous love letters to Marietta continued for the next two decades. In January 1966 he wrote, "I long to see you & be with you once again." In January 1977 he wooed her by praising her hidden, visceral qualities: "What excitement you create all around you. It can't be just your classic beauty—it's got to be your insides which cause people around you to catch fire." Eloise Hardt, a close if rather caustic observer, said that "the only woman he ever cared for was Marietta—and that became a fantasy of what a woman should be. . . . She had all he required: beauty, intelligence, social status; someone of great importance. Others were for possession only, but he actually wanted to marry her. If he could have loved, he would have loved her."[7]

Marietta remained his unattainable ideal. In two simple but heartfelt statements in his autobiography of 1980, Huston declared that she "was the most beautiful and desirable woman I had ever known . . . the closest woman friend I've ever had." He continued to exalt her, and in a sketch of 1982 he connected her to his youth and confessed, "When I have doubts, I go to see her, and naturally, she is the same charming young girl. I fall in love all over again." Huston's lifelong obsession with Marietta answered Yeats' searching question in "The Tower": "Does the imagination dwell the most / Upon a woman won or woman lost?" As the poet Robert Lowell wrote to his poet-friend Elizabeth Bishop, whose wise rejection of his marriage proposal was one of the great turning points of his life, "Asking you is *the* might have been for me, the one towering change, the other life that might have been had."[8]

· III ·

Evelyn Keyes had played Scarlett O'Hara's younger sister in *Gone with the Wind*. She knew Walter Huston before she met John, and remembered the father proudly showing her photos of the son and talking enthusiastically about him. Evelyn said both she and John had been married twice, which gave them something in common—though not much. When they first met in 1946 John asked, "How would you like an adventure?" And of course, the twenty-seven-year-old actress, whom he described as vivacious and companionable, could not resist his challenge of a romantic evening. Soon afterward, during dinner at Romanoff's, Evelyn asked *him* a startling question: "John, why don't we get married?" Well—why not? Mike Romanoff, rising to the occasion, retrieved a wedding ring someone had lost in his pool; Huston chartered a plane from a stunt pilot; they flew to Reno and got married that night. Like Marietta, Celeste and many other women, Evelyn felt "his lovemaking was sure, with authority, and cool as always. And it was fun. Isn't this an amusing thing we're doing! Was the tone of the action."

When Huston told Eloise, his in-house companion and wrangler, that he had gotten married, she was taken by surprise and exclaimed, "Are you out of your mind?" He assured her that nothing was going to change between them, that she could stay on and manage the horses in Tarzana. She did stay on, but she was heartbroken. She thought Evelyn was a sweet girl, but "didn't have real dimensions and wasn't good enough—or bad enough—for John." The married couple never had a peaceful moment. When Huston, jealous as always, disapproved of the skimpy halter top that showed off Evelyn's breasts, he reached out and tore it off. He then calmly said, "Put on something, honey, and let's go to dinner." John once turned up at a Hollywood party with a clinging red-haired companion. Evelyn and John's current girlfriend, Ricki Soma, were also in the room. Used to constant competition and frequently irritated, Evelyn told the new arrival: "Listen, you, I'm his wife, and that's his mistress over there, and you are one too many."⁹

Lauren Bacall was with Bogart when he made *The Treasure of the Sierra Madre* in Mexico. She often saw Huston pointlessly assert his power over Evelyn—though she posed no threat—and put her down in public: "John displayed his disdain for women—his wife in particular. Poor Evelyn would say something and John would say, 'What? What was that, Evelyn? Now, wait a minute—I want everyone to hear this,' and Evelyn was on the block. Any casual, innocent, occasionally thoughtless remark was magnified and she was made to look like a fool. It was humiliating."

Evelyn remained permanently insecure about her rash, impulsive marriage. She doted on John's every attention, letter and phone call, and always wondered if he loved her. He suggested having a baby and took hormone injections for a low sperm count (he later had three children), but they failed to conceive. In any case, she never knew if he really wanted a baby and feared she would be left with the child if he abandoned her. Walter, always fond of her, provided emotional support. Huston continued to see his past and current lovers, even when she was present, and Ricki Soma was waiting in the wings.

Evelyn had to compete not only with other women, but also with children and animals. When Huston was making *Sierra Madre* in Mexico, he found a thirteen-year-old Indian orphan, Pablo Albarran, who attached himself to the film company and made himself useful. Evelyn described him as "very attractive . . . with an alive, smiling face, bright black eyes, intelligence shining through." Huston told Pablo that he wanted to adopt him and bring him back to America, educate him and give him a chance to escape from hopeless poverty. According to Pablo, "He said he'd be my father and I would live like his son." Pablo, desperate for affection, would now get what he'd always wanted: a full stomach and a good life. Without informing Evelyn (who'd gone home earlier), Huston turned up in Los Angeles with Pablo and suddenly presented her with a grown-up son who had never been to school and spoke no English. Huston had impulsively acquired the boy the same way he acquired art, then handed him over to Evelyn, who was also an impulsive acquisition. Pablo soon became very attached to her, and, she said, "at every opportunity he would snuggle close and flick my nipples with his finger, grinning at me all the while."[10]

Huston painted a portrait of the young Pablo. His wide, flat, dark, masklike Indian face has stylized features: slanted eyes, wide nose, thin lips and pillar-shaped neck. He wears a white jacket and holds a guitar flat on his lap; his thick black hair, parted in the middle, hangs down the sides of his forehead. This picture of a typical rather than individual Mexican suggests Huston's emotional distance from Pablo.

Pablo was a sweet boy, but it was a long way from the streets of his village to the lush surroundings of Tarzana, and he was way out of his depth. As he grew up, friends described him as "very outgoing, excitable. He acted like a big man, John Huston's son . . . [yet] was essentially a peon." He clearly worshipped Huston, but "was a total failure, poor little devil." After boarding school in Ojai, California, and a year at a Los Angeles community college, he went back to Mexico and became a sports reporter for a local newspaper. Torn between a desire to return to Mexico, where he faced an impoverished future, and a glamorous world where he could not fit in, between limited ability and great expectations, Pablo could not hold a job or sustain a marriage. He drifted around and was often incompetent. He was, for short spells, a used car dealer, a photographer and owner of a comic book kiosk. He sold car insurance and personal insurance to tour guides in Mexico City, dabbled in real estate and became a caretaker on a small farm. To raise cash, he once rented a car in California and sold it in Mexico.

Pablo married an Irish girl named Olga and had three children with her. But his marriage broke up, he left his children and was plagued by bad luck. He constantly tried but could never please his new father. In May and June 1964, after his divorce from Olga, he wrote Huston,

"I am sorry I have failed you and caused you a lot of headaches. . . . I hope that you won't think too badly of me." After Huston severely replied, "It's all right to leave a wife, but you don't leave a wife and children," Pablo tried to explain his impossible situation: "Dear Father, The tighter things got the more she nagged. . . . Within the last six months, she has told me about 15 times to get out of the house, that I'm not good enough for her as a man and as a provider. . . . I think that Olga believes that you should support us in luxury for the rest of our lives." His troubles continued when, in 1977, his third wife died of cancer and left him with a debt of $60,000. None of his four children would have anything to do with him. Huston felt instinctive sympathy for orphans and outcasts like Pablo, and gave in to the temptation to make the grand gesture. He liked an entourage and a household, but Pablo could not stay a child forever. He eventually lost interest in Pablo, grew impatient with his problems and became estranged from him.

In a well-meaning gesture, Evelyn provoked another crisis by giving Huston a baby capuchin monkey. Emboldened by her present, he trumped her by acquiring a pet chimpanzee called Trudy. Not surprisingly, the ape invaded and wrecked Evelyn's apartment, borrowed from Paulette Goddard, which had been lavishly decorated entirely in white. Huston, amused by the chimp's exploits and Evelyn's horror, recalled: "The dark glass counter was shattered. The perfumes and unguents were pools on the rug. The curtains had apparently been used as trapezes—they were ripped from the walls and shredded. And all over there was chimp shit, even in the open drawers. The stench was overpowering." Peter Viertel quoted Huston's nonchalant response: "Oh, they'll make friends sooner or later. Things were a little tense last night when we got home, but that was only their first meeting." As Huston introduced his wife to his latest "mistress," "they just stared at each other . . . then Evelyn put out her hand, and Trudy bit her."[11]

Evelyn called Huston "the best director and the worst husband in Hollywood." When she forced him to choose between Trudy and herself, he chose the chimp. They divorced in Mexico in February 1950, and she extracted crippling alimony. In contrast to the modest $50 a week for three years that he'd paid to Dorothy Harvey, he had to fork out $42,000 in 525 installments of $80; $7,500 in quarterly installments of $1,875; and $10,000 for every six months that she didn't earn that amount. Though Evelyn was a well-paid professional actress, he agreed, if she decided to stop working, to support her.[12]

On top of the alimony, Evelyn also got his ranch and livestock, his paintings and works of art. She told me that when they flipped a coin for his precious pre-Columbian art collection, her luck held out and she won all that as well. It's not clear exactly why Huston agreed to such a rack-and-thumbscrew settlement. She undoubtedly had a better lawyer; he probably felt guilty about the way he'd treated her, thought she deserved whatever she asked for and didn't really care that much about money or property. He could always earn more and acquire more.

· IV ·

During his marriage to Evelyn, Huston continued to see his old and new lovers. Pauline Potter, like Marietta Tree, had an illustrious background and married a very rich husband. Born in Paris in 1908, she was descended from Pocahontas, Thomas Jefferson and Francis Scott Key. She was the top designer for the fashion entrepreneur Hattie Carnegie and one of the leading hostesses in New York. After a youthful four-year marriage to an alcoholic homosexual, she had affairs with a lesbian as well as with the stage director Jed Harris, the Belgian prime minister Paul-Henri Spaak and the Russian Grand Duke Dmitri, who'd murdered Rasputin. As the second wife of Baron Philippe de Rothschild, the immensely wealthy owner of the famous Château Mouton vineyards, she acquired a title and entertained on a grand scale. (Huston drew the label for the exceptional 1982 vintage of their Bordeaux: a curved, yellow-horned, rampant ram—the *mouton*—dancing in the blue sky between a fiery orange sun and a bunch of purple grapes hanging beneath a green vine leaf.) Pauline, an accomplished woman, designed the costumes for the Broadway production of Jean-Paul Sartre's *No Exit* (directed by Huston in 1946), wrote articles on fashion and travel for *Vogue* and *Harper's Bazaar,* and translated Elizabethan poetry and the plays of Christopher Fry into French.

At Pauline's house Huston enjoyed being treated as a literary and cinematic lion. It was obvious to Evelyn, when she met Pauline in New York, that she was Huston's "very special friend." As if to apologize for showing up with a wife, he bought Pauline an expensive eighteenth-century bedspread. Evelyn wrote that Pauline had an exquisite town house in the East Sixties, "everything in it carefully chosen and arranged. As she was herself." For all her upper-class manners, Pauline was deliberately rude to the younger and prettier Evelyn. After giving her guest a frosty reception, the gracious hostess actually declared, *de haut en bas,* "This—person is allowed in our houses, John, only because of you." Huston habitually demeaned Evelyn's opinions, and Pauline did the same. In a pretentious dinner-table conversation about Picasso, she sneered at Evelyn's views.

Doris Lilly, at the other end of the social scale from Pauline, was another of Huston's girlfriends. He'd met her in 1939, when she was seventeen and clearly on the make, and continued to see her during the war years. Truman Capote gave a rapturous description of Doris, a model for Holly Golightly in *Breakfast at Tiffany's* (1958): "Tall and pretty, with long legs and streaked blond hair, she belonged to a species that was soon to become extinct: the good-time party girl whose only goal, openly and honestly stated, was to make a rich catch. . . . She was bouncy and buoyant, not subject to moods or given to silences of more than thirty seconds . . . [and had a] madcap sense of fun and adventure."

Doris, like most women, was impressed by Huston's success and magnetic charm. "You felt you were hitching your wagon to a star," she said. "And nobody ever said no to him, he got anything he ever wanted from anybody. . . . He didn't give a damn about money. Never had a money clip or a wallet in his life. He used to put his hand in his pocket and bring out little balls of money." In December 1944 he sent her a letter criticizing Hollywood and paying flattering attention to every part of her delightful body: "This place I like least of anywhere. The sun shines all the time and everybody has beautiful tans and it's all simply terrible. I called you several times but you are always out being unfaithful. Are you pretty as ever? And your feet? And your bottom?"

Doris got angry when he refused to react to her infidelity: "You could never make him mad, no matter what you did. It infuriated me. So I started going out with Errol Flynn" (another bond with Huston) and with Ronald Reagan.[13] She later became a gossip columnist and wrote the do-it-yourself comedy *How to Marry a Millionaire,* which was made into a successful movie with Marilyn Monroe.

Always, in the background, there was Eloise Hardt, a key figure in Huston's life. Born in 1917 in the Oklahoma Indian territory (the same year as Marietta, but in a completely different world), she had a German father and Cherokee mother. She lived on the reservation until she was thirteen, when her desperately poor family moved to California with the dust bowl Okies. An exceptionally beautiful Nordic blonde, she did not look as if she had Indian blood. In her teens she began working as a Powers model, supporting her mother and three young siblings. She also modeled for Tom Kelley, who took the famous nude calendar photo of Marilyn Monroe and who introduced her to Huston.

Huston was a friend and lover. He helped her out when she needed money and said, "Come and bring your family any time you want to ride horses." She came to live in the house in Tarzana and became totally at home there, but Huston didn't invite her to the dinner table, except for special occasions when he wanted to show her off. Despite her beauty, she still felt she was an Okie Indian, embarrassed and ill at ease with "mucky muck people." But when she got a contract at Columbia Pictures, the studio gave her free training with the best teachers in speech, voice, dance and deportment. She finally learned to speak educated English, and became a minor actress in the 1930s and 1940s. Huston gave her bit parts in *The Asphalt Jungle* and *The Night of the Iguana.*

Huston and Eloise were very attached to each other. When she phoned him he would always take her call (even during an important script conference), greet her with "Hi, honey," and keep important people waiting while he spoke to her. He invariably gave her the impression that it was great to be with her and to get away from all the awful Hollywood types—even if they were only going out for a hamburger. All her boyfriends got angry when she responded to his summons. He was a marvelous entertainer, and she knew she would always have a better time with him than with anyone else.

In 1945 Eloise (in her late twenties) began to see his limitations. Unlike Marietta, Evelyn, Celeste and many others, who gave his sexual performance rave reviews, Eloise cast a dissenting vote. She thought he was more interested in the seduction than in the climax and was critical of him as a lover: "When I wanted my romantic fill and my idea of a man to sleep with, it was not John. I truly loved John, but I was not in love physically. . . . I loved cuddling and being with him and I loved everything he represented, but I didn't particularly like the sex. He filled every other bill, except he wasn't romantic. We could love each other without sexual love very easily, because he was a bad lover. He didn't love the physical part of you." Recalling his jealousy, Eloise also felt that "John didn't want me but didn't want anyone else to want me. He wanted total control, but would not commit himself to any woman." In 1949, when she was having an affair with Gilbert Roland, who was acting in Huston's Cuban movie *We Were Strangers,* Huston (according to Eloise) went out of his way to mistreat him.

Eloise was vulnerable beneath her tough carapace, and an ugly incident seemed to turn her against Hudson and make her his harshest critic. Huston didn't drive after his 1933 accident that killed the Brazilian dancer and was nervous, as always, when she was driving him. She recalled that in Ireland in 1968, "I put the car in the wrong gear and went up against a tree. And this monster sitting next to me turned and said, 'What the fuck! You always say you can do something, you can't do *anything*! Go back to the farm! You're ignorant, you're dumb, you're stupid! You've never done anything with your life and you never will.' " In my recent interview with her, Eloise concluded that Huston was "the most inconsiderate, selfish and diabolical man I've ever known." Yet only six years after he insulted her in Ireland, when he was shooting *The Man Who Would Be King,* he made a characteristically generous offer. He asked Eloise if she wanted to see Morocco, invited her to visit him there, and gave her a few lines in the movie so the studio would pay her fare and expenses. As usual, whenever he called, she dropped everything and followed him.

In about 1972, when Eloise married Paul MacNamara, Selznick's publicist, she assumed the role of hostess and invited Huston to come to *her* house whenever he liked, to gamble and spend the night. He told her, rather surprisingly, that he now yearned for a stable domestic life: "I want a house like yours, with backgammon, a fireplace and a good cook, who'd make bacon and eggs at midnight."[14] But it would take two more wives and many more women before Huston would be ready to settle down—in a rather unexpected way.

NINE

WITCH HUNTS,

1947

· I ·

Huston's documentaries had contributed to the war effort, and he had no idea that his political views and loyalty to the United States had ever been questioned. Like many other returning veterans in 1945, he found that the political alignment of the government had changed. The advent of the Cold War had turned Stalin from the genial Uncle Joe to an evil tyrant (which, of course, he always had been). This shift in attitudes created and fostered fear of Communism, and left-wing views were now considered antipatriotic. Bogart had said, "If you want to get [Huston] roused, tell him something that appeals to his sense of justice and courage." The anti-Communist witch hunts in Hollywood, which persecuted liberals and Communist Party members alike, tested both these qualities. Huston—at his best in a crisis—was active in speaking out, mobilizing opinion and organizing actors, writers and directors against the collective madness of Cold War politics.

In March 1947 Richard Nixon, serving his freshman term (in a Republican-dominated Congress) as a representative from southern California, wrote to Eric Johnston, president of the right-wing Motion Picture Association that represented the Hollywood executives. Nixon, a prominent member of the House Un-American Activities Committee (HUAC), was hostile to the left-wing Screen Writers Guild. By asking Johnston, "Is the motion picture industry doing anything to stop the infiltration of Communist influence in Hollywood, or to root out any of those who are . . . sympathizers and use their positions in some

subtle manner to affect the film?," he laid the groundwork for the persecution of many people, including the Hollywood Ten, the "unfriendly"
writers and directors who refused to cooperate with HUAC.

One of the most controversial wartime propaganda movies was *Mission to Moscow* (1943), a film biography of Ambassador Joseph Davies,
written by Howard Koch and starring Walter Huston. It portrayed Stalin and the Soviet Union as warm-hearted allies and presented the horrific Moscow show trials of 1936–38—in which forty-seven innocent,
high-ranking political and military leaders were sentenced to death—as
just punishment for guilty traitors. In his autobiography, Jack Warner
quoted President Roosevelt's personal plea: "Jack, this picture *must* be
made, and I am asking you to make it." But Warner's superficial, even
frivolous book said nothing about his own subsequent denunciation of
the film and those who made it.

John Houseman explained how "the brothers—Harry and Jack—
summoned [Koch] and begged and bullied him into doing it: they
assured him that he was uniquely qualified to undertake a patriotic
assignment that, they implied, was particularly dear to the heart of
the President of the United States." Then the studio executives, fearful of being denounced during the Cold War for this pro-Communist
picture, protected themselves by accusing their innocent employee:
"Five years later these same brothers denounced Koch as a notorious
Red, citing his connection with *Mission to Moscow* as clear evidence of
his Communist sympathies." Evelyn Keyes, married to Huston and
standing with him in the events that followed, described the sense of
betrayal felt by the studio employees: "The heads of studios, instead
of closing ranks and protecting their own people—who had earned
them millions of dollars—fell all over themselves declaring what good
Americans *they* were."[1]

The conservative studio heads had always controlled the content
of films, and writers could not introduce political ideas without their
approval. Nevertheless HUAC, chaired by Nixon's colleague J. Parnell Thomas, saw political conspiracies everywhere and felt anything
that opposed right-wing thought was pro-Communist. They wanted

to undo Roosevelt's social policies, weaken trade unions and outlaw the Communist Party. The Committee feared artists and intellectuals, thought films were a dangerous propaganda weapon and wished to eliminate all liberal content from motion pictures. HUAC used the threat of blackmail, imposed ideological censorship, persecuted people for their political beliefs and often convicted the accused without giving them a chance to defend themselves. After the hearings, present and former members of the party, who had not committed any crime, were punished, without evidence or a trial, immediately blacklisted by the studios and professionally ruined. Real, alleged or merely suspected Communists were being condemned for their thoughts and speech rather than for their acts.

In September 1947 HUAC subpoenaed forty-three producers, directors, writers and actors, who were required to appear at the Committee's hearings in Washington the following month. Most people in Hollywood felt that HUAC was a serious threat and that the film industry had to be defended. Artists and intellectuals feared the oppressive social and intellectual climate; studio heads worried that political attacks would hurt business. While the executives assumed a patriotic role, cooperated with HUAC and denounced their colleagues, Huston did everything in his power to oppose it. With William Wyler and the screenwriter Philip Dunne, he responded to the subpoenas by setting up the Committee for the First Amendment (CFA). Its name referred to the part of the Constitution that guarantees that "Congress shall make no law . . . abridging the freedom of speech . . . or the right of the people peaceably to assemble." Dunne said that the CFA was established to fight four specific abuses: "the threat of a blacklist, the threat of censorship, official inquiry under threat of contempt of any citizen's legal political beliefs and affiliations, and the indiscriminate trial and conviction by headline of hundreds of persons deprived of any legal opportunity to defend themselves."

Disgusted by the attack on political freedom, Huston felt morally obliged to take a stand: "People were being persecuted for their beliefs, and nobody was coming to their defense. I felt ashamed of

Americans. I saw the thing that was coming and I wanted to cut it dead." In a fiery statement, Huston declared that the CFA "deplored the Congressional investigation, predicted that it would endanger the jobs and livelihood of many loyal Americans, cause anguish to others and throw the motion-picture industry as a whole into disrepute. . . . We stated our opposition to Communism, but argued that mass hysteria was no way to fight it." The CFA eventually attracted five hundred members, from leading film stars to distinguished intellectuals like Albert Einstein and Thomas Mann. The screenwriter Dalton Trumbo wrote that the CFA "had sensed the House committee's purpose more accurately than the rest of the country, and were willing, at that time and in those circumstances, to stake their reputations in a fight against it."[2]

The FBI, keeping a wary eye on Huston and noting his leadership of the CFA, cited his challenging statement of October 20, 1947, which they considered subversive: "We hold that these hearings are undemocratic because (1) any investigation into the political beliefs of the individual is contrary to the basic principles of our democracy, and (2) any attempt to curb the freedom of expression and to set arbitrary standards of Americanism is in itself disloyal to both the spirit and the letter of our Constitution." The FBI had to be vigilant, however, for the CFA was surprisingly effective. As Ceplair and Englund explained in *The Inquisition in Hollywood,* "Dunne, Wyler, and Huston *were* the Committee for the First Amendment. They wrote all its publicity and press releases, conducted its liaison work with the Nineteen [subpoenaed witnesses], the producers, liberal congressmen. . . . Given the CFA's resources of funds and personnel, these activities were widespread and highly visible: two national radio broadcasts, a series of one- and two-page ads in the trade papers, and a highly publicized, star-studded trip to Washington, D.C., on a chartered airplane."

Of the forty-three Hollywood people subpoenaed, nineteen were labeled by HUAC as "unfriendly" witnesses. They refused to cooperate with the investigating committee, to state whether they were members of the Communist Party or to name other party members and sympathizers. Eleven "unfriendly witnesses" actually testified. The German playwright Bertolt Brecht falsely denied he was a Communist and immediately left the country. The remaining Americans became known as the Hollywood Ten. Despite Huston's clear statement of the CFA's opposition to Communism, the Hollywood Ten mistakenly assumed that its protest against HUAC meant personal solidarity with their political beliefs. As Ceplair and Englund wrote, "While liberals had loyally stepped forward, it was not to support suspected Communists, whom many regarded as 'agents of a foreign power,' but to defend civil liberties and oppose political reaction."

Huston and Bogart interrupted their preparations for *Key Largo* and joined the fifty actors (many others were making films and could not leave) on the CFA flight from Los Angeles to Washington. Press photos showed Evelyn Keyes, Richard Conte, Danny Kaye, Gene Kelly, Bacall, Bogart, Marsha Hunt, June Havoc, Paul Henreid and Geraldine Brooks standing on the steps leading to the plane. In addition to Huston and Dunne, Ira Gershwin, John Garfield and Sterling Hayden were also on the flight. Gene Kelly's biographer wrote that the mood on the plane was both festive and serious: "In the air, a party-like atmosphere took over, but with strange, even tense, overtones. To Gene it was like a wrap celebration of a film production, glee and relief tempered by concern for what lay ahead."[3]

Huston and Dunne spoke to the press and placed Bogart and Bacall, the most charismatic couple, at the head of the group. The plane stopped along the way in Kansas City, St. Louis and Chicago, where throngs of people turned up—sometimes in the middle of the night—to greet them. Huston, Bogart, Bacall, Kelly and Kaye made short speeches to counter the negative publicity about Hollywood and arouse support for their cause. They explained why they were making the trip and why the charges of Communist subversion were absurd, denounced HUAC and reaffirmed the right to free speech. All the actors were well established and did not need publicity or controversy. They had decided to fly into the eye of the storm to set the record straight. No one dreamed that they would become victims and that some careers would be destroyed when public sympathy turned against the Hollywood Ten and the CFA was smeared as a Communist front.

· II ·

The October 1947 hearings, which (in Max Lerner's words) tried "to track down the footprints of Karl Marx in movieland," were the "most flamboyant and widely publicized" in HUAC's history. The investigation of Communist infiltration in Hollywood began on October 20, a week before the CFA flight, in the crowded Caucus Room in the Old House Office Building. Nixon attended the opening session and then, because his Californian constituents were being accused, withdrew from the subsequent sessions. The "friendly" witnesses, who deplored the Communist influence in Hollywood and named prominent Communist sympathizers, were called during the first week. They included the actors Ronald Reagan, George Murphy (elected U.S. senator for California in 1964), Gary Cooper, Robert Montgomery, Robert Taylor and Adolphe Menjou as well as the studio executives Walt Disney, Louis Mayer and Jack Warner. Ceplair and Englund wrote that these actors "had cast themselves in the role of 'concerned patriotic citizens' defending a shrinking studio beachhead against an invading Bolshevik menace. . . . [They] related how they had vigilantly scrutinized prospective scripts for their 'Communistic' content, tried to warn their colleagues and superiors of 'subversive' activity, and generally tried to set a high standard of patriotic Americanism."[4]

The most significant testimony, from Huston's point of view, was that of Jack Warner, who was called first. Eager to display his patriotic credentials, he launched into a long-winded, incoherent attack on Communism and told HUAC that "Communists injected 95% of their propaganda into films through the medium of writers." Though he admitted that he had never actually seen a Communist and "wouldn't know one if I saw one," he mentioned the names of twelve "Reds" (including Howard Koch and five of the Hollywood Ten) whom he had somehow spotted and fired from his studio. Joining the hysteria about a secret conspiracy, Warner also exclaimed that "ideological termites have burrowed into many American industries, organizations, and societies. Wherever they may be, I say let us dig them out and get rid of them. My brothers and I will be happy to subscribe generously to a pest-removal fund."

Warner's willingness to betray his own screenwriters on admittedly flimsy evidence horrified the Hollywood Ten, the CFA and his colleagues at the studio and intensified Huston's hatred of his boss. Even Eric Johnston told the writers that the producers were "embarrassed by the fact that Jack Warner ... made a stupid ass of himself." Warner, later appalled by his own testimony, told Huston: " 'They wanted to know the names of people I thought might be Communists out here.' 'What did you say?' 'Well ... I told them the names of a few. . . . I guess I shouldn't have, should I? . . . I guess I'm a squealer, huh?' "[5] Unwilling to let his boss off the hook, Huston mercilessly replied: "Yes, you are!" Nevertheless, Warner's testimony was extremely damaging. It emphasized the split between executives and actors, reinforced the suspicion that Communists were indeed making propaganda films and served to justify the witch hunt that threatened to destroy his own industry.

Huston and the CFA resented not only the testimony of Warner and other "friendly" witnesses, but also HUAC's quite different treatment of the witnesses. The "friendly" witnesses confirmed the existence of Communist infiltration in Hollywood; the "unfriendly" ones were accused of subversion. The former did not know the names of Communist Party members; the latter refused to give them. The former were allowed to read speeches and testify at great length; the latter were cut off before they could speak and sometimes dragged from the room by armed guards. The chairman J. Parnell Thomas was loud, vulgar, aggressive and hostile.

The large, drafty stone hall, with its mass of bright lights and whirring cameras, its grim interrogators, screaming witnesses and gavel pounding right next to the microphone created a theatrical atmosphere. It had fierce dialogue, intense drama and a highly emotional audience. The CFA had agreed, Dunne wrote, on the basic premise that "any *official* inquiry into political beliefs and affiliations was unconstitutional." If any of them were called to the stand and asked the crucial question, "Are you now or have you ever been a member of the Communist Party?" they would reply, "I must respectfully decline to answer that question, on the grounds that the information is privileged under the First Amendment to the Constitution." Though all of the Ten were professional writers and directors, with extensive experience in plays and films, they completely miscalculated the effect of their performance.

After belligerently challenging the Committee and acting as rudely and vulgarly as the chairman, the screenwriter John Howard Lawson, the leading Communist in Hollywood, was cited for contempt and roughly removed from the stand by the police. Huston was appalled and outraged by Thomas' arbitrary treatment of the witness, but he was also disgusted by Lawson's undignified behavior and disdain for the congressional hearing. His arrogant refusal to answer the questions alienated the public and smeared the stars with his own Communist views. The other nine witnesses, like sheep rushing over a cliff, followed Lawson's example and made an equally disastrous impression. Dunne felt that the transparent ploy "of pretending to answer the questions while actually evading them and indulging in combative political speeches . . . inevitably—and perhaps deservedly—backfired." He also said that "this blustering and shouting—getting in the gutter with the committee, and it was a gutter committee"—obscured the real issue and missed the chance to defend an important principle. Victor Navasky agreed that Lawson's aggression had upset the audience, "who thought they had come to cheer on a group of civil libertarians and instead found themselves listening to what sounded suspiciously like Party rhetoric." Only Ring Lardner, Jr., who said, "I could answer [the question], but if I did, I would hate myself in the morning," replied in a dignified manner.[6]

In his definitive book on HUAC Robert Carr concluded: "The Hollywood hearings revealed the committee at its worst. . . . No other major investigation of the committee ever ended so anti-climactically or produced so little tangible evidence in support of a thesis which the committee set out to prove." Thomas—who had been criticized by the press but felt he had achieved his political aims—indefinitely adjourned the hearings after only ten of the nineteen "unfriendly" witnesses had been called. The CFA, feeling victorious, had a celebratory party at "21," one of Huston's favorite hangouts in New York.

Yet the discreditable performances of Lawson and his colleagues had suddenly turned editorials against the Hollywood Ten and their supporters. Since the Hollywood Ten had obscured the constitutional issue in a cloud of leftist jargon, the CFA now seemed to be defending Communism rather than democracy. Evelyn Keyes said, "We faced a hostile, sophisticated, worldly press who made us look like stupid children interfering with grownup problems." David Selznick, Mayer and even Warner had originally contributed to the CFA. Louella Parsons had publicly supported them. President Truman had invited them to lunch. But, as Paul Henreid recalled, "We woke up the next morning to find that the press, which had praised us so fully, had done a complete about-face. We were no longer knights in shining armor. We were 'dupes and fellow-travellers,' 'pinkos,' who were trying to undermine the country." The strategy of the Ten had played directly into the hands of HUAC, whose propaganda victory would have far-reaching effects.

The studio heads met at the Waldorf-Astoria Hotel on November 24 and reversed their previous stance. They announced that they would not employ Communists and would fire the Hollywood Ten; they would not rehire any of them until they had cleared themselves of contempt and declared under oath that they were not members of the party. HUAC listed the CFA as a "Communist front" and its members, now tainted and threatened by the prospect of unemployment, felt betrayed by the men they had come to Washington to help. The CFA quickly dissolved, and within a few weeks there was almost no one left in the fight. As Navasky observed, "Liberal Hollywood, which had been with the Ten on arrival in the East, abandoned them as they left— partly out of shock at the confrontation with the Committee, partly in reaction to the indictment for contempt of Congress, and partly out of fear, after the Waldorf meeting, that they themselves would be tainted. The Committtee for the First Amendment, which had announced a major propaganda campaign on behalf of the Ten, folded almost as fast as it had formed."[7] Huston and other prominent figures came under public and private pressure from journalists, gossip columnists, studio executives, financial backers, managers, agents, family and friends. To save their careers, they had to withdraw their opposition to HUAC and obtain an official clearance from the FBI—as if acting were equivalent to working for the State Department or doing atomic research.

· III ·

According to the FBI report, "HUSTON was very aggressive in his efforts to recruit individuals and in fact kept HUMPHREY BOGART up until 6:00 o'clock in the morning getting him 'fired up to get behind the movement.' " But their friendship was severely strained when the badly battered CFA returned to Hollywood and Bogart defected from the movement while Huston kept up the good fight. Ceplair and Englund wrote, "Once the producers decided to blacklist the 'unfriendly' witnesses, the CFA lost its rallying cry and the vast majority of its troops. . . . In connection with the dissolution of the CFA . . . the Committee's founding triumvirate of Dunne, Huston, and Wyler by no means collapsed under pressure, but continued to struggle 'in the only ways available to us. We lobbied, pressured, pleaded, argued, fought within our guilds and signed the *amicus curiae* brief.' "

Like everyone else on the CFA, Bogart was pressured by friends and business associates, the studio and the press, to dissociate himself from the now-tainted organization. The key figure in Bogart's recantation was the right-wing journalist George Sokolsky, who was influential in deciding which people were worthy of immediate absolution. The FBI quoted a newspaper article, addressed to "Dear Bogey," saying that "SOKOLSKY suggests that you're sticking with the Committee because you're afraid to offend HUSTON, or maybe [SOKOLSKY] thinks you're suspect for making a movie with [HUSTON] who has spoken up for civil liberties."[8]

By caving in to the pressure exerted by all his associates, Bogart followed what turned out to be good advice. Ian Hamilton described how the political winds had changed: "The Committee for the First Amendment had gone to Washington in support of what had seemed a glorious cause, the cause of free expression, and had found themselves lined up with a group of writers who had come across as shifty, ill-mannered, fanatical, and—well, frankly, un-American." Since Bogart had already dissociated himself from the Communists and was not close to any of the Hollywood Ten, there was no point, with the press now hostile to him, in destroying his career to uphold a principle that few others were willing to defend. In a letter that Sokolsky published in his *New York Daily Mirror* column on December 6, 1947, Bogart reaffirmed the constitutional principle that had originally inspired him to join the CFA, but he was forced to swallow the toad and disavow his own behavior, to make the CFA seem trivial, even absurd. In his letter (its addressee blacked out) he announced: "I went to Washington because I thought fellow Americans were being deprived of their constitutional rights, and for that reason alone. That [the] trip was ill advised, even foolish, I am very ready to admit. At the time it seemed like the thing to do. I have absolutely no use for Communism nor for anyone who serves that philosophy."

Though Bogart's statement was a direct refutation of everything Huston stood for on this crucial issue, Huston—who'd recruited him—was surprisingly tolerant and understanding. He thought personal friendship, and their future films together, were more important than Bogart's lack of principle. In a letter included in his FBI file, Huston rather mildly recalled, "I was considerably surprised at this change of attitude on his part, because when I had last seen him, shortly before the interview, he seemed undismayed at the role he had played in the aeroplane junket." He later mentioned, when discussing Bogart's defection, the financial considerations: "Bogie owns a fifty-four-foot yawl. When you own a fifty-four-foot yawl, you've got to provide for her upkeep."[9]

After the failure of the CFA, the controversy boiled on. While being investigated by the FBI and under great pressure to recant, Huston took another brave stand. Joseph Mankiewicz, president of the Screen Directors Guild, had opposed the loyalty oath for its members.

Cecil B. De Mille, a fervent anti-Communist, was in favor of the oath and tried to get rid of Mankiewicz. Huston thought De Mille "was a thoroughly bad director. A dreadful showoff. Terrible. To diseased proportions." During a seven-hour meeting at the Beverly Hills Hotel in October 1950, Huston made a brilliant speech that persuaded guild members to support Mankiewicz and forced De Mille and his supporters to resign from the board. Billy Wilder, one of Huston's staunchest allies, said that Huston had "applied a samurai sword to Mr. De Mille's withered neck."

Huston was never called to testify before HUAC, but since he was not a Communist, he would have welcomed the chance to attack the Committee in person. Nevertheless, his extensive FBI file reveals that he was under constant scrutiny and falsely accused both of crimes and of subversive acts. The FBI habitually recorded negative testimony without confirming the accuracy of the reports, and hostile informants could easily slander anyone they disliked. One report, going back to 1935, was a complete fabrication: "While in England, after deciding not to go to Spain, HUSTON indulged in the 'fruit shakedown' racket in London parks, financing himself in this manner. He would permit a pervert to approach him, and they would agree on a rendezvous, and when they arrived at this point, after a certain length of time, HUSTON's confederates would appear and would proceed to shake the victim down for whatever money was obtainable. HUSTON was characterized by the informant as 'a sadist and a pervert and a man of no principles.' . . . The informant continued that HUSTON is scatterbrained and irresponsible."[10]

A letter of August 2, 1949, written by J. Edgar Hoover himself two years after the CFA debacle, reveals that the FBI was still trying to nail Huston. Hoover notes that in 1936, at the start of the Spanish Civil War, Huston signed a cable to Léon Blum, the French Socialist prime minister and head of the Popular Front government. He urged Blum, as part of the democratic fight against fascism, "to abandon the ineffectual policy of non-intervention [in the Spanish War] and open the [French] border for the purchase of vitally necessary supplies by Loyalist Spain." Hoover deliberately ignored the fact that the Loyalists were fighting Francisco Franco, who was supported by his allies in Nazi Germany and fascist Italy.

In the same letter Hoover repeated another completely phony story, vaguely based on Huston's support for Spain in the cable to Blum: "A confidential source, indicated to be reliable, stated that Huston was once a member of the Communist Party preceding the Spanish Civil War. This source stated that under orders from the Party, Huston went to Europe to fight in the Abraham Lincoln Brigade but 'lost his nerve in London and didn't leave England.' . . . He blamed his apparent desertion in London on liquor. It was stated that his fondness for liquor was well known and apparently the Party accepted this excuse." Any source was acceptable to the FBI if it contained damaging material about their suspects. Hoover was exceptionally fond of supposedly "reliable" and "apparently" true information. Huston was never a member of the Communist Party, he never planned to fight in Spain, he could not desert a unit he'd never joined, drunkenness was never an acceptable excuse for disobeying the orders of the party and his courage under fire in World War II was well documented. In a letter of January 29, 1953, to an unknown recipient (whose name was blacked out by the FBI), Huston clearly stated his political beliefs in the 1930s: "My sympathies during the Spanish Revolution were entirely with the Loyalists, for the simple reason that Germany and Italy had thrown in against them. . . . I was all for declaring war against the Nazis the first time they chased their first Jew down an alley."

Huston, like many others, didn't realize at the time that some of the committees he supported may have been Communist front organizations. The FBI took a dim view of Huston attending a July 1944 reception at the Soviet consulate in Los Angeles "in honor of the Actors Committee of Russian War Relief," even though the Russians were an essential wartime ally. It also criticized him for merely being asked "by the United Nations to make a motion picture based on the idea of 'one world' with no war and no hate." (Hoover, according to reliable informants, was apparently pro-war and pro-hate.) All these idealistic causes became highly suspect during the Cold War. If liberals agreed with

Communists on any political issue, they were immediately stigmatized as Communists. The FBI kept recycling the same false information about Huston in many different reports until, after frequent repetitions, it seemed to be true. The file reveals more about the methods and mindset of the FBI than it does about Huston himself.

Recalling the witch hunts, Huston later declared, "Suddenly people were made into circus performers. If they didn't jump through hoops, they were disgraced, ruined, and destroyed." The ugly anti-Communist campaigns went on for years. In December 1952, when Huston and his star José Ferrer, well known for his left-wing views but not a Communist, traveled from Paris to Los Angeles for the premiere of *Moulin Rouge*, they found splinter groups from the American Legion, incited by attacks in Hedda Hopper's columns, marching in front of the theater with placards that claimed Huston and Ferrer were Communists. By this time Huston had formed his own production company, had married again and had two children. The extreme right-wing pressure increased to the point where he had to follow Bogart's example. Forced to bend the knee, to repent and confess, he wrote a formal recantation regretting some of his actions and declaring that he was not a Communist.

In his typed, single-spaced, six-page letter of January 29, 1953, drawn up in consultation with a lawyer and sent from the Soho Square office of his English partner Romulus Films, Huston made four essential points. He defended the principles and integrity of the CFA; he dissociated himself from the Hollywood Ten, who refused to admit they were Communists and exploited the CFA for their own ends; he regretted his connection with Communist front organizations that had secretly followed the party line; and he categorically rejected the Communists and their ideology:

> The Committee for the First Amendment was most certainly not a Communist front. I say this with some authority, because I started it.

> When I believed [the Hollywood Ten] to have engaged to defend the freedom of the individual, they were really looking after their own skins.

I have come into possession of information regarding the true nature of certain organizations to which I gave my name and support. There can be no question but that, in so doing, I was unwittingly following the Communist party line, and giving unconscious aid to subversive elements within our own country. To the extent that this occurred, I am profoundly regretful. For no one is more opposed than I to the Russian system of government by falsehood and violence.

I wholeheartedly pledge my energies in the struggle against Communist aggressions the world over.

The FBI accepted his honest (if coerced) declaration, but cited an informant's statement that cast doubt on his idealistic intentions. By forming the CFA, the anonymous informant said, "HUSTON has made a studied effort to appear to be in the guise of correcting an injustice and has not openly identified himself as espousing Communism." The FBI strangely asserted, after compiling a large dossier of lies, that "HUSTON has not been the subject of a Bureau investigation," but concluded—as the army had done during the war—that the "case on HUSTON is being placed in a closed status."

One of the most sickening effects of the witch hunts was that mediocre people gained power over superior talents by allying themselves with HUAC and promoting themselves as superpatriots. Huston's screenwriter-friend Nunnally Johnson expressed disgust about the way the witch hunts had polluted Hollywood and his disdain for Ward Bond, who'd played the good cop in *The Maltese Falcon* and became an influential anti-Communist: "So many outrageous things went on that made me ashamed of the whole industry. . . . Think of John Huston having to go and debase himself to an oaf like Ward Bond and promise never to be a bad boy again, and Ward Bond would say, 'All right, then, we clear you, but we've got our eye on you.' "[11]

TEN

GOLD IN MEXICO,
1948

· I ·

Huston had a great deal in common with Billy Pearson, who was fourteen years younger and a foot shorter. The jockey, joker, art dealer and con man was one of his closest friends. Like Huston, he was raised by a single mother and grew up in Los Angeles in the 1920s. As with Huston (wrote Nat Moss in a *Vanity Fair* profile of Pearson), Billy's "grandfather became the boy's early role model, regaling him with stories of his own grandfather's gold-rush adventures, while educating Pearson in the subjects of gambling and women." Like Huston, Billy was extremely intelligent but never finished high school. Huston had five wives; Billy trumped him with six. Both men loved women, gambling, drinking and tall stories. Both were passionate about horses (Billy began his career by exercising horses for Harry Warner) and about pre-Columbian art.

Billy understood the misery of Huston's long recuperation from his boyhood illness. In 1941, Moss noted, "Pearson's career took a drastic turn one day at the Hollywood Park racetrack when he was knocked off his saddle and trapped beneath five horses. He lay in the hospital for nearly six months with a shattered collarbone and shoulder." Like Huston, Billy made a spectacular recovery. Between 1949 and 1954 he won more than three hundred races on the West Coast and earned nearly $1.3 million. He even won a race on Huston's restive filly Bargain Lass and was paid with his choice of pre-Columbian art from Huston's collection. While making *Moulin Rouge* Huston brought him to France, where he also raced successfully. More talented than Huston in a sport they both loved, Billy praised him as "absolutely horse-crazy; he didn't know any normal fears and was a natural-born rider."

A collector and connoisseur, like Huston, Pearson took up a third lucrative career in the spring of 1956. He appeared as an art expert on the television programs *The $64,000 Question* and *The $64,000 Challenge* and won nearly $180,000. In his 1959 article "How I Squandered a Million Dollars," he declared (again like Huston) that money was meant to be spent. Pearson, a self-taught con man, was clever, but not *that* smart. The questions he answered demanded a vast knowledge of minute details, and the television shows he appeared in, like the ones that followed, were probably fixed.

Huston first met Pearson, appropriately enough, at the Santa Anita racetrack in Los Angeles, and soon made him part of his entourage. He described Pearson as "one of the most entertaining persons alive. He has a gift of being able to go beyond the limits of acceptable behavior and yet never lose his membership in human society. . . . His accounts of our experiences together are infinitely better than what really happened."[1] Always a great antidote to boredom, Pearson would do anything to amuse Huston and Huston was always amused by anything Pearson did. Huston relished his storytelling and wit, and let him get away with all kinds of outrageous behavior. Pearson might bring Huston a monkey to liven things up, and thought nothing of brashly entering the bedroom where Huston lay naked with his fourth wife. In his role as courtier and clown, Billy would make himself comfortable on the four-poster and start to tell jokes.

Pearson was always on the lookout for a shady deal. When Dr. George Hodel, the Black Dahlia murderer, had to sell his art collection to pay urgent legal fees, Pearson bought most of it. But his real specialty, with Huston's collusion, was finding his own archeological sites in Mexico and smuggling pre-Columbian art into California. While Huston was making *The Treasure of the Sierra Madre*, Pearson used one of his sound trucks to sneak contraband out of the country. He hid Aztec statues in coffins and in the false bottoms of boats, paid lavish bribes and swept past the border guards. Jan Lavender, an art dealer and friend in Puerto Vallarta, questioned Huston about the authenticity of some pieces. "How do you know it's real?" she would ask, and he confidently replied, "You just feel it's real." Huston relied on his own knowledge and intuition rather than on provenance, documentation, hard facts and expert advice. He was easily duped by Pearson, a sponger and exploiter, who sold his friend a lot of fake art.

Pearson once wanted to sell a precious Navajo necklace to Bill Gardner, a Hollywood publicist and friend of Huston. Gardner took it to an appraiser on La Cienega Boulevard in Los Angeles and was informed that the old buffalo nickels had been made the previous week. In 1974, with Pearson's help, Huston sold his three best Veracruz pieces to a Texas collector, who gave them to the Dallas Museum of Art. When they were exhibited in 1987, the experts said they were fakes. Pearson maintained that he had seen and even filmed the statues being excavated, but the curators thought he'd been deceived by a staged scenario. Angry and vexed as he must have been, Huston (who could have directed the scene) was probably amused by the idea of a swindler swindled by an elaborate hoax. Pearson's plots were like Huston movies. Like the Maltese falcon, smuggled in from Hong Kong, a great deal of the art he smuggled in from Mexico turned out to be bogus. Pearson stealing art from Mexico was like the three miners stealing gold in *Sierra Madre*.

Partly deluded and partly aware of being cheated, Huston was amused rather than outraged by Pearson's shameless cheek. As the Huston character in *White Hunter, Black Heart* says, "You can't con anyone unless they're part crook, or willing to play along in a shady deal." Huston didn't care much about money, valued Pearson's friendship and let him get away with his cunning deceptions. The two friends were like the reclusive Boston diarist Arthur Inman and his engaging chauffeur, Eddie, who "lied to him and sweet-talked him out of a lot of cash, but Eddie's petty dishonesties mattered less in the long run than his sympathy, understanding, and loyalty, and he [was fascinated by] Eddie's feckless life."[2] Pearson was a lively presence, and Huston's way of life encouraged a certain degree of excess. He enjoyed hearing Pearson's rascally tales and didn't mind if he was sometimes the butt of his jokes.

· II ·

The making of *The Treasure of the Sierra Madre* (1948) was closely connected to Huston's personal relations with another strange character, the author of the novel that was originally published in German in 1927. B. Traven—like J. D. Salinger and Thomas Pynchon today—aroused public interest and enhanced his reputation by creating his own legend and becoming an ostentatious recluse. Born Otto Feige in East Prussia in 1882, he was an actor, reporter and political activist, and took part in the Communist revolution in Munich that was crushed in 1919. Persecuted for his radical beliefs, he escaped to Mexico, adopted the name of Traven and became a citizen of that country in 1951.

Huston's screenplay pleased Traven by remaining faithful to the novel. In the book Howard (the old prospector, played in the film by Walter Huston) expresses the theme when he warns his partners that the "eternal curse on gold changes the soul of man in a second." In the film he says, "I know what gold does to men's souls. . . . You lose your sense of values and your character changes entirely. Your soul stops being the same as it was before." In the book, when Howard first discovers the gold, he jubilantly berates his partners: "You two are so dumb, so immensely stupid and dumb. . . . You two are so dumb that you don't even see the millions when treading upon them with your own feet." In the film he does a manic dance by bouncing from his heels to his toes and tells them, "You two are so dumb you don't see the riches you're treading on with your own feet." (It's often been said that John told Walter to take out his false teeth in order to look older, but Walter's mouth is not sunken and you can see his teeth when he laughs.) Traven was a defiant Red; and the FBI noted that Huston's film, according to a Communist informant, "contains a speech on gold which is practically a direct quotation from MARX." The FBI, not noted for its literary insights, had no clue that the idea "money is the root of evil" goes back to 1 Timothy 6:10 and was quoted in Chaucer's "Pardoner's Tale."

Huston's agent, Paul Kohner, was married to the well-known Mexican actress Lupita Tovar, who helped him get in touch with the elusive

Traven. The author was enthusiastic about Bogart playing the lead-ing role, and in 1946 sent Huston many long-winded and sometimes tedious letters. Applauding the script, Traven told Huston: "By the first rapid look, I realized that an expert had handled it. . . . I must say that pp. 48 to 58 is just super excellent writing and letting the whole script flash through my mind for a few seconds I simply feel obliged to say that I don't know anybody or can imagine anybody who could have written a script better liked by me than the one you wrote." Like a pro-ducer, Traven could not leave well enough alone and asked for unneces-sary alterations: "Your script is so good, almost too good, that it could remain as it is without change. However, a few changes will, and of this I am positive, make the picture better still."[3] But he also made several useful suggestions about Mexican details that Huston adopted—the price and number of Bogart's lottery ticket, the cost and outdoor prem-ises of his barber—which added authentic touches.

Though Traven wanted no personal publicity and refused to be photographed or interviewed, he could not resist coming to the locale as a paid consultant and impersonating his own secretary, Hal Croves. Evelyn Keyes said the nondescript Croves was "small, no taller than I, with pale, pale hair that blended with his pale skin. His eyes were blue and small, his nose large." Huston found him equally unimpressive and described him as "a thin little guy with gray hair, dressed in faded khaki. . . . Croves had a slight accent. It didn't sound German to me, but certainly European. I thought he might very well be Traven, but out of delicacy I didn't ask." Unlike Traven, who was assertive and dog-matic in his correspondence, "Croves was very tight and guarded in his manner of speaking. He was nothing at all as I had imagined Traven."[4] So Traven, the author of the novel, acted a role for Huston, the author of the script and actor in the film.

Puzzled by the contrast between Traven and Croves, Huston told Arthur Schlesinger that "Traven's emphatic letters were very different from the bland and studiously furtive Croves. [Huston thought] that Traven may have died at some point and that Croves assumed his iden-tity." Writing in 1948 to an editor at *Time*, who was trying to solve the mystery of Traven's identity, Huston said, "Traven is as awkward in his relationships with casual acquaintances as he is adroit at dealing with his characters on paper." Traven got only $5,000 for the screen rights; and when "a member of my crew asked him point-blank, 'Are you B. Traven?,' he answered that surely if he were Traven, he would not be working for so small a salary." In the end, Huston preferred to draw an artistic veil over Traven and didn't want to know his real identity: "I would deplore any definite proof that Croves and Traven are one. In the first place, Traven has worked very hard at being mysterious, and I'd hate to see so much effort go for nothing. But more important, the Sweet Mystery of Traven makes for fascinating speculation in a world where too much is known about too many."

Always the tease, Traven left considerable evidence to suggest that Croves was, in fact, Traven. Croves was the maiden name of Traven's mother. Both names have six letters; three of them—R, V and E—are identical and in the same place in their names: tRaVEn and cRoVEs. If the first letters are switched, the names hint at the themes of the novel: *craven* behavior and treasure *troves*. Traven's letters stopped coming when Croves was with Huston. And Evelyn shrewdly concluded, "Of course it was B. Traven himself. He gave himself away in countless ways, saying 'I' when it should have been 'he,' using phrases similar to those he used in his letters to John." In her introduction to the 1976 edition of his novel *The Bridge in the Jungle*, Traven's Mexican wife settled the question by confirming that Croves and Traven were the same man.

· III ·

The Treasure of the Sierra Madre marked Huston's reentry into film-making after his wartime adventures: he wrote, directed and acted in it. The film united several of his passions: a Mexican setting, on-location shooting, violent action during the revolutionary period and a rugged story of male adventurers. One of the first American movies to be made outside the United States, *Sierra Madre* had a budget of nearly $2 million and was filmed between mid-February and late July 1947. Apart from the mining scenes, which were shot in ten days near Kernville, in the Sequoia National Forest of central California, it was made in the mountainous country near San José de Perua, a few hours west of Mexico City. The remote little spa was off the main highway and at the end of a road leading nowhere.

Huston complained that "somebody else always owns the picture, and there's always somebody ready to take it away from you and screw it up."[5] As he gained power, he broke the stranglehold of the studios, first by moving up from writer to director, and then by shooting in remote places, far from their absolute control. After filming in the Aleutians and in Italy, he knew the value of realistic settings. In *Sierra Madre* Huston used the menacing, desolate landscape to create a sense of urgency and danger and to reveal the shifting allegiances and tensions in the isolated group of predatory miners.

On May 2 the unit manager sent the producer, Henry Blanke, a lively description of the inedible food, which sometimes made the company sick, and the homely women at the Mexican watering hole: "This headquarters is as dull a spot you'll find this side of Forest Lawn [cemetery]. It is a mineral spa enlivened only with the creak of arthritic joints. The food, strangely enough, is poor and monotonous, but as no one ever seems to get very hungry the squawks aren't too loud. . . . The morale is as good as you'll find on any location trip where the few girls look like they've been raised on a steady diet of dog food." Lauren Bacall occupied herself by shopping for canned goods and organizing better meals for everyone. Though Bogart liked to work in the studio and go home at six, he had to suffer prolonged absence from home, bad food and extreme discomfort if he wanted to make a first-rate film with Huston. The actors and crew spent their days working outdoors in the rough countryside, their nights bowling and drinking. The Mexican actor Alfonso Bedoya, who played the evil bandit Gold Hat, livened things up. One night he ran naked through the hotel, chased by a big blond woman who brandished a knife and screamed, "You Mexican bastard!" Bedoya, still running, replied, "You don't say that when you suck my cock!"

Bacall noted Huston's tender, respectful behavior with his father, and said that "John was a man who did not openly or easily deal with his emotions." But with Walter he softened up and became "somewhat vulnerable, therefore more human, more connected" to another person. "It was a revelation to see that he was capable of feeling strongly about another human being."[6] Yet Huston, a rugged athlete, drove the actors (including his father) relentlessly. Bogart believed that the realistic setting enhanced the atmosphere of the film and said, "It's always better to shoot a hot-weather picture in a hot country. You get a different expression on your face." But he also resented the unnecessary discomfort and felt that Huston had forced him to suffer: "John wanted everything perfect. I have to admire him for that but it was plenty rough on our troupe. If we could get to a location site without fording a couple of streams and walking through rattlesnake-infested areas in the scorching sun, then it wasn't quite right. . . . We'd stumble over rocks and stones and cactus and sagebrush. We'd dodge snakes and scorpions and things that must have been Gila monsters. The guy was a bundle of energy and I was a bundle of old, tired, left-over atoms." Walter Huston agreed that "acting is not supposed to be done outdoors." An old Mexican cavalryman, John Huston loved the colorful, barbaric country. In an amusing press release written for Warner Bros., he recalled the recruitment of some all-too-eager horsemen: "I said my company would be willing to pay up to 40 pesos a day for trick riders. [The Mexican leader] said, 'For that amount they would let you shoot them in the arms and legs. Not to kill, you understand.' He waved a warning finger at me. 'No killing. We can't have any of that.' "[7]

While Huston gloried in the hardships of Mexico, Bogart couldn't wait to get home. Huston had promised that they'd finish in time for Bogart to race his boat to Honolulu. When Bogart complained about the delays, Huston risked their close and profitable friendship by insulting and humiliating him in front of Bacall. While making this picture, Huston wrote, with no trace of regret,

Bogie and I had our one and only quarrel. Bogie was very eager to get his boat, the *Santana,* into a race to Honolulu. The race was soon to be run, so he was always trying to pin me down to a finish date. I refused to let Bogie's race schedule interfere with my picture, and told him so. Bogie sulked and became progressively less cooperative. . . .

One evening at the dinner table he started in on me again about the race. Suddenly I'd had as much as I could take. Bogie leaned across the table toward me to make a point, and I reached out and took his nose between my first two fingers and closed them into a fist. There was silence at the table.

Finally, Betty Bogart couldn't stand it. "John," she said, "you're hurting him."

"Yes, I know. I mean to." I gave one more twist, and let go.

Bogie came to me later and said, "John, for heaven's sake, what are we doing? Let things be with us as they have always been."

For all Bogart's pleas, the picture wasn't finished until July 22 and he missed the yacht race. "Bogey the Beefer" lived up to his name, but may have felt he had gone too far with his complaints. In Huston's version of the story, despite the final cruel twist, the *victim* offers to make up the quarrel. Though he was notorious for losing interest in his weaker projects, Huston was deadly serious about this film and determined to make it as perfect as possible. Once in Mexico and out of Jack Warner's control, he took five and a half months on production and finished twenty-nine days over schedule. Huston didn't seem to like sailing, perhaps because he could not be in command, and there's no evidence that he ever went out on Bogart's beloved *Santana*.

The film opens in Tampico, on the Gulf of Mexico, in August 1924, as the American oil companies are closing down their operations. Expatriate laborers like Fred C. Dobbs (Bogart) are thrown out of work and, when destitute, are forced to beg for money. Like Hemingway in *For Whom the Bell Tolls* (1940), Huston achieved realism by including Spanish dialogue that is made clear in the context of the film. He sent Walter recordings of what he had to say in Spanish and Walter learned to make his speech colloquial. The scenes in which masses of peasants dressed in black and white take the prisoners out to be executed and the hanging sickle that appears to announce the arrival of the Indians vividly evoke the menacing atmosphere of the country that John had known in 1926.

In the early scenes Bogart, playing Dobbs and parodying his gangster roles, bites a toothpick, twitches his lips and hitches up his trousers. Grimacing but humbly keeping his eyes down, he repeatedly asks for money from a prosperous American, whose white hat, white suit and long cigar recall Mark Twain. After Dobbs' third request, the American (played by Huston as if he were discussing the Honolulu race) condescendingly tells him in his best lordly voice: "Go occasionally to somebody else. This is beginning to get tiresome. . . . From now on you are to try your best to make your way in life without my assistance." Huston had been a bum in London; Bogart played a bum in Tampico. Huston had a winning lottery ticket to the Irish Sweepstakes when he was down and out; Bogart's winning ticket allows him to buy a stake in the search for gold. (The young Robert Blake, playing the persistent Mexican boy who sells Bogart the lottery ticket, would later have the leading role in *In Cold Blood*.) And Bogart, in another witty allusion, carries a large package wrapped in newspaper, just as he did in *The Maltese Falcon*. Huston's screenplay is tightly structured. Dobbs asks the white-suited American for money three times, and there are also three miners and three bandits. Dobbs tries twice to shoot Gold Hat and is finally shot by him, and the bandits' quarreling over Dobbs' possessions recalls the miners' quarrel over the gold. The miners find, transport and lose the gold amid growing suspicion, dissension and violence.

Huston composed several scenes with an artist's eye. When Dobbs is about to kill Curtin (played by Tim Holt), Curtin rolls his eyes like a Christian saint about to be martyred. Huston told the interloper Cody (Bruce Bennett), who tries to grab his share of the gold, "You're smarter than those guys." Though Cody survives for a while, he's finally killed by the bandits. James Agee, in a fine analysis, shows how Huston arranged the actors in a painter's tableau: "The three prospectors come to identify the man [Bennett] they themselves were on the verge of shooting. Bogart, the would-be tough guy, cocks one foot up on a rock and tries to look at the corpse as casually as if it were fresh-killed game. Tim Holt, the essentially decent young man, comes past behind him and, innocent and unaware of it, clasps his hands as he looks down, in the respectful manner of a boy who used to go to church. Walter Huston, the experienced old man, steps quietly behind both, leans to the dead man as professionally as a doctor to a patient and gently rifles him for papers."[8]

In one scene, Huston tried to play a diabolical trick on Bogart. Dobbs becomes suspicious and then paranoid about his partners' attempts to steal his share. When he accuses Curtin of searching for the gold he's hidden under a rock, Curtin says he's been looking for a Gila monster that has crawled underneath. He dares Dobbs to reach in and get his treasure. When he's too frightened to do so, Curtin levers up the rock with a piece of timber and reveals the monster belly-up on a pile of Dobbs' gold. Though Bogart never actually put his hand under the rock, Huston claimed, in a typically tall tale, "I got a camera clamp and I climbed underneath the set, which was made of that material which rocks are composed of in studios, and when Bogart put his hand in I put on the clamp while the cameras were running and he screamed, thought he had a Gila monster on his hand."

After madly shooting Curtin, who manages to recover, Dobbs delivers a fine soliloquy that recalls the guilt-tormented speeches of Shakespearean murderers: "Conscience. Conscience. What a thing. If you believe you've got a conscience, it'll pester you to death. But if you don't believe you've got one, what can it do to you?" A little later, just as he thinks he's reached a safe refuge, he lies down to drink from a pool of water. In a striking image, he sees the frightening face of Gold Hat, who's pursued him through the film, reflected in the water. Gold Hat (who has the same large protruding teeth as his mule) then hacks him to death with his machete and strips the clothes off his body. But mistaking the packs on Dobbs' burros for sand, he scatters the gold dust to the winds. His act recalls the traditional "ashes to ashes, dust to dust" of the burial service and suggests the many deaths, of both miners and bandits, that the gold has cost.

At the end of the film, Howard—laughing as he did when he first found the gold—explains: "The bandits thought there were bags of sand hidden in among the hides to make them weigh more. . . . They poured our goods out on the ground. The wind has carried all of it away. . . . It's a great joke played on us by the Lord or fate or by nature. . . . The gold has gone back to where we got it." Walter based Howard's manic, even diabolical laughter on his own reaction to a personal disaster in 1937, an episode that taught John an important lesson about the vanity of human wishes. John recalled: "The morning after he opened in *Othello,* in New York, I went around to see him at his hotel. The reviews were just terrible. Through the door, I heard Dad laughing. 'Ho! Ho! Ho!' I went in, and there stood Dad, the tears running down his face, and he was laughing. . . . He was laughing at the reviews! He was laughing at himself! All those years of work and planning that had gone into his Othello . . . down the drain! This was to have been his definitive performance. The joke was on him. Pretty soon he had me laughing, too."⁹ Walter's example encouraged John to ignore the critics, laugh at failure and move on to the next project. In the film, Walter's laughter shows the triumph of the human spirit, transcending the greed that has driven and destroyed the miners.

One defect in the picture is the discovery, after Cody has been killed, of a long, sentimental letter from his wife, which was meant to soften the brutality of the story. As Pauline Kael wrote, the reading of the letter "is so false and virtuous that it's hard to believe that it's in the same movie as those scenes in Tampico." The film should have ended with Howard's laughter after the gold dust blows away, instead of with the anticlimactic scene in which Howard persuades Curtin to visit Cody's wife in Dallas. But Jack Warner exclaimed, "This is the best picture we ever made," and the critics agreed. The London *Spectator* declared, "It is grueling toil, greed, fear and tragedy brilliantly acted under brilliant direction."¹⁰ The film magazine *Sequence* concluded that it was "made with such intelligence, such uncompromising vigour and savagery, that one is astonished that it was made at all." Agee was also wildly enthusiastic about the picture. He called it "one of the most visually alive and beautiful movies I have ever seen" and declared the story was rich "in themes, semi-symbols, possible implications, and potentialities as a movie." He concluded by defining its theme: "This is, after all, about gold and its effects on those who seek it, and so it is also a fable about all human life in this world and about much of the essence of good and evil."

Helped by Agee's influential review, *The Treasure of the Sierra Madre* was nominated by the Academy for best picture. Walter Huston won the award for best supporting actor, and in an extraordinary triple father-and-son victory, John Huston got Oscars for best screenplay *and* best director. In his acceptance speech Walter delighted the audience by recalling, "Many years ago I raised a son and I said to him, 'If you ever become a writer or director, please find a good part for your old man.' "[11] Despite the awards, the film was not at first financially successful and took a number of years to recover the cost. The stark location, the lack of women and love interest, the absence of a hero and the dark conclusion all had an adverse effect on its earnings. But it is now considered one of the greatest American films ever made.

ELEVEN

CRIME AND THE CITY,
1948–1950

· I ·

Huston's double-Oscar triumph vaulted him to the top of his profession, and he was acknowledged as one of the very best directors in Hollywood. His celebrity made him a hot topic for the press and gossip columnists and a more prominent target for right-wing politicians. He co-wrote his next films: *Key Largo* (1948), a gangster movie set in postwar Florida; *We Were Strangers* (1949), a political thriller set in Cuba in the 1930s; and *The Asphalt Jungle* (1950), one of his best pictures, a crime thriller set in a big city. All three were tense and violent, with a political dimension that reflected his current involvement with the Committee for the First Amendment.

Key Largo, a Maxwell Anderson play in blank verse, was first produced in 1939. In a prologue on a Spanish hillside, the central character, King McCloud, an American volunteer in the Spanish Civil War, believes the Loyalists are losing and deserts from the army. The main action takes place when, back in America and guilty about abandoning his men, he finds the family of one of his dead comrades. They are running a small hotel in Key Largo and menaced by gangsters; he redeems himself by defending the family and dying to save them. Huston, who did not find the play at all appealing, disliked the confined drama and the dialogue in verse. He declared, "I hate this kind of play, I don't like free [*sic*] verse. I don't like Maxwell Anderson's work. I don't like *him*." But with his collaborator Richard Brooks, he completely transformed the rather stodgy and sententious play into a tense thriller that leads up to a burst of violent action. Huston moved the time from after the Spanish Civil War to after World War II, and he retained the play's setting in what was essentially one long scene during one night. His McCloud is a disillusioned but heroic veteran who moves from apathy to action and then explodes. He finally takes the gang on a boat to Cuba and confronts them in a fatal battle. In Huston's version the gang are killed one by one and the hero survives to win the girl in an upbeat ending. Huston took the climax directly from the last chapters of Hemingway's *To Have and Have Not* (1937), which had been cut from Howard Hawks' 1944 film of the novel.

Richard Brooks, six years younger than Huston, had been a sports reporter, radio announcer and Marine in the war, and he would later direct film adaptations of Williams' *Cat on a Hot Tin Roof,* Conrad's *Lord Jim* and Capote's *In Cold Blood.* They traveled to the Keys, a string of tiny islands off the southwest coast of Florida, to soak up the atmosphere in an out-of-season hotel. Following his usual method, Huston let his coauthor write the first drafts and, after casual but incisive discussions, dictated the revisions. Huston liked to ponder the material and take his time to dramatize the story. Brooks recalled, "John would go out on the pier and fish, then come in, read what I had written, take a little nap, wake up, go to the end of the pier and smoke. . . . John was clinical most of the time. He'd force me to find the truth according to the nature of the characters. It was the finding of the solution that excited him."

Huston liked to shoot in exotic settings, both in and out of the studio, and tropical locales featured in most of his early films: the American Deep South in *In This Our Life,* Panama in *Across the Pacific,* Mexico in *Sierra Madre,* the Florida Keys in *Key Largo* and Cuba in *We Were Strangers.* The hurricane that approaches and effectively isolates all the characters in the hotel is a familiar theatrical device, yet it is also a realistic natural event. The hotel owner (played by Lionel Barrymore, in considerable pain and confined to a wheelchair in the film, as he was in real life) mentions that eight hundred men had been washed out to sea in a previous storm. When living in Key West, Hemingway had brilliantly described the hurricane that took place on September 2, 1935, killed hundreds of railroad workers, who had had no warning, and devastated the Matecumbe Keys, only twenty-five miles from Key Largo. In "Who Murdered the Vets?," Hemingway angrily wrote: "The wind makes a noise like a locomotive passing, with a shriek on top of that, because the wind has a scream exactly as it has in books, and then the . . . high water rolls you over and over . . . and we find you, now of no importance . . . stinking in the mangroves."[1]

In *Key Largo* Huston includes the subplot of the Osceola brothers, played by the Seminole Indians Jay Silverheels and Rodric Redwing, to represent the poor victims of the hurricane. The two Indians, with only thirty days left to serve in prison, could no longer bear confinement and have escaped. The gangsters, who've killed a sheriff's deputy, force them to remain outdoors during the violent storm while one of their women, 106 years old, calmly smokes a thin cigar. The gangster (Edward G. Robinson) tells the police that the escaped Indians have killed their deputy and the cops take revenge by killing them. Barrymore, who'd been their protector, reflects that it "seems like we can't do anything but hurt these people even when we try to help them."

Since shooting *The Treasure of the Sierra Madre* on location had inflated the original budget by $600,000, Jack Warner insisted that *Key Largo*, apart from the opening shot, be filmed indoors at the studio in Burbank. It was made in three months from December 1947 to early March 1948 and cunningly captured the mood of tropical menace. It opens with an aerial shot of the Florida Keys and the sound of the police siren in pursuit of the Indian escapees, then homes in on the hotel. Describing the special effects, John Brosnan wrote that a good deal of the action was "centered around a sea-front setting which includes a jetty extending out into the water, several launches moored nearby, and a large yacht moored in the distance. Actually the 'sea' is a studio tank and the launches vary in size from full-scale to miniature (the 'large' yacht is only a few feet in length) in an attempt to force the perspective and to create the illusion that the horizon is miles away. . . . The later scenes in the same film which supposedly take place on a launch at sea were also filmed in a tank, but in this case the horizon had been camouflaged with a studio-made fog which makes the whole thing much more effective."

Key Largo is nevertheless more theatrical than cinematic, and Huston had nine actors on the set: five principal players and four other gangsters. He united an effective ensemble of familiar actors: Bogart, who had become a great star after *Casablanca* (1943); Edward G. Robinson; Claire Trevor, who had appeared with Bogart in *The Amazing Dr. Clitterhouse*. Lauren Bacall, who'd married Bogart and knew Huston well, had acted with Bogart in *To Have and Have Not* (1944), *The Big Sleep* (1946) and *Dark Passage* (1947). Frank McCloud (Bogart), a former army major, visits and consoles his wartime comrade's elderly father James Temple (Barrymore) and his young widow Nora (Lauren Bacall). McCloud, a war hero in Italy, tells the Temples that their son and husband died in the battle of San Pietro. They are menaced by a notorious racketeer and counterfeiter Johnny Rocco (Robinson), accompanied by his gun moll Gaye Dawn (Trevor) and his four henchmen. The struggle between good and evil is perfectly clear: the good are powerless, one in a wheelchair, the others unarmed; the gangsters, who have all evaded military service, threaten the civilians with guns.

Though there is some effective dialogue in the movie, Huston and Brooks did not completely eliminate the talky staginess of the original play. On December 10, 1947, the day shooting began, one of the producers noted the weaknesses in the pace and dialogue: "You forgive Barrymore for his big talk because he is old and a kind of prophet. However, Bogart and Bacall . . . should talk in the idiom of normal, every day people. If Brooks will do this he will remove a rather irritating preachiness in the script." The acting styles do not always combine well. Barrymore, a well-known stage actor, speaks his noble lines in a quavering voice and hams it up. Bogart and Bacall do not have their usual flirtatious banter. Bogart is never very effective as a crusading knight; the wasp-waisted Bacall, who has little to do but look worried, seems stiff and ill at ease in the role of a devoted helpmate. Just as Huston had forced Mary Astor to run breathlessly around the set of *The*

Maltese Falcon, so in *Key Largo*, to pump some real emotion into Bacall, he twisted her arm and made her wince.

Robinson—with his flashy clothes, guns, hoods, mistress and violent behavior—steals the film. Bogart is restrained and passive until the very end, while Robinson's colorful character (modeled on the gangster "Lucky" Luciano, recently convicted and deported to Cuba) is intriguingly evil. Robinson's character had originally been called Muriello (which was considered too close to Luciano) but became Johnny Rocco, after Little Rico (his first major role) in *Little Caesar* (1930). Gaye Dawn corresponds to Luciano's alcoholic mistress, Gay Orlova, who had loyally followed him to Cuba. Huston revealed his shrewd insight into the gangster character when he said he wanted to expose the "crustacean with its shell off," the soft, flabby man beneath the vicious exterior. He first showed Robinson in a strikingly original scene—naked, smoking a cigar, holding a drink and a fan, and sweltering in a steamy bathtub.[2] Bogart caustically characterizes him as "the master of the fix. When he couldn't corrupt, he terrified. When he couldn't terrify, he murdered."

The villainous Robinson—who wears two-toned shoes, a cowboy belt and a hideous tie—forcibly kisses the young widow and whispers suggestively to her (perhaps to get her into the bathtub with him). He humiliates the drunken Trevor by forcing her to sing "Moanin' Low" for a drink, though her condition has clearly been caused by their bitter relations and the humiliating life he's forced her to lead. Explaining her character, Huston told Claire Trevor: "You're the kind of drunken dame whose elbows are always a little too big. Your voice is a little too loud; and you're a little too polite. You're very sad, very resigned." When her voice cracks in a pathetic performance of the bitterly ironic words— "He's the kind of man needs the kind of woman like me"—Robinson snarls "you're rotten" and refuses to give her the drink. Bogart defies Rocco and pours it out for her; Robinson then slaps his face and Bogart has to accept his share of abuse before he takes revenge. Robinson bullies Trevor, but is terrified by the natural force of the hurricane which batters against the hotel, prevents his escape and foreshadows the violence that will be turned against the gang. Bogart, referring to the hurricane, ironically tells him, "If it doesn't stop, shoot it."

Huston wrote that "the action ending in the boat was something which would not only appeal to the star, Humphrey Bogart, who is a boat owner and has made one of his big successes in *To Have and Have Not*, but it would also show him in the kind of action which his fans expect of him." Our hero moves from cynicism to idealism (as Bogart had done in *Casablanca*), defeats a group of evil criminals and returns to claim Bacall. Despite its conventional romantic plot, *Key Largo* has enduring dramatic power. Huston told *Time* that he "tried to make all the characters old-fashioned (the gangster's moll is out of the 1920s), to brand them as familiar figures, and to suggest they were ready to take over again."[3] The film derives its emotional intensity from its controlling idea: that after the war Americans had to turn their attention to the grave social problems at home. Huston made Bogart and Robinson effective and enthralling adversaries. Robinson, the gangster as fascist, capitalizes on social apathy and personifies the evils that Bogart, the returning soldier, had fought against in the war. By killing the criminals, Bogart avenges the death of his friend and expresses the themes of brotherhood and loyalty. Reversing the courageous speech of La Pasionaria in the Spanish Civil War, "Better to die on your feet than live on your knees," Trevor tells Bogart, "Better to be a live coward, than a dead hero." But he rejects this idea, and moves from egoistic indifference about the corruption of the world, "I fight nobody's battles but my own," to the almost biblical prophecy: "We're fighting to cleanse the world of ancient evils, ancient ills."

James Agee, alert as always to Huston's achievement, said the film conveys "heat, suspense, enclosedness, the illusion of some eighteen hours of continuous action in two hours' playing time. The lighting is stickily fungoid. The camera is sneakily 'personal'; working close and in almost continuous motion, it enlarges the ambiguous suspensefulness of almost every human move." But Huston felt the film could have been much better. He was furious that Jack Warner lopped out the "thematically most necessary speeches" after the director had finished the picture and exclaimed, "Goddamit, they cut the very gizzard out of it."[4] *Key Largo* was the last film Huston made for Warners.

· II ·

Huston's next two movies were more morally ambiguous. *We Were Strangers* was his first film co-written with the screenwriter Peter Viertel, who became a close friend, and made with the producer Sam Spiegel, a contentious associate. It was based on the 1933 revolt against the Cuban dictator Gerardo Machado who, after a general strike and the loss of military support, was overthrown by Fulgencio Batista and forced to flee the country. The story is told from the point of view of a Cuban-American revolutionary, played by John Garfield (an "unfriendly" HUAC witness, blacklisted after this picture). The revolutionaries tunnel under a cemetery in an attempt to blow up the evil dictator, the police chief and several other brutal officials at the state funeral of a prominent senator, whom they've assassinated. Their plan fails when the funeral is unexpectedly moved to another location. At the end, the heroic Garfield is shot by the police and dies in the arms of Jennifer Jones as the revolution breaks out in Havana. The Cuban revolution succeeds, but the picture, made during the oppressive Batista regime, ignores the fact that one dictator merely replaced another. Huston had a cameo role as a bank teller, and George Antheil, the American composer and self-styled "Bad Boy of Music," did the score.

Huston tried to spark the claustrophobic action with a sexual undercurrent. The bomb-maker, who's told his girlfriends that he's not married, cynically boasts to his cronies, "I haven't lied so much since my wife went to live with her mother." In the best scene, the sweaty, repulsive police chief (Pedro Armendariz) tries to bed Jennifer Jones with a machismo display of excessive eating and drinking. He plays Russian roulette and claims he's a man of honor, but passes out before he can rape her. After persecuting Jones throughout the movie, he's hanged upside down like Mussolini. Huston said the theme was that "violence under certain circumstances may become a duty and be morally justified," a controversial point of view in 1950s America.

In January 1950—thinking perhaps of the talky, slow and sententious scenes—Huston told the future director Lindsay Anderson, then a film critic on the British magazine *Sequence,* "There are parts of it that I like very much, but I'm rather afraid it missed on the whole." Critics on both the Right and the Left attacked the movie's politics. The *Hollywood Reporter,* recalling the accusation that *Sierra Madre* had a Communist bias, called it "a shameful handbook of Marxian dialectics. . . . It is the heaviest dish of Red theory ever served to an audience outside the Soviet Union."[5] Despite the supposed dose of Red theory, the *Daily Worker* reviewer condemned the portrayal of the heroic Cuban revolutionaries: "We feel constrained to object here to using a putschist bombing as characteristic of the fight for national independence. . . . *We Were Strangers* contends that freedom returned to Cuba with Machado's ouster. That was not the case: Wall Street simply commanded another figurehead. It was years before any political democracy was gained." Though the *New York Daily News* thought it was *anti*-Communist and described it as "a testament against dictators in general and Stalin in particular," the FBI feared it might inspire revolutionaries to overthrow the American government, and the State Department refused Huston's request to show it at the International Film Festival in Prague.[6] Though it is not one of Huston's best films, it shows his original and independent thought. It was the kind of serious political film that European directors made in the postwar period.

· III ·

In *The Asphalt Jungle* (1950), a crime story set in a big midwestern city west of Chicago, Huston created a new kind of gangster movie and made the criminals quite different from the ruthless killers in *Key Largo.* The gang steals, but each has his own dream of a life free of crime; they are betrayed by a crooked lawyer and caught by corrupt police. The title *The Asphalt Jungle,* adapted from the novel by W. R.

Burnett, recalls Bertolt Brecht's play *In the Jungle of Cities* (1923). A key motif in the film is the contrast between the sinful, corrupt city and the innocent, healthy countryside. Huston wanted to shoot the film on location and hoped for cooperation from the police in Kansas City or Minneapolis, but was turned down. He finally decided not to identify the specific city, used stock shots of New York for the opening scene and shot most of the film in the MGM studio.

Huston collaborated on the script with Ben Maddow, a left-wing graduate of Columbia University who'd made newsreels and documentaries before becoming a screenwriter in the 1940s. In a letter of January 9, 1950, Huston wrote, "Maddow would take one scene and I would take another. We wrote concurrently and then would read the scenes to each other and discuss them." If both writers were satisfied, the scene would remain. If not, they would exchange and rewrite them as many as three or four times. Their superb script is tautly structured into two halves. In the first half the criminals plan to steal jewels from a store, in a plan masterminded by Doc Riedenschneider (Huston's old friend Sam Jaffe), who's aided by the safeblower Louis Ciavelli (Anthony Caruso) and the tough country boy Dix Handley (Sterling Hayden). A crooked lawyer, Alonzo Emmerich (Louis Calhern), agrees to fence the goods. In the second half they complete the robbery but Emmerich double-crosses them. At the end the central character, Dix Handley, who has resorted to crime to survive in the city, is badly wounded in the shootout. Accompanied by his faithful gun moll, he drives all the way back to his family's lost farm in Kentucky and dies in the paddock as the horses gather mournfully around him. In the screenplay Huston emphasizes the sharp contrast between the dark, gritty streets of the city at the beginning of the film,

> The asphalt road, the cement sidewalks, the dark store windows and brick sides of the four-or-five-story tenements, are now all the same color and texture: wet, black and shiny,

and the open sky and green hills at the end,

a rich landscape of rolling farm country extends to the horizon, white houses set in the valleys and connected by lines of fences or trees set in order between fields.

Like B. Traven, W. R. Burnett (who'd collaborated with Huston on *High Sierra*) was pleased with the screenplay, but had one important reservation: "Huston is an adept at putting a property he likes on the screen—how to dramatize its essence, what it is really saying. And he did this very successfully with *The Asphalt Jungle*. He stayed close to the characters, the action, and the atmosphere. Nothing was invented, nor was the story changed in any respect. . . . [But] I was unhappy with the end of Dix Handley, the Southern strong-arm heister—half-dead, but chasing horses around in a field."[7]

While writing the script, Huston asked MGM for police equipment, technical information on how to crack a safe, and a list of likely winners at the Belmont and Pimlico racetracks. He created a credible underworld, with its own hierarchy. Dix Handley is described as "a small town hooligan who's crazy for horses." A rival criminal mocks him as a hick and remarks, "If he makes a crooked move, he'll never pitch another forkful of manure." The dialogue of the elegant, silver-tongued Emmerich and the educated, articulate Doc Riedenschneider provides a sharp contrast to the inarticulate and naïve Hayden and his rough gang. When Emmerich, with waxed mustache and suave manners, is told that the robbery is foolproof, he sardonically warns them, "I've made a lot of money getting [boys like you] out of jail." As if to signal the similarity of the criminals and the police, the thieves—like Emmerich, the police commissioner and the detectives—all wear hats, jackets and ties.

Huston's casting was particularly astute. The hard-drinking Sterling Hayden was an ex-Marine and highly decorated war hero, who'd fought the Nazis as a special commando alongside Tito's partisans in Yugoslavia. He admired his wartime comrades and had briefly joined the Communist Party after the war. Then, repudiating his political beliefs, he cooperated with HUAC and named names, but soon regretted his testimony and emphasized the bitter self-contempt he'd felt since the day he testified. In a generous gesture, Huston hired the repentant Hayden, who described his casual audition for the film. Huston said, " 'Kid, play it the way it feels best. Lie down, sit up, walk around, do any damn thing you please. Wherever you go, we'll follow. Take your time. Let me know when you're ready.' He drops in a canvas chair and starts to read a book." When the picture was completed, Hayden gratefully wrote Huston that working with him had been "a pleasure, a privilege and an education all in one."

Marilyn Monroe, in her first important role, was perfectly cast as Emmerich's blond mistress, Angela Phinlay. Burnett's novel described Angela as "voluptuously made; and there was something about her walk—something lazy, careless, and insolently assured—that was impossible to ignore."[8] Marilyn's glowing skin and soft, dreamy sensuality contrasts sharply with the hard, striving male characters who surround her, and she remains rather vague about what's really going on. Emmerich twice calls Angela "some sweet kid"—the second time, after she's betrayed him, with sharp irony. She first defies the cop and tells him, "Haven't you bothered me enough you big . . . banana head?," but then breaks down under interrogation and fails to protect Emmerich with a prearranged alibi. When she's disappointed that they won't be able to go on holiday, Emmerich caustically reassures her that she'll soon find another protector, "Don't worry baby, you'll have plenty of trips." The writer Budd Schulberg, praising Huston's acute delineation of character, told him that he "made us feel Calhern was really on the spot, trying to hide naked nerves with charm; and with Hayden you went farther into an understanding of violence than I have seen on the screen before. . . . The thought-processes of the little kept blonde were for once accurate."[9]

Sam Jaffe's character was originally named Rie*m*enschneider, after the great sixteenth-century German sculptor (whose work Huston knew), but was changed to Rie*d*enschneider to shed the positive connotation. Doc has a strong German accent, rolls his guttural *r*'s and says *v* for *w*—as in "vork." He has a mustache, sagging jowls and wrinkled neck, and wears an elegant homburg hat. Emmerich has a sexy mistress; Doc dreams that the stolen jewels will enable him to flee to

Mexico and "have nothing to do all day long but chase [girls]—in the sunlight." The classy lawyer and classy criminal are connected by their taste for women, educated speech, natty clothes and German names (which, only five years after the war, still had negative associations) that emphasize the shadowy line between thieves and supposedly honest men.

None of the deadbeat criminals has hit pay dirt for a long time. Handley lives in a shabby rented room and wants to regain his horse farm in Kentucky. Emmerich, now bankrupt, wants to leave his invalid wife and take a Cuban holiday with Angela. Doc, just out of prison and broke, wants to squander his wealth on beautiful women. (He's easily excited after a long confinement and, considering his decrepit appearance, will need a lot of money to get those women.) Ciavelli, the explosives expert, wants to liberate his wife and children from their squalid tenement. But none of them gets what he wants. Each of the distinctly portrayed characters has a fatal weakness—Handley: horses, Emmerich: money, Riedenschneider: women, Handley's hunchback friend Gus: deformity, Ciavelli: family. In a grotesquely vivid scene the cops, trying to capture Ciavelli (who's been fatally shot in the robbery), kick down a door and interrupt his funeral.

Huston created a strikingly innovative film despite the moralistic Production Code, which drained a lot of originality and interest from the eccentric cast of characters. The censor Joseph Breen insisted Huston make absolutely clear that Handley, who shares a room with his girl Doll (Jean Hagen), does not sleep with her. Doc, the lubricious mastermind of the robbery, is caught by the police while watching young girls dance in a roadside café. In a letter of October 1949 to the studio head Louis Mayer, Breen demanded that Doc be one-dimensional and "be played as a pitiful character trying to recapture his youth, not at all as a lecherous man." As the studio was forced to make concessions on these issues, Breen did all he could to cramp Marilyn's physical assets and sexy style. "It is mandatory," he declared, "that the intimate parts of the body—specifically the breasts of women—be fully covered at all times." There must be no "indication that [Emmerich] follows her into the bedroom, or any more definite suggestion of intimacy."[10] After saying goodnight to her sugar daddy, Marilyn—in her lazy, careless walk—sways down the hallway to the alluring bedroom, leaving her nocturnal adventures to our imagination.

When the thieves first enter the jewelry store, they seem tentative, as if walking into the lobby of an expensive hotel where they don't belong but hope (someday) to be able to afford. Huston noted that "the sequence where they break open the safe, which was totally visual without any dialogue whatsoever, has been imitated many times since"—especially in Jules Dassin's *Rififi* (1955). Two bits of staging in the exciting robbery must have reminded Huston of incidents in his early life. He wrote that when he was twelve years old and living in Los Angeles, he stole sticks of dynamite from building sites and boiled them to distill nitroglycerin for homemade bombs: "With an eyedropper we trickled it into three-ounce bottles held slantwise. We filled them all the way up so the nitro couldn't shake around, and put a cork in the bottle." Just before the explosive is set, Ciavelli takes the small bottle hanging from a string around Handley's neck and exclaims, "It's going to take a lot to blow this baby."[11] In Mexico the young Huston said he'd played a kind of Russian roulette by throwing a cocked pistol against the ceiling and making it go off when it hit the floor. During the robbery Ciavelli is shot when Handley punches the night watchman and the gun flies out of his hand, strikes the stone floor and fires.

There are some notable similarities between *The Asphalt Jungle* and *Sierra Madre*. Riedenschneider warns his cohorts about the possibility of disillusionment and failure, just as the prospector Howard warns his partners not to be too greedy. The well-dressed Doc wants to spend his money on beautiful women; Fred C. Dobbs dreams of expensive clothes, swell cafés and sexy dames. Emmerich has exactly the kind of sexy mistress that Doc and Dobbs merely dream about, and that Howard actually has when he goes back to the Indian village to resume his blissful life as a revered healer. The thieves get the jewels but can't fence them; the miners get the gold but lose it. The endings of both films are sentimental, tacked on to soften the dark view and please the audience.

MGM knew they had a winner, felt like celebrating and spent $2,800 on the lavish wrap party. Several distinguished writers living in Los Angeles—Thomas Mann, Aldous Huxley, Christopher Isher-wood, John Steinbeck and Norman Mailer—were invited to a special showing. The report cards at the Pickwood Theater preview in West Los Angeles got commendably high marks: 273 out of 281 were Good, Very Good, Excellent and Outstanding. Nobody walked out. The crit-ics raved and *Newsweek* declared, "Between pranks Huston has demon-strated that he is certainly the most creative director in Hollywood." His colleagues agreed and sent enthusiastic letters. José Ferrer wrote, "I've just sat through two consecutive showings of *The Asphalt Jungle* and can't tell you how it thrilled me."

Huston's realistic dialogue and expert casting differentiated the thieves' characters and made the audience sympathize with their aspi-rations. He exposed the depths of corruption in the story; and the powerful lawyer and the police commissioner, more venal than the ordinary crooks, gave the movie unusual depth. The screenwriter and director Dudley Nichols, another old pro, sent Huston an appreciation of his achievement: "To take a story pattern that is as old as the hills and make it into a film so fresh and original and hard-hitting that one has the illusion of seeing something that has never been written before is a real triumph."[12]

TWELVE

Sultanate of St. Clerans,
1950–1960

· I ·

Though Evelyn Keyes was accustomed to Huston's flirtations and infidelities, she was shocked by his reaction to Ricki Soma. She angrily recalled her humiliation when Huston met Ricki at David Selznick's party in Hollywood in 1949: "He was all over her. They were embracing with all these people around. . . . John had flipped out and was necking in public." Someone asked, "Who's that with John? I guess it's his wife." "No," Evelyn said, "I'm his wife." Ricki, in full pursuit, didn't seem to mind that John was married, that his wife was present and that people might disapprove of her behavior. Huston was probably amused to recall that "soma" was Aldous Huxley's name for the dream-inducing drug that soothed all human cares in *Brave New World* (1932). As his third marriage disintegrated under the strain of his wild behavior, he thought Ricki would provide an escape from Evelyn and offer him a new life.

Enrica Soma, born on May 6, 1929, was twenty-three years younger than Huston and barely out of her teens when they met. Her father, Tony Soma, fond of singing Italian operatic arias while standing on his head, owned speakeasies and then restaurants in New York that catered to Broadway clientele. (Later on, when Tony kept demanding money, Huston would call him "the demented old dago.") Ricki had a striking Italian Renaissance oval face, with sharp nose, thin lips and dark hair pulled back from her forehead, and her tense manner suggested a nervous temperament. She had studied ballet with the Russian master

George Balanchine and danced with the Ballet Russe de Monte Carlo, but at five feet six and 120 pounds she was rather heavy for an aspiring prima ballerina. She began modeling at sixteen and had appeared on the cover of *Seventeen*. On June 9, 1947, the producer David Selznick saw her stunning photo on the cover of *Life* magazine and offered her a seven-year movie contract, which brought her to Hollywood. She never appeared in a movie, and instead chose a life with Huston.

The twenty-year-old Ricki soon got pregnant, and when Evelyn asked, "Are you sure it's yours, John?" he replied with characteristic nonchalance, "It doesn't matter."[1] He had had no children with Dorothy or (despite the hormone treatments) with Evelyn, and Lesley's child was stillborn. He desperately wanted a child and was tolerant about its paternity. He had slept with scores of mistresses and none of them had ever got pregnant. Later on, when Billy Pearson forbade his third wife, Queta, to have children, Ricki "poked holes in her diaphragm" and Queta became pregnant. Knowing that John would marry her if she became pregnant, Ricki may have tried the same ruse to capture him. Bayard Veiller, the son of Huston's collaborator and friend Tony Veiller, recalled that Ricki was very pregnant when she married John on February 10, 1950. She was charming and lovely, but awfully young and knew nobody and nothing. John was worldly and cultured, and knew everyone and everything. Veiller thought John would never have married her if she hadn't been pregnant, and that they didn't have much of a marriage. Ricki was starry-eyed, in love, eager to be a companion to her famous and handsome husband, and to explore the glamorous world he inhabited. But Huston tired of her soon after their children were born, and did little to bridge the gap between their ages and backgrounds. Like many a trophy wife, she would find herself marooned in a grand house with sole responsibility for the children, while her husband was free to travel and pursue his career and his women. Anjelica said that in the Belgian Congo, John "contrived to have himself photographed with a native naked woman and her seven children, and when a businessman would produce his own picture [of his wife and kids] my father would reach for his wallet and produce this picture!"

On April 6, soon after the wedding, John arranged a sixty-sixth birthday party for Walter at Mike Romanoff's fashionable restaurant on Rodeo Drive in Beverly Hills. But Walter suddenly became too ill to attend and sent his regrets. John returned to Walter's hotel and stayed with him in the hospital until he died of an aneurysm of the abdominal aorta the following day. Idealizing his father, John said, "He died peacefully and without a struggle. I have never seen so quiet a death. He died as modestly as he lived. . . . He was too good a man to get sick. When the time came, he just died." After his death, Walter continued to take care of John. He got a $30,000 trust fund from his father's estate and also inherited money from Walter's sister.

On April 16 John's son Walter Anthony (called Tony) was born and, in a way, the son replaced his father. Huston's hero James Joyce, whose father had also died at the same time his son was born, wrote a moving poem, "Ecce Puer" (Behold the Boy) about it: "A child is sleeping: / An old man gone. / O, father forsaken, / Forgive your son."[2] Fifteen months later, on July 9, 1951, his daughter Anjelica was born; and would later take up the acting career her mother never had.

· II ·

Around the time of his marriage to Ricki, Huston began to think about moving to Ireland. Walter's death had severed an important tie to America. The anti-Communist witch hunts continued with full force until the downfall of Senator Joseph McCarthy in 1954 and certainly influenced his mood. The right-wing press had absurdly labeled him "the brains of the Communist Party in the West." *We Were Strangers* and *Sierra Madre* were falsely condemned as crude Communist propaganda, and even the nonpolitical *Moulin Rouge* would be attacked. Huston, moreover, had some significant connections with Ireland. Walter's father was Irish, John had been attracted by Dorothy Harvey's Irish looks and Lesley Black was Irish. It also seemed to be a lucky place: when he was poor in London, he'd won £100 in the Irish Sweepstakes, which helped him to live in Paris and then sail home to resume his career in Hollywood. He wanted to do more work in Europe, and Ireland would be a more convenient home base.

Most important of all, perhaps, was the fact that Ireland was a tax-free haven for artists. It was a poor country, still mostly rural, where Huston could live a traditional life in the grand style, far from Hollywood and its censorious press. In 1952 he rented Courtown House, in Kilcock (an inappropriately detumescent name), County Kildare, about twenty-five miles northwest of Dublin. It had three hundred acres and a staff of servants, but the unceasing heavy rains made it seem like a ship plowing through a heavy storm. Peter Viertel thought the house lacked aesthetic appeal and "had the look of a correction center for juvenile delinquents." Huston agreed it was a "monstrosity" but gallantly maintained that "unlike most Irish country houses, it was warm and comfortable."

While living in Courtown, Huston discovered St. Clerans, named after a seventh-century bishop who was martyred at Vienne, in France, and became the patron saint of prisons. A typical ruined Georgian manor, it had been built in the Palladian style in 1784, on a mound near the remains of a Norman castle. The "Big House" had seventeen rooms, and there was a "Little House" about half a mile away. Standing on one hundred acres of land, it was sixteen miles from Galway, in the west of Ireland, and 120 miles from Dublin. In 1953 Huston bought the crumbling mansion for £10,000 and spent another million dollars on renovations. "The house was in utter disrepair," he wrote. "The roof was leaking and the flooring gone, but the stonework was beautiful and the proportions were classic." Eloise Hardt remembered Huston, like a child playing with a stage set, showing her the elaborate plans for St. Clerans, and telling her where all the art and furniture would go. He didn't move into the Big House until the summer of 1959, when the fifteen servants—including butlers, cooks, maids, gardeners and grooms, along with his Irish wolfhound Seamus—gathered at the entrance to welcome the master. He lived there until 1973. The man who'd once been homeless in London and slept rough on the Embankment was now the owner of a grand estate in Ireland, where he could arrange and admire all the objets d'art he'd collected.

Visitors were impressed by the plashing fountain and lime-stained lions that guarded the four-columned gray stone entrance. There was a tennis court, trout stream, grazing cows and galloping foals in the green, green meadow, unspoiled by fences but protected by a *ha-ha,* an invisible barrier ditch. Huston proudly wrote: "St. Clerans had three stories. The main entrance was on the second floor. The lower floor had a stone-and-concrete moat—a surround—that permitted full windows and plenty of light. It was here that I had the Japanese bath. I also installed a gallery for pre-Columbian art. There was an office for the estate manager, a storeroom, the wine cellar, an apartment for members of the staff and a lovely room we called the TV room. We only visited the TV room to see world soccer, horseracing, boxing matches, events we'd watch in groups, betting fiercely." The living room suggested both comfort and luxury, with a marble fireplace, thick carpet, velvety olive-green sofa and chairs, and an elaborate chandelier hanging from the white ceiling. There was a huge bookcase, with library steps, and deep niches for the Inca and Aztec statues on one wall and Huston's own paintings on the other.

Huston's *horror vacui* compelled him to fill the vast spaces of his mansion, to create an aesthetic autobiography in which material objects represented the phases of his taste and testified to his obsessive enthusiasm. After passing through the black marble hallway, guests were dazzled by the pre-Columbian figures, the Spanish Colonial chairs, the ornately carved four-poster Florentine-Napoleonic bed, and the silk screens from Japan. The manor seemed like a classier if more modest version of William Randolph Hearst's Castle in San Simeon, California, which was re-created as Xanadu in Orson Welles' *Citizen Kane.* One English writer, referring to the local fox hunters and to Peter Shaffer's 1964 play about the conquest and plundering of Peru, penned a rather satiric account of Huston's eclectic superabundance:

Beyond the moat, the fountain, and the huge stone lions
were rooms that held his collection of Impressionists,
original posters by Lautrec, a medieval wooden Christ astride
a donkey, Indian jade deities, African sculptures, heads from

New Guinea, six-foot high candles . . . and everywhere so
much gleam of gold that it looked as if it wasn't the Galway
Blazers that the host followed, but the Royal Hunt of the
Sun. Such movie mementoes as "Oscars" and scripts were
tucked away, invisible, in a dusty remove room downstairs.
The effect upstairs was of a well-ordered treasure house into
which the living Pharaoh would ultimately retire himself. He
had arranged his own pyramid.[3]

As a collector, Huston certainly had catholic taste. He made a
great deal of money, but never saved it and was always in debt. He
acquired art, as he acquired lovers, wives and exotic pets, while roam-
ing all over the world to make his movies. He preferred primitive to
Greco-Roman art, and owned a lot of easily obtainable pre-Columbian
statues and many West African tribal masks. This "heavy blood stuff"
from cultures that practiced human sacrifice and cannibalism matched
his taste for hunting foxes and shooting big game. He had a classical
third-century B.C. horse's head, a eighth-century Chinese Tang horseman and a fifteenth-century wooden Christ figure.

Huston's art collection equaled the best in Hollywood, and included paintings by Paul Klee, Maurice Utrillo, Amedeo Modigliani,
Chaim Soutine, Rufino Tamayo and the American Expressionist Morris Graves. He also collected flamboyant posters by Toulouse-Lautrec,
and may have owned works that portrayed the very people who were
characters in his film: the performers La Goulue, Jane Avril and Aris-
tide Bruant. In 1952, while making *Moulin Rouge* in France, he bought
one of Monet's huge *Red Water Lilies* (1914–17) from a dealer in Deauville for the unusually low price of $10,000. Billy Pearson, who claimed
to work as an agent for wealthy clients and promised to bring the seller
more business, persuaded her to lower the original price. But Huston,
who didn't have the money in hand for this tempting bargain, repaired
to the local casino and won the necessary cash. The six-by-four-foot
oil painting, not signed or dated, portrays two groups of round, green,
floating water lilies with darkly outlined pinkish red flowers on top of

them, separated by a gentle channel of blue water. There's no horizon in the picture, but the reflected sky and its patch of yellow cloud dance on the shimmering surface. Monet painted it both with thick impasto and thin washes of pigment, and gave it a soothing, dreamy quality.

The only other painting we can precisely identify as belonging to Huston (Sotheby's, which sold some of his collection, has no record of Huston's art sales) is Juan Gris' *Arlequin* (1925), a present from Lesley Black. This traditional character in the Italian commedia dell'arte is a tall, powerful, standing figure, with dark skin, thick Roman nose and bull-like neck. He wears a wide, curved, two-pointed, black Napoleonic hat, apron collar and diamond-patterned costume with a buckled black belt. He rests his huge right hand on his hip and with his huge left hand opens a stage curtain to begin the show. Huston was clearly drawn to this popular theatrical figure.

Huston sometimes converted his salary into objects and possessions that reflected his taste and enhanced his collection. While acting in *The Cardinal,* directed by Otto Preminger in 1963, he took two paintings by Jack Yeats (brother of W. B. Yeats) instead of a fee. In 1966 he got $50,000 worth of art for playing Noah in *The Bible.* He owned a bronze head, sculpted by Jacob Epstein in 1963, of the American film-maker Robert Flaherty, who'd made a greatly admired documentary of the Aran Islands. Epstein's biographer called it "a heroic portrait, the portrait of a visionary, the portrait of an Irishman [*sic*]."

Huston also owned works by the tall, handsome, aristocratic and adventurous Russian-born Parisian painter Nicolas de Staël, who'd joined the cavalry of the French Foreign Legion during World War II. An abstract artist who returned to brightly colored realism, he killed himself in 1955 by jumping out of his studio window in Antibes. Douglas Cooper's description of de Staël, who sounds like Huston, explains why he was drawn to this artist: "He was a complex and in many ways contradictory character: autocratic, exacting, exuberant, morose, charming, witty and uncompromising."[4] A conquistador of art, Huston captured sculpture from Mexico, Africa, Greece, China and Japan, and bought paintings by artists from Spain, France, Italy, Switzerland,

Russia, England, Ireland, America and Mexico. Most of his great collection was sold when he left St. Clerans in 1973; the rest mysteriously disappeared after his death.

· III ·

Huston was both a connoisseur and a serious artist. He liked to share his interests, and he put his girlfriends at ease by showing them illustrated art books and impressing them with perceptive explanations of the pictures. He loved the colorful work of the Impressionists, but his favorite painting, Rembrandt's *Night Watch* (1642), in the Rijksmuseum in Amsterdam, reveals his attraction to character and conflict. Rembrandt's group portrait of an armed burgher company on their way to a shooting contest has the striking realism, complex movement, pictorial spectacle and glowing chiaroscuro that Huston achieved in many of his films.

Throughout his life he sought refuge from the hectic process of filmmaking, from directing many people on a complex project. He found tranquillity at St. Clerans, where he could enjoy the solitary, private, self-communing and peaceful relaxation of painting. In April 1967 his secretary at St. Clerans wrote, "John is painting morning, noon and afternoon. Good canvases that absorb him completely. The only thing that brings him to the surface is the tinkle of ice and the promise of the coldest martini possible around 8 P.M." Photographs show Huston painting a bowl of fruit and his son's pet falcon. When Olivia de Havilland visited St. Clerans, Betty O'Kelly, his estate manager and mistress, welcomed her to the estate. The religious and stoic, slender and stylish O'Kelly smoked heavily and wore beautiful head scarves. Olivia was shocked to see Huston's portrait of O'Kelly, who had posed for him while eating an apple and lying naked on the floor. Far from keeping his affair with Betty secret while his wife was in residence, he celebrated it in his art.

Huston's two most ambitious paintings were the portrait of his tall daughter Anjelica (no date) and *The Spirit of St. Clerans* (1960s). Anjelica, her elongated body in sharp profile, appears with long black hair and long black dress, and emerges from a cloudy blue background. Her left arm is extended to her knee, her right arm is bent back on her shoulder and her huge feet protrude to the edge of the frame. In this unflattering, even hostile portrait of an attractive young woman, her eyes are obscured, her nose is prominent, her face shadowy and dark.

The second picture, painted in hot reds and oranges, vividly evokes with symbolic images his fox hunts and fishing trips. The stylized figure has hoof-shaped feet and rides a leaping horse with a feathery mane. His oversize, egg-shaped, masklike face, with large, black, almond-shaped eyes, is surrounded by a glowing halo. Following the traditional iconography of St. George and the Dragon, the rider's hand emerges from behind his tight head of dark hair, grasps a thin spear and pierces the neck of the threatening monster as the horse's hooves are about to trample it. A bare tree trunk with limblike branches appears in the upper-left background, and a realistic, curved and open-mouthed trout leaps up in the lower-left corner. When he was making *Moby Dick* in 1955 Huston drew another picture that alluded to his local fox hunters, the Galway Blazers. It showed a rider, with long rein and bridle, on top of a giant whale.[5]

Though Huston did not follow the contemporary movement toward abstract art, he maintained a cool, impersonal distance from his subjects (and himself) and seemed unwilling, after his first *Self-Portrait*, to realistically portray their faces. His painter's eye, and combination of artistic and literary talent, contributed significantly to his career as a director, and his films testify to the tradition of art behind them.

· IV ·

With a touch of self-pity, Huston said, "I go back to Ireland to lick the wounds that have been inflicted on me in the outer world." He told an Irish journalist that he had no wish to become a farmer: "There's a stream and plenty of rough shooting, and enough pasture to turn the horses out on. It's all I want." He tended to glamorize St. Clerans, especially when trying to lure women to his seraglio, and was ecstatic about its tranquillity and natural beauty when writing to Marietta Tree, who visited on several occasions: "The quiet of this place is wonderful & deep—so that you can hear a fish jump in the river a hundred yards away during the night. And snuffling of the horses & now & then a hoof banging against the stall door. I feel as though I could spend the rest of my life here & never want to leave—except to come to you my dearest."[6] After living in hotels and rented flats for most of the year, he particularly welcomed the space and the silence.

Huston idealized Ireland and blanked out everything that James Joyce, who fled the country, had criticized and condemned in his fiction. He never mentioned the Catholic Church's censorship and oppression or Ireland's poverty and ignorance, backwardness and narrowness, bigotry and fanaticism, sectarian hatreds and acts of terrorism. In his life as in his films, Ireland was all high art and ceremonial hospitality, genteel country life and colorful characters in congenial pubs. Its poverty and unemployment meant he could always find a willing array of servants, ranging from his estate manager to his grooms, gardeners, housekeepers and cooks.

Always the actor, Huston put on a delightful performance for the benefit of his guests and entertained in grand style. The amiable Count Dracula lorded it over his castle and drank (instead of blood) only the finest red burgundy. St. Clerans was like a big movie set, with John the magical director. The congenial host captured his friends, charmed his colleagues and seduced his lovers. The producer Carter De Haven said Huston couldn't have been more gracious and made his pampered visitors feel immediately at home. The pièce de résistance was a long collective soak in the huge, deep Japanese bath installed on the lower floor, which relaxed the mind, soothed the body and provided erotic hydrotherapy. The bath, according to his Irish publicist, had "not only the boiler and tub, which seated six comfortably, but also all the plumbing, the screens, the kimonos, and the clogs, and even the sand and Japanese stones for a proper Oriental setting."

Huston would appear in an impressive array of costumes. John Steinbeck's young son was shown "an amazing closet filled with riding gear." The son of Claud Cockburn (the author of the novel *Beat the Devil*, who lived in Ireland) described the effect Huston had on his more conservative neighbors: "When he would appear at hunt balls in full ceremonial hunting rig and foxes' masks embossed in gold thread on his pumps, the Anglo-Irish gentry would snigger, but he hypnotised them all the same." The actor John Hurt recalled that Huston would turn up for dinner in a fancy velvet suit and on another occasion, as a joke, put on a long red nightdress and soft pointed cap with a wool bobble on top. "Put it this way," Hurt said, "he was perverse."[7]

Huston usually kept about six horses and joined the landed gentry by providing money for the fox hunts and becoming Master of the Galway Blazers. They were named for the occasion when their celebrations got out of hand and they burned down a local pub. Quoting Jorrocks, the sporting character in the nineteenth-century novels of R. S. Surtees, he said, "Foxhunting is the very image of war, with none of the guilt and only seventy percent of the danger." He told Peter Viertel, who joined him on the frantic chase, that foxhunting, the ultimate test of horsemanship for nonprofessionals, was "more exciting than polo or show jumping, only one step removed from steeplechasing and perhaps even more difficult, as a rider had to choose his own route over the natural obstacles of the Irish countryside. . . . It was like stepping into the pages of Siegfried Sassoon's *Memoirs of a Fox-Hunting Man*." Billy Pearson said Huston had no fear and refused to wear protective headgear even when riding a dangerous horse. To Celeste Shane, an expert equestrian, Irish foxhunting as the locals practiced it was alcoholic, rough and reckless. The riders would make their horses jump over barbed wire and on to asphalt, and their abuse of the animals repelled her.

Following the example of the Canadian-born Walter, who became an American citizen in 1922, John solidified his ties to his adopted country by becoming an Irish citizen in 1964. Charles Haughey—the minister of justice who later became prime minister—officiated at the ceremony, which was noticed in the Irish press. At the same time Huston revealed his diplomatic skills and ability to live in two different, even opposing worlds: official and revolutionary Ireland. When John Hurt visited St. Clerans in 1969, the only other guest was Dan Breen, feared as the notorious IRA "Gunman" during the time of the

Troubles from 1916 to 1923. In October 1972, when Huston was planning to make *The Mackintosh Man* in Ireland, he received a threatening letter, ostensibly from the IRA. He made contact with the organization, who assured him that the letter had been sent by a crackpot, that his people would be welcome in Ireland and that foreign film crews would not be molested.[8] Between 1956 and 1987 Huston shot parts of six other movies in Ireland—*Moby Dick*, *The List of Adrian Messenger*, *Casino Royale*, *Sinful Davey*, *The Mackintosh Man* and *The Dead*—and helped establish the Irish film industry.

Despite Huston's flirtation with the IRA and rumors that they had held secret meetings in the basement of his manor, on July 10, 1970, Trinity College, Dublin, awarded him an honorary Litt.D. that made him a Doctor of Letters. The recipients traditionally brought their wives. But Huston, then between his fourth and fifth marriages, brought two of his loyal support group: Gladys Hill and Betty O'Kelly. The citation read:

[Our University] has chosen to honour an artist whose works have been viewed with approbation all over the world, JOHN HUSTON. Everyone must remember such powerful films directed by him. . . . Besides directing other actors, he himself, like the ancient Athenian dramatists, has been an actor, and also, as the spirit moved him, painter, writer, and soldier. Recently—and this is a particular reason for us to rejoice—he has become an Irish citizen and lives in Galway, where, they say, the local foxes have learned to fear his prowess as a hunter. We think it most fitting, then, that a man who has enriched our minds and delighted our eyes with so many colourful scenes and stories should be robed in our brightest academic scarlet *honoris causa* and received with our liveliest applause.

The original Latin also had a witty description of six of his films: "No one certainly has created such vehemently depicted stories about that excitable and fatal whale, or navigating the dangerous African river, or the Parisian tavern called the Red Windmill, or the lost treasure, or the Asiatic land or the Holy Scriptures."

He was particularly pleased by the reference to his skill as a hunter and by the fact that he could now be addressed as Dr. Huston as well as Major Huston. Abandoning all modesty, he wrote a gracious letter to the chancellor: "Yesterday's honors and celebration have left me full of unholy pride. I've tried drowning it with scornful assurance that I am entirely unworthy, but it's no use. Decent humility has fled. I'm unbearably full of myself and you, Sir, are responsible."[9] It was the acme of his time as an Irish gentleman and lord of the manor.

· V ·

When in residence at St. Clerans—usually part of the summer, the odd week or two between projects, and Christmas—Huston would get up late and have breakfast in bed while reading the Paris *Herald Tribune*. While he resided in stately splendor in the Big House, Ricki and the children lived in the damp Little House, separated by a stream and half a mile away. They came to the Big House for more formal luncheons and by invitation only. His relations with Ricki became polite but icy. On weekends Tony and Anjelica would be asked to spend an hour with him. They would also come to the Big House at night to perform Shakespeare and other plays for his guests. He loved to show off Anjelica and praised the children if he thought they performed well.

Some people felt he neglected and mistreated Ricki. But she remained loyal to him and seemed sufficiently content to lead the life he'd created for her in the home she'd helped create for him. She had supervised the renovations and the decor, the delivery and placement of the furniture and works of art. The war cartoonist Bill Mauldin recalled an example of his harsh treatment: "One night we went fishing and she wanted to go along. John told her to get lost. He treated her in some ways more like a gruff father than a husband. I don't think he liked women very much. He tended to be mean to them. He was sort of a man's man." The well-known photographer Inge Morath thought Ricki was unfulfilled and unhappy: "There was some lamentation of her own on not achieving something. That was the undertone in her life." An actor-friend agreed that Ricki had become disillusioned: "She was an extraordinary and charming woman, but there was a kind of sadness to her, a melancholy and resignation. She made me understand what it was to have been a very young woman—starry-eyed, and married to an old man."

Eloise Hardt, as usual, was Huston's severest critic. She thought "Ricki really tried to make a home in Ireland: to get all the art into it and please him. But he treated her badly, was so disrespectful. She lived down below like a servant. . . . Ricki was spending all her time chasing John and John couldn't care. It was a horrible marriage, a classic example of the kids caught in a crossfire between two people who were so involved with themselves."[10] But Ricki was far less egoistic than John. She tried to secure him in marriage, first with two children, then with the grandeur of St. Clerans, but neither could transform the roving rake into a devoted husband and father.

A restless wanderer and obsessive worker who had his first child at forty-four and his third at fifty-six, Huston was rather old to become a family man. Like Walter, John was a mainly absent father and didn't have much to do with his children when they were growing up. They made emotional demands he could not meet, and he had more urgent interests and pressing needs. He found children boring and didn't know how to play with them. Though John was not demonstrative with anyone, Tony complained about his lack of affection. He could "never remember being in Dad's arms. He never was a physical father in any way. It just didn't come naturally to him. But I can remember sitting in his lap when we were making *The List of Adrian Messenger.*" A photo taken at the time shows the bearded John—in his canvas director's chair, smoking a cigarette and staring pensively into space—and the gawky, bespectacled, twelve-year-old Tony, still craving affection, sitting in John's lap, looking at the camera and embracing his father.

All his attempts to get closer to Tony—by giving him gifts and horses, and making him responsible for chores—failed. Like many rich and busy fathers, he would turn up with an armful of expensive presents, then disappear to his next remote location. Tony became a good rider and even jumped a fence when he appeared during the fox hunt in *Adrian Messenger,* but as a child he was also seriously injured. He fell off his pony, caught his foot in the stirrup, was dragged up the gravel driveway to the front of the house and suffered severe lacerations of the scalp. John's inconsistencies, his sudden swings between harshness and leniency, were also confusing. When Tony, age eight, failed to clean the pigsty, his pet piglet was taken away from him and turned into bacon— an extreme and traumatic punishment. Yet whenever Tony misbehaved at school, John, always allied with the rebels, defended him against his teachers. On one occasion the young Tony, who'd learned to sing Irish Republican songs, got his revenge. He removed the guns from the gun room and made it seem as if the rack had been forced. In a maneuver worthy of John, he tricked his father into believing that the IRA had broken into the house and stolen all the guns.

As an adult Tony, mistaking John's motives, bitterly criticized his frightening severity:

If you did something wrong, he assumed that you were
doing it because you were evil. It was almost Victorian.
And he would take you to bits. Not only me, but my sister.
He drove Anjelica out of the room crying on any number
of occasions. . . . This was a scary man. He was absolutely
terrifying. . . .
    Between the foxhunting, trips to the bogs of
Connemara, evenings in oyster bars, visits to the Japanese
bath, and dress-up nights, he'd make attempts at instant
fatherhood that usually ended badly. Particularly during
adolescence, we were subjected to the most devastating
criticism. Surrounded as he was by a more or less
sycophantic court, it became a spectator sport to see
who would be taken apart next, who would rush out of
the room in tears.

Thom Steinbeck, who had a rough time with his own hard-drinking father, and visited St. Clerans as a boy, confirmed that Huston was "always dissatisfied with his children. Anjelica, and especially Tony, caught a lot of shit from the old man. He constantly criticized Tony to toughen him and 'make him a man.' He made life difficult for Tony; slapped him around with a clip on the head to humiliate him."[11] John may have thought that Ricki coddled and spoiled the children. Tony felt estranged from John when he was absent and apprehensive when he was at home. Isolated in the manor and with few friends at school, he became obsessed with falconry and took refuge in his birds of prey. Marietta Tree, always loyal to John, thought he *tried* to be a good father, but was disappointed by Tony's weak character and lack of ambition: "He did everything he could to make Tony enjoy nature, be a good fisherman, man the hounds, be an Irish gentleman. Of course, when he turned out to be like an Irish gentleman, John was disgusted"— because Tony didn't want to be anything more than that.

Huston treated Anjelica—a pretty girl, and younger, named for her late grandmother—more gently than Tony, though she too felt ignored and neglected. "I was so sorry," she said, "that he was too busy caring for a whole lot of things that he couldn't get to us except for one week in a year." When he left home to return to work, she and Tony would hold on to his legs as he walked out the front door. She missed her father so much that she'd walk into his vast closets to touch and smell his smoke-filled clothes. She showed precocious talent as an actress and at nine years old gave a perfect imitation of a gypsy woman who came begging at the back door. Anjelica went to a convent school, and when she dramatically found her vocation and said she wanted to be a nun, John knew she wasn't serious and cavalierly said, "That's great. . . . When are you going to start?" There were so many mysteries in their household—parents in separate houses, mistresses both visiting and in residence—that Anjelica, to avoid confusion and pain, thought silence was safest. "I never asked my father anything," she said, "because I was so afraid he'd tell me the answer." She later confessed that she still had emotional scars: "My father was extremely loving to me and funny and wise and understanding, and at other times extremely demanding, calculating, exacting. When you're a young woman, I think you want to please a lot, so maybe you accept more criticism than you would as an older person. But criticism can be very wounding. It certainly was to me."[12]

Despite well-intentioned but sporadic efforts, Huston was an emotionally detached, distant and disappointing father. Eloise said that Ricki raised Tony and Anjelica, and Huston never looked after them: that wouldn't have left "enough time [for others] to worship him." Celeste Shane believed (with some exaggeration) that "Tony and Anjelica were terrified of him. Anjelica was full of hatred because of [the way he treated] her mother. And Tony was full of lots of hatred." Thom Steinbeck agreed: "The children felt he treated Ricki badly. They loved him, but it was not easy to be around him. Everyone was afraid of Huston." When he was in a bad mood, he could be the terror of his family and of anyone else who crossed him.[13]

· VI ·

Though Huston—like most famous artists—neglected his children, he assiduously courted the women in his life. He had a beautiful, devoted and sequestered young wife to display, run his household and care for the children, and was free to sleep in the Big House with as many women as he wanted. He directed his life as well as his films; he loved the confusion created when his women, past and present, came together at St. Clerans; and he sometimes had a wife, long-term mistress and current lover in his private zenana at the same time. The sexual sultan encouraged them to compete for his favor and circulate through his bedroom, and he made (as John Dryden wrote of the biblical patriarchs) "promiscuous use of concubine and bride."

John Steinbeck enviously noted how Huston fulfilled a male fantasy and got away with it. While married to Ricki, he'd also sleep with Gladys Hill, Betty O'Kelly, Zoe Sallis, Valeria Alberti and many other women who responded to his urgent pleas and summons. Every woman had their moment on stage before passing out of the spotlight. "The more intriguing and involved and black Irish it got," Eloise remarked, "the better he liked it." Unlike the furtive, squalid and guilt-ridden adulteries of contemporary religiose politicians, Huston carried on his affairs with grace and panache. He knew how to please women, most of them accepted a time-share rather than exclusive rights and almost all of them continued to love him after the liaison had ended. Sometimes, however, passions ran high and the competition became rather fierce. Marietta Tree, always very healthy and physically tough, had a strong stomach. But after her first meal at St. Clerans, she vomited for the next twenty-four hours. She was "absolutely sure" that Betty O'Kelly or Gladys Hill, jealous of Huston's adoration, had given her a powerful emetic.

One woman, Afdera Franchetti, claimed to be immune to the erotic ambience. The daughter of a Venetian baron and African explorer, and named after an Ethiopian volcano, she was a close friend of Adriana Ivancich, who inspired the heroine of Hemingway's *Across the River and into the Trees*. Afdera had been married to Henry Fonda, who described her as blond, glamorous and sensuous, effervescent, unpredictable and volatile. Mistaking the Japanese bath for a swimming pool, Afdera somewhat unconvincingly wrote:

The setting was ideal: a fairy castle in the middle of rolling green hills and woodlands, the clean rain and, below ground in the cellars, the most amazing Japanese garden, big plants, a sauna, a swimming-pool where everyone swam naked. It was all very erotic. John had decided that, finally, this was the time but, when it came to it, I couldn't. It was impossible. I felt a mental chemistry, but not a physical one. Everything about John was too long: his arms, his legs, his prehistoric monkey face—everything! [as she could see when he was naked]. It was most embarrassing—in fact, I had to tell him a little lie—that I had a strange illness. He didn't believe me, but he had to pretend to

—though he could have believed she had the clap.

At St. Clerans, Huston lived like a lord and well beyond his means, graciously commanding his family and friends, servants and lovers. John Milton's lines about God apply to Huston's worldwide entourage as well as to his devoted wife:

> His State
> Is Kingly. Thousands at his bidding speed
> And post o'er Land and Ocean without rest:
> They also serve who only stand and waite.[14]

THIRTEEN

HEART OF DARKNESS,

1951–1952

· I ·

Huston's *The Red Badge of Courage* (1951), based on Stephen Crane's classic 1895 novella about a young man's cowardice and bravery in the American Civil War, had no stars, no women, no love scenes and not much dialogue. It came out while America was fighting the Communists in the Korean War and starred Audie Murphy, a real-life hero of World War II. Louis B. Mayer, the head of MGM, had not liked *The Asphalt Jungle* (a financial success) and did not want the studio to make *Red Badge*. Mayer favored warm-hearted, homespun fare and protested, "It has got no laughs, no songs, no entertainment value" and predicted, "It will be ugly and not make money." It was such a bad idea, he insisted, that he wouldn't even make the picture "with Sam Goldwyn's money." The movie as commercially released was indeed a failure, but it was not the movie that Huston wrote, narrated and directed.

Dore Schary, the new head of production, wanted to make the film and, backed by Nicholas Schenck, the president of MGM's parent company in New York, won out over Mayer. On June 9, 1950, Huston thanked Schary for his support and, referring to the producer Gottfried Reinhardt (the son of the theatrical director Max Reinhardt, who'd discovered Olivia de Havilland), wrote:

> L.B. had Gottfried and me in to see him today and as a result of your letter, which he allowed me to read, he has withdrawn all pressures against the making of the film.

More, if I am any judge, he is really rooting for us now. The honesty and courage of your letter hit him right where it should, and I feel that he is with us even if it doesn't turn out all that we hope it will be. I told L.B. that I was going to do everything in my power to prove him wrong, and he told me that he hoped I would succeed, and I tell you again, honey, I'm going to break my ass.[1]

The screenplay of *Red Badge* was an extreme example of Huston's fidelity to the book. The plot of the picture, following the novella, is simple—too simple for a movie, which demands drama and conflict. A new conscript, Henry Fleming, is a thoughtful, sensitive, brooding youth who's afraid that he might run under fire. His Union regiment is ordered up river to cut behind Confederate lines. Most of the soldiers accept their situation; he has doubts about it. He runs away from the first battle, but his side wins. He envies the wounded who've won their "red badge." He's comforted by the Cheery Soldier (played by the lovable Andy Devine). During a fight he's hit on the head by a rifle, but claims he was grazed by a bullet. Now hardened and unafraid, he does well in the second battle. In the third battle he leads troops, rescues their flag and captures the Confederate banner. He confesses that he was scared in the first battle, but still hides the extent of his fear and shameful flight.

Huston echoes the tedious rural accents and euphemisms of the original novella (and the dialect in *Frankie and Johnny*) with expressions like "By Jiminy, I'll be durned." One of the better lines, spoken by a survivor of the battle—"Ain't no holes in me 'cept the ones that were intended"—is rather corny. Some of the actors had to bite their cheeks to keep from laughing when they spoke the absurd dialogue: "Th' boys ain't had no fair chancet up t' now, but this time they showed what they was. I knowed it'd turn out this way. Yeh can't lick them boys. No, sir! They're fighters, they be. Where yeh hit, ol' boy?" The hillbilly speech seems left over from the script Huston wrote in 1941 about Sergeant York, the backwoods hero who won the Medal of Honor in World War I. Disappointed with the result, the studio added an obtrusive voice-over narration, which Huston based directly on Crane's text. The words sound rhetorical, stagey, even hollow.

Whenever Huston took up the challenge of transforming a literary work into film, he imagined its visual appeal. He composed every scene—the frame of the shot, the focus, lighting and atmosphere—with the scrupulous care of a painter. He said, "I've always felt I learned a lot about film by studying art. It's very important, for example, to use your lighting to capture the mood of the scene.... Paintings have a frame the same as those shadows you see on the screen." He researched the artistic record of the Civil War era and, taking his cue from Mathew Brady's photography, decided to intensify the emotional effect by shooting *Red Badge* in black and white. A historian noted that Brady composed his scenes to create a morbid theatrical effect: "Civil War photographers frequently resorted to stagecraft, arranging scenes of daily life in camp to convey a *look* of informality, posing groups of soldiers on picket duty—perhaps moving corpses into more advantageous positions for dramatic close-ups of littered battlefields." He added that in his novel Crane, who'd never seen actual battles, "made use of [Brady's] reproduced photographs.... He studied [them] as the equivalent of first-hand accounts." Like Crane, Huston borrowed images from Brady.

With his cumbersome equipment, Brady couldn't film the actual battles, but recorded in horrifying images the blighted landscapes and rows of neatly arranged dead bodies. There was a striking, ironic contrast between the heroically posed commanders before the battles and the carnage of war that followed. A contemporary report in the *New York Times* said that Brady's shocking photographs had "done something to bring home to us the terrible reality and earnestness of war. If he has not brought bodies and laid them in our door-yards and along the streets, he has done something very like it."[2] Huston's battle scenes achieved the same verismo effect. Like Brady's photographs and Crane's story, Huston's film was not a clear celebration of courage in battle.

Huston wanted to reveal the emotions of men in war, the thin line between bravery and cowardice, and "the pointlessness of [Henry's] courage in helping to capture, near the end of the picture, a fragment of wall." The dominant themes of the picture are the initiation to blood and war, the soldier's desire for redemption after running away and the need for strength to confront the possibility of death. As the Union soldiers lined up in a shallow trench and the Confederates charged into their lines, Huston shot the scene from above, through clouds of gun smoke, with sharp cuts to show the close-up faces of wounded soldiers. Yet the battle scenes in *Red Badge* are surprisingly static and unexciting.

James Agee—who'd been exalting Huston's films in *Time* magazine and was about to publish an enthusiastic essay about him in *Life* on September 18, 1950—was keen to observe his hero at work. On July 6 he wrote to Huston from his farm in New York, "I'd give anything if I could come down for a while and watch some of the shooting. Is that possible from your end? Or am I doing wrong in asking? Regardless of that I repeat, I hope to God you can do it in the East." But the picture was shot on Huston's ranch in the San Fernando Valley, on a $2 million budget, between August 25 and mid-October 1950. Agee could not escape from his blocked novel, or his emotional entanglements with his wife and mistress, till early October.

Huston had met the popular war cartoonist Bill Mauldin while filming *The Battle of San Pietro*. Always keen to use nonprofessional actors and employ old comrades, he hired Mauldin to play one of the Union soldiers and paid him a handsome $2,000 a week salary during the forty-nine-day schedule. Mauldin called Audie Murphy, the hero of the movie, "a scrappy little sonofabitch, a wary little bobcat, lonely and angry."[3] The short, twenty-six-year-old Murphy, the son of a poor Texas sharecropper who'd abandoned his twelve children when Audie was ten, had a boyish freckled face, reddish-brown hair and gray eyes. The most decorated soldier in American history, he'd destroyed six tanks and killed 240 German soldiers, and won every combat medal in the army, including the Medal of Honor. He'd never played a major role in a movie, but his autobiography *To Hell and Back* had been a great success in 1949. Having seen both combat and casualties, Huston fully understood Murphy's violent character and heroic achievement.

It was ironic to cast Murphy as the fearful Henry Fleming. Despite his heroic deeds, the hair-trigger Murphy, emotionally burnt out by all the slaughter and unable to slake his taste for killing, resembled one of the traumatized patients in *Let There Be Light*. In Huston's 1946 documentary a hospitalized soldier, lamenting his current apathy, had said, "I used to always have fun. . . . I used to be going places . . . don't go no more." In a postwar interview Murphy had confessed, "Seems as if nothing can get me excited any more—you know, enthused? Before the war, I'd get excited and enthused about a lot of things, but not any more." For Murphy, nothing could ever be as exciting as the perils and carnage of war. The stress of battle had left him feeling empty and unable to engage with other people.

The English novelist and screenwriter Christopher Isherwood, a gentle pacifist, was watching the shoot. He noted that Murphy was still surprisingly volatile and dangerous, with a constant need to rev up the action: "He was still amazingly aggressive. Whenever he wasn't actually in front of the camera, he kept playing practical jokes on his fellow actors. These jokes weren't fun, they were full of hostility and the object of them, clearly, was to provoke their victims to fight. Since Murphy was The Star, and also smaller, the other actors were unwilling to tangle with him; but he usually managed to annoy them into doing so. When they did, Murphy fought back in deadly earnest. His face was grim, and he looked capable of pulling a knife. Most people seemed afraid of him." This was exactly the way Huston wanted him to be—the way he could get the best performance out of him. Isherwood also saw the dark side of Huston's personality and gave a good example of how he "broke his ass" to make the picture: "Huston was Murphy's opposite—large, charming, popular, relaxed. (He was also a far greater and deadlier monster than Murphy could ever be.) On this picture, Huston was so relaxed that he actually sat chatting with [me] under a tree while his assistant director shot one of the battle scenes."[4]

The movie was savaged at the previews and the studio lost faith. They demanded changes, but Huston had left immediately to shoot his next film in Africa and Gottfried Reinhardt was left to defend the crumbling fort. MGM cut more than an hour of Huston's version, eliminated every hint of ambiguity and irony, and made it an artistic as well as a commercial failure. They deleted a scene in which Huston appeared as a campaign-hardened veteran who jeered at Henry Fleming and the new recruits and offered some cynical advice, "Hang your clothes on a hickory limb and don't go near the battle!" They also eliminated the death of the Tattered Soldier, which Huston thought was the most powerful moment in the movie. Bitterly disappointed, he complained, "*The Red Badge of Courage* was edited so barbarously by the studio, reducing the 135 minutes to barely sixty-nine, that the picture was deprived of the force it had possessed initially." In a telegram to Reinhardt, responding to the news of the mutilations, he said, "Know you fought the good fight. Hope you're not too bloody on my account."[5]

Lillian Ross had been on the set to observe the work on the film. Just before shooting began, she had published a destructively satirical piece on Hemingway in the *New Yorker* of May 13, 1950. In their interview Hemingway had deliberately played the fool and presented himself as a boring braggart, and Ross accepted his behavior at face value. She repaid his generosity with meanness, portrayed him as an arrogant, anti-intellectual and free-spending celebrity, and established her reputation at his expense. When he read the essay Hemingway was shocked and horrified. True to form, Ross' article on the making and breaking of *Red Badge* consistently assumed a superior, even mocking attitude, and made most of the people involved look foolish, even absurd. Ross, however, was charmed and infatuated by Huston, who did not create a public façade or fake persona for her *New Yorker* profile in May–June 1952. Confident of his talent and indifferent to what other people thought of him, Huston was not as vulnerable as Hemingway. He didn't give a damn how Ross portrayed him or criticized him for abandoning the picture, as long as he appeared as a lively, dramatic and colorful character.

· II ·

In December 1949, before starting *The Red Badge of Courage*, Huston and James Agee wrote the screenplay of *The African Queen* (1951)—based on the 1935 novel by C. S. Forester—so it would be ready to shoot as soon as he finished the Civil War picture. The Tennessee-born,

Harvard-educated Agee, three years younger than Huston, had published a famous social history of Alabama sharecroppers during the Depression, *Let Us Now Praise Famous Men* (1941). Huston described him as "about six-two and heavy but neither muscular nor fat—a mountaineer's body. His hair was dark brown, his eyes blue and his skin pale. His hands were big and slab-like in their thickness. He was very strong, and . . . gentle towards his fellow humans." In contrast to Huston's sublimely relaxed manner, Agee, a novice at screenwriting, was contorted and tense. "I can see him sitting on the edge of a chair," Huston continued, "bunched forward, elbows on knees, arms upraised, the fingers of one of the slab-like hands pointing at those of the other and working as if they were trying to untie a knot. His forehead is furrowed and his mouth is twisted in concentration. His head is nodding in sympathy and understanding." Agee's friend Christopher Isherwood recorded his worshipful attitude to the Master. "Jim Agee [was] big, handsome, sentimentally alcoholic, terribly anxious to be liked. . . . He made a hero of Huston and eagerly, indeed desperately, tried to keep up with Huston in any activity or amusement he proposed."[6]

In a variant of Huston's procedure with Richard Brooks, he and Agee would discuss a sequence, plan it and compose alternate scenes. They'd then exchange scenes and rewrite each other's work. Agee found their collaboration both exhilarating and instructive and told his friends, Father James Flye and James Stern: "The work is a great deal of fun: treating it fundamentally as high comedy with deeply ribald overtones, and trying to blend extraordinary things—poetry, mysticism, realism, romance, tragedy, with the comedy. . . . Working double is exciting and fascinating, and so is watching that particular intelligence and instinct work. And so is learning from him—any number of basic things a day, which had only vaguely occurred to me before, about good craftsmanship and taste and imagination."

When Agee was slow to pick up the new technique, Huston became exasperated at his pretensions and gave him a brief lesson on the essentials of the art: "Oh, Christ, Jim. Tell me something I can understand. This isn't like a novel. This is a screenplay. You've got to demonstrate everything, Jim. People on the screen are gods and goddesses. We know all about them. Their habits. Their caprices. But we can't touch them. They're not real. They stand for something, rather than being something. They're symbols. You can't have symbolism within symbolism." On January 15, 1950, while Huston was in San Francisco looking at Billy Pearson's priceless new finds, Agee—overweight, smoking, drinking heavily and trying to keep up with Huston's strenuous activities—had a heart attack.

Since they had not yet found an effective ending, Huston took his old companion Peter Viertel to work on the script in Africa. Viertel, describing Huston's method, told the film historian Rudy Behlmer: "Huston's imprint and view of and on the story were decisive. As with most of his movies, he was the biggest creative force involved. I worked with him previously on WE WERE STRANGERS and the script of Frank Harris' REMINISCENCES OF A COWBOY. His method on all three of these projects was the same. He used the writer or writers as creative mules which were guided by him; checked and reversed, and occasionally led by hand on foot through the bad passages."[7]

In 1950, following a new trend that moved away from the soul-destroying domination of the studios, Huston and the producer Sam Spiegel formed an independent production company, Horizon Pictures, to make *The African Queen*. They were an odd couple, physical and temperamental opposites. Spiegel, born in Austria in 1904, a graduate of the University of Vienna, seemed like a caricature of the typical Hollywood producer: a Middle European émigré with a strong accent; short, pot-bellied and physically unattractive; fond of Rolls-Royces, yachts and ostentatious luxury; surrounded by beautiful young women he'd bought to amuse and satisfy himself; financially unscrupulous, always operating on the verge of bankruptcy and sometimes even jailed for bouncing checks. Billy Wilder, always on target, called Spiegel "a modern day Robin Hood . . . he steals from the rich and he steals from the poor." Justifying his own lack of scruple with typical panache, Spiegel exclaimed, "If I hadn't lied during all these years, I would now be a cake of soap."

Spiegel was flamboyant, cultured and sharp-witted, with a charming manner, continental polish and inherent melancholy, but Huston hated his high-handed manner, luxurious habits and shady activities.

Huston would interrupt his long pronouncements with a practical joke or a cutting jest. Commenting on Spiegel's gluttony and obesity, he remarked during dinner, "I'll wait until my partner has finished going down on the asparagus and then proceed." Spiegel's biographer wrote that the ebullient producer "sensed a certain coldness in [Huston]. 'He seems to hate me for some unknown reason,' Spiegel admitted to Viertel. Was it the lack of payment for several weeks?"[8] He also cut an absurd figure when he turned up in Africa and tried to interfere with the shooting. But most of all, as Richard Brooks observed, Huston disliked any excessive displays of emotion: "He knew Sam was very bright, erudite, spoke four languages, knew about painting. But even though he had old-world mannerisms, Sam was half an inch away from hysteria most of the time and hysteria bothered John. He didn't like to handle it and he didn't want to be around it." Though he found Sam intensely irritating, Huston was amused by his endless financial catastrophes and concluded, "I really can't help liking [him]. He's such a desperate man." Viertel recognized Spiegel's faults but also liked and valued him: "He had the ability to appear as a father figure, was a good listener, and, like everyone else in the world, loved to give advice. He was shrewd, not only in business, but in his dealings with his friends as well. His greatest weakness was obvious: he was attracted to women chiefly for their looks."

The director Joseph Losey described Spiegel as "a highly educated man and a very bright and not insensitive man. He is a megalomaniac and I think impossible for most directors to work with because he wants his films to be 'Spiegel' pictures."[9] A well-known survivor in a cutthroat world, he wanted to make great movies and took bold risks to do so. Adventurous and ambitious, able to tolerate extreme financial pressure, he recognized Huston's genius, and was willing to give in to his quixotic and expensive decision to make the film in a remote and dangerous place. Spiegel used the names of Huston, Bogart and Hepburn to secure the funding with John and James Woolf, who owned Romulus Films in England. The original budget was about £400,000; Huston was supposed to get $87,000 and half the profits. A brilliant innovator, Spiegel went on to produce *On the Waterfront*, *The Bridge on the River Kwai* and *Lawrence of Arabia*.

· III ·

In 1890 Joseph Conrad had traveled a thousand miles inland from Léopoldville to Stanley Falls in the Congo, the heart of darkness, to take command of a "battered, twisted, ruined tin-pot steamboat," the *Roi des Belges*. In his "Congo Diary" Conrad recorded some of the hardships that Huston would experience sixty years later: the hot gloomy days and cold sleepless nights; long steep climbs up hilly ravines; stabbing mosquitoes, foul drinking water and menacing drums beating in the dark. Conrad had mentioned the close proximity to the Arab slave traders and the bloodthirsty history of the jungle, and recalled, "The subdued thundering mutter of Stanley Falls hung in the heavy night air of the last navigable reach of the Upper Congo, while no more than ten miles away, in Reshid's camp just above the Falls, the yet unbroken powers of the Congo Arabs slumbered uneasily." Huston and his film company, traveling from the asphalt to the African jungle, went beyond Conrad's perilous journey.

Huston had traveled 25,000 miles by plane to scout sites in Kenya, Tanganyika and Northern Rhodesia and rejected Lake Victoria, which "looked like suburban Maidenhead" and was too pretty for a jungle setting. He finally chose Uganda and the Belgian Congo, where banking, communications and logistics were infinitely more difficult to arrange than in British territory. But he liked the challenge of a primitive setting and wanted to be as far as possible from Spiegel's control. He believed (as he did in Mexico) that the film would have more character and the actors would give better performances if they actually suffered on location. Huston, Hepburn, Bogart and Bacall (who accompanied her husband), with a production staff of thirty-four British technicians, spent ten weeks (early April to mid-June) in the middle of Africa.

. Before he met Huston, Bogart rarely went beyond the 120 miles from Beverly Hills to Palm Springs. Once again under the monster's spell, he agreed to travel 12,000 miles into the Belgian Congo. The actors flew from Europe to Léopoldville (now Kinshasa), the capital of the colony, about 200 miles upriver from the Atlantic coast, and on to Stanleyville in the center of the continent. Viertel met them at Stanleyville airport and broke the news that Huston was not there to welcome them. He'd left an hour before to hunt elephants near the makeshift village that had been constructed for the cast and crew. Hepburn—extremely anxious about the unfinished script, the lack of funds and the slapdash preparations—thought "it was an utterly piggish thing to do and it makes me mad to think of it even now—goddamn—goddamn." A few days later they crossed the Congo River and took an eight-hour, hundred-mile ride on a wood-burning train, past the still unnavigable Stanley Falls. They reached Ponthierville, a cluster of huts and warehouses at the end of the railway line, and traveled the final stretch by car to Biondo, a village on the Ruiki River.

Huston wanted a close jungle and narrow river for filming. The Ruiki, a thin winding tributary of the Congo with trees and thick vines forming a canopy between stream and sky, was perfect. Admitting the difficulties on location, he wrote Ricki, about to give birth to their daughter in California: "We're about thirty miles from Ponthierville and the Lualaba [River]. But what a long thirty miles it is. Once a week provisions are brought in and the exposed film is taken out. There hasn't been very much rain (for the Congo) and the river has fallen several feet so that now it's just barely navigable."[10] In an article and in *Open Book,* however, he tended to idealize the setting. "Biondo was a romantic-looking place," he wrote, "huts all thatched with palms, little paths lined with bamboo and a dining room big enough to hold seventy-five people. We even had shower baths. . . . Most of the shooting was done on a raft made of planks laid across pirogues. . . . All in all, for a film where everything we needed had to be flown in or shipped in laboriously overland, things went quite smoothly. We lacked luxuries, but we had basic comforts." Huston could not see the rushes in Africa. He sent the film to Nairobi and had it flown to London, and the Woolfs cabled back their favorable reaction.

After shooting the jungle scenes in Biondo, they traveled by Jeep, truck and rail back to Stanleyville. They then flew to Masindi and drove thirty miles by car to their second location, Butiaba, a railroad terminal on the shore of Lake Albert in western Uganda. Their third location was the Niagara-like Murchison Falls, about fifty miles from Butiaba.

The filming was tough and the moves from one place to another just as strenuous. The cinematographer Jack Cardiff rather grimly wrote that the evenings in the rough villages were "desperately festive . . . like being in a prisoner-of-war camp without guards."

Peter Viertel's fine Hemingwayesque novel *White Hunter, Black Heart* (made into a 1990 film with Clint Eastwood), describes the making of *The African Queen* and portrays the main characters in the Africa expedition. It focuses on John Wilson (Huston), famous for his skill at directing but notorious for his renegade overspending. When Wilson, a great womanizer, fails to show up as expected, Philip Duncan (Bogart) tries to explain his absence: "Where's the ogre? Why wasn't he there to meet us? I bet he's shacked up with one of these black ladies and has forgotten all about us." Mrs. Duncan (Bacall), who'd come to Paris with a mountain of luggage, is also sceptical about his motives and worried about his fondness for practical jokes: "I'm sure that bastard John is thinking up some horrible gag for us. He wants to get us off in some horrible hole, and then just stay and stay and watch us all suffer." This is the key to Wilson's character, and in the novel Verrill (Viertel) tells him: "You know what your success is based on? . . . Your deep-seated sadism. You love to torture people, the audience included. You love to put them through hell and reward them with futility and disappointment. Your cruelty is your biggest box-office quality."[11]

Excited by reading John Taylor's *Big Game and Big Game Rifles* (1948) and more interested in hunting elephants than in finishing the picture, Huston was willing to stay in Africa indefinitely. Bogart's boat race to Honolulu had not been important to Huston during the filming of *Sierra Madre*, but his own obsession with elephant hunting had top priority during the making of *The African Queen*. Bacall noted that Huston was a serious hunter but a terrible shot, which made his quest more hopeless and more endearing. In his second letter to Ricki from the Congo, he described his search for a trophy and admitted his failure:

Last year there were some man-eating lions about and they seized the natives out of their huts and dined on them. Every morning and evening we go out after elephant. I'd like to get one with really big tusks. In fact, we've got him all picked out. But so far something has always happened so that I couldn't get a shot. Stalking elephant is most exciting. They don't see at all well and if one stays down wind of them one can get very close. Yesterday morning we were after them in some forest and we weren't more than six or eight yards away from them finally. Just a little wall of vines between us and them. I tell you it gave me a very funny feeling. . . . [But] I didn't get my elephant. Never saw the big tusker again.

After two frustrating months in the Congo jungle, where he never even got a shot at an elephant, Huston was surrounded by elephants in Uganda. But hunting in the game preserve was strictly prohibited. As in Huston's films, the quest was more important than the prize.

The company soon discovered that it was as difficult to film in Africa as to live there. Every morning five cars and trucks drove the actors three miles from Biondo to the banks of the river. Then the thirty-foot *African Queen*—which they had found in derelict condition on Lake Albert, repaired and transported 600 miles from Uganda to the Congo—pulled four rafts up the river. The first, Huston wrote, was "a replica of the *Queen*. That raft itself became our stage. We could put cameras and equipment on it and move around, photographing Katie and Bogie in the mock-up with as much facility as we'd have had on a studio floor. The second raft carried all of the equipment, lights and props. The third was for the generator. The fourth was Katie's, equipped with a privy, a full-length mirror and a private dressing room."

Huston posted an African night watchman next to the boat, telling him to observe it closely and make sure nothing was stolen. One night, as he looked at it very carefully, it slowly sank to the bottom of the river. It took two hundred Congolese workers three days to haul it to the surface. In the midst of these disasters Sam Spiegel turned up, looking ludicrously out of place with his white shorts, knee socks, protruding belly and huge cigar. Though desperately worried, he managed to survive all the chaos and hold the project together by wheedling more and more cash out of the backers.

The unusual color photography of scenery and animals was spectacular. Huston, making excellent use of the river, showed monkeys, crocodiles, hippos, elephants and, most improbably in the jungle, lions and giraffes. Though the setting enhances the story, the film is not about Africa but about two people in Africa. Charlie Allnut (Bogart), the dissolute skipper of a decrepit river boat, and Rose Sayer (Hepburn), the straitlaced sister of an English missionary, are thrown together at the outbreak of World War I after her brother (Robert Morley) dies of a heart attack following the German raid on his compound. Allnut, concerned about her welfare, stops by and rescues her from the now-deserted mission house. Though Rose knows nothing about handling boats or navigating the river, she takes the upper hand. To avenge her brother's death, she persuades Allnut to run a series of dangerous rapids. She intends to blow up the German gunboat that dominates the lake and blocks the invasion route of the British forces. Allnut's boat, in alternating scenes of crisis and calm, navigates the swirling river, slips past the German fort and sails into the lake to carry out its mission. (In fact, rivers don't run into lakes—they flow away from lakes and into the sea.)

The essence of the wonderfully comic film is the contrast between the two irritable, middle-aged characters. Isolated and forced to be intimate on the boat, they find it difficult to maintain the proprieties. They clash bitterly as she condemns his character and spurs him into action, while he mocks her affected speech and resists her orders. During a particularly fierce dispute, he calls her a "crazy, psalm-singin', skinny old maid." But when they survive the cataracts and gorges, she reveals her sexual awakening by confessing that she loved the excitement: "I'd never dreamed that any—any mere—er—*physical* experience could be so—so *stimulating* . . . so *exhilarating*."[12] After overcoming a series of increasingly perilous obstacles, each one bringing them closer together, they transcend their differences of class and character. As her brittle crust melts and reveals an emotional core, they fall in love.

Bogart's personal relations with Hepburn in real life were strikingly similar to the relations of the characters in the movie. He was the hard-drinking cynic, she the preachy spinster. He was annoyed when Hepburn, a strict teetotaler who'd struggled for years to control Spencer

Tracy's heavy drinking, ranted for hours about the evils of alcohol and the need for temperance. They suffered the same illnesses and dangers in the compound as in the film. They began with prejudice and suspicion, and endured many hardships. Confined in a narrow space and an isolated setting, they overcame mutual hostility and eventually became very fond of each other.

Both stars agreed that Huston was a brilliant director. After he showed Bogart by gesture and expression what Allnut should be like, Bogart became enthusiastic and said, "John, don't let me lose it. Watch me. Don't let me lose it." Hepburn wrote, "He has a kind of lanky charm and he inherited enough of Walter's showmanship so that he's fun." She played her part with dour seriousness until Huston suggested how to make her character more comical and congenial. He reminded her that Eleanor Roosevelt always smiled serenely when she visited soldiers in hospitals and told her, when condescending to Bogart's character, to imitate that ladylike "society smile." Hepburn effectively used the familiar gesture in an exotic context and felt his "awfully clever piece of direction" improved her performance. Huston—who didn't use a daily plan or a list of shots—was "the most laid-back director" Jack Cardiff had ever worked with. Nothing bothered him and he was always perfectly calm. He even fished while shooting a scene and when Hepburn complained, he said, "Honey, I don't have to watch. I'm listening, and you sound just great!"[13] In the film Hepburn *is* the African Queen: at tea with Morley and Bogart, alone on the boat with Bogart, with the German captain who is about to execute her, and triumphantly with Bogart when they're finally married.

· IV ·

Huston, Agee and Viertel had a great deal of trouble with the ending, and the contrived conclusion is the weakest part of the picture. They'd rejected the ending of Forester's novel when, after Charlie and Rose are captured, the chivalrous German captain cannot bring himself to hang her and cannot legally hang Charlie without her. An English gunboat suddenly appears and sinks the *Königen Luise,* and Charlie and

Rose survive to marry. Viertel noted that this conclusion did not satisfy either the writers or the censors:

> I worked with Huston on several endings, which were supposed to please the Breen Office, as well as ourselves. As the characters had slept together without being married, the code required they end badly, if not unhappily. But as the material was essentially comic and romantic, neither Huston nor I felt a tragic ending was in keeping with the rest of the piece. Therefore the bogus wedding ceremony was devised on board the German ship. Prior to that we had various other endings: one that I recall was to have the film end with the couple arguing in the water, once they had lost *The African Queen.*

The restrictions of the censors forced Charlie and Rose to marry *in order to* survive. As John Woolf explained, "It seemed to us all that for a film it was preferable for the two main characters to be rescued after their trials and tribulations, and to sink the German ship, rather than that their mission should fail and they should be executed." In the movie Charlie loads his boat with explosives and intends to ram the Germans. But before he can do so, the boat is swamped and overturned during a storm on the lake. They manage to swim away from their capsized craft, but are captured and taken aboard the enemy ship. They are sentenced to death for spying, but the captain agrees to Charlie's sentimental request to marry them before they are hanged. After a brief ceremony he proclaims: "I now pronounce you man and wife. Proceed with the execution." As the film suddenly shifts from realism to fantasy, the *Luise* rams the abandoned *African Queen* and is fatally damaged. Charlie and Rose jump ship, swim toward the shore and glide out of the last frame to a blissful future.

Bogart said Huston was "murder to work with during the last three weeks of shooting. Always restless, wanting to quit for some new idea." Huston's script girl, noting his characteristic restlessness and unwillingness to perfect his work, observed that he was "bent on self-destruction.

So frequently in his pictures he made a wonderful film, but when it came to the end he did something that kind of blew it. And he knew that he was doing it. . . . He got too bored to think up a good end. It wasn't on a par with the rest of the film. It's a wonderful picture, but the end is a bore."[14] Agee also disapproved of the hasty and jarring conclusion, which violated the carefully planned mood and structure of the movie. Audiences, however, liked the upbeat conclusion, and Bogart won an Oscar for best actor. The picture cost $4 million to make and earned more than $40 million.

Huston never collected his share of the millions of dollars that made Spiegel a very rich man. In February 1952 he warned his business manager, Morgan Maree, about one of Spiegel's characteristic swindles. He was delaying Huston's payment and using Huston's money to repay his ravenous creditors: "Spiegel's offer is a transparent piece of phony manipulation whereby he would be using my money to meet his obligations and repaying me from my own profits. This sort of thing has stopped being funny and I again ask you to bear down with all your weight." But Maree's weight was not sufficient to extract the money from the cunningly evasive Spiegel. Huston received only $25,000 of his director's fee and never got his percentage. Finally, to cancel his contract with Horizon and escape from his repulsive partner, he surrendered all financial claims.

Viertel, puzzled by Huston's gullibility, tolerance and indifference to money, asked why he'd become Spiegel's partner when he had had so many other attractive offers. Huston replied, "Because it was the wrong thing to do, kid." When the money disappeared like the gold dust in *Sierra Madre*, Huston philosophically accepted his fate and moved on to the next project. Strangely enough, he continued to admire (as well as to hate) the paternal Spiegel, who "needed to steal in order to live," and refused to sue him. In 1961, when Huston was trying to lure the talented art director Stephen Grimes away from *Lawrence of Arabia* in order to make his own film about Sigmund Freud, he wryly remarked, "I'd love to steal something from old Sambo Spiegel for a change."[15]

FOURTEEN

Paris and Italy,

1953–1954

· I ·

When Huston planned to make a movie about the nineteenth-century French painter Henri Toulouse-Lautrec, he was told "nobody wants to finance a picture about a dwarf." But José Ferrer, who'd recently won an Oscar for best actor in *Cyrano de Bergerac* (1950), used his new box-office power to attract funding for *Moulin Rouge* (1952). He owned the rights to a fictionalized biography of the artist and wanted to play Lautrec in the film (he also played Lautrec's father). He became a dwarf star with the aid of an orthopedic brace and walked on his knees, reducing his height by more than a foot, from five feet ten inches to four feet eight inches.

Huston was delighted to make the movie in Paris. The home of the Impressionist painters, the Fauves and the Cubists, it had a thriving art scene. It was also a romantic city, recovering from the war years, but full of pent-up creative energy. Americans had a special feeling for Paris, and films with European locations were popular at a time when few people could afford to travel. Huston was amused that the maid Ricki had brought from Los Angeles to take care of the children was under the impression that France "was Mexico because they speak another language. She kept saying, 'I just gotta learn Spanish.' " Wherever Huston was, horses were not far away. He rented a villa in Chantilly, forty miles north of the city, which (he told Katharine Hepburn) was "the Kentucky of France. All the big training stables are here. They work their horses in the forest, where they have straightaways that go as far as five miles." At Huston's urging, his jockey friend Billy Pearson came to Chantilly and entered several races. Huston even managed, at the beginning of the film, to work in a foxhunting scene on Lautrec's ancestral estate. Though Huston was still active in racing, his health was beginning to break down. Pearson, next door to him in the Lancaster Hotel in Paris, was alarmed to see him cough up blood, but Huston reassured him by asking "doesn't everyone?"[1]

Huston wrote the script with Tony Veiller, whom he called his favorite American screenwriter. Like Huston, Tony came from a show business family. His father, Bayard Veiller, wrote three superior thrillers that were big hits on the stage and are still performed today. His mother, Margaret Wycherly, played Gary Cooper's devoted mom in *Sergeant York* and James Cagney's malevolent ma in *White Heat* (1949). Three years older than Huston, Tony attended Union College for a year and, more briefly, Antioch College, but when his father failed to pay the overdue bills, he had to leave. He was a short, heavyset man with silvery hair, olive skin and piercing black eyes. Also like Huston, he'd worked as a newspaper reporter and theater manager before becoming a writer, and was an amusing raconteur who used humor to connect with people. But Tony had a completely different personality. Like Bogart and Jules Buck, he envied Huston's way of life and always wanted to be like him: a buccaneer, wildly magnetic and with a great theatrical style. Huston defied convention and seemed to stride through life doing exactly as he pleased, indifferent to contracts and money, unencumbered by wives and children.

Huston first met Tony in the 1930s when they were both writing for different studios. They became good friends during the war in the Signal Corps, where they worked for the director Frank Capra on the series of propaganda films called *Why We Fight*. Their light duties at the end of the war allowed them to collaborate on *The Killers* (1946), based on Hemingway's story, and on *The Stranger* (1946), directed by and starring Orson Welles. Tony, demobbed first, made those two movie deals; Huston, still in the army, could not accept a screen credit. During their collaboration on *Moulin Rouge* they'd discuss the story and agree on the content and structure; then Tony would write the first draft, and they'd go over it together. The censorship board's strictures showed how puritanical and insular American life was at the time. Joe Breen tested their ingenuity by insisting that solicitation and prostitution— are these not the same thing?—the very core of Lautrec's emotional and sexual life—were "a problem and would have to be omitted."

"One of the things I look for in a colored film is the palette," Huston remarked, "just as a painter, when he approaches a subject, decides what colors and tonalities" to use. The visual impact of *Moulin Rouge* is overwhelming—a total contrast to the black-and-white thrillers that had made Huston famous. The film opens with gorgeous titles in art nouveau lettering and a stunning display of the vivid cabaret posters that made Lautrec instantly famous. Huston shows Lautrec working in his studio and portrays the rather decadent ambience that inspired him. In the musical cabaret scenes he re-created the flat planes of discrete colors and subtle chromatic palette of the artist's posters, and contrasted it to his personal deformity and squalid surroundings.

Technicolor is a three-color process in which three different negatives—individually sensitive to red, green and blue—are run through the camera and printed together. Huston's cinematographer, Oswald Morris, removed one color negative and replaced it with a black and white one to get the special texture Huston wanted. Huston explained that Technicolor wished "to make everything equally bright and sharp and clear," but he wanted to create more subtle effects. His color "was hazy in some places, was light or dark according to one's mood, sometimes showed the central figures clear and then let the background go into vagueness." After the picture was released, Morris wrote a furious letter to the photographer Eliot Elisofon, condemning him for repeatedly telling journalists that *he* had invented the color and *he* had been the cameraman on *Moulin Rouge:* "I really do not think you are serious when you expect any of us back here to believe any of your excuses . . . for taking the credit for other people's honest efforts to create something a little different in the world of Cinema."[2]

But Huston and Veiller ran into the problem that afflicts many biographical films about creative artists. To write or paint you need to sit down or stand still, and this does not make for dramatic action.

Lautrec's repetitive sketching and the frilly underwear of the can-can dancers were not enough to sustain the picture, which had to offer considerably more than a lavish display of art. In the clichéd plot, familiar from the nineteenth-century fiction of Balzac and Zola, an ugly crippled man falls in love with a whore (played by Colette Marchand) and with an elegant woman (Suzanne Flon), both of whom abandon him as a hopeless case. There's no explanation of why he loves the whore, except that she's the first woman who pays any attention to him. Zsa Zsa Gabor is decorative but plastic as the dancer Jane Avril.

Though most of the actors speak with a French accent, Ferrer, who carries the film, does not. He exclaims, "I know I drink too much, but I cannot stop myself. . . . I use cognac to escape my loneliness, my ugliness and the agonizing pain in my legs." Recognizing his self-destructive way of life but unable to do anything about it, he quotes Oscar Wilde's aphorism, "Each man kills the thing he loves." In the end, drinking himself to death while mourning for his lost loves, he goes home to die. He starts to gas himself, but begins to paint and regains the will to live. The dominant themes of the movie are unrequited love, pain as a stimulus to creation and art as a substitute for life.

As usual, Huston had trouble with the ending, and later told a journalist that he'd rejected a ludicrous finale: "I thought, my God, how could I let Toulouse-Lautrec commit suicide because he was turned down by a whore." The actors did not get the last page of the screenplay until the final day of shooting. In a dream sequence at the end, Lautrec has a vision of all his friends from the Moulin Rouge coming into his room and dancing up to his bed. The script girl protested that the conclusion did not make any sense, but that was the best Huston could come up with—and that was it.

The movie critic of the Paris edition of the *Herald Tribune* wrote, with gentle restraint, that "such a beautiful film deserved a stronger story." Nunnally Johnson loyally told Bogart that the innovative color and portrayal of art in the film compensated for its defects: "Please tell John that I saw *Moulin Rouge* the other night and thought it wonderful. The truth is, I hated every actor in it, but the accumulation of story and beauty made up for this personal prejudice. But perhaps I should except Zsa Zsa. I simply cannot hate any woman that pretty." After being swindled by Spiegel, Huston was grateful to the Mirisch brothers at Allied Artists: "The producers were scrupulously honest: instead of trying to conceal profits, they took pleasure in giving me my dues."[3]

· II ·

While in France, Huston bought several Lautrec posters and Monet's painting of *Red Water Lilies,* but his greatest acquisition was the French actress Suzanne Flon. Born in a working-class district near Paris in 1918, the daughter of a railway laborer, she'd been employed as an English translator in the Printemps department store and as secretary to the popular cabaret singer Edith Piaf before becoming a stage actress. *Moulin Rouge* was her first film. There's an astonishing resemblance between the graceful Latin looks of Ricki Soma at age eighteen and the young-looking Suzanne at age thirty-five. Both women have dark hair parted in the middle, an oval face, broad forehead, widely spaced dark eyes, long straight nose and thin lips. Bayard Veiller said everyone thought Colette Marchand would become Huston's lover, but he chose Suzanne (who could speak English). She was delicate, lovely and sweet; they got on wonderfully well together and seemed like an old married couple.

That was not the way Suzanne's jealous lover saw it. When the drunken Huston took her back one night to her flat in the rue Vaneau in Saint-Germain, a man suddenly jumped into their taxi and beat him up rather badly. Huston finally managed to knee him in the groin; Suzanne (realizing the danger) screamed for Huston to go; the man left and then reappeared in the dimly lit courtyard with a pistol in his hand. Standing only a few feet away, he aimed at Huston's heart and pulled the trigger—but the gun misfired. The next day Huston turned up, sober this time and with a bodyguard, found his rival and started to beat *him* up. After taking a few hard blows, the man stopped trying to defend himself, began to weep and had to be taken to a hospital. Huston's assistant on the movie (Kirk Douglas' future wife), exasperated by the emotional turmoil, recalled, "I got my fill on *Moulin Rouge,* having to deal with John Huston's affair with the leading lady, and her jealous husband [i.e., lover] and everybody getting black eyes and chasing around and shooting guns."

After the movie was completed, Suzanne appeared on the French stage as Joan of Arc in Jean Anouilh's *The Lark* (1953). Huston hoped to direct her both on the New York stage and in the Hollywood adaptation of the play, but these projects were never realized. Suzanne rarely reappeared in his life after his passion had subsided (though on one occasion she barely missed coinciding with Marietta Tree at St. Clerans), but Huston continued to correspond with her and remained deeply in love. He idealized her from a distance and spoke of her even more rapturously than he did about Marietta, whom he still actively courted. When asked if there was any woman he wished he'd married, he named Suzanne. But Ricki would not give him a divorce, so he could never marry his French saint and Suzanne remained on a pedestal. Praising her with uncharacteristic emotion, he exclaimed, "I have enormous respect and regard for her intelligence and humanity. . . . She was the most extraordinary woman I have ever known. . . . Her affection over the years has been my blessing on earth. . . . It's better that no official ties have bound us. Suzanne is like my wife and our relations like the best of my marriages. The most precious qualities that a woman can possess are found deep in her character. She has tenderness, fidelity, gaiety, depth of emotion and that rare form of simplicity that is truth incarnate."[4]

Huston's love for Suzanne did not preclude other distractions and adventures while he was in Paris. Pauline Potter Rothschild or even Suzanne herself may have introduced him to Marie-Louise Bousquet, who ran the Paris office of *Harper's Bazaar,* maintained a fashionable literary salon, and was a friend of Gertrude Stein, the photographer Cecil Beaton and the Duchess of Windsor. In a suggestive passage, Helena Rubinstein's biographer wrote that during a boisterous party at Marie-Louise's house, "wedged in a succession of tiny, smoke-filled rooms was a wild human scrimmage," which incongruously included Audrey Hepburn and the criminal-turned-writer Jean Genet. Guests at the orgy then observed "Madame Bousquet emerging from beneath a pair of legs belonging to John Huston." His pleasure must have been limited, however, by the fact that Marie-Louise was more than thirty years his senior.

While hanging around with the American crowd in Paris, Huston became friends with John Steinbeck, who would win the Nobel Prize for Literature in 1962. His son Thom recalled that they'd first met in Hollywood in the 1930s when Huston began as a screenwriter. Both were tall, tough men and had a lot of interests in common: literature, theater, Spain, Mexico and bullfights. Steinbeck was not a keen hunter or fisherman and didn't care about these pursuits, but he found Huston terribly entertaining and thought he had a first-rate mind. They got along well and discussed many film projects, including an adaptation of Steinbeck's *Cannery Row*. Thom said that "both men had the worst taste in women (including my mother)" but Steinbeck, who tended to be gallant, disapproved of the way Huston criticized and mistreated women. Steinbeck, who wrote to friends with the language he thought would appeal to them, felt obliged to adopt a macho swagger when corresponding with Huston. Three years before his death, he sounded like a parody of a punch-drunk Hemingway: "I can still lift a fairly accurate left and counter with a neat, tucked-close right hook. And if worse came to worst, I guess I could rumble somebody who would find me tolerable. . . . I'm a guy with lots of friends, good friends."[5]

· III ·

In September 1951 Huston suggested that Bogart's Santana film company pay $10,000 for the rights to *Beat the Devil*, a novel written by Claud Cockburn under the pseudonym of James Helvick. It was not an especially promising property. But Cockburn, who had been a London *Times* correspondent in the 1930s and had belonged to the Communist Party for a time, was now impoverished and living with his family near Huston in Ireland. Bogart replied by telegram with his own proposal and a Swahili flourish that recalled their journey to Africa: "Have advised [business manager] Morgan Maree purchase *Beat the*

Devil at terms stated in your cable. Would you be interested in directing same for Santana partnership? Deal object to make a buck for both of us. *Habari. Mzuri* too. ["How are you? I'm fine"] Bogart." In October Huston urged him to pay Cockburn promptly, as he desperately needed the cash, and accepted the offer to make the film. He got $175,000 to write, direct and (with Bogart) co-produce it. Bogart would pay almost anything in order to work with his talented friend. "The monster is stimulating," he said in 1950. "Offbeat kind of mind. Off center. He's brilliant and unpredictable. Never dull. When I work with John, I think about acting. I don't worry about business." But after putting half a million dollars of his own money into *Beat the Devil,* he had plenty to worry about.

Postwar Italy offered filmmakers warm weather, a six-day work week and cheap labor. Huston made *Beat the Devil* (1954) from February to April 1953 in Ravello, a town of curving streets and terraced vineyards, high above the Amalfi coast, south of Naples and not far from the battlefield of San Pietro. Though Huston and Bogart amused themselves by having both prostitutes and aspiring actresses sent down from Rome, the work began inauspiciously. On February 6, while they were driving down the Appian Way from Rome to Naples, Bogart's Italian chauffeur got into an accident that foreshadowed the car crash in the film. Though the picture was delayed while Bogart had his mouth repaired, Huston found the whole incident quite hilarious: "The driver couldn't make up his mind which road to take, so he went straight ahead, right over an island, through a heavy stone wall and into a ditch. I was up front, so I had a chance to brace myself, but Bogie was asleep on the back seat. . . . 'Chrith, no! Somethin'th happen t' my tongue!' He stuck out his tongue out. A piece of it was split over into a flap like a little trapdoor. Moreover, all his front teeth—actually a full bridge— had been knocked out. When I realized he wasn't seriously hurt, I couldn't help laughing. Bogie glared at me. 'John, you thun-of-a-bith! You dirty, no-good thun-of-a-bith!' " Bogart needed several stitches, and a German doctor in Naples sewed up his "little trapdoor" without an anesthetic. "Bogie had guts," Huston said. "Not bravura. Real courage." After the accident Peter Sellers, not yet in the movies, dubbed

John Huston's birthplace,
402 S. Adams Street,
Nevada, Missouri

Walter (left) and John Huston,
early 1930s

Dorothy Harvey,
c. 1943

John's house
in Tarzana

Eloise Hardt,
late 1930s

Marietta Tree,
mid-1940s

Above:
Peter Viertel,
John and
Ernest Hemingway,
1954

Ricki Huston,
1960s

Above:
St. Clerans

John with
Marilyn
Monroe and
Arthur Miller
on the set of
The Misfits,
1961

Anna
van der Heide,
early 1960s

Zoe Sallis,
early 1960s

John as Noah in *The Bible*, 1966

John directing George Sanders in *The Kremlin Letter*, 1970

John and
Celeste Huston,
1972

John and
Marciela Hernandez,
1973

John with
Anjelica,
Tony, Danny
and Allegra at
Tony's wedding,
1978

John and Danny Huston,
early 1980s

some of Bogart's speech as well as the dialogue of the Italian actors who couldn't speak English.[6]

Huston had a more urgent problem—the intractable script. He'd quickly discarded the first version of the screenplay, written by Claud Cockburn; the second draft had been done by Peter Viertel and Tony Veiller. Viertel did not get on with Veiller, described him as "a high-strung man in his early fifties, plagued by high blood pressure, a self-confessed Anglophile whose presence even in his beloved London did little to calm his growing irritability." He added that Huston, disenchanted with their effort and rapidly losing patience, "was thinking of abandoning the project and was concerned only with the damage this might do to his friendship with Bogey."

A week before shooting was to start David Selznick, whose wife Jennifer Jones was the costar, suggested that Huston collaborate with the twenty-nine-year-old Truman Capote: "He is, in my opinion, one of the freshest and *most original* and most exciting writing talents of our time. . . . He is easy to work with, needing only to be stepped on good-naturedly, like the wonderful but bad little boy he is, when he starts to whine." Capote, then living in Rome, agreed to work on the script for $1,500 a week. The weird-looking writer startled Huston by turning up in a velvet suit, reminding him of "Little T.C." in Andrew Marvell's poem. Huston exclaimed, "I immediately fell for him—it didn't take me five minutes to be won over completely, as he [won over] everyone I ever saw him encounter. He had a charm that was ineffable. . . . His effeminacy didn't in any way affect his strength or his courage."[7] Capote, a flamboyant homosexual, shared a hotel room with Huston, which prompted Bogart to invent a number of scurrilous stories about them. Much tougher than he looked, Capote beat Bogart in several arm-wrestling contests at $50 a throw. "At first you can't believe him, he's so odd," Bogart wrote Bacall (in California with their young children), "and then you want to carry him around with you always."

Portraying himself as an innocent among debauchees, Capote claimed that Huston and Bogart had "nearly killed me with their dissipations . . . half-drunk all day and dead drunk all night." He called Huston "a cowboy as imagined by Aubrey Beardsley" and—in a series of clashing characteristics—created a brilliant portrait of the director. He captured Huston's lethal mix of warmth and callousness, and said he had a "riverboat gambler's suavity overlaid with roughneck buffooning, the hearty mirthless laughter that rises toward but never reaches his warmly crinkled and ungentle eyes, eyes bored as sunbathing lizards."[8]

Like Huston, Capote disliked the Viertel-Veiller script and called it a "stinker." He recalled: "I found the story impossible as it stood, a straight and rather incredible melodrama. Both John and I felt that the best thing to do was to kid the story as we went along. The only trouble was that shooting had to begin the following week. . . . When I started, only John and I knew what the story was, and I have a suspicion that John wasn't too clear about it." The story concerns a quartet of inept crooks in search of uranium deposits in British East Africa. To get there they must "beat the devil" and surmount a series of diabolical obstacles that prevent them from reaching their goal: their ship breaks down and they are stranded in an obscure Italian port; they have a car accident; the ship they sail on explodes (an allusion to *The African Queen*); they are shipwrecked and captured by Arabs—an exotic episode that goes all the way back to Samuel Johnson's *Rasselas* (1759) and to Mozart's *Abduction from the Seraglio* (1782). There is also plenty of lies, deception, treachery, betrayal and murder. In *The Asphalt Jungle* the criminals are caught at the end of the film; in *Beat the Devil* they are caught at the beginning. Contrary to Huston's usual practice of telling a linear story, most of *Beat the Devil* is a flashback that explains why the gang of four has been arrested. Like Faust and Don Juan, the characters finally learn that you *cannot* beat the devil. The movie, like many of Huston's works, portrays a grandiose quest that ends in tragicomic failure.

The script was a continuous work in progress, and Capote and Huston were rarely more than two or three days ahead of the shooting. They tried to establish the tone and mood of the picture by telling the actors what they *planned* to do. Then, writing frantically to keep up with the schedule, they wrestled with the complications of characters and plot. But it was difficult to know if the constantly evolving movie was a melodrama, satire, comedy or farce. Despite the intense pressure and considerable confusion, Capote and Huston had a good time together. "At least one picture I wrote, *Beat the Devil*, was tremendous fun," said Capote. "Sometimes scenes that were just about to be shot were written right on the set. The cast was completely bewildered—sometimes even Huston didn't seem to know what was going on. Naturally the scenes had to be written out of sequence, and there were peculiar moments when I was carrying around in my head the only real outline of the so-called plot. . . . It's a marvelous joke. Though I'm afraid the producer didn't laugh."[9] The situation did not improve when Capote interrupted work and returned to Rome to visit his pet raven, which (he said) refused to talk to him on the telephone and seemed to be quite ill. (The excuse was absurd—there must have been more pressing business. In his essay on his pet raven, "Lola," Capote revealed that the bird—like all of its kind—did not have the power of speech.)

Beat the Devil, in which all the characters are absurd, is a parody of Huston's *The Maltese Falcon*. A beautiful woman lies to everyone, a group of rogues pursue unobtainable riches and the quest for uranium reprises the search for the falcon. Though the picturesque setting could have been shot in color, Huston used black and white to allude to the earlier film. The lying Jennifer Jones parallels the deceitful Mary Astor. Robert Morley, an equally rotund but more genial villain, replaces the ailing Sydney Greenstreet. Ivor Barnard, the irrational and violent Major Ross, has the same function as the gunsel Elisha Cook, Jr. In *The Maltese Falcon*, Lorre has British, French and Greek passports; in *Beat the Devil*, he's a cosmopolitan German-Irish Chilean. In Cockburn's novel, O'Hara (played by Lorre) says, like Greenstreet continuing his pursuit of the black falcon, "Although our present venture is wrecked, one can always, as it were, pop up again." Captivated by Capote's blond hair and bangs, Huston had Lorre's hair bleached and cut to make him look like a grotesque version of the writer. The wild card in this eccentric enterprise, as W. R. Burnett had pointed out, was the temperamental director: "If Huston really likes a property, there's no person who can put it on the screen better. But if he is not entirely sold on the thing he is doing, he can make a bomb."

When the picture was finished in May 1953, Huston realized that he might be in trouble. Whistling in the dark to keep up his spirits, he wrote Morgan Maree, "It is now an out-and-out comedy. . . . Anyway, it has a good smell to it, and everybody connected with the picture seems to feel that we have something." But no one, unfortunately, knew what they actually had. A month later, when he began to hear the negative reactions, he tried to explain what went wrong and even sought divine intervention: "So much of the writing was done the night before, and there was so much invented on the set. Its complexion actually underwent a change, and it wasn't at all the kind of picture it started out to be. . . . If the joke should fall flat—well, God help us." David Selznick, worried as always about the impact on his wife's career, was apoplectic: "I can't tell what is going to happen with this mad picture. . . . It is so utterly insane, it is such a complete defiance of all the rules."[10] But the absolute absurdity was precisely the point of the satire.

Huston showed the film to his old friend William Wyler, who regretfully said, "Well, John, that's the kind of movie that, when you've finished making it, you should make another one as quickly as possible." Peter Viertel "was amazed at how philosophically Huston had accepted Wyler's words. He had in all probability realized that *Beat the Devil* was doomed early on to be a failure." Peter Lorre attributed the failure not only to its confusing tone and structure, but also to its flat-footed marketing campaign: "It was a flop in New York. Why shouldn't it be? It was a deliciously sardonic comedy, meant for art houses, and they opened it with a blood-and-thunder campaign. People just didn't get it."[11] Huston agreed that "its off-the-wall humor left viewers bewildered and confused. . . . It was generally conceded to be a minor disaster, frivolous, self-indulgent, and all the rest of it." A theater owner in Michigan placed an ad in the local newspaper apologizing to his patrons for showing the baffling movie and offering to refund the price of admission. Annoyed that he had spent a lot of money for what turned out to be a gigantic private joke, Bogart bitterly complained that "only phonies think it's funny."[12]

Moulin Rouge had been a great success, partly because the marketing campaign was so effective. *Beat the Devil* was a flop, chiefly because the publicity was completely wrong. Sixty years on, *Moulin Rouge* is a maudlin bore, while *Beat the Devil* is still witty and entertaining, with excellent character roles and vivid, sun-bleached crime scenes. The film is much more amusing the second and third time around when the viewer has a clearer idea of its satiric comedy.

· IV ·

Huston had made six pictures with Bogart (three of them superb), and *Beat the Devil* was their finale. In February 1956, aged fifty-seven and a heavy smoker, Bogart learned he had cancer of the esophagus—a particularly painful disease with a high fatality rate. An operation to remove the tumor revealed (though he was never told the truth) that the cancer had spread to the nearby lymph nodes and that he would die within a year.

Remembering Bogart, Huston emphasized his urge to survive and willingness to endure the ghastly chemotherapy: "We all knew he wasn't going to live, but he was still having those goddamn treatments. He wouldn't give up the ghost. We had a drink and Bogie said, 'Look, fellas, come clean. Am I gonna make it or not? Tell me the truth.' And Morgan Maree said, 'Of course you are, Bogie. We're not kidding you.' Lying through his teeth. Which was all right. Bogie looked relieved and prepared to go on with it. . . . He didn't want to know. And Betty didn't want him to read in the paper that he was going to die, so everyone who knew him put the best face on they could." Bogart met death with bravado and panache. During his last months he would stay in bed for most of the day, and at the cocktail hour he would slowly make his way downstairs to greet his daily guests. When he could no longer walk, the butler would lift him into a wheelchair. He died, as the doctors had predicted, in January 1957.

Huston's eulogy of his closest friend, the most moving and memorable part of the funeral service, was spoken with a honeyed voice and made many people weep for the extraordinary man they had lost. He emphasized, with a striking analogy, Bogart's lively attacks on complacency, his generosity of spirit and his bravery when faced with death:

In each of the fountains at Versailles there is a pike which keeps all the carp active, otherwise they would grow over-fat and die. Bogie took rare delight in performing a similar duty in the fountains of Hollywood. . . . His shafts were fashioned only to prick the outer layer of complacency, and not to penetrate through to the regions of the spirit where real injuries are done. . . . Bogart's hospitality went far beyond food and drink. He fed a guest's spirit as well as his body, plied him with good will until he became drunk in the heart as well as in the legs. . . .

No one who sat in his presence during the final weeks would ever forget. It was a unique display of sheer animal courage. After the first visit—it took that to get over the initial shock of wasted appearance—one quickened to the grandeur of it, felt strangely elated, proud to be there, proud to be his friend, a friend of such a brave man. . . . He got all that he asked for out of life and more. We have no reason to feel any sorrow for him—only for ourselves for having lost him. He is quite irreplaceable. There will never be another like him.[13]

FIFTEEN

White Whale,

1955–1956

· I ·

Warners had made two earlier versions of *Moby Dick* with John Barrymore: *The Sea Beast* (1926), a silent film, and *Moby Dick* (1930), an early talkie. A critic found the whale in the talkie "a particularly lifeless example of poor studio machinery, as ferocious and menacing as a ferry boat." Though techniques in the 1950s were far more sophisticated, Huston also had to use a chartered whaling vessel and rubber whales, and to shoot the exteriors on the ocean. But filming in the Irish Sea was very different than off the coast of Catalina.

An epic novel about an obsessive hunt, with no love scenes, hard to condense into a screenplay, difficult and dangerous to make—all these ingredients strongly appealed to Huston. Peter Viertel saw the similarities between Captain Ahab and Director Huston, who was also a kind of maniac, pursuing the completion of the movie as Ahab had pursued the white whale: "*Moby Dick* was an account of a man's obsession, a character trait that fascinated Huston because he recognized a similar strain in himself. His wanting to kill an African elephant was in a small way similar to Ahab's insane desire to kill the white whale that had bitten off his leg." His collaborator Ray Bradbury put it more crudely when he created a fictional character based on Huston: "You ever figure, kid, how much the Beast is like me? The hero plowing the seas, plowing women left and right, off round the world with no stops."[1] To Huston, making a film was an exciting journey on which he could lead a caravan of assorted writers, actors and crew. As soon as he passed his electrocardiogram test—needed to obtain medical insurance and work under arduous conditions—he began the mad pursuit of his goal.

Most writers were eager to work with Huston, an amusing companion and master of both filmscripts and directing. He always expected people to answer his call when summoned and was extremely annoyed when they failed to respond. The British-born Roald Dahl, author of aviator stories and not yet famous, did not accept. The worshipful James Agee, torn by a prior agreement, offended Huston by his refusal to commit to *Moby Dick,* changed his mind when it was too late and then apologized for his disloyalty: "I knew it was the job of a lifetime. . . . I sweated around trying to be 'honorable' just too damned long; and within literally hours after I made myself sufficiently 'dishonorable,' I learned the *Moby Dick* job was lost."

In January 1953 Ray Bradbury, a leading science fiction writer and author of *Fahrenheit 451,* sent Huston an ingratiating letter that extolled *Moulin Rouge* and offered himself as a collaborator: "I have the very certain feeling that some day, some how, in some way, I want to work with you. I *must* work with you on a picture. I have never been more sincere and I have never spoken more urgently in my life." Responsive, like most people, to flattery, Huston read and liked Bradbury's recent story "Fog Horn" (1951), in which the resonant warnings of a lighthouse attract a sea monster that destroys it. Bradbury hyperbolically claimed, "The reason John Huston selected me to write the screenplay of *Moby Dick* is that he saw in my own books a kinship with Melville. Melville is a poet and a Shakespearean, and I've been influenced by poetry and Shakespeare all my life"—an absurd claim followed by an even more absurd non sequitur.[2] As preposterous as Bradbury's boast may seem, Celeste Huston thought that John would have said anything, even compared him to Shakespeare and Melville, to get Bradbury (who didn't need much encouragement) when he wanted him. Bradbury would earn a lucrative $12,500 plus $3,400 for living expenses for seventeen weeks, and $750 a week if they went beyond that time.

Both men had used excessive flattery during their distant courtship and were bound to be disappointed when they actually met. Huston was certainly disillusioned when Bradbury finally turned up in Ireland. It was hard to imagine anyone more different from the rough, sea-seasoned Melville—or from the seigneurial Huston himself—than the short, unappealing, timid and obsequious Bradbury. He sent adventurers to Mars in his stories, but was afraid to fly in an airplane. Huston was bored by Bradbury, who spoke entirely in clichés and platitudes, and told Celeste, "You'd never think he could write anything." Bradbury's satiric description of Huston, whom he first worshipped and then came to dislike, made the director seem grotesque: "He stood there in boots and riding pants and a silk shirt open at the neck to reveal an ascot. His eyes bulged like eggs to see me here. His chimpanzee mouth fell down a few inches, and the air came out of his lungs in an alcohol-tinged rush." Bradbury got right down to business by suggesting that they throw Fedallah, the Parsee harpooner, overboard and give all the good lines to Ahab. Huston agreed by lifting his wine glass and saying, "He's *thrown!*"

Huston was then living in Courtown, Bradbury in a Dublin hotel. Every day, alone in his room, Bradbury would hammer away at the major scenes: "the sailor falling from the mast, the sea becalmed, the arrival of the Whale, the almost-deaths of Queequeg and Ishmael, the lowering, the pursuit, the harpooning, the roping of Ahab to the Beast, the plunge, the death, and Ahab arisen, dead, beckoning from the side of the Whale for his men to follow, follow . . . into the deep." Every night Bradbury would take a twenty-five-mile taxi ride to discuss the eight pages he'd written that day. Though not clubable, Bradbury was hard-working and cranked out more than a thousand pages before paring down the script to a filmable 150.

Huston loved to cut pretentious people down to size. He constantly teased and mocked the rather naïve Bradbury, who never quite knew where he stood. To liven things up, Huston offered fulsome praise, telling his collaborator, "You have just written the finest scenes you ever wrote in your life for your truly great screenplay," then instantly deflated him by adding, "Let's spend an hour cutting this brilliant, superb scene of yours." When Bradbury was stymied by a scene, Huston pretended that Jack Warner (who was releasing the picture) wanted him to sex up the script and add a sultry love interest for the lonely Captain Ahab. After yet another provocative remark that pushed him over the edge, Bradbury finally exploded and punched him. Huston was quite pleased by this unexpected assault and proud of Bradbury for lashing out. He may even have felt that he deserved it.

After months of toiling together, Bradbury was furious, refused to recognize Huston's contribution and claimed sole screen credit. Angry at the injustice, Huston wrote Paul Kohner that he'd spent months "working on the screenplay step by step with Ray and spending every day with him discussing and writing the scenes with him."[3] The Screen Writers Guild at first gave sole credit to Bradbury; then, swayed by Huston's argument, it awarded co-credit to both writers. When Bradbury lost the arbitration, he suddenly reversed himself, said he loved their film and claimed he was pleased that Huston got the credit he deserved. An authentic touch was added to the script when Burl Ives, known as a heavyweight folksinger before playing Big Daddy in *Cat on a Hot Tin Roof* in 1958, supplied the sea chanteys that are sung at the New Bedford inn and as the *Pequod* gets under way.

After Bradbury left Ireland, some problems remained with the script, so Huston drafted one of his cronies, Baron John Kilbracken— an eccentric and impoverished Irish aristocrat—as his next collaborator. Kilbracken, with no experience as an actor, began by trying out for the part of Ishmael, the sole survivor and narrator of the story (eventually played by Richard Basehart). While they were writing together in April 1954, Huston's attempt to improve Kilbracken's appearance provoked an amusing letter to Huston's secretary and revealed the type of oddball character Huston loved: "I've received the enclosed bill for the *teeth* you told me to buy.—I think that John ought to pay me for them as I never wear the damn things and anyway I haven't got twenty-five guineas."

Kilbracken gave a lively account of how Huston took over the actual writing and tried out his ideas on his new collaborator: "He would write a phrase, then delete part of it, then add to it, then delete the whole phrase and try a different one, and so on, smoking rapidly, continuously sipping Scotch, gazing for inspiration at the ceiling, pacing about the room, muttering to himself, then writing again." He also gave a perceptive analysis of the contradictions in Huston's character: "Huston, to work with, is the final epitome of quixotry, unpredictability, inconsistency, and volatility. He is one of these men of fantastic personal magnetism and charm, who can behave completely outrageously, and then, with a smile and a gesture, make one again instantly devoted to him. . . . In his moments of inspiration, one stands aghast at his virtuosity. Yet, at times, he makes errors of judgement, of taste, of understanding, so gross that one feels it cannot be the same man."[4]

· II ·

Huston had first worked with Orson Welles, who directed *The Stranger,* in 1946. The self-styled genius of Hollywood, Welles conceived a number of brilliant projects, but failed to complete most of them. He was famous for collaborating with Howard Koch on the frighteningly realistic broadcast, *The War of the Worlds,* in 1938; for starring in and directing *Citizen Kane* in 1941, a satire on the press tycoon William Randolph Hearst; and for his striking appearance as Harry Lime in Carol Reed's *The Third Man* in 1949. In his autobiography Huston, thinking of himself as well as of his talented friend, observed that Welles' genius was intimidating: "People are afraid of Orson. People who haven't his stamina, his force or his talent. Standing close to him, their own inadequacies show up all too clearly. They're afraid of being overwhelmed by him." In May 1954 the producer Harold Mirisch warned Huston that Warners was certainly worried about using Welles: "None of the Hearst papers throughout the country will give the picture any break whatsoever if Welles is in it."

But Huston wanted Welles to play Father Mapple, and he was paid £6,000 for two days' work. The hardest part of the role seemed to be heaving his vast, 350-pound bulk up the wiggling rope ladder and into the New Bedford pulpit. He then pulled the hanging ladder up after him, grasped the edge of the lectern with his thick fingers and—with stiff, jutting beard and underslung jaw—orated in a deep, resonant, Huston-like voice. His fiery, menacing sermon from Jonah 1:17, "Now the Lord had prepared a great fish to swallow up Jonah," warned of the power of the whale, and foreshadowed the doom of the *Pequod* and its crew. In a passage that may have given Welles more credit than he wished him to have and that was omitted from *An Open Book,* Huston wrote that before shooting his big scene, Welles pretended to be nervous and asked for brandy. He then "went through those five pages without one single error. He was letter perfect. . . . We had the whole thing in the first shot. . . . We were scheduled to be in the church for three days. We finished with Orson that same morning." In a letter to a potential biographer of Welles, Huston said that the actor not only spoke the words but also wrote them: "Orson had accomplished in a few hours what Bradbury and I had failed to do over a period of months. Word for word what he wrote is now in the picture."[5]

The big-bellied Robert Morley thought Huston might ask him to play the whale in *Moby Dick,* but the real search was for Captain Ahab, the supreme lord and dictator of the ship. John had originally wanted Walter, who'd died in the planning stage. He also wanted Welles, who was considered too unreliable. Montgomery Clift refused to play either Ishmael or Ahab. Huston also offered the part to Laurence Olivier, who had other commitments. James Mason, who'd played Captain Nemo in *20,000 Leagues Under the Sea* (1954), did not want to appear in a remake and did not change his mind after reading the script. Kirk Douglas' name came up, but Huston didn't think he was right for the part.

Finally, Huston compromised with Gregory Peck, who'd played Captain Horatio Hornblower in 1951. Peck was a bankable name that got the picture started, but he looked like a seafaring Lincoln, with stovepipe hat and facial scar. He was as wooden as his peg leg, and in the finale the supposedly tyrannical oppressor seemed bound to the whale like a slave. The handsome actor was hardly the type to strike down the sun "if it insulted him." After the movie was made, Bradbury thought of a different approach to Ahab's character, which might have been more suited to Peck. He thought the actor could have more effectively portrayed "a quiet madness that's very inner, very intense, so that you don't have to try for the big thing. I think Peck could have carried that off and you'd have had a different kind of Ahab." Peck had a respectable and honorable aura, but lacked the demonic fire of a Richard Burton or Jack Nicholson, even of a Lee Marvin or Jack Palance. In our time, Ahab could be well played by Daniel Day-Lewis or by Russell Crowe, a convincing captain in *Master and Commander*. Huston himself could have portrayed Ahab as well as any of these actors, but it was impossible both to direct and play the leading role in this demanding picture.

As if to compensate for the safe choice of Peck for Ahab, Huston boldly hired his friend Friedrich von Ledebur to play the harpooner Queequeg, the tattooed South Seas cannibal. A handsome, adventurous aristocrat, born in 1900 and standing over six feet seven inches tall, Ledebur, after graduating from the University of Vienna as an agricultural engineer, had been a mounted lancer in the Austrian army in World War I, a big game hunter in Africa and a whaling harpooner in the Marquesas Islands. Huston called his companion "one of the finest horsemen in the world. His knowledge of riding ranges from the Austrian Haute École to bronco busting."

Ledebur was married to the poet, actress and adventuress Iris Tree, the mother of the screenwriter Ivan Moffat, who gave a vivid account of his impressive stepfather: "Count Friedrich, considered by many to be the handsomest man in Europe, had dark wavy hair, skin that years in the South Seas had turned the color of mahogany, and eyes blue as the turquoise on his rings and silver belt. He had a deep, resonant, almost echoing voice. He sang . . . American cowboy songs that he learned when he worked as a horse trainer on ranches in the Far West." He also described the impoverished and frustrating life of the young Ledebur, when he was living with Iris before their marriage: "They subsisted on the dwindling remains of her trust fund, the occasional money he earned as a horse trainer, and the hospitality of friends. As Friedrich had hopes of becoming a movie actor, they settled in California for a while, living mainly in a trailer, but he had to wait fifteen years before a couple of small parts in Italian movies launched his modest career."[6] Ledebur was exactly the kind of character that Huston admired. He was not only poor and living in Ireland, but also had a colorful background, knew how to handle horses, and was cosmopolitan, masculine and tough.

Huston liked to exercise his power and torment his friends. He had one of his assistants, Jeanie Sims (who'd worked for the Woolf brothers at Romulus Films), inform Ledebur that his dark wavy hair would have to go. "John asked me to break the news to you as gently as possible," she told him. "Queequeg should have his head completely shaved. . . . John has reluctantly agreed that the tattoo marks need not be genuine." Ledebur enjoyed the experience, despite the ordeals, and told the director it was "certainly fascinating to see the wolf [Huston] driving the sheeps along." When *Newsweek* called Ledebur a "playboy," he fiercely disputed the charge. Making *Moby Dick* had been tough, he said, and "to be stripped and shorn on the icy Irish seas, with the undaunted Captain Ahab at the helm and John Huston on deck, is not exactly playboy's stuff."[7]

· III ·

The Mirisch brothers, who'd earned a lot of money on *Moulin Rouge*, also invested in *Moby Dick*. Walter Mirisch found Huston a larger-than-life figure and was impressed by his ambitious plans for the film. Once again Huston used unusual color to get an authentic period look. The color in *Moulin Rouge* had had a soft edge; the color in *Moby Dick* had the hard edge of the nineteenth-century steel engravings of whale hunts that appeared behind the opening titles. These pictures showed the small whaleboats, with harpooners standing in the bow and sailors pulling at the oars, fighting the giant leviathan. Huston and his technicians developed a new silvering process that softened and toned down the Technicolor images, and fortified them with a sharp, clearly defined appearance. He explained, "From the color film we made two sets of negatives—one in color, one in black and white. The two negatives were printed together on the final print, achieving a completely new tonality."

Huston said that *Moby Dick* (1956) was the most difficult picture he ever made. He chose to film off the coast of Ireland during the season of rough seas, but he had not reckoned with the danger and unpredictability of the weather. He refused at first to use ship models for the long shots of the *Pequod* tossing in the storm. In a letter of November 1953 to Harold Mirisch, Huston seemed unaware of the potential problems in what he called a "temperate latitude." To save money on hotels and encourage a comradely spirit, he saw "no reason why we all just couldn't sleep on deck." Intent on creating as much realism as possible, he came up with another (semiserious) idea that unnerved the producers—a shark in whale's clothing. Walter Mirisch wrote that "John made an extraordinary suggestion about avoiding models and having a shark, which would be encased in a whale suit, put into the water, and somehow or other controlled on some kind of wires. In that way we might avoid having a phony-looking whale"—though they would still have a ravenous shark.[8] Writing to Harold, Huston found the perfect candidate for this hazardous task: "We need somebody, God knows who, to cajole man-eating sharks into letting men fit them into rubber union-suits. Come to think of it, Harold, I think you are the very guy for that job."

Shooting began in mid-July 1954 and was scheduled for twenty weeks, but the film was plagued by difficulties and took more than twenty-eight weeks to complete. The New Bedford scenes were shot in Youghal (pronounced "Yawl"), east of Cork, on the Irish Sea. They then moved to Fishguard, on the southwest coast of Wales, for two weeks of maritime scenes, but the heavy seas broke three masts on the *Pequod*. In September Richard Basehart fractured some bones in his foot while jumping from the ship to the whaling boat, and Leo Genn (playing Starbuck) injured his back and had to be sent to a doctor in London. The cameraman Ossie Morris recalled Huston's innovative but demanding and dangerous methods: "John has always guarded most strongly the right and privilege of complete freedom on his part to shoot a sequence as he likes. . . . If he wants a camera on the water, in the water, up the mast or hanging from the bowsprit, then I feel he must be allowed to have it there."

The technicians simulated gale-force winds with the propellers of World War II de Havilland Mosquito airplanes, and created huge waves by filling old gravel-tip trucks with water and sending torrents down the chute. But, Morris wrote, they were constantly cursed by the perversely uncooperative weather: "Every day at sea, wind, sun, and land combined against us: If there was no coastline showing (always desirable) and the sun was where we needed it, invariably the wind was in the wrong quarter and made the ship look becalmed. If the sails were billowing correctly and the sun was right, then we could still see the bloody coastline! If the sails were right and the land was out of sight, the sun would be on the wrong side. It was a total nightmare."[9] Finally, the stormy winter seas on the Welsh coast capsized their boats and proved impossible, and the unit had to spend several more weeks in the Spanish-owned Canary Islands, off the northwest coast of Africa.

Huston's greatest difficulty was the eighty-five-foot, sea-shouldering rubber whale, which had an internal engine that enabled it to spout water, and a mixture of chemicals and dyes under its latex skin that allowed it to bleed when harpooned. The amazing grayish-white whale dived, resurfaced, opened its mouth and showed its ferocious teeth. It was built in several sections so that the most perilous scenes—Ahab riding the leviathan's back or lashed to its side—could be shot with at least some measure of control. Four men were specially trained to manipulate the whale under water. But Gladys Hill told the anxious London producer that it was still very difficult to handle: "They have been scouting like mad for a place to put the whale so that we can go to him rather than have to tow him out every day. John doesn't believe that it would stand a four-hour journey out and back and also a full day's shooting. If the structure is anything like the one at Fishguard, I'm sure he is more than right." Huston never managed to solve that tricky problem. One day a life-size twenty-five-foot section of the whale, carried on a large pontoon and towed by a tug, broke loose in the rough sea and was carried away by the powerful current.

The scene in which Ahab drowns and emerges from the sea in a grotesque resurrection was filmed in a tank in Elstree studios outside London. Peck was actually lashed to the whale, and Huston could well have drowned his star. When asked about this, he responded with joking bravado that it may have been risky, "but it was the last shot of the picture." Peck said, "I could have *really* come up dead, which I think would have secretly pleased John—providing the last touch of realism he was after." Huston later listed all the disasters they'd endured: "It was the worst winter in maritime history. Three of our lifeboats capsized. We just had one storm after another, wretched storms. . . . We had started out with three mechanical whales, and we lost two of them. And I knew that if we lost the third one, we were shit out of luck."[10] To see things for himself—playing Jonah, as he would later play Noah—he went down into its belly, knowing the crew would never let *him* sink.

As they fell six weeks behind schedule, at the expense of £8,000 a day, the total cost of the film ballooned from $3 million to $4.5 million, and all the profits the Mirisch brothers had made on *Moulin Rouge* were consumed by *Moby Dick*. Defending himself, Huston maintained that the producers' attempts to cut costs had caused some of the problems. The generator was put in the wrong place on the ship and interfered with the sound recording; the little harbor at Youghal was not dug deep enough, so he could shoot only at high tide.

Peck, loyal to the end, sent Huston a handwritten note saying, "I will work for nothing, indefinitely, to finish the picture in the way that you want it." Unfortunately, things ended badly between them. When Huston sent flowers to Peck's beautiful young French wife, Véronique, and kissed her on the cheek when they met, Peck was offended by his innocent behavior, turned cool and refused to answer his calls. In a variant passage from *An Open Book,* Huston (who didn't poach on friends' wives) speculated on the cause of the breach: "Very often new wives try to depose their husband's old friends and, in the process, create or magnify situations."[11]

· IV ·

Huston made a serious effort to dramatize the major themes of Melville's complex novel. In the beginning Starbuck, the first mate, represents everything that is sane and lawful. He sees that the ship and crew are not doing what they are supposed to do—capture the whales that furnish oil to light the lamps of the world—but are engaged in a devilish undertaking. He maintains, "I came here to hunt whales, not to satisfy my commander's lust for vengeance," and hints that Ahab is intent on retribution that belongs to God alone (in Romans 12:19, the Lord declares, "Vengeance is mine; I will repay"). Starbuck realizes that the crew, driven by the monomaniacal will of the captain, are headed for destruction. With both admiration and fear, he tells how Ahab "called the typhoon's bluff and stood toe to toe against it. . . . Let Ahab beware Ahab. . . . If Ahab has his way, none of us will ever see home again." But, like a doomed tragic hero, Starbuck cannot bring himself to kill the mad Ahab, take over the *Pequod* and save the ship from its predestined fate.

The whale that bit off Ahab's leg has also marked his mind. In one of his great speeches Ahab cries out that "Moby Dick tore my soul and body until they bled into each other. . . . I'll follow him around the horn and around the Norway maelstrom and around perdition's flames before I give him up." He wants to possess the souls of his men, but his own soul is devoted to the destruction of the whale. Yet even Ahab, in a lucid moment, wonders what drives him on and into hell: "Why this madness of the chase, this boiling blood and smoking brow?"

Huston and Bradbury devised a conclusion that was even more dramatic than Melville's. In the novel, Ahab is caught by a rope and dragged into the depths of the sea. In the film, the dead Ahab emerges from the sea and seems to summon the crew, with a still moving arm, to follow him into watery extinction. As Starbuck observes, "He's dead, but he beckons." Huston and Bradbury thought it was appropriate for Ahab and the white whale to be joined forever through eternity. In the novel, after Ahab's death, Starbuck tries to steer the ship away from the murderous whale. In the film, Starbuck takes over the fanatical fight and tells his crew, "Now I'm captain. Turn the boats around. . . . We're going back for the whale." As in the end of *The Maltese Falcon* and *Beat the Devil*, the men continue their impossible quest.

Huston thought it was also possible to see Ahab's pursuit in a positive light. His search for the pernicious whale is an attempt to extinguish the epitome of evil that God allows to exist in the world. Huston said, "Ahab speaks for Melville, and through him he is raging at the deity. . . . The whale is the mask of a malignant deity who torments mankind. Ahab pits himself against this evil power. . . . There was the general idea that Ahab was a ranting madman, wild and distraught and fanatical, whereas Melville would have him as a kind of Anti-Christ, noble in his blasphemy. It is the story of a blasphemy, of course, it's an assault on God."

Moby Dick, rubber whales and all, has a screenplay that captures the essence of Melville's story and remains one of Huston's most ambitious achievements. It has an austere maritime atmosphere, a magnificent climax and fine performances by the supporting cast. Huston was particularly moved by two appreciative letters from men he respected. The maverick producer Walter Wanger wrote, "Personally, I was overwhelmed by the beauty of the picture, the depth of feeling, the tremendous imagination, and the respect for detail. The authenticity of atmosphere was inspirational." The eighty-three-year-old poet Carl Sandburg, then at the height of his reputation, praised Huston's "intelligence, perception and true courage. In a sense it is better than the book because children, to whom the book would be too heavy, can enjoy the picture. Your father would have had pride about it."[12]

SIXTEEN

Tobago, Japan and Africa,
1957–1958

· I ·

A ttracted to the exotic locales, the adventurous stories and (with one exception) the congenial actors, Huston made three relatively weak movies in the late 1950s. His Irish estate was expensive to maintain, and since he usually spent more than he earned and had almost no savings, he continually needed the money. *Heaven Knows, Mr. Allison* (1957) takes place, like *Across the Pacific,* during the fight against the Japanese in World War II. *The Barbarian and the Geisha* (1958) portrays Japanese hostility to an American diplomatic incursion in the mid-nineteenth century. *The Roots of Heaven* (also 1958), shot in a remote part of Africa, shows a Huston hero on another impossible quest. The mediocre script of *Heaven Knows,* constrained by censorship, failed to realize the emotional potential of the story. Poor casting and changes made by the studio, against Huston's will, wrecked *Barbarian. Roots,* much better than the other two pictures, was hurt by widespread illness in the hostile climate and by emotional conflicts between the producer Darryl Zanuck and his volatile French mistress, Juliette Gréco.

After scouting locations in Tahiti and Samoa, Huston decided to make *Heaven Knows, Mr. Allison* (a soppy title) on Tobago, a Caribbean island off the coast of Venezuela. Most unusually, he brought Ricki and his young children to the island and rented a house for them far from the set. A strange incident occurred at the Blue Haven Hotel when Ricki first arrived. Huston was talking to Robert Mitchum and his wife, and Ricki sat down next to them. "John looked up and smiled," Mitchum said, "and you had the feeling he hadn't a clue as to who she was. When the kids walked in, it all came back to him." Anjelica recalled that they knew their father was making a movie, but rarely saw him.

A newspaper interview revealed that Huston's lungs were in poor condition as early as May 1957 (though he managed to live for another thirty years). The reporter noted how he studiously ignored his illness: "At this point, Huston's vitality was temporarily sapped as he shook his head in a coughing fit. With theatrical instinct, he made capital out of the situation by remarking, 'I got this cough since I stopped smoking. I lost my appetite and can't sleep. I can't wait to get back to smoking just for the sake of my health,' he said as he settled back into his unsettled position."[1]

The movie opens with a distant shot of a life raft in the open sea and (as the camera moves in) with Mitchum floating on it. He plays a Marine who falls in love with a nun (Deborah Kerr) while they're stranded on a South Pacific island. Like Sterling Hayden, whom Huston also liked as a man and admired as an actor, Mitchum was a hulking tough guy and heavy drinker. Huston was drawn to his wildness, thought they'd get on well and was merely amused when the actor consumed most of a bottle of vodka by ten in the morning. In a letter to Buddy Adler, head of production at Twentieth Century-Fox, Huston reported that Mitchum (though still drinking heavily) was as well behaved as a choirboy: "I had various reports . . . how on the last picture he raised hell at the company's expense and made life miserable for everyone around him. . . . [But] he couldn't possibly be more cooperative. He is always letter perfect in his lines and he's never a minute late on the set."

Huston's guidance was characteristically minimal. His most specific direction came at the end of a take when he said, "I think, kid . . . *even more.*" Mitchum found that Huston tried to extract a better performance by making him suffer. He claimed to have cut his chest while crawling through the jungly underbrush and swimming through a coral reef filled with broken coconut shells and sharp discarded bedsprings. But he accepted the challenge and was determined to show Huston he could take it. When the director asked, "Think it'll kill ya, kid?," Mitchum stoically replied, "We'll find out."[2] He is especially good when he proposes marriage to Kerr and begs her not to take her final vows. His ecstatic war dance when the American forces capture the island imitates Walter's joyous dance when he discovers the gold in *Sierra Madre*.

Ethnic Japanese were scarce in the Caribbean islands. Huston recruited eight émigrés who worked on a farm colony in Brazil, but (as in *Across the Pacific*) most of the Japanese were played by Chinese waiters and laundrymen from nearby Trinidad. The climactic scene, in which the Americans bombarded the island, made the cameraman extremely nervous. Ossie Morris wrote that "the American powder man didn't exactly fill me with confidence—he had only one eye and had lost fingers off each hand." When rain shorted the wires, the bombs exploded simultaneously instead of sequentially and fifty pseudo-Japanese, fleeing the detonations, were nearly blown up.

Deborah Kerr (who would marry Peter Viertel in 1960) had played a nun in *Black Narcissus* (1947). In this picture her sensitive, perhaps sunburned or rash-ridden skin looked terrible, and Huston avoided close-ups of her face. In the novel by Charles Shaw, the nun has sensual thoughts; in the movie, she's pure in mind and body. In a variant screenplay, which would have been more interesting, Sister Angela reveals that she's not really a nun, but had stolen a habit to disguise herself and help her escape. Fed up with the Hollywood censor who came to Tobago, Huston staged a fake scene. He had Mitchum lift Kerr's skirts and attempt to rape her, which sent the moral guardian fleeing in horror.

Heaven Knows is a reprise of *The African Queen*. In both films two contrasting characters—a rough-hewn but good-hearted man and a very proper religious lady—are thrown together in an isolated and dangerous place. They work harmoniously to defeat the enemy, triumph in battle and fall in love. But *African Queen* was fast-paced and dynamic, *Heaven Knows* slow and sentimental, and Huston was unable to stamp his distinctive image on the story.

· II ·

In *The Barbarian and the Geisha* Huston moved from the Japanese war in 1944 to Japanese resistance to the American mission in 1856, two years after Commodore Matthew Perry "opened" Japan to the West. A historian described Townsend Harris, a considerable figure and hero of the movie, as

> a New York merchant who had already been engaged in the Far Eastern trade, and was to prove a unique figure in American diplomatic history. . . . His mission was to negotiate the first commercial treaty between the United States and Japan, one which would assure normal rights of residence and trade. . . . Harris was patient, tolerant, and understanding. . . . He lived alone in a small, poor, desolate port, housed in a shabby Buddhist temple, without the amenities, comforts, even necessities of the normal life of an Occidental. He was deprived of normal human intercourse. . . . The Japanese kept him at a distance, spied on all his movements, frustrated him by all the devices known to them. . . . They sought thus to wear him down and by isolation and discomfort to force him to surrender and go home. They failed.

Another historian called him "a stubborn, shrewd, doggedly coura-geous, and, at the same time, fairly sensitive man, who . . . with con-siderable skill, played on Japanese fears of British intrusion . . . and overcame obstruction and prevarication."[3] The original title of the movie was *The Townsend Harris Story,* but since nobody had ever heard of him, it was changed to something more suggestive and exotic.

The movie was set in the fishing village of Kawana, on the jagged coast of the Izu Peninsula, about seventy miles southwest of Tokyo. The barbarian-foreigner (John Wayne) arrives with his interpreter Henry Heusken, whose name sounds just like "Huston" and who is played by his Japanese-size friend Sam Jaffe. The film provides a realistic and visually beautiful portrait of Japanese life and customs. Once Wayne reaches the shogun's court, there's a great deal of bowing and a certain amount of scraping, and many short-stepping processions and elaborate ceremonials. Wayne, deprived of sexual but not human intercourse, is provided with a geisha who enhances his life and spies on him. He inevitably falls in love with her but, like the also-isolated Mitchum in *Heaven Knows,* treats her with decorous formality.

When American sailors jump ship and infect the village with cholera, "the demon of death goes from door to door." With destructive Western ingenuity, Wayne burns down the village to stop the epidemic, but in doing so makes even more enemies. When a high official asks the geisha to help kill Wayne, she's forced to agree but cannot bring herself to do it. She prevents the official from killing Wayne; the dishonored official must kill himself; and she then prefers to kill *herself* for breaking her vow. According to the legend, Townsend Harris fell in love with the geisha, who committed suicide after he left Japan. But the screenwriter Charlie Grayson—Huston's old crony, who wrote thirty-six mediocre scripts between 1936 and 1957—did not use this promising romantic material. The movie suggests—thirteen years after the end of World War II and only six years after the end of the American occupation of Japan—that this self-destructive samurai mentality had propelled Japan into the war and foreshadowed its defeat.

Huston earned $300,000 for the twenty-six-week shooting schedule; Wayne got a hefty $700,000. When a reporter asked why he chose Wayne for the role, Huston playfully replied, "Because he's the biggest goy of all." He actually liked the idea of "this massive figure, with his bluff innocence and naiveté, with his edges rough, moving among those minute people"—like Gulliver in Lilliput. But Wayne was a disastrous choice. Though physically impressive, he spoke the flat dialogue like a weary robot. Unhappy with the part, despite his huge fee, Wayne complained, "Huston has me walking through a series of Japanese pastels. Hell, my fans expect me to be tall in the saddle."[4] But he never got into the saddle with the geisha.

Though Grayson stated, "It would be unthinkable for [Huston] to show any human failing, like anxiety or doubt, that might put his judgment in question," Huston also showed surprising flexibility. Wayne told Grayson, just before shooting, " 'A line's been cut that's valuable. . . . I think it should go back in.' John turned a look of concentrated annoyance when we approached him. But he listened attentively, and agreed that Duke's point was valid." Huston had a hard time with the blustering Wayne. Their politics were antithetical; the casting against type misfired. Wayne, used to specific direction from John Ford, disliked the freedom Huston gave his actors, and his on-screen relationship with the geisha was a nonstarter.

Huston also had trouble with the Japanese actors. Sô Yamamura, playing the official who conceives the plot to kill Wayne, wrote to demand honorable compensation for the jobs he had lost because the movie was not completed on time: "I am standing on the last stage to decide whether I continue to play in *The Townsend Harris Story* or not. . . . If 20th Century-Fox does not accept my request, I have to discontinue my performance reluctantly. I am not making any business negotiation like a merchant does nor any intimidation." Since he did not want a career in Hollywood, he was in a strong position to carry out his threat and force the studio to spend a great deal of money to replace him. Realizing this, Fox agreed to double his salary from the eleventh week to the end of the shoot.

Huston's oriental plunder while making this picture included Japanese masks, folding screens, the hydro-erotic bath and Eiko Ando, who'd been a stripper and singer in a Tokyo music hall. She played the geisha in the movie and, in this *Mikado*-like setting, also played the disconsolate Madama Butterfly to Huston's callous Pinkerton. After Huston, having trouble dealing simultaneously with Suzanne Flon and Eiko Ando, had disappeared into Africa to make *The Roots of Heaven*, the miserable Eiko went on a publicity tour in California. Romain Gary, the novelist and French consul-general in Los Angeles, then had a fling with Eiko. Jealous of her passion for Huston and angry about the way Huston had adapted his novel, *The Roots of Heaven*, Gary behaved treacherously. Eiko's emotional upheavals led to the nannylike intervention of a producer at Fox, who feared a scandal and informed Huston: "For the last two weeks Eiko was very unhappy and heart-broken.

About two or three weeks ago she called me up and said [Romain Gary] asked her to have dinner with him. . . . Unfortunately during this meeting he told her certain things . . . about your friendship with Suzanne [Flon], and as far as I can learn his motive was pure malice. This made her very unhappy. . . . The whole thing is none of my goddam business but her behavior is so impeccable and she is such a very nice and decent person I feel a moral responsibility toward her."[5] Huston usually let his lovers down more gently, but Eiko seems to have had unrealistic expectations about their future together and took it all rather hard.

The final blow on this disastrous project was a reprise of the debacle after he left *The Red Badge of Courage*. When the picture was completed and Huston departed for Africa, Wayne bullied the studio into making changes that enhanced his role. Sensing big trouble ahead, Huston had wired Buddy Adler, "Stop fiddling and fixing as seems to be going on." Adler, who had spent $4 million on the picture and now controlled it, shot back, "With the amount of money we have invested in this project, I can hardly call what I am trying to do fiddling and fixing. We are attempting to strengthen the personal story by adding a few scenes [with Wayne]." Defending himself, Huston later lamented, "The studio altered *The Barbarian and the Geisha* so it was unrecognizable. . . . [It] turned out to be a bad picture, but it was a good picture before it became a bad picture. I've made pictures that were not good, for which I was responsible, but this was not one of them."[6]

· III ·

Romain Gary's *The Roots of Heaven* had won the prestigious Prix Goncourt in France. As an ecological *African Queen* or *Out of Africa*, it could have been an important and successful film. It had a gorgeous setting, an adventurous story and an idealistic hero (played by Trevor Howard), passionately committed to protecting endangered elephants from poachers and freeing the Africans from colonial oppression. Darryl Zanuck produced the film because his current girlfriend, Juliette Gréco, an enormously popular French singer, wanted him to give her the starring role. She also persuaded him that the center of French

Equatorial Africa would be a cheaper place to shoot the film and a more authentic locale than the healthier but more touristic Kenya. The French colonial authorities eagerly offered their help.

On March 2, 1958, the cast flew from Paris to Fort Lamy (now in western Chad) and from there traveled southeast to Fort Archambault in the southern part of the country. They then moved northwest to Maroua (now in northern Cameroon, south of Lake Chad) and, moving southeast, finally wound up in Bangui, a river town (now on the southern border of the Central African Republic). After making *The African Queen* in the Belgian Congo and Uganda, Huston liked the idea of a new hardship post in Africa—though the big-game hunting was better in British than in French territory. He loved adversity and never took the easy route, but the choice of Equatorial Africa was a terrible mistake. Food and bottled water had to be flown in from France; cast and crew lived in a kind of grass-hut hotel and ate in a communal dining room. Gréco's French biographer described what he called the Dantesque conditions: aggressive insects, astonishing reptiles and dust that penetrated everywhere. Soon after they arrived the medical problems and repatriations multiplied, and like casualties in a losing war, the sick or wounded technicians had to be replaced by new arrivals. The numerous problems were both comic and pathetic, with alcoholic shipwrecks, amorous heartbreaks and wounded egos.

The heat was so intense and so many people passed out that it was impossible to work between 11 A.M. and 4 P.M. Nearly everyone suffered from sunstroke, heat exhaustion, viral infections, blood diseases, malaria or other mysterious symptoms. Juliette Gréco was sick for weeks at a time. Zanuck was particularly upset when Gréco's tame mongoose ate a box of his precious cigars. Several people cracked up. Eddie Albert walked out in the midday sun, conversed with witch doctors and "went absolutely bananas"; one crew member saw a threatening hurricane in the clear blue skies; a second thought he was directing traffic in Piccadilly Circus; a third stripped stark naked and disappeared without telling anyone. Resigned to failure, Huston summarized the savage conditions: "The location was one of the most difficult I have ever been on. Temperatures were killing; the thermometer got up to

125° during the day, and seldom fell below 100° at night. People started dropping right and left."

Their compound, called Zanuckville and constructed in Fort Archambault, had streets named after the fashionable thoroughfares in Paris, Rome and Los Angeles: rue la Boétie, via Veneto and Sunset Boulevard. In May 1958 Diana Cooper—the aristocrat, actress and famous beauty of the 1920s—told Evelyn Waugh that she had been seriously tempted to join Huston on location: "I nearly broke all dates and did a bunk to the centre of central Africa—in fact to Zanuckville—John Huston disarmingly invited me to be his guest—I should have seen animals as Noah saw them in much the same surroundings."[7]

The handsome and adventurous travel writer Patrick Leigh Fermor—who'd fought on the side of Greek guerrillas and captured a German general during the war in Crete—wrote the screenplay. In London he had a bizarre encounter with Zanuck, who roundly condemned the script and told him, " 'It's a whole heap of crap. . . . IT'S NO GOOD!' " Fermor recalled, "Oddly enough I felt rather relieved. It wasn't my world, after all. . . . He went on, 'We go to Paris tomorrow and I'll get you a suite like mine in the Hôtel Prince de Galles and a bottle of whisky and a nice-looking typist, and we'll get down to it. Is your passport OK for French Equatorial Africa?' "

Exaggerating a bit to shock the Duchess of Devonshire, his correspondent in comfy England, Fermor described Fort Lamy, below Lake Chad, on the edge of the Sahara Desert, as "a fly-blown town of mud walls inhabited by dejected looking Negroes, the air a-swoop and a-flutter with vultures, the heat giving you a straight left like a boxing glove." Used to roughing it, Fermor took a more positive view of the second location and told me that he found the camp-like setting reasonably comfortable:

I think Darryl Zanuck was advised to use Fort Archambault because it was the largest town—but not very large—in the area, with many inhabitants who could be used as extras, and forests not too far off where elephants could be found. The conditions there. Not too bad. There was a large stockaded compound filled with quite comfortable huts, and a large marquee where we had very respectable meals flown out from Paris to a nearby aerodrome. The top echelons— Darryl, John Huston, Errol Flynn, a man called Eddie Albert, whom we thought rather wet, Trevor Howard, Juliette Gréco, (I think) Friedrich Ledebur and (luckily) me, all lived in a slightly grander part of the compound.

With characteristic English understatement, Fermor described the conditions in Maroua as "very hot." He wrote Deborah Devonshire that it was more colorful than the other places and reminded him of the pageantry of the Middle Ages:

The town is a labyrinth of mud walls surrounding conical thatched huts and the population consists entirely of coal black enormous Foulbés, very fine looking, clad in splendid robes—their faces slashed by ceremonial scars, and they ride horses with medieval tilting saddles and black-and-white checked caparisons down to their fetlocks. Curly scimitars glitter from the saddles. . . . [The feudal chieftain's] subjects approach him kneeling and when he sallies forth surrounded by his horsemen, trumpeters sound fanfares. He has many slaves and concubines and a subterranean jail where his prisoners lie in chains. . . .

Halfway through our time at Maroua, Ramadan began, and the local extras began fainting from the heat and their total fasting; to such an extent that Darryl suggested to the French *chef de région* that he was prepared to pay a large sum of money if they could put Ramadan forward, or back, for two weeks. The *chef de région* was astonished and rather shocked at the proposal. Some of the neighbouring hill-people were stark-naked animists.

Bangui (Fermor told me) was the roughest and most primitive place of all:

The forests near Bangui were inhabited by very intelligent
pygmies. We were "shooting" in the forest when the clouds
broke and a deluge of rain came down. Our procession of
vehicles headed back to the ultra-modern hotel, like an up-
ended mouth-organ on the banks of the Shari river, which
was full of crocodiles. I got there with Errol and his girl,
and we were astonished to find the whole of the ground
floor a foot deep in termites, over which small bright green
frogs from the Shari were leaping about in parabolas,
while Juliette's mongoose ran riot among them, killing and
swallowing as many as he could, two legs sticking out of his
mouth. A strange sight.[8]

Huston and Fermor admired each other, but were also wary when
they worked together, testing their strength like giants shaking hands.
Huston put Fermor in the Hayden-Mitchum class of exuberant imbib-
ers: "Paddy could drink with the titans, but there weren't any titans
around, so he drank by himself. And he would go drunken-walking.
He'd walk in the jungle. There were man-eaters around." After psych-
ing out Huston's weak points, Fermor—a forceful personality, well
matched against his adversary—found a way to handle the dominating
maverick: "*John Huston:* Wildly bogus, charming, complicated, boast-
ful and ham. I like him very much and don't trust him a yard. He has
to be kept under pretty strict control; he would trample on one if he
saw the faintest flicker of a flinch, and does so when he does see it.
This entails keeping on the offensive quite a lot, i.e., diagnosing his
weak points and, when the occasion arises, hitting hard and often. This
establishes an equivocal and amusing kind of truce and makes life quite
fun, a rather dangerous game."[9]

Huston, who could be surprisingly indifferent to his own films,
seemed to write this one off, remarking, "The pictures that turn out to
be the most difficult to make, usually turn out to be the worst—like
Roots of Heaven." He had gone straight to central Africa after making
The Barbarian and the Geisha and, still wearing his kimonos, arrived just

before shooting started. He knew the script (which had many preachy, undramatic speeches) was bad. But instead of scrapping it and starting again (as he'd done with *Beat the Devil*), he tried to rewrite it as he went along and began to shoot before it was ready. He then gave up on the script and considered the film a dead loss. The English cinematographer Ossie Morris recalled the general air of defeat about the whole project. He remarked, with some exaggeration, that nobody was any good in the movie. It was all a bit embarrassing. Everyone thought: "Why are we here?" It didn't seem worth enduring such appalling conditions to make such a poor picture. Huston didn't seem to try very hard. He needed the money and did it merely for money. Zanuck, as usual, created more problems than he solved. He tried to control the notoriously rebellious Huston by sitting right next to him as he was directing the picture. When Huston told the actors, "Make it a little louder," Zanuck, like a parody of a Hollywood producer, would repeat the instruction in a more emphatic way. Huston simply ignored him.

The thirty-year-old Juliette Gréco—a friend of Sartre and Jean Cocteau—was a politically active singer in the Existentialist caves and cafés of Saint-Germain. Her mother had taken part in the French Resistance; as a teenager Juliette had been arrested and jailed by the Gestapo, and was saved only by her youth from deportation to a concentration camp. In 1957 she had appeared with Errol Flynn in Zanuck's production of Hemingway's *The Sun Also Rises*. Still unsure of herself in an English-speaking role and (like John Wayne) uneasy about Huston's *laisser-faire* attitude, Gréco remarked, "He never say I am good or I am bad. First, I think he must hate me. Then he look at me like a snake with little slitted eyes, and he say through his teeth, 'Fine, honey, fine.' Then I know he like me."[10]

Zanuck, twenty-five years older than Gréco, was jealous and possessive. Each tried to exploit the other, and their relationship became intense and volatile. When a crew member made an unguarded remark about Gréco, he was instantly fired and sent home. Huston observed that "Darryl had made no secret of his infatuation with Juliette Gréco, but I realized fairly soon that it was a one-sided affair. She was openly rude to him and spoke slightingly of him behind his back—even to me, until I set her straight. Paddy Leigh Fermor also fell in love with Juliette."

Fermor called her interesting, "extremely well read, unspoilable, wild, rather like a panther, a tremendous sense of humour," and noted some toxic details about her relations with Zanuck: "It is quite obvious that she can't bear to be touched by him any more. This leads to scenes and blows. Last night he knocked her out cold, then, in a fit of anxiety, threw a bucket of water over her and sobbed for an hour. It's all rather pathetic and awful." Juliette herself described an unpleasant encounter with Zanuck. When she returned to the camp after a late night out with her French friends, she found him clad in his Baby Doll nightshirt and with his sleeping mask pushed to the top of his head. He asked where she'd been, and her laughter at his question released his pent-up fury: " 'It signaled the start of the most extraordinary behavior I have ever witnessed,' she said later. 'He insulted me. He raised his hand. Unluckily for him, all the hot quick strength of my youth boiled up inside me.' "[11] She was furious that he dared to treat her like an errant wife—or errant daughter. To avoid antagonizing the producer on his own turf, Fermor made no advances to Gréco, but the art director, Stephen Grimes, boldly poached on Zanuck's prize.

The grandiloquent Orson Welles—wasted in the role of a smug, cynical and boorish American newsman—stirred up this heady mixture. Flynn had worked with Welles and known him in Rome, and both shared a taste for drugs and drink. In his unpublished diary of February 1953, he recorded his analysis of Welles' impressive but deeply flawed character: "Welles, fat & bloated as Nero . . . [was] at his hedonistic best, seemingly enchanted with himself and life. . . . I would like to know Orson better. Intelligent, aggressive and no servant of bromides in life . . . a man of large, perhaps great ability, able to dominate others, who is at the same time quite a bit of a fool. . . . No self-sanctity in Orson. But until he grows up mentally he is a fool. *La bêtise* is precisely his strong point."

Huston and Flynn, old friends and adversaries, had a great deal in common. Like Huston, Flynn had had extensive worldly experience before coming to Hollywood. As a young man in New Guinea, he had been a tobacco planter, bird trapper, gold prospector, diamond smuggler and slave trader. Both men were athletic and keen boxers, and wrote fiction and lively autobiographies. They had similar personalities: they were insatiably curious searchers for extremes of experience, reckless risk-takers and high-stakes gamblers, defiant rebels against authority and notorious seducers of movie stars. They had both been lovers of Olivia de Havilland. Huston liked Flynn and was willing to work with him, but now, when he failed to remember his lines, he found him a rather pathetic and irritating character. Huston thought Flynn was in terrible shape and didn't want to take him out hunting, but he insisted on going, behaved perfectly and was a great companion. Flynn wrote that Huston "was obviously very good in the jungle. I thought I was pretty good, on foot, but this fellow Huston, no youngster, leaped along like a big spider swinging through the trees."

Roots was Flynn's last movie, and he died the following year. Huston later wrote a sympathetic account of Flynn on location and suggested that the actor knew his end was near:

> Errol Flynn was truly ill, but it had nothing to do with Africa. He had a vastly enlarged liver. He continued to drink, however, and he was also on drugs. . . . I remember seeing Errol sitting alone night after night in the middle of the compound with a book, reading by the light of a Coleman lantern. There was always a bottle of vodka on the camp table beside him. When I went to sleep he was there, and when I'd wake up in the middle of the night I'd see him still sitting there—the book open, but Errol not reading any longer, just looking into his future, I think, of which there wasn't much left.[12]

Fermor, perceptive as always, saw the more serious side of Flynn and found him a congenial companion: "He poses as the most tremendous bounder—glories in being a cad—but is intelligent, perceptive and, in a freak way, immensely likeable. We are rather chums, to my bewilderment. Sex rules his life." Welles was mightily impressed by Flynn's ability to endure the intense tropical heat, take heavy doses of heroin and still satisfy the teenaged girlfriend he'd flown in from California. In his autobiography Flynn wrote, with amused self-deprecation, that in *Roots* he played "a once-handsome man, now decadent, a shadow of his former self and who has taken to the bottle. . . . I know that must be me. . . . I make more today being a shadow of my former self than I did when I *was* my former self."[13]

· IV ·

In *Roots of Heaven*, Flynn plays a character with a guilty past, a Conradian hero in search of self-redemption. In the Balkans during World War II he had commanded a group of men who were captured by the Nazis. All the others refused to provide information and were shot. Flynn talked, survived and ended up an alcoholic, in love with Gréco (who's in love with Trevor Howard) in this remote part of Africa. She urges him to quit drinking and to help Howard, who's trying to save the elephants, and Flynn explains: "I'll start tapering off as soon as we get to the elephants. It's only the coming of man that drives me to drink." Playing the washed-up loser who still has some pathetic dignity, he tries to express his feelings for Gréco. With his famous crooked smile, he tells her, "Odd, isn't it? The things you most want to touch in life don't want you to touch them." Like Trevor Howard, Flynn embodies the theme of self-sacrificial idealism and tries to preserve the elephants that symbolize "the very image of freedom."

The old desire to hunt had brought Huston back to Africa, though he was no longer obsessed with the elephants he'd failed to kill on his previous trip. He was now making a movie about saving elephants instead of trying to slaughter them. In *White Hunter, Black Heart* Viertel expressed the same feeling about these huge beasts that Romain Gary had dramatized in *Roots:* "The elephants had something to do with God, with the miracle of creation. They made you feel that you were passing into another age, into a world that no longer existed. They transmitted, not so much the idea of jungle and wilderness, as the feeling of unconquerable time."

Romain Gary believed that men themselves must suffer before they could dedicate themselves to saving the elephants. Both Gréco and Trevor Howard have been victims and are bonded by their suffering. She'd been forced into sexual slavery in a German prison camp; he'd been a prisoner of war in Germany, dreaming of freeing the elephants when he was finally freed. Howard insists, "I'd give anything to become an elephant myself. . . . People must be made to understand [their plight]," but an unsympathetic priest refuses to sign his petition and tells him, "You're fed up with men, so you've gone over to the animals." A crusading idealist, Howard opposes the poachers who think "the killing will go on, it's in our blood," with the belief that "the elephants are our largest and greatest friends on earth. They are docile unless harmed. We slaughter them for their valuable ivory tusks. This must be stopped—with force if necessary." The title of the movie suggests that elephants—like the oceans, forests and mankind itself—are the roots of heaven on earth. "Poison heaven at its roots," Howard explains, "and the tree will wither and die. The stars will go out and heaven will be destroyed."

Sustained by this noble belief, Howard battles a small army of ivory poachers and saves the elephants (this time, at least) by stampeding the herd and trampling his white enemy. In the long, climactic gunfight, Flynn is killed. Howard is captured with his companion, played by Friedrich Ledebur, a great physical presence, muscular and with a deeply lined face, who is impressively dignified in this role. They're freed by the African rebel leader and, though weak and ineffective, survive to continue their hopeless Hustonian struggle.

Instead of blaming each other (as directors and producers usually do), Huston and Zanuck both took responsibility for the comparative failure of *The Roots of Heaven*. Huston regretted that the film did not reach the story's potential and called the adventure tale one of the most unfortunate pictures he ever made: "I regret that failure as much as any sin I've committed in my time. *The Roots of Heaven* could have been a very fine film. And largely owing to me it was not a good film at all." Huston's sudden transition from Japan to Africa, his unfocused script that made Howard too preachy and cranky, and the rush into production before they were ready to shoot were certainly negative factors. But he was not responsible for all the difficulties. The disastrously unhealthy climate and poor accommodations were hard on everyone. Gréco was a poor actress (out of her depth with old pros like Welles, Howard and Flynn), and her constant fights with Zanuck—an intrusive and irritating presence—created intolerable tension.

Nunnally Johnson wrote, with considerable *Schadenfreude*, "When the first money reports on *The Roots of Heaven* reached Darryl, Darryl didn't leave his room for two days. *Look* had a layout this week of John Huston's simultaneous double blockbuster on Broadway [*Barbarian* and *Roots*]. No mention was made of the amounts of money that these two pictures will lose. If a studio wants to commit suicide I have the perfect arrangement for it. Get Leland Hayward to do the producing and Huston to do the directing."[14] But Huston and Johnson were too severe, and the picture was not really an artistic failure. It has held up well in the last fifty years, seems more relevant today than ever before and would be perfect for a contemporary remake.

SEVENTEEN

MUSTANGS AND MISFITS,

1959–1961

· I ·

In the early 1960s Huston made his first two westerns. *The Unforgiven* (1960), set in Texas in the 1870s, was about fighting Indians; *The Misfits* (1961), set in contemporary Nevada, was about capturing mustangs. The first repeated all the clichés about the old homestead, wavered unsteadily between low comedy, sentimentality and melodrama, and failed. The second, which had unusual intelligence, complexity and depth, was a brilliant artistic success. In the former, Burt Lancaster and Audrey Hepburn were wasted in mediocre parts; in the latter, Clark Gable and Marilyn Monroe gave the best dramatic performances of their careers. *The Unforgiven* was the only one of the four films Huston shot in Mexico that was not set in Mexico.

The script of *The Unforgiven*—no one ever knew what the title meant—was written by Ben Maddow, who'd collaborated with Huston on *The Asphalt Jungle*. The movie was originally meant to explore the subject of racial prejudice, which Huston had done previously in *In This Our Life*, but the story is ludicrous. Lancaster's independent company produced the picture and forced Huston to compromise his principles and make a standard western, in which the white characters are heroic pioneers and the Indians are bloodthirsty and absurd. Lancaster and his sister Hepburn, living out on the prairie with their ma (Lillian Gish), are strangely and seemingly incestuously attracted to each other, but discover she was actually a lost Indian child, adopted by the family. They have to fight off an attempt to rescue her from the Kiowas, whose buffalo-horn headgear make them look like refugees from a Wagnerian opera. In a pointlessly suicidal attack, the Indians drive their cattle over the sod roof of Lancaster's cabin as he warns Audie Murphy, "Wake up Cash, we've got company." After Hepburn shoots *her* Indian brother to show she's white at heart, she and Lancaster are finally free to express their love and get married.

The budget for the twenty-two-week shoot was $6 million. Huston got $300,000, but he knew from the start that the movie would be terrible. At odds with the producers and the star, he recalled, "the entire picture turned sour. Everything went to hell. It was as if some celestial vengeance had been loosed upon me." Fierce sun, tormenting fleas, unhealthy water, horrible food and local bandits in Durango made everyone's life miserable, and Huston was in a sour mood. Inge Morath, photographing *The Unforgiven* for *Paris Match* and *Life,* noticed that he seemed detached and distracted. A writer saw that "he pitted people against each other. He was demanding and mean-spirited." The actor John Saxon observed, "Huston delighted in finding challenges on the set, as if he were trying to stave off boredom or show his disdain for producers or both." He constantly clashed with Lancaster, who tried to usurp his authority by telling him where to place the camera.

Two accidents nearly killed the leading actors. Audie Murphy, as explosive and aggressive as ever, was more vulnerable than he seemed. When he was out on a duck-hunting expedition with Huston and some of the actors, Inge Morath saw two helpless men struggling around a rocking boat. Arthur Miller (who later married her), described how the slim, slight Inge courageously "got out of her clothes, and in panties and bra slipped into the cold lake and after swimming nearly half a mile found Murphy flailing desperately in the final stages of exhaustion, too weak to climb into the boat he had fallen out of. . . . She got Murphy to grasp her bra strap and towed him back to land."

Hepburn, fresh from *The Nun's Story* (1959), certainly earned her $200,000 fee. Stripped of both religious habit and high-fashion gowns (her fringed buckskin was not designed by Givenchy), she was absurdly miscast as an Indian girl. In a scene with Lillian Gish—who resembles the waxworks woman in Grant Wood's painting *American Gothic*

(1950)—Hepburn sees geese flying overhead and profoundly exclaims, "They're human too, Maw. They just fly a mite higher than us, that's all." Hepburn, who was pregnant at the time, didn't know how to ride a horse. When her mount suddenly bolted and "some idiot" tried to stop it by putting up his hands, she was thrown, badly sprained her foot, fractured four vertebrae in her back and thought she'd lose her baby. The picture was delayed for three weeks while she recovered, and she finished the picture in an orthopedic brace.

The movie got predictably poor reviews. The critic Dwight Macdonald called it "a work of profound phoniness, part adult Western . . . part *Oklahoma!* kind of folksy Americana. It is limp as drama, every situation is built up until it soggily collapses, even the final Indian attack is tedious." Huston agreed with the critics and lamented, "Some of my pictures I don't care for, but *The Unforgiven* is the only one I actually dislike. Despite some good performances, the overall tone is bombastic and over-inflated."[1]

· II ·

Once again, a new location produced a new lover—with an exotic background. En route to Durango, Huston met the fiery Maka Czernichew—a beautiful and talented dancer, painter, writer and equestrian—at a party at the French embassy in Mexico City. Wearing his safari suit, smoking a long Cuban cigar and telling the well-honed story of how an excremental chimpanzee ruined his marriage to Evelyn Keyes, he stared intensely at Maka, who thought, "God, what is this? Something very strange and tumultuous." Their affair lasted while he made *The Unforgiven* and, like many of Huston's liaisons, continued on and off for three decades.

Maka's father was a Russian count who'd met her mother, a wealthy Mexican, when he was in the diplomatic service and she was in a Swiss convent school. Both families were opposed to their marriage. During the war her father collaborated with the Nazis and worked for them as a translator. At the same time (according to her story) Maka worked for the Resistance in Paris and met Camus, Sartre and de Beauvoir. After the war she married an Austrian in order to smuggle her father out of France and into Mexico. Her parents ended up in Cuernavaca, somehow managing to exist on his charm and her sewing. Maka made three more expedient marriages: to a Frenchman when she became pregnant and, later on, to two other rich bourgeois. She regretfully said, "I always married for someone else—my parents or my two sons." Guy Gallo, who met Maka when he was working in Mexico with Huston on the script of *Under the Volcano,* wrote, "It is interesting that this woman, who speaks so fiercely of freedom and violence and whim and recklessness, has married for advantage (not her own) four times."

Temperamentally Huston and Maka, a strong woman with fierce eyes, were well matched. He was fascinated by her mélange of revolutionary spirit, primitive ferocity and beguiling witchcraft, and wrote, "There is some other transcendental substance mixed into her flesh. Look at her mouth when she smiles: it is the Olmec jaguar's mouth. Her eyes are too shiny. She is undoubtedly a *bruja.*" Later in life, echoing what Patrick Leigh Fermor had said about never showing any weakness to Huston, Maka recalled the pleasure, pain and danger of being his lover: "At the beginning we had a very tender relationship, but it then became a challenge, mixed up with a lot of love. If you were weak in front of John, you were through. I am not the type to become weak. With John, you had no time to go to pieces, to reason. He would talk beautifully in front of people, but in private it was more difficult. We lived around the bed or in the bed, eating sandwiches, playing dominoes." In a break from the filming, Maka and Huston went on a turkey shoot, and she had a miscarriage. Audie Murphy offered to fly her to Mexico City in his own plane, but Huston refused to let her go. (He may well have felt that Murphy was unreliable, and he was right to be cautious. Murphy died in a private plane crash in 1971.) Instead, his driver took her back to the capital by a much slower route. At the time Maka thought, "He didn't care. Much later, after knowing John for years and years, then [I knew] he would take care of me whenever I needed help." But "he could be very cruel, and he had a very tough character, but I had, too. That's the way we could survive for almost thirty years."

After observing Huston and Maka together in 1982–83, Guy Gallo noted, "They were friendly and familiar. But I would not say overtly close or in any way affectionate. In appearance she was strong and self-confident. In conversation perhaps more at ease with me than she was with John. . . . She told me a bit of their 30-year history by way of illustrating John's personality. Specifically his sadism and wild west ego. . . . I asked her why she put up with Huston's brutal treatment. She shrugged and said how life was living [to the hilt] all the time."[2]

· III ·

On July 14, 1958, Arthur Miller had sent a description of his *Misfits* story to Huston at St. Clerans: "I'm writing to you to offer you an original screenplay I've written. . . . The setting is the Nevada back country, concerns two cowboys, a bush pilot, a girl, and the last of the mustangs up in the mountains. . . . The script is an early draft. If you are interested I'd want to sit and talk over my notions of further developments and of course would like to hear yours." Miller had based the original story on the character of his wife, Marilyn Monroe, and written the screenplay for her. In a rather muddled apology, he blamed her former photographer and business partner, Milton Greene, for hurting her relations with Huston after he'd directed her first significant picture, *The Asphalt Jungle:* "Marilyn is available for the girl, and since her break-up with one Milton Greene she has sometimes wanted somehow to let you know she was put in a position vis-à-vis you which was not of her doing and for which she felt and still feels badly. Tell you the truth I can't recall what it was all about but it probably no longer matters anyway." Huston was drawn to the rough life of the competitive but closely bonded male characters and to the challenge of shooting the exciting scenes with wild horses. He read the script and, eager to direct the film, cabled back a single word: "Magnificent."

Miller continued to work on the draft and in the spring of 1960, while Marilyn was shooting *Let's Make Love* with Yves Montand, Miller flew from New York to Ireland to work on the script with Huston. A French journalist, dispatched to interview the authors at work, offered a romantic picture of great minds writing as one: "Miraculously and all at once, these two completely different and often opposed characters are marvelously in agreement in the clear, quiet and hard-working atmosphere of St. Clerans."[3] Though Huston had called the screenplay "magnificent," he always pushed his writers to revise. He was a skilled screenwriter, but wouldn't rewrite an author he respected and kept prodding Miller to do the work himself. They went on and on, month after month, year after year, but had great difficulty deciding on the best ending. During the shooting Huston insisted that Miller revise the dialogue every day and late into the night (which made it much more difficult for Marilyn to memorize the constantly changing lines). Miller continued to revise some scenes that had to be reshot even *after* the film was finished.

Like the characters in Hemingway's *The Sun Also Rises,* wounded and traumatized by the Great War, the three pathetic and lonely men in *The Misfits* are psychologically damaged and unable to adjust to ordinary life. (Courage is tested in the novel by the bullfight and in the film by the mustang hunt.) "The striking thing about these characters," Miller said, "was they were internally drifting without it being painful to them. They had a wonderful independence and at the same time they weren't tough." All the characters suffer from disappointed ambitions. The pilot Guido (Eli Wallach) had wanted to be a doctor, the rodeo rider Perce (Montgomery Clift) a champion and rancher, the cowboy and part-time gigolo Gay (Clark Gable) a husband and father, Roslyn (Monroe) a serious dancer until it got "changed around into something bad." But their domestic life has been destroyed. Guido has lost his wife and baby in childbirth, Perce has lost his father in a hunting accident. Gay has been betrayed by his wife, who divorced him, Perce by the stepfather who stole the family ranch. Even Roslyn's friend Isabelle (Thelma Ritter) was divorced by her husband, who married her best friend.

Miller called *The Misfits* an "Eastern Western" that described the meaninglessness of life. The men engage in debased versions of two archetypal western experiences: the rodeo and the roundup. In the rodeo, where a bucking-strap with nails digs into the horse's belly and makes him furious, Perce gets thrown and battered, and the drunken Gay finds and then loses his estranged children in the crowd. In the roundup, the last cowboys kill the last mustangs—both are a dying breed—and transform the beautiful wild horses into canned meat.

In the beginning of *The Misfits,* at the courthouse and in the casino, Roslyn wears a black hat, black dress and high heels; at the end, acclimatized to the roughhouse and sweltering desert, she has pigtails and western clothes. None of the men understands the naïve yet enigmatic Roslyn, but they all fall in love with her. Anxious, frightened, suffering, angry and in pain, she expresses simple, sometimes simple-minded, New Age wisdom. She says that the garden seeds, though tiny, "still know they're supposed to be lettuces!" and that "Birds must be brave to live out here. Especially at night. . . . Whereas they're so small, you know?" Intuitive rather than rational, sympathizing with all hunted creatures and haunted men, she passionately undermines the mustangers' macho beliefs. She makes the cowboys, whom Isabelle calls the last real men left in the world, feel guilty about their primitive instincts and participation in the exhilarating hunt.

All the men try to prove their masculinity: Perce by riding a bronco in the rodeo, Gay by lassoing mustangs from a truck, Guido by daredevil flying in his decrepit plane. But Perce is a physical wreck; Guido's plane leaks oil, needs repairs, and like Gay's truck, is falling apart. Guido, who'd been an army air force pilot, performs a parodic reprise of his glorious exploits. He sees his military combat as heroic; Roslyn, unimpressed by his wartime missions, equates bombing with mustanging. Both, in her view, butcher helpless victims. Using machines—a plane and a truck—to capture the six mustangs, makes the vital animals seem helpless and tragic. Gay echoes Roslyn and voices their desperation by exclaiming, "It just got changed around, see? I'm doin' the same thing I ever did. It's just that they . . . they changed it around. . . . They smeared it all over with blood, turned it into shit and money just like everything else."[4]

The Misfits reaches its emotional and dramatic climax in the mustang hunt, and Huston, as always, filmed the horses brilliantly. Like Hemingway and his hunting companions in *Green Hills of Africa,* the mustangers bond in male friendship and express their love for wild creatures by slaughtering them. Huston thought "what they're doing is pointless, if not ugly." Gable, Marilyn's idol and father figure, said, "I didn't like the original ending of the screenplay (in which the stallion defeats Gay and leaves him lying on the lake bed, arousing Roslyn's compassion) but I didn't know the solution. I think Arthur's new ending is the answer." After being dragged across the burning desert while trying to tie up the stallion, Gay finally captures it by himself to prove his manly power. He then cuts it loose to show his love for Roslyn and gain her respect. Roslyn calls the stallion, mares and colt (which parallel Roslyn and her three "stallions": Gay, Perce and Guido) a "family," and when they are freed she urges them to "go home." Though the horses are freed, the men, whose freedom is an illusion, are still trapped.

Roslyn and Gay are both poignant in their loneliness, and their love becomes a forlorn poetry uniting their solitudes. When Gay chooses love for Roslyn over a roving life and freedom with horses, he returns to domestic and economic responsibility. This is especially difficult, for he has no way of earning a living (apart from escorting wealthy divorcées) and will be forced into humiliating work in a supermarket, laundromat or service station. The finale of the film, like the end of the story, is ironic. Marriage, like mustanging, had better be "better than wages" because Gay will need wages to provide for his wife and the children they hope to have. Gay transforms Roslyn, who finds herself and discovers she has the "gift of life," and *The Misfits* ends positively.

The writers' strike delayed the completion of *Let's Make Love,* so the cast and crew arrived in the Nevada desert at the hottest time of the year. They stayed at the Mapes Hotel on North Virginia Street in Reno, and began the first stage of shooting on July 20, 1960. As sand blew into their eyes and into the cameras, they worked in Nevada until September 21 in temperatures of 110° Fahrenheit. There was a lot of dusty driving, in real life and in the film, from Reno to the distant locations. They piled into cars, trucks and buses, and drove through the desert for the mustang hunt at Pyramid Lake. The picture, most unusually, was filmed in black and white, and in chronological sequence. The scenes in Guido's unfinished house were shot in Quail Canyon, about twenty miles from the lake, and the rodeo scenes were filmed in Dayton, about twenty miles southeast of the city. The rest of the film was completed in the Hollywood studio.

Huston thrived on discomfort and took advantage of the location by taking every risk that came his way. Alongside Billy Pearson, he gamely rode in an exciting Labor Day camel race in Virginia City. His camel took off like a shot and beat all the horses, which were supposed to win, to the finish line. After his triumph Huston exclaimed, "I owe my splendid victory to a deep understanding of the camel. You're really living when you're up there between those humps. It has its ups and downs, but so has life." He often stayed up all night gambling in the casinos. The cautious and careful Miller, greatly impressed by Huston's reckless character and indifference to money, observed: "One night, he lost twenty-five thousand dollars, which he didn't have, of course. John used to spend his money as soon as he got it. The gangsters who ran the place told him politely that he was never going to leave town unless he paid that bill. So, one evening, I left him around nine o'clock after dinner at the table. . . . I came down the next morning around six, and there he was. He had made his money back! Plus about five hundred or a thousand dollars!"[5]

Huston, his stylish clothes always neatly pressed, turned up on time for work the next morning but, all too relaxed, sometimes fell asleep on location. When he woke up and forgot what scene he was directing, he'd say, as if still in control, "Now we'll shoot scene twelve." The script girl would whisper, "We've already done that one," and he'd casually declare, "Fine, just fine, then we'll do the next one." Miller, who found it all completely crazy but very exciting, concluded, "The Huston I saw, whatever his reputed faults, relied on a certain ultimate resiliency or even courage in people, probably because he saw himself as a lifelong fighter against impossible odds."

The drama off the set of *The Misfits* was as great as the drama portrayed in the script. Huston had to contend again with searing heat and arduous drives, forest fires and power cuts, difficulties with shooting the rodeo and the wild mustangs, reckless pilots and fragile planes, and he calmly dealt with every crisis. But three of his actors were always on the edge. Gable's health was a serious concern and Clift indulged in lethal drinking bouts. Monroe caused frequent delays and huge cost overruns, and her wrangles with Miller led to endless revisions of the script. Paula Strasberg, her influential acting coach, constantly interfered with Huston's direction. Despite all the chaos, Huston encouraged spontaneity and had an intuitive understanding of his cast. His own commanding presence and creative temperament inspired fine performances and kept the whole show together.

Monroe thought Huston was the only director who gave her the proper respect and treated her like a serious actress. He did not discuss motivation and provided minimal direction, but was always gentle— the only way to deal with her—and encouraged her by saying, "That's okay, darling." The photographer Eve Arnold recalled that "in the love scene on a bed with Gable, when he, fully dressed, woke her with a kiss, she, nude and covered only in a sheet, sat up and dropped the sheet, showing her breasts. . . . Huston let her finish the scene her way, didn't say 'Cut' to the cameraman until she was through, but he did cut it in the editing. And when she looked at him for approval, all he said was 'I've seen 'em before.' "

In a passage deleted from *An Open Book*, Huston wrote that he had *wanted* to show Monroe's exposed breasts (of which she was justly proud) but was overruled: "It was in keeping with the scene, and there was nothing lewd about it. Later that take was cut from the final print, over my objections." But James Goode, on the scene for the shoot, noted that Huston did not like sex scenes in his films, opposed the nude shot and dismissively said, "I've always known that girls have breasts."[6] According to Curtice Taylor, son of the producer Frank Taylor, when Monroe exposed her breasts in that scene Huston, citing external constraints, stated, "You must hold that up. The censors won't approve it. We can't print it." Frank Taylor strongly disagreed and maintained, "It's the best take. Let's use it and let *them* take it out." Gable agreed with Monroe and Taylor; the argument went on and got heated; and after seeing the rushes, Huston and Taylor had a real row in the theater lobby. In the end, either because of Huston's insistence or the censors' insuperable opposition, the scene *was* cut from the film.

· IV ·

Robert Mitchum was considered for the leading role, but Clark Gable got the part. The rodeo and roundup were the most difficult and dangerous to shoot, and both Clift and Gable were injured in these scenes. Directors almost never allowed movie stars to do their own stunts—the risk was far too great. If an accident occurred, the actors would not be covered by insurance and the costs would be catastrophic. But both Huston and Gable were swaggering machos.[7] Despite his illness and the warnings of his fifth wife, pregnant with his son, Gable insisted on doing some of his stunts in the exceptionally fierce heat. Though it seemed in the picture as if the wild stallion were dragging him across the dry lake bed, he was actually holding on to a rope attached to a moving camera truck. When the driver asked Huston how fast he should go, Huston—enjoying the spectacle of Gable's discomfort and testing his strength, as he did Mitchum's in *Heaven Knows, Mr. Allison*—replied, "About thirty-five, the speed of a horse, or until Clark begins to smoke." Gable was covered with an armor of "chaps, shoulder pads, gloves and a sort of all-over corset to be worn underneath . . . to protect him from bruises and sand burns." But it was extremely tough work, and he was cut and bruised.

In 1957, three years before appearing in *The Misfits*, Clift had smashed up his handsome face in a near-fatal car crash and had to have it rebuilt. In the film, the scars from his plastic surgery fitted his character and seem to have come from his frequent falls and fractures in the rodeos. (He reassures his mother, on the telephone, that she'll still recognize him after all his injuries.) Goode described how Clift also hurt himself when catching the mustangs: "For some unknown reason, Clift had not been wearing gloves when the sequences began and could not put them on now. . . . He was forced to throw the mare barehanded with his single rope. . . . His hands were lacerated and bleeding, but there was nothing anyone could do about it." A covert homosexual and heavy drinker, with a tortured personal life, Clift was delicately balanced on an emotional high wire. Huston said, "Clift was very fragile. He was a mess; he was gone," and called him "the male counterpart of

Marilyn—of that thing in her that touched people . . . a sense that she was headed for disaster."[8] Nevertheless, his performance was perfect.

Monroe's mental state had a greater impact on the making of *The Misfits* than all the other problems put together. Huston lamented, "We get so little done. It's not that there are so many setups. We don't have that many. It's just that we get so little done. It's unthinkable for an actor not to start at nine in the morning." Often sick and depressed, drinking heavily and addicted to prescription drugs, Monroe was usually four or five hours late. After the assistant producer picked her up in Reno, he'd drive ahead of her chauffeured car to announce her imminent arrival. But the actors and crew were astonished to find, after she got to the site, that she needed yet another hour before she could appear. They were forced to wait patiently and never dared utter a word of criticism. Her coming late, forgetting her lines and needing an infinite number of takes cost the studio a great deal of money, and her entire entourage was on the payroll. She had, a journalist satirically noted, "ten people to take care of her: a masseur for her body; a drama coach for her psyche; a make-up man for her face; a make-up woman for her limbs; a secretary for her affairs; a maid for her convenience; a lady to comb her hair; three wardrobe women for her clothes."

As she constantly sought direction from Paula Strasberg and relied entirely on her judgment, Monroe's conflicts with Huston and Miller intensified. Strasberg would hold up bizarre, simple-minded signs, meant to guide her disciple, that said, "You're a branch on a tree. . . . You're a bird in the sky."[9] When Monroe did something as ordinary as walking down a staircase, she looked to Strasberg (not Huston) for approval. If Strasberg didn't like the way she walked, they'd have to shoot the scene over and over again. At the end, even Huston was forced to communicate with Monroe through Strasberg.

Blaming Miller for Monroe's addiction, Huston told him that it was irresponsible, even criminal, to allow her to take any drugs. But he soon realized that that she wouldn't listen to Miller and he couldn't control her. One morning Frank Taylor's wife, Nan, went to their hotel suite "and found Arthur sleepless, his nerves raw. He was shaking with fatigue. He'd been up all night with Marilyn. Marilyn was in no better shape, but everyone was very protective toward her, very considerate. . . . We watched those two tearing themselves to bits." Marilyn was so high in one scene that Huston, after trying a few takes, gave up.

After Miller, at Monroe's request, moved out of their suite and into a different room, her addiction intensified. Huston inspected the damage and, in a passage too severe to be included in his autobiography, expressed his revulsion: "I was never so shocked. She was obviously on drugs, and euphoric in a drunken way. Her appearance was worse than I'd ever seen her. She was wearing only a short nightgown, her hands and feet were grubby, her hair was a tangle, and she looked as if she hadn't showered for days. . . . Marilyn was on her way out. Not only of the picture, but of life."[10] In late August 1960, suffering from complete physical exhaustion, Monroe had a nervous breakdown, took an overdose of sleeping pills and collapsed on the set. Huston sent for medical help and took personal responsibility for getting her off the drugs. She was rushed to Westside Hospital in Los Angeles and, while there, saw her psychiatrist every day.

When she returned, Monroe fell back into her old addiction and behaved as badly as ever. Huston, tough with women and allied with Miller in their struggle against Strasberg and Monroe, squirmed when Monroe used her tyrannical power to insult Miller in public:

> She'd talk out against Arthur Miller, right in his presence, to me, and with others around. And say things that embarrassed me, and certainly must have made him cringe. He would pretend he wasn't listening. And all my sympathies were with him. . . . I didn't like what she was doing to him. . . .
>
> I saw him humiliated a couple of times, not only by Marilyn but by some of her hangers-on. I think they hoped to demonstrate their loyalty to Marilyn by being impertinent to Arthur. On these occasions Arthur never changed expression. One evening I was about to drive away from the location—miles out in the desert—when I saw Arthur standing alone. Marilyn and her friends hadn't offered him a ride back; they'd just left him. If I hadn't happened to see

him, he would have been stranded out there. My sympathies
were more and more with him.

Miller had always hoped to restore Monroe's self-confidence. In his
endless revisions, he enhanced her role and made her character more
and more appealing. He had the Gable, Clift and Eli Wallach characters fall in love with her, and express their admiration for her sweetness,
charm and beauty. Yet, in a terrible psychological bind, Monroe lost all
trust in Miller, hated her role and believed she was being victimized.
As the shooting progressed, the marriage of Gay (Gable) and Roslyn
(Monroe), which ran counter to the heartbreaking events in real life,
seemed bitterly ironic to the actors and crew: Gable, Miller's surrogate,
wins Monroe at the very moment that Miller loses her.

Linking Huston with her estranged husband and unaware of how
tolerant he'd been with her, Monroe lashed out at them: "I think that
Arthur's been complaining to Huston about everything he thinks is
wrong with me, that I'm mental or something. And that's why Huston treats me like an idiot."[11] Though Monroe was indeed mentally
and physically ill, looked slightly chubby in the swim scene, affect-
edly twitched her lips and had great trouble remembering her lines,
she gave a poignant portrayal of a wounded woman who understands
suffering. At the end of the film, furious about the imminent slaughter of the mustangs, Roslyn screams at Gay, *"I hate you!,"* which also
expresses Monroe's public condemnation of both Miller and his
script. Instead of using a traditional close-up, Huston filmed her in
a long shot as a tiny figure, standing alone amid the sun-charred and
eroded rocks of the lunar landscape. She rages not only against the
cowboys, who need all this wilderness to feel free, but also against the
hostile universe.

· V ·

The Misfits finished shooting on November 4, 1960, and the following day Gable had a heart attack. He entered a Los Angeles hospital and,
after a second massive attack almost two weeks later, died on November

16. The Hollywood columnist Hedda Hopper, who hated Huston's liberal politics, spread the false rumor that he had killed Gable. After his death his wife rather bitterly told the *Los Angeles Mirror-News:* "It wasn't the physical exertion that did it. It was the horrible tension, that eternal waiting, waiting, waiting." But Gable himself, who was paid $48,000 a week for working overtime, had said that he didn't mind waiting. He told Miller that *The Misfits* was the best picture he ever made. There were other casualties soon after the film was completed. Monroe never made another movie and, her career in ruins, died of a drug overdose in 1962. Clift made only one more picture—*Freud* with Huston—but also died of a heart attack, at the age of forty-five, in 1966.

Huston "was absolutely certain that Marilyn was doomed." He agreed with Miller that "she was incapable of rescuing herself or of being rescued by anyone else."[12] In 1960 he correctly predicted, "She'll be dead or in an institution within three years." Huston had always liked and respected Miller when they worked together on the film, but later on he turned against him. He strongly objected to Miller's portrayal of Monroe in his notorious play, *After the Fall*, written two years after her death. Huston seemed genuinely surprised when in 1977 his friend Marietta Tree recalled how badly Monroe had behaved during the making of the film:

My one jolt came when you told me about how awful
Marilyn Monroe was during *The Misfits*. I know it's true
because you observed it first hand. I wouldn't have believed
Billy Wilder & Tony Curtis [who'd complained about her
after making *Some Like It Hot*]—I know how easily a director
gets angry when an actress holds up production or makes
difficult demands. I wouldn't believe Arthur Miller because
I believe him to be fundamentally a light weight man—an
opportunist. He was trying to get a passport at the time he
met Marilyn & I'm sure his world fame at the marriage was
not a detriment to the trip he made almost at once. Also,
the horrid picture he drew of her in *After the Fall* was deeply
offensive to me, true or fabricated.

In an interview that same year Huston gave an incisive analysis of Marilyn's troubled history, her unstable personality and her betrayal by the studios:

> Here was a child, scarcely educated, her upbringing a pretty scattered proposition, ill-prepared for the role she was to play, that of a sex symbol. It takes background and character to stand the assault on that kind of career. Marilyn certainly had nothing good in the way of background. Little disasters had begun when she was still a child. . . . She had no mental preparation for what was to come, just a great innocence, a childishness, the kind of faith that was very often betrayed, too, because people began to exploit her, use her. The studio used her to its purposes, individuals tried to get her to serve their purposes . . . some carnal, some fiscal—and Marilyn was the victim of that system.[13]

His sympathy for the innocent victim obliterated his anger about her behavior on *The Misfits*.

EIGHTEEN

MYSTERIES OF THE MIND,

1962

· I ·

Huston's difficulties with the recalcitrant Jean-Paul Sartre and the broken-down Montgomery Clift when making *Freud: The Secret Passion* (1962) were worse than filming under fire in *The Battle of San Pietro,* the heat and disease of the jungle in *The African Queen* and *The Roots of Heaven,* the raging ocean storms in *Moby Dick,* the desert winds and wild mustangs in *The Misfits,* and the dangerous animals entering the ark in *The Bible.* As with *Moby Dick, The Roots of Heaven* and *The Bible,* Huston's ambitious attempt in *Freud* was far greater than his actual achievement, and the backstory of this film is more interesting than the film itself.

The studios were always looking for the next big subject, and the 1950s saw the rise of popular and fashionable interest in the father of psychoanalysis. The challenge of making the ideas of one of the seminal thinkers of the century available to a wide audience appealed to Huston, and *Freud* was one of the earliest films with a psychoanalytic theme. He knew very little about Freud when he first considered the project, though his aunt Margaret had sent her husband to Freud to be analyzed and "cured" of his homosexuality.

Like Huston's wartime documentary *Let There Be Light, Freud* showed the effect of trauma on the human mind, offered a simplified explanation of psychological processes, and emphasized the possibility of quasi-miraculous cures through drugs and hypnosis. The mentally ill soldier who exclaims "I can see" after treatment in *Let There Be Light* resembles Freud's patient who is cured of hysterical paralysis and declares, "I can walk." Huston himself did not believe it was possible to explore the unconscious. Commenting on his own nightmares about the war, he wrote, "We really don't know what goes on beneath the surface." Nevertheless, he saw the dramatic potential of stories about the repression and revelation of traumatic memories. In an interview to publicize the picture, he alluded to its subtitle and thematic prologue and melodramatically called the movie "a reminder of all unpleasant memories carefully forgotten. *Freud* is the image leading [the audience] down into the hell of their own secret passions." Publication in 1953–57 of a major three-volume biography of Freud by his devoted disciple, Ernest Jones, renewed Huston's interest in this subject.

When looking for a writer, Huston went right to the top and sought out the French philosopher Jean-Paul Sartre. Then at the height of his fame, Sartre (like Freud) had a profound influence on twentieth-century thought. The author of *Being and Nothingness* (1943) and many novels and plays, Sartre went on to win—and refuse—the Nobel Prize for Literature in 1964. Huston was attracted to Sartre's ethic of action and his belief that every individual is "condemned to be free," that he is responsible for his decisions and that his choices authenticate his existence. In November 1946, after completing *Let There Be Light,* Huston directed Sartre's play *No Exit* in New York, boldly introducing Existentialism to America when few people had even heard of it.

Huston's direction of the play did not meet with Sartre's approval and foreshadowed their conflicts when they began to work on *Freud.* Paul Bowles, the translator, wrote that Sartre was angry with Huston for tampering with his text and treating it like a screenplay that could be constantly revised: "Sartre was annoyed because I was unable to keep the director of *No Exit* from changing the script. . . . He sent telegrams of protest from Paris before we opened, and I was obliged to send back replies that were dictated by John Huston. His anger should have been directed against John, not me."[1] Huston violently opposed the changes the studios made to *his* films. But in his autobiography Bowles revealed how Huston justified the changes he made to Sartre's play:

> John wanted to particularize the references made to his
> past life by the male character upon his arrival in hell; by
> substituting political for metaphysical motivations he hoped
> to enliven the argument for the American public, which
> he considered generally incapable of appreciating the play's
> existentialist basis. . . . Sartre got wind of what was afoot
> and sent me a cable of protest from Paris. John's opinion,
> however, was that Sartre was surrounded by busybodies who
> hoped to sabotage the American production. He believed
> that he was clarifying the play rather than weakening it. Very
> likely the drama was made more immediately interesting to
> a great portion of the New York public by being presented
> in this way.

No Exit contains three characters, who know each other all too well, trapped in an ugly hotel room. They gradually learn that they are in fact in hell, forever doomed to judge each other as well as themselves, and that, in Sartre's famous line, "hell is other people." Huston's version, with the French actor Claude Dauphin in the leading role, had a poor reception. "The critics were confounded by it," Huston said. "They thought it was just another French triangle play." But the most influential critic, Brooks Atkinson of the *New York Times,* praised Huston's evocative direction and the powerful acting he inspired: "Inside a vividly claustrophobic setting . . . one man and two women faced one another in hell. They were looking to one another for help. But there was no help. They were doomed to confront one another eternally. In the existential philosophy of Sartre, every person is responsible to himself and can expect nothing from other people. *No Exit* was ruthlessly staged by John Huston and acted with great vehemence and bitterness."[2] Despite the favorable reviews, the static and intellectual succès d'estime closed after four weeks.

· II ·

The failure of *No Exit* in New York did not change Huston's mind about Sartre's genius, and he failed to notice that Sartre's novels lacked dramatic power. His first meeting with the unattractive literary lion did not shake his confidence. His lover Suzanne Flon knew Sartre from the French theater and had introduced them in Paris in 1952 when Huston was making *Moulin Rouge*. He found Sartre physically repulsive and in his autobiography described him as "a little barrel of a man, and as ugly as a human being can be. His face was both bloated and pitted, his teeth were yellowed and he was wall-eyed." Sartre's biographer called his mésalliance with Huston "a perfect Kafkaesque play, far more absurd than *No Exit* and *The Misfits* combined." Huston paid him $25,000 to write the *Freud* script, and each was completely mistaken about the other. Sartre assumed that Huston was an expert on Freud, while Huston believed that Sartre, one of the leading minds in Europe, had read deeply in psychology and was intimately acquainted with Freud's works. In fact, Sartre was not really interested in him and had only a superficial knowledge of the Viennese sage.

When Sartre came to Huston's mansion in Ireland for ten days in October 1959 to work on the script, they discovered another intellectual gap. Huston did not speak or read French and Sartre's English was . . . nonexistent. Not to be outdone by Huston's harem, Sartre brought along his Jewish-Algerian mistress, Arlette Elkaïm, who was thirty years younger and served as his interpreter and secretary. (Later on she became his legally adopted daughter and editor of his posthumous works.) After each meeting she typed the English translation of Sartre's notes and suggestions. The visit was brief but excruciating for both men. Sartre sent frequent reports to Simone de Beauvoir, his senior mistress and intellectual companion back in Paris, detailing his host's bizarre behavior and his own snobbish and bewildered reaction to life in an Irish country house.

Their script conferences were interminable and unintelligible. Sartre spoke with such torrential rapidity that Huston, even with the aid of his own interpreter, could not follow what he was saying. Their failure to understand each other did not prevent Sartre from plunging ahead with astonishing energy and persistence. Contrasting his guest's vitality with his own weariness, Huston recalled his boredom and irritation: "He did not have any discipline. He would not even listen to what people [i.e., Huston] would tell him and would keep on writing and talking without getting tired. . . . Sometimes I'd leave the room in desperation—on the verge of exhaustion from trying to follow what he was saying; the drone of his voice followed me until I was out of earshot and, when I'd return, he wouldn't even have noticed that I'd been gone." But Sartre *did* notice, and thought Huston was very rude to leave suddenly and disappear for hours at a time. Huston continued his onslaught by condemning Sartre with Bogart's favorite nickname for Huston himself: "He is not in any way a joyful companion! He works with a single-mindedness that's impressive and frightening. . . . He was a bit of a *monster*, Sartre—a monster of the mind. . . . He proves unsuitable only because he has really no idea of what the film medium actually requires."[3] In fact, Sartre *did* know how to write a screenplay; in 1956 he had done *Les Sorcières (The Witches of Salem)*, an effective French version of Arthur Miller's *The Crucible*.

Sartre was even more of a mismatch than the unclubable Ray Bradbury had been on *Moby Dick*. Huston found him personally overbearing and intellectually secretive, more boring than brilliant. An impossible collaborator and uncongenial guest, Sartre was not, like almost everyone else, seduced by the aesthetic allure, lush landscape and sporting life at St. Clerans. He would have agreed with Oscar Wilde that foxhunting was "the unspeakable in full pursuit of the uneatable." His letters to de Beauvoir were savagely critical and unexpectedly funny. Not au courant about the sexual complexities of wives and mistresses at St. Clerans (he didn't mention Ricki Huston and their children), he scrutinized the scene with the jaded eye of a displaced boulevardier and isolated flâneur, lost in an alien landscape of endless green. He mocked Huston's choice of headgear and thought exercising his horse and pony (surely not a "prancing donkey") was a pointless and depressing activity: "My windows overlook a green prairie that seems to stretch for miles and miles. On the prairie, there are cows and a few horses, which our host, a cap on his head, rides every afternoon. He trots or gallops near his house followed by a small prancing donkey, which turns the ride into ridicule."

When Sartre's camera-eye scanned the drawing room, he zeroed in on the strange array of guests ("hell is other people"), whom the gracious host was pleased to embarrass or ignore:

> This is exactly what makes up the interior landscape of my boss, the great Huston. Ruins, abandoned houses, wastelands, marshes, a thousand traces of the human presence, but the man himself has left, I don't know where. . . . Almost every night he invites the strangest sort of guests: the richest heir in England, a rajah who is also an innkeeper (a big hotel in Kashmir), an Irish master of fox-hounds, an American producer, an English director. And he says *nothing* [significant] to them. Arlette and I came into the drawing room at a moment when Huston was chatting languidly to the master of hounds, a broadbacked young man with a red nose, *très* gentleman farmer. We were introduced and the "major" said that he didn't know French. Huston banged him on the shoulder and said, "Well, I'll leave you to practise your French," and went off leaving us there feeling stupid. Panic-stricken, the major rolled his eyes and finally said, "Churchill is funny when he speaks French." I said "Ha, Ha" and silence fell until we were called into dinner.

Huston enjoyed discomfiting people, and Sartre was bored by what he called their "shared solitude." Sartre felt existence at St. Clerans was superficially jolly but really quite moribund, and lapsed into Freudian expressions: "What a business! Dear, oh, dear! what a business! Such systematic lying here. Everyone with their complexes, ranging from masochism to savagery. But don't imagine we're in hell. More like a vast cemetery. Everybody dead, with frozen complexes. So little life—so very, very little."

The famous Huston charm failed to seduce old Jean-Paul. He ignored the art treasures in the individually named and decorated rooms, which he called "identical," and shifted from the defects of the grand house to those of its imperious master. He emphasized Huston's sudden withdrawals, his vanity, his Byronic melancholy, his inability to concentrate on their work and his lord-of-the-manor persona. Taking Huston literally, he described him as simply vacuous:

> Huston used an odd expression to describe his "unconscious," when speaking of Freud: "In mine, there's nothing." And the tone made his meaning clear; nothing *any longer*, not even any old, unmentionable desires. A big void. You can just imagine how easy it is to get him to work. He shuns thought because it makes him sad. We'll all be together in some smoking-room, we'll all be talking, and then suddenly in mid-discussion he'll disappear. Very lucky if he's seen again before lunch or dinner. . . .
>
> Through this immensity of identical rooms, a great Romantic, melancholic and lonely, aimlessly roams. Our friend Huston is absent, aged, and literally unable to speak to his guests. . . .
>
> Huston isn't even sad, he is empty, except for those moments of childish vanity when he wears a red tuxedo, or rides one of his horses, or reviews his paintings or orders his workers about. It is impossible to keep his attention for more than five minutes at a time: he is unable to keep on working, refuses to think. . . . His emptiness is purer than death.[4]

There clearly wasn't sufficient air in the room for these two gigantic egos who deeply loathed each other. They got on each other's nerves, built up a venomous resentment and were headed for certain disaster.

Before going to Ireland, Sartre had written a ninety-five-page synopsis that included a detailed but de trop discussion of the costumes, lighting and camera angles. The film, which generally follows Sartre's outline, dramatizes Freud's discoveries from 1885 to 1890, when he was between twenty-nine and thirty-four years old and recently married. It opens with his fateful decision to leave neurology, and portrays him as a kind of Sherlock Freud—the psychiatrist as detective—who explores the theory of the unconscious and develops the techniques of psychoanalysis. But in the movie Freud himself, more like a patient than a doctor, is ill. He discovers new ideas and methods in order to resolve his own conflicts, especially his repressed hostility to his overbearing father, and to cure himself of his own neurosis. Sartre's script ridicules those who oppose Freud and transforms the scholarly doctor into an Existential hero whose daring beliefs shock and threaten the medical establishment in Vienna. The validity of Freud's theories is never questioned.

Sartre then completed his film script and gave it to Huston, who had it translated and suggested extensive revisions. Bradbury's original script of *Moby Dick* had been 1,200 pages long, but he had reduced it to a manageable 150 before giving it to Huston. Instead of making extensive cuts as requested, Sartre actually expanded his film script to 1,600 pages, which could have run to sixteen hours of film. Huston was also shocked to find many scenes with sensational material, which in 1962 could never be included in a commercial movie: prostitution, masturbation, homosexuality, child abuse, incest and a *mélange choisi* of sexual perversions.

In desperate need of help with this impossible script, Huston called in the fire brigade. Wolfgang Reinhardt (older brother of Gottfried, the producer of *The Red Badge of Courage*) and Charles Kaufman (his coauthor on *Let There Be Light*) reduced the script by seven-eighths to 200 pages. Huston then sent it to Sartre, who'd returned to Paris, and asked for still more radical changes. Sartre made some revisions, but then grew bored with the whole project. Reinhardt and Kaufman then rewrote Sartre's script. Huston, by now desperate for cash, had to sign his financial interest in the picture over to Universal International. Sartre became furious at Huston's requests for rewrites, his loss of control over the script and the inevitable censorship.

On August 24, 1961, Sartre sent a telegram that took Huston, not used to being rejected by a coauthor, by surprise: "Am in complete disagreement with unrealized treatment and totally distorted solution. Am obliged to withdraw my name since I recognize nothing of the initial project." He followed this message up with a devastating seven-page letter that explained his reasons for accepting the commission and vented the grievances he'd expressed in his correspondence with de Beauvoir: "I only realized your near total ignorance of the subject in St. Clerans, when it was too late. Why did I let myself make this mistake?—because I liked you, because the subject pleased me, because I needed money. . . . You never collaborated with me, in this work, you have only destroyed and you have contributed nothing. . . . You were negative, absent, with inner resistances which gave you the appearance of laziness."

In an angry telegram to Reinhardt (not Sartre), Huston angrily condemned Sartre's abandonment of the project and blasted his former coauthor: "I am shocked at such a demonstration of irresponsibility by a foremost authority on ethics. You might inquire of him how a manuscript of some four times the length of *Ben-Hur*'s could be reduced without considerable rewriting. You and I undertook to do what Sartre in all conscience should have done himself, but instead of giving us sincere thanks and an offer of his ready aid, he dismisses such obligations with a few unconscionable words."[5] But it was surely illogical of Huston to expect a philosopher to behave more morally than anyone else, or to be grateful for what he felt was the mutilation and ruin of his work. Since Sartre's name had little commercial value and they heartily disliked each other, it's odd that Huston regretted rather than rejoiced in his departure.

In an interview with the English playwright and critic Kenneth Tynan, Sartre acknowledged that his script was far too long and explained his ambitious attempt to dramatize Freud's exploration of the human mind:

> Except in construction, the final script has little resemblance
> to what I wrote. The fault is partly mine, and partly Freud's.
> My scenario would have been impossible to shoot; it would
> have lasted seven or eight hours. As you know, one can make

a film four hours long if it has to do with Ben Hur, but a
Texas audience won't sit through four hours of complexes.
Hence the script was cut down to ninety minutes or so.
I haven't seen the final version, and I don't know if I shall
leave my name on it; that depends on the contract.

However, what we tried to do—and this is what
interested Huston especially—was to show Freud not when
his theories had made him famous, but at the time, around
the age of thirty, when he was utterly wrong; when his ideas
had led him into hopeless error. You know that at one point
he seriously believed that what caused hysteria was fathers
raping their daughters. We begin in that period, and follow
his career up to the discovery of the Oedipus complex.

That, for me, is the most enthralling time in the life of a
great discoverer—where he seems muddled and lost, but has
the genius to collect himself and put everything in order.

Despite all the emotional conflict and chaos, the final script *did* follow
Sartre's essential outline and interpretation. In his autobiography, Huston generously gave credit to the uncredited writer and said, "Much of
what Sartre had done was in our version—in fact, it was the backbone
of it. In some scenes the dialogue was left intact."[6]

· III ·

Sartre, rather surprisingly, thought Marilyn Monroe was the finest
actress alive. Despite the agonizing trouble he'd had with her in *The Misfits,* Huston was bravely willing to take her on again. After many years
of psychoanalysis (which would lead to her suicide rather than to her
recovery), Monroe wanted, appropriately enough, to appear as Freud's
principal patient. But she withdrew when Freud's analyst-daughter
Anna, the mentor of Monroe's analyst Ralph Greenson, did not want
the picture to be made. She was afraid that Freud might be portrayed
negatively and that popularizing his ideas would debase them. In her
magisterial condemnation of the project, Anna Freud (using the royal

our) wrote, "In our opinion neither historic nor scientific truth about the person, Sigmund Freud, or his work, can be conveyed by the film, contrary to the pretensions made by the producers."

Following this commandment from on high, Monroe regretfully told Huston, in an illogical letter, composed with stilted formality and probably dictated by Greenson, "I have it on good authority that the Freud family does not approve of anyone working on a picture of the life of Freud—so I wouldn't want to be part of it, first because of his great contribution to humanity and secondly, my personal regard for his work. Thank you for offering me the part of 'Anna O.' and I wish you the best in this and all other endeavors. Yours, Marilyn."[7] The twenty-year-old English actress Susannah York, who'd played teenagers in three previous pictures, secured the role of Anna O., now called Cecily, and earned $70,000. Wary of the legal minefield, Huston was very careful not to portray any living member of the Freud family or to use any material copyrighted by Freud or by Ernest Jones. All the characters in the movie were either fictitious or based on dead people.

Throughout his career Huston had often helped personal friends who needed money—Claud Cockburn in *Beat the Devil,* John Kilbracken in *Moby Dick,* Friedrich von Ledebur in *The Roots of Heaven*—as well as actors, like John Garfield in *We Were Strangers,* who were accused of being Communists and blacklisted. He now hired Larry Parks to play Freud's sympathetic colleague Dr. Joseph Breuer. After his success in *The Jolson Story* (1946) with Huston's ex-wife Evelyn Keyes, Parks had been summoned by the House Un-American Activities Committee and forced, against his will, to name names. Despite his cooperative testimony, he was blacklisted and dropped by Columbia. Parks was stiff and unconvincing as Breuer, and his undiluted American accent jarred with all the others, who seemed more Central European. *Freud* was his last film. Freud's devoted wife, Martha, was played by Susan Kohner, the daughter of Huston's agent, who often asked him, "Do you have anything suitable for my little Suzy?"

Shot in Munich and Vienna, the picture had mostly American actors, English cameramen and German crew. It took five months to complete and cost $4 million—double the original estimate of time and money. For the part of Freud, Huston considered Marlon Brando (often his first choice), the Australian Peter Finch, the Englishmen Albert Finney and Peter Sellers, and the Austrian Maximilian Schell. Montgomery Clift, who'd played a neurosurgeon and psychiatrist who cures Elizabeth Taylor in Tennessee Williams' *Suddenly Last Summer* (1959) and had performed well in *The Misfits*, finally got the part and earned $200,000.

Though Huston was a sexual adventurer and sophisticated man of the world, he had a deep-rooted puritanical streak and felt uneasy with homosexuals. He could accept and work with flamboyant and obvious gays like Truman Capote and Tennessee Williams, but was deeply troubled by covert, guilt-ridden and tormented homosexuals like Monty Clift. An incident that occurred when Clift was visiting St. Clerans, between finishing *The Misfits* and starting *Freud*, shocked Huston to the core and caused a rift between them. Huston opened Clift's guest-room door without knocking and was horrified to discover Clift's French lover, Jean, in bed with him. When they met in Munich, Huston asked Reinhardt, " 'Did you know this about Monty?' 'Yes, of course I knew,' Reinhardt said. 'I think it's disgusting! Why didn't you tell me?' " It's hard to believe that Huston could be so naïve, but it seems that he really was. In any case, Huston, who imported many mistresses to St. Clerans while his wife was in residence, was highly offended and felt his house had been polluted. Ignoring the fact that his wife and children were safely sequestered a half-mile away in the Little House, he told Clift's biographer: "The incident seemed trashy—I felt Monty had insulted me. It was messy. I wish he'd considered my family and how I felt about it. I can't say I'm able to deal with homosexuals."

Huston's attitude toward Clift was similar to the disdain that Bogart (Sam Spade) felt for the effeminate Peter Lorre (Joel Cairo) in *The Maltese Falcon*, but after *Freud* Huston became more tolerant. He would sympathetically portray both the repressed and the overt homosexuals (played by Marlon Brando and Zorro David) in *Reflections in a Golden Eye* (1967) and the homosexual transvestite (George Sanders) in drag—knitting and picking up male prostitutes in squalid bars in

The Kremlin Letter (1970). Anthony Perkins, another covert homosexual, would appear in *The Life and Times of Judge Roy Bean* (1972). Huston later said the "funny thing about Clift [was that] he only propositioned men when he was drunk. There was nothing abnormal about him when he was sober. I found him a delight to work with, which is why I put him in *Freud*."[8]

Huston had a lot of experience working with actors who were complete wrecks and found it difficult to remember their lines, and his film sets were partly rehab centers. Errol Flynn in *The Roots of Heaven*, Monroe in *The Misfits* and Clift in *Freud* all had grave problems with drink and drugs. But Clift had radically deteriorated since *The Misfits,* and his poor health, eye troubles, psychological problems, alcoholism and addiction to pills caused expensive delays on *Freud*. Clift told friends that "he wasn't afraid of working with Huston—he could take care of himself. . . . [Clift] disliked his game playing, his false heartiness; but he admired his relish for life." But Huston, afraid that Clift's homosexuality would affect his performance and provoke bad publicity if Freud were portrayed as gay, began to lay down impossible rules for the conduct of Clift's private life: "Monty was not to behave in a homosexual manner, or to have any kind of homosexual relationships while he worked on the film. He was to behave in a normal manner. He was not to drink or take pills. He was not to have dependent friendships with older women." In other words, Monty must not be Monty.

Three important differences between *The Misfits* and *Freud* made conditions much more difficult for Clift. The close-ups of his smashed-in and badly scarred face after his near-fatal car accident of 1957 were appropriate for a rodeo rider, but not—even when partly covered by a beard—for the intellectual Freud. The dialogue was also quite different in these two movies. In the contemporary western, Clift was at ease with the idiomatic talk. But Freud spoke a new scientific language with turn-of-the-century cadences. In one typical speech, an uneasy mixture of the ideas of Jean-Jacques Rousseau and John Calvin, Freud observes: "Cecily, you are not guilty. Or if you are, your guilt is shared by every human being. The innocent is born into a world in which it cannot help but lose its innocence. Every child is foredoomed to become a sinner. I sinned too. I dreamed of killing my father." Lastly, neither Huston nor Clift was aware that his vision was defective.

Huston later summarized the formidable obstacles he'd faced with Clift and exonerated the actor, who'd become a battered version of his former self: "I shied away from him. He was, or had been, a wonderful actor, but I got the remnants of him, not the man himself. He was pretty shredded by the time he came to me. The troubles I had with him were not his fault. He was just not capable any more. The accident to his face had done great interior damage to him. He had been very good in *The Misfits,* but he had very few lines in it, mostly colloquialisms, and I was taken by his performance and thought he could do *Freud.*"

But Clift couldn't memorize the more complex and elaborate dialogue. As Huston recalled, he tried to do everything possible to help Clift remember his lines, "We had dialogue written all over the set, on the back of doors, walls, on boards, in front of the camera. But it soon became obvious that on top of everything else Monty really *couldn't* see—it was macabre." When they finally discovered that Clift had cataracts that blurred his vision, he was sent to London to see his doctor, and as soon as the movie was completed he had an eye operation. Defending himself, Clift rightly said, "They kept changing the script on me. I'd go to bed knowing one set of lines and wake up to another whole new scene!" Other actors could deal with all these sudden changes; Clift, in his fragile condition, could not. Reinhardt agreed that "it was *terribly* hard for Monty to learn these rewrites given to him just hours before photography. Monty had already told John that he was a slow study. He was the sort of actor who needed to ponder and study; and, remember, these were complicated psychiatric terms. Some actors of Monty's stature would simply walk off the film if scripts were handed to them in that haphazard way."

Huston's treatment of Clift during the making of *Freud,* which several observers have called sadistic, is the most contentious episode in his entire professional career. In *Freud* Clift hurt his hands, just as he had in *The Misfits* when he mistakenly started a sequence without gloves and had to hold the mustang's rope with his bare hands until they were lacerated. His biographer Patricia Bosworth stated that in the cave-dream sequence in *Freud*, in which Clift is pulled by a rope, "Huston forced Monty to pass the rope through his hands without stopping, until by the ninth take his palms were raw and bleeding and he was in obvious pain." In his autobiography, Huston categorically denied this and blamed Clift for the self-inflicted injury: "After each shot, when I called 'Cut!' Monty proceeded to slide down the rope, holding tightly. In this way, he burned his hands horribly. . . . Monty's defenders have charged that I did this to him deliberately, going so far as to demand take after take while blood from Monty's hands streamed onto the rope. Unthinkable nonsense!"[10]

In later interviews Huston tried to clarify the situation and occasionally contradicted himself. He admitted that his attitude toward Clift was ambivalent but essentially hostile: "I liked him and detested him. His behavior was just so offensive. Belching and farting and, you know, stinking. He was awful, awful. I couldn't bear him." But he insisted that he had been gentle rather than cruel: "I was never kinder to anybody than I was to Clift. Sometimes I spoke harshly to him, but it was an attempt to awaken something in him. The combination of drugs, drink, and being homosexual was . . . just too much" for Clift. Frustrated by the actor, Huston admitted that he adopted a risky strategy to scare him into giving a better performance. In a dramatic event, in which he played actor as well as director, he "decided to stage a fight to frighten him into shaping up. I even considered using physical violence. I wasn't trying to destroy him. I wanted to save my movie! . . . Nothing worked. Finally I decided I would get rough with him. I went to his dressing room, opened the door and slammed it behind me so hard that a mirror fell from the wall and shattered, showering glass shards all over the room. . . . I wanted him to feel my anger. . . . I was trying to scare him, thinking fear would do something."[11] Though this violent and frightening treatment was anything but "kind," Huston believed that he was attempting to help Clift and save the picture, that his behavior was constructive rather than cruel.

The fractious cast and crew split into pro-Clift and pro-Huston factions. The former felt Huston was treating Clift in a brutal manner, terrifying him for not learning his lines and torturing him on the rope until his hands bled. The latter, mostly the production crew, felt it was all Clift's fault for failing to learn his lines, demanding script revisions, and destroying himself with drugs and drink. To resolve this crisis, Huston called in an eminent British psychiatrist, Sir David Stafford-Clark (future author of *What Freud Really Said,* 1967), to treat the troubled actor who played the troubled psychiatrist in the movie. As soon as Stafford-Clark arrived, Clift's partisans bombarded him with complaints about Huston's treatment of the actor. Despite two visits, Stafford-Clark did not offer his professional opinion and was not much help.

Robert LaGuardia, a biographer of Clift who defended the actor and attacked Huston, wrote that "Monty's friends thought him extremely courageous in his determination to finish what was so obviously an impossible film. . . . Three or four times, he broke down completely and rushed off the set sobbing." Since Huston insisted on long takes and Clift couldn't remember his lines, they kept repeating this humiliating process. LaGuardia argued that Huston completely ruined Clift: "The filming of *Freud* destroyed whatever was left of Monty's life. When the five months of celluloid grotesqueries were done, Monty was a walking cadaver." Speaking of Angela Allen, LaGuardia got carried away and claimed that "for years, she had been Huston's confidante and script girl, but after *Freud* she announced bitterly that she would never work with him again."[12] In fact, she *did* work with him again on two more films. Clift made only one more movie before dying of a heart attack.

· IV ·

In a recent interview the principled, strong-minded Susannah York, who also clashed with Huston, threw some light on this controversial episode. She said that *Freud* had been a big step up in her nascent career, and that she had been flattered, proud and thrilled to appear in the film. She gave Huston enormous credit for being perceptive enough to see her potential, pick her out of nowhere and realize that she could play such a complex part. She was then unfamiliar with psychology and "afraid of making a fool of myself, and so I had to learn quickly. I had lived a sheltered life. *Hypnosis* was a new word to me. I didn't know anything about Freud or the dark, labyrinthine corners of the soul. I must have known them instinctively, of course, but plunging into them was another matter."

York was very fond of Clift and loved acting with him. She admired his perfectionism, his passion for doing the very best work and the way he encouraged her to realize her full potential. After dinner together, they would rehearse their scenes until very late at night. She would get up at 5 A.M., after only a few hours of sleep, and was not vain or concerned about her appearance on camera. Both she and Clift struggled with the infinite number of rewrites, which in her view did *not* improve the film. It was especially difficult to relearn, for the second or third time, what already had been learned. As they struggled together, she became very protective, even a bit maternal, about him.

In a rare criticism of an actress, Huston called York a "spoiled young lady, and I had difficulty with her." He expected the novice to be obedient and was furious when she stood up to him. She compared Clift to a steel rapier who could bend but still remain strong, while Huston, though an overwhelming figure, seemed like a marble column with an awful hollowness inside.[13] Huston was completely immersed in the film and at the same time strangely detached from it: "During my scenes, John would be doodling and drawing. He didn't seem to be focused. He'd removed himself, and I found that terribly destroying for me." Huston preferred to listen rather than to watch, which upset many actors. York thought that he was wrong, even stupid, to keep his head down during filming and not watch Clift's takes, not look at his work. She was puzzled and critical when Huston kept saying, for no apparent reason, "Do it again, do it again, do it again." She was upset and angered by his bullying, believed he was unjust and savage, and felt that he forced people to be for or against him, which caused a lot of dissension on the set.

The breaking point for York came when Huston, mocking Clift's defective vision, enraged her by cruelly remarking, "We'll form a club to get a Seeing Eye dog for Monty." Like Ray Bradbury, a short and slight man who finally exploded and punched Huston while working on the script of *Moby Dick*, York suddenly went berserk, threw herself at Huston and—taking both of them by surprise—hit him with her fists. When she returned to her hotel, she found her room filled with vases and vases of red roses. She thanked Huston for the flowers, but couldn't accept his apology. She was not aggressive, but had a reactive temper. She was very much in awe of Huston and had not begun the film in a fighting mode, but she was forced into it by the fearful and disruptive conditions he'd created.

Huston believed that "tearing down an actor's ego doesn't work." Why, then, would he alienate half the cast and crew, as well as the leading actors, by bullying and frightening the fragile and vulnerable Clift? York answered, "Why, indeed? I do not know." In response to Huston's assertion that he was trying to get a good performance out of Clift, she said he could have gotten a fine performance (as he had with Monroe) without being cruel. She was adamant that Huston's defense was untrue: there were too many instances of his unnecessary cruelty. He would not allow Clift to wear gloves, and she herself saw that his hands were torn and bleeding. But there was no doubt in her mind that Huston and Clift "perversely played to each other's dark side."[14] Both director and actor were complicit: Huston's sadism was a perfect match for Clift's masochism. Huston wanted to punish Clift for his homosexuality and Clift felt he deserved punishment for being a homosexual. Like Bogart in *The African Queen*, Gregory Peck in *Moby Dick* and Robert Mitchum in *Heaven Knows, Mr. Allison*, who were all treated roughly, Clift also wanted to show Huston that he could take it. In some bizarre, inexplicable way, Huston's strategy succeeded. His rough treatment of Clift *did* make his eyes more expressive and produced a superb performance. As another British psychiatrist observed, Clift's Freud broke with the traditional portrayal of doctors in fiction and film. He "is not mature, reassuring and paternal, but instead [like the patients he's trying to cure] neurotic, jittery and curmudgeonly."

Commenting on Huston's direction, Woody Allen observed, "Whatever he was doing, he was doing right. If imposing himself on the actors was how he got those performances, then I have to say that that was the perfect way for him to work, because the performances in Huston's movies are often superb."[15]

York said there was an awful lot of suffering on the set, but she wouldn't have missed that tense, disturbing experience. She later recalled, "I was shattered at the end of *Freud*. It took me more than a year to recover my nerve, and I'm not sure I've really done so yet. *Freud* was an incredible experience, though. And it did more to make me understand myself—as a person and as an actress—than anything I have ever done. At times I really hated it. After violent arguments with John Huston, I would [like Clift] go to my dressing room in floods of tears." After considering this episode, Huston disingenuously concluded, "Apart from Montgomery Clift and—through association—Susannah York, I don't think I've ever had a conflict with an artist—certainly not an important conflict, or one that persisted."[16] Huston certainly got on well with most of the greatest actors of his time, from Bogart to Brando, but he did have serious conflicts with John Wayne in *The Barbarian and the Geisha*, Burt Lancaster in *The Unforgiven* and Marilyn Monroe in *The Misfits*, and he would clash with George C. Scott and Michael Parks in *The Bible*, Sylvester Stallone in *Victory* and Anthony Andrews in *Under the Volcano*. His conflict with Clift was more subtle and complex, more traumatic and disturbing, more destructive but also more positive, than those he had with stronger stars.

· V ·

Freud opens with a rather pedantic prologue spoken by Huston, whose voiceover continues throughout the film to express Freud's thoughts when he makes a startling discovery. Like the old man in Hemingway's "A Clean, Well-Lighted Place," Freud is "with those acquainted with the dark." Alluding to Christ's harrowing of hell and the description of Christ in Matthew 5:14 as "the light of the world," Huston and Reinhardt state, this is "the story of Freud's descent into a region almost as black as hell itself—man's unconscious—and how he let in the light." As Freud faces fierce opposition from his medical colleagues, Dr. Theodore Meynert publicly ridicules him after his lecture and tells him that the unconscious, like the symbolic scorpions that Meynert keeps confined in a box in his office, "must be kept locked up in darkness." The film's narrative technique, alternating conventional interiors with exotic dream sequences, maintains the contrast between dark and light, unconscious and conscious.

The script is surprisingly forthright about Freud's theories of infant sexuality. At the same time, the major speeches convey their meaning through intellectual allusions, whose heavyweight style is more like Sartre's and Reinhardt's than like Huston's lean, fast-paced scripts. After first opposing Freud, Meynert becomes an ally, calls him to his deathbed and urges him to continue his bold research. In a brief but densely packed speech—whose allusions are far beyond the comprehension of the movie's audience—Meynert hints at Joseph Conrad, St. George, Faust, Virgil and Dante: "Go to the heart of our darkness and hunt out the dragon. . . . If you lack the strength, make a pact with the devil. What a splendid thing to descend to hell and light your torch from its fires."

Susannah York plays Cecily Koertner, who suffers at various times from a variety of psychosomatic illnesses: hysterical paralysis, false pregnancy and temporary blindness. Tense and sickly, she believes that her father has sexually molested her. She is jung and easily freudened, and plays Beethoven's Appassionata Sonata when Freud visits her. In one of the most effective scenes, Cecily dreams she's in a hospital in which whores are dressed in nurses' uniforms (though Catholic hospitals in Austria would have been staffed with nuns, not lay nurses) and sit in suggestive poses with their legs spread apart. Policemen, who seem to be investigating venereal diseases, take the place of doctors. Freud's hypnosis reveals two of Cecily's suppressed memories: the sight of her beloved father soliciting prostitutes and the revelation that he died not in a hospital, but in a brothel. (Cecily's father liked to go driving, but put the whores before the cart.) After several visits, Freud discovers that Cecily's symptoms were caused by the guilt she feels about her repressed sexual desires. Toward the end of the picture, Freud tells his wife that his patient has transferred her own anguished feelings to her father: "Cecily claimed that her father seduced her! False! It was she who wanted him! And it was not a memory that she had repressed! No! It was a fantasy!"

In the final thematic sequence, Freud once again lectures a hostile audience—a pedantic way for the movie to explain his basic psychological principles. He compares benighted mankind to the aged Oedipus in Colonus at the end of Sophocles' trilogy: "It is in the Oedipus Complex, the child's fixation on the parent of the opposite sex, that infantile eroticism reaches its climax. Each human being is confronted with the task of overcoming this complex within himself. If he succeeds, he will be a whole individual; if he fails, he will become a neurotic and himself wander forever, blind and homeless."

The film closes with Freud's visit to his father's grave. After acknowledging and accepting his own sexual jealousy about his mother, Freud is finally reconciled with him. His speech begins with a classical Greek maxim, and alludes both to Apocalypse 6:17 ("the beginning of wisdom") and to Ecclesiastes 1:2 ("all is vanity"): "Know thyself. Two thousand years ago these words were carved on the temple at Delphi: Know thyself. They're the beginning of wisdom. In them lies the single hope of victory over man's oldest enemy: his vanity. This knowledge is now within our grasp. Will we use it? Let us hope." Freud finally performs a son's duty to his father—"the eyes shall be closed"—at the same time that he opens the eyes of the living to the mysteries of the mind.

· VI ·

In *Freud* Huston used visual allusions to paintings and films in order to represent the abstract principles of psychology. To achieve this aesthetic effect in the sequences portraying Freud's studies in Paris, Huston carefully reproduced the appearance, costumes and setting of the figures in Pierre-André Brouillet's painting *A Clinical Lecture at the Salpêtrière* (1887). In this home for aged and mentally afflicted women,

Freud's teacher, Dr. Jean-Martin Charcot—surrounded by students, interns, hospital staff, journalists and politicians—demonstrates that the symptoms of hysteria are as real as those of organic disease. His patient is the classically hysterical Blanche, her blouse lowered in a striking décolletage, swooning into the arms of an astonished doctor. The black and white photography and heavy, murky Biedermeyer interiors suggest the oppressive conventions that Freud's work contravened.

The cinematographer Douglas Slocombe revealed that Huston enhanced the mood by combining two distinct photographic modes. Huston wanted "an overall style, and within that two separate styles, one for the dreams and one for the flashbacks, which would be so different that the audience always knew where they were. I used very sharp photography for the main part of the film, to give the clarity of steel etchings, and help the period feeling. For flashbacks I shot through a glass plate, treated to fuzz out all the details." The dream scenes were influenced by German Expressionist films of the 1920s, by Luis Buñuel's *Un Chien Andalou* (1928) and by Ingmar Bergman's *Wild Strawberries* (1957). The philosopher Roger Scruton gave a fine description of Bergman's dreamlike techniques, which Huston adopted in *Freud:* "The images, often grainy, with sharply foregrounded details, leave many objects lingering like ghosts in the out-of-focus hinterland. Things, like people, are saturated with the psychic states of their observers, drawn into the drama by the camera which endows each detail with a consciousness of its own."[17]

After finishing the film, Huston faced still more difficulties with the censors, the studio and the critics. The censors, in a comic attempt at repression that Freud himself would have appreciated, told Universal International that the picture was "too clinically lurid" and insisted they "reduce the words 'sexual' and 'sexuality' to avoid the impression that the treatment of this theme is somehow saturated with sex." Huston cut half an hour, reducing it to two hours and fifty minutes, and felt he had vastly improved it. Considering the intellectual content, pedantic speeches and lack of drama, the preview was surprisingly favorable. More than 200 out of 226 responses were "good," "very good" or "excellent." Nevertheless, the studio panicked and cut Huston's version by another half hour, to two hours twenty minutes, without regard for either logic or continuity.

The critics who saw the studio's cut were more severe than the preview audience. The habitually caustic John Simon was restrained but discouraging. Noting the film's ponderous quality, he said, "Huston and his scenarists have made conscientious efforts in the direction of integrity. . . . The film is respectful and, Lord knows, serious." *Newsweek* unkindly compared it to "a movie about Bach with a musical score by Dimitri Tiomkin." The more highbrow *Films and Filming,* alluding to Huston's screenplay about another pioneering Germanic physician, *Dr. Ehrlich's Magic Bullet,* called it "a period piece in every sense of the word. . . . [It] looks and sounds exactly like a belated addition to the Warner waxworks of the late thirties."[18]

When the picture was completed, the Fireman's Insurance Company paid Universal $373,500 for the cost of Clift's illnesses and absences. He was responsible for $112,500, or thirty percent of this payment—more than half his original fee. Huston, ever the gambling man, had changed his deal with the studio from a safe percentage of the gross to a risky share of the future profits. But he was always unlucky with money and, after the drastic cuts and poor reviews, he lost his bet.

NINETEEN

LOVERS,

1962

· I ·

Huston was continually on the lookout for his next movie project and always alive to the prospect of a new romance. He was not only a fascinating and charming companion, but also had a lot to offer. He led a glamorous life, with access to celebrities and movie stars, and many young women were keen on a film career. He traveled in luxury to exotic places, where he would often invite a likely young lady. There was always the chance to visit St. Clerans, or even more exciting locales around the world. Huston surrounded himself with women. His wife, Ricki, reigned at St. Clerans but did not live in the main house; short-term lovers could visit him in Ireland or join him on location; an intensely loyal cadre of secretaries followed and invariably fell in love with him; and long-term lovers in Europe, Mexico and America could be visited or summoned from time to time. Like Alec Guinness in *The Captain's Paradise* (1953), he had various women in different locations who adored him. But unlike the movie character, he had no need to dissemble and quite enjoyed the imbroglio when his mistresses collided with one another.

In liaisons, Huston was a kind and generous lover, as well as an attentive, unaggressive and subtle seducer. In a more protracted affair he remained interested in his lover, valued her opinions, solicited her ideas and enjoyed her correspondence. He had the gift of making his romantic partner feel that she was the only woman in the world—until she found out otherwise. He was usually able to maintain friendly relations once the affair had ended. Many people who knew him felt he was essentially a cold person, despite his charm, and when in love he seemed to remain somewhat detached. Like many of Huston's friends, the mild-mannered and uxorious Ray Bradbury envied his bacchanalian life at St. Clerans. While Ricki was safely tucked away on the estate, Huston might fly to Paris to spend a weekend with Suzanne Flon, go out riding for a plein air frolic with Betty O'Kelly (she of the nude portrait), preside over a dinner table with a pretty new guest, or remain sequestered in his office with one of his obliging secretaries, Gladys Hill, Jeanie Sims or Lorrie Sherwood.

Though Betty would sulk with hurt feelings and Gladys would weep in her room, Huston was usually quite adept at managing his harem. But his numerous lovers were also intensely jealous and fought, sometimes violently, for his favor. Lorrie Sherwood, who'd worked for Howard Hawks, had the qualities that Huston admired in a woman. Sam Jaffe's wife called her "very bright, very attractive, and mad about John." In about 1959, when her rival secretary Jilda Smith tried to bogart her turf, Lorrie threatened her, screaming, "I'm here with my Johnny, and I love my Johnny and he loves me and I don't want you here. If you don't leave I'm going to kill you now and then kill him later." After a terrible row in Mexico, Lorrie attacked Huston with a knife and tried to cut him up because she was "outraged at his alleged infidelity." Invulnerable as always, he escaped injury, as he did when Suzanne's lover shot at him, and greatly enjoyed provoking her operatic bloodlust.

· II ·

Freud brought three new women and a second son into Huston's life. There are many contradictory accounts of the character of Monty Clift and of Huston himself, but there's remarkable unanimity about the personality of Gladys Hill (born in 1920), who was very close to him from the making of *Freud* until the end of her life. Portraying Gladys in his novel about Huston, William Hamilton wrote, "Doris had been raised in dire, ignorant, West Virginia poverty. She was enormously proud of how meticulously she had erased every smudge of that gaunt, toothless, dirty, rickety past." His "secretary for twenty-seven years, she was plain, faithful, and hopelessly enamored of her employer." The intelligent and efficient Gladys had worked on *The Stranger* (1946) when Huston was writing that script, and had been Sam Spiegel's secretary until her marriage and move to Mexico in 1952. After her divorce, Huston asked her to come to Ireland and work for him "forever."

Anjelica remembered Gladys, a rather colorless figure with a mousy manner, as being "very mild, upstanding, kind, solemn. She had her wild side, too, but she was very West Virginian. She would laugh, but she was controlled. A good-hearted woman. Not ebullient, but she had personal pride."[1] Her wild side came out when she helped Billy Pearson smuggle art out of Mexico. Huston's adopted daughter, Allegra, described Gladys more poetically: "She was his moon, her orbit sometimes closer, sometimes farther, but always held by his gravity. She was ageless, as if she'd managed to keep the harshness of life at one remove, the way she'd kept the skin of her face untouched by the sun. Her severe hair and black-rimmed glasses were not designed to attract a man; she wore lipstick only because she would have been half dressed without it. There was something wraithlike about her paleness."

Stacy Keach, the star of *Fat City* (1972), remembered that Gladys anticipated Huston's moods and wishes, and was totally devoted to him. She was rewarded with her own flat above the stables at St. Clerans. Keach added that her pallor reminded him of "a ghost drifting in and out of the set," and she was actually mistaken for the ghost that haunted St. Clerans as she wandered through the halls of the manor house late at night. To the young Celeste Huston, she was Mrs. Danvers, the evil housekeeper hostile to the master's new wife in Daphne du Maurier's *Rebecca*. The actor John Hurt, who called Gladys "an *eminence*, not so *grise*," said you would not want to get on the wrong side of her.[2]

The indispensable Gladys, the steady element in Huston's chaotic life, remained with him through various wives, movies and medical crises. Quietly arranging all the practical details, she kept track of birthdays and sent presents, made his appointments and answered his letters, took care of his money and bought his art, typed his screenplays and eventually helped write them. Always there when needed, she respected, adored and was obsessed by Huston. He treated her as an equal, and she protected him as if he were a South American dictator. He slept with Gladys, at least at the beginning, acting on his belief that it would ensure her loyalty. He thought she expected sex, and when she fell in love with him, he obliged her. Eloise Hardt said Gladys gave her life to Huston, did everything possible for him and was perfectly happy to be his servant.

Gladys got screen credit as assistant to Huston in thirteen movies, from *Freud* to *Annie*. She had bit parts in *The Night of the Iguana* and *Wise Blood*, and acted with Huston as his secretary in *Winter Kills*. She collaborated with Chapman Mortimer on *Reflections in a Golden Eye*, and with Huston on *The Kremlin Letter* and *The Man Who Would Be King*. He always talked things over with Gladys when she was typing his scripts, and she eventually graduated from sounding board to coauthor. Both Walter Mirisch and Bayard Veiller agreed that her credits as script-writer were his beau geste for her long years of faithful service. When describing how they worked together, Gladys shifted from "John" to "Mr. Huston" and explained, "If we are adapting a novel, I will first break the novel down, scene by scene. I then memorize the book, so when John and I are discussing a scene, action or sequence, I can say, 'Remember, John, such and such happened.' . . . From there we talk about it and then I write it. I put in the description and the dialogue. Then I take it to Mr. Huston to read. And if it has to be redone, it's redone and we discuss it again."[3] Gladys loved Huston more than most of his women, and vainly hoped she would outlast all the others and finally capture him. But in 1981 she died unexpectedly of a heart attack in a New York hotel room.

· III ·

Huston met Anna van der Heide in 1961, when filming *Freud* in Munich, through her Los Angeles school friend Susan Kohner. Susan invited Anna to come down from Denmark (where she was then living) to visit her and introduced her to Huston. Born in Holland in 1937, the daughter of a Jewish mother and Gentile father, Anna came to America two years later. Her father was a Freudian psychoanalyst and named her after Freud's daughter. He joined the U.S. forces, treating pilots for shell shock during the war, and she was an air force brat on both coasts. After the war he practiced in Beverly Hills and analyzed Ava Gardner, James Dean and many other movie stars. She went to the Westlake School for Girls, Wellesley College and, after two years, the University of California at Berkeley. Shortly before meeting Huston she'd spent a year in Crete. Anna (who spoke Dutch and French) said that Huston, rather ashamed about never finishing high school, always wanted to be around intellectual and well-educated people. In 1961 she had seen very few American movies, had never heard of Huston and didn't know how famous he was. Her naïveté intrigued him, and he was also attracted to Anna's lovely Dutch features, her blond hair, blue eyes, high cheekbones, delicate nose and thin sensitive lips.

Anna—whose role in Huston's life has been completely unknown until now—recalled, "The first time we met, he asked me whether I'd like to play a role [Grete Hübner] in the film. He wanted someone who looked European but could speak English. It was just a very small part, a short scene with Monty Clift. I was one of the patients being hypnotized by Freud." When asked how she wound up in bed with Huston, she replied that it seemed to happen quite effortlessly. "I don't know exactly how he seduced other women. I don't even remember exactly how he seduced me except that he invited me to the 'wrap-up' party for *Freud*. I went to the party with him, came home with him, and before I knew it I was in his bed, and he invited me to spend the Christmas holiday at his home in Ireland."

Anna found life at St. Clerans intriguing. Ricki not only had to tolerate Huston's lovers, but also play the gracious hostess. Anna wrote that the beautiful Ricki, wearing a dark cape, "welcomed me to the house when I arrived after midnight on my flight from Munich. I was very naïve and didn't even know (or ask) if he was married. I didn't even know that she was John's wife. I'm sure *she* knew why I was there and what relationship I had with John. His elegant toilet boasted three wall-to-wall bookshelves crammed with his favorite reading: Conrad and Kipling, Hemingway and Sartre, Tennessee Williams and Carson McCullers. My room was quite gorgeous and, as I found out, in the closet there was a door that led through a secret corridor to John's bedroom. Hmmmm. He was a hedonist and sensualist who loved women and their bodies. I wasn't very experienced sexually. We had pretty straightforward missionary position love-making. He was always a gentleman. There was nothing kinky or untoward."

After leaving St. Clerans and returning to California, Anna asked John, in a letter of January 14, 1962, about her brief, hypnotic moment in *Freud*. She said that after enjoying her freedom and adventures in Europe, she was now troubled by her parents' divorce and her father's illness: "I haven't heard from you and I am so very anxious to know if that little scene came out as you wanted it. All I want to know is if you liked it. Beverly Hills is terrible. Life here with my family is complicated and at the moment very sad. I'm not too happy at all. I wish I could run away back to Europe but it's time for a needed sacrifice. I'm doing my best. With much love, Anna."

Their affair was intense for two years. Huston was then fifty-five, Anna twenty-four, but he did not seem thirty years older to her and, she said, "The gap in our ages didn't seem to make a difference. Although he told me that he was polygamous, when he was in the U.S. and with me, he was *with me*. He treated me well, was generous with money— always left me some when he went abroad. He appreciated me and respected me, and liked lying in bed and sketching me as I played the violin. I think my innocence and guilelessness made me attractive to him. We related well and had good conversations. I liked his practical jokes and capers, his nostalgia for the danger and excitement of World War II. I enjoyed listening to his stories of poker and horse racing, hunts and adventures in Africa, escapades and scandals on film sets."

Anna gave a lively description of the things they did together— Huston knew how to romance his lover—and of how she was able to assist him in his work: "When John played a cardinal in *The Cardinal* [1963], shot in Boston, I helped him with his lines and costume changes (there were 181 buttons on his priestly robes, we counted them). We also drove around Mexico City in search of pre-Columbian treasures,

and went marlin fishing on the tip of Baja California. We traveled to
Key West to visit Tennessee Williams, who was slightly terrified of
John's 'macho-ness,' and we flew around Mexico in a four-seater plane
in search of a location for *The Night of the Iguana*, which we finally
found in Puerto Vallarta. When he was preparing to film *Iguana*, we
talked about the play and its meaning. He couldn't really understand
the character Richard Burton played, but then I don't think John knew
what it was to be insecure and lose your way. He didn't know the word
fear, or *anxiety*, nor understand the bonds that hold a man back from
living out his fantasies. In a way, it was very 'domestic.' He sent me
wool from Ireland and I knitted scarves for him. We wrote letters from
time to time. We even went to see a movie together in New York. After
he had an operation, I stayed with him in a house in Palm Springs for
a week while he recuperated. Although we had a maid, I cooked for
him a few times. He was good company. It wasn't just about sex. It was
deeper, I think."

Anna also had a bit part in another Huston movie: "I did a short
stint as an airplane stewardess in *The List of Adrian Messenger* [1963]. I
was floating on a piece of the airplane after it crashed. We shot that in
a studio in L.A. in a large pool of water with a gigantic wave machine
and pieces of an airplane. But the scene was cut. He never promoted
my work as an actress because he thought I was 'too good' to live that
kind of life. He eschewed the Hollywood mentality. A lot of young
girls would press themselves on him when we were out—they were
seeking some kind of part in his movies. I wasn't that kind of girl and I
think he liked that about me. I think he liked me because I was modest,
naïve, intelligent and good company. He was entertaining and lusty,
and appreciated—more than anything else—my ability to listen to
him talk about things of interest."

In 1964–65, while absorbed with preparations for *The Bible*, Huston
expressed genuine concern about Anna's welfare, encouraged her to be
more positive and generously offered his assistance: "Anna dear—How
good to hear from you. Although you speak of unhappy incidents, the
tone of your letter itself is anything but. It's infectiously gay. Yet I'm
concerned that things haven't gone better for you. It's time they should

start going well—high time. Maybe you need a breather. . . . [Your] silences, I've learned, usually mean one of two things—a stroke of very good luck or of very bad luck. In either case, you might tell me *now*. If it's good I'd like to share it with you—if it's bad, to help."

Their affair came to an end in about 1963, Anna explained, when Huston "went off to Egypt to film *The Bible*. He asked me to join him there, but by that time I was more involved with my own life in Greenwich Village, studying acting, working as a temp waitress, and finding other boyfriends closer by. In order to be a mistress, you really have to have some money and a comfortable life for yourself while the 'man' is gone. Because John came to the U.S. on his own time schedule (and always sent a telegram to me to come join him at the St. Regis hotel in New York), it was getting difficult for me to keep up with him."

They stayed in touch. In a valedictory letter of March 30, 1987, John expressed his lasting affection and admiration for Anna. He thought of the creation of man in Genesis as he faced the imminent prospect of his own death, which came only five months later: "Anna dear—As ever, a joy hearing from you, and having once again one's wish confirmed that there are things and people in this life who simply refuse to change or give up their innocence, much less bend a knee, in these oppressive times. [It] is a distinguishing characteristic of your breed, that they refuse to be involved in the confusions of the moment, but continue to face up to those great questions of love, fear, and death that have confronted man since he was assembled organ by organ."[4]

· IV ·

Huston met Zoe Ismail, who bore his son and radically changed his relations with Ricki, in Paris in 1961. Perhaps the most beautiful of all Huston's beautiful women, Zoe was born in Lucknow, India, in 1939, of mixed English-Persian and Indian background. She was slim and had a Mediterranean complexion, thick black hair, large widely spaced brown eyes, perfect nose, expressive mouth and dazzling white teeth. She wrote, "My father was a successful industrialist and we enjoyed a very privileged life style. I remember wonderful carriage rides every afternoon, birthday parties with bears, elephants and monkeys that entertained us on the lawns of our huge, elegant house. All this was shattered during the partition of India in 1948 when my parents felt it would be safer to come to England, where we could get a better education." Zoe attended the fashionable and expensive Cheltenham Ladies College. After leaving Cheltenham she won a scholarship to a London drama school, but stayed for only a few months. Her father strongly disapproved of an acting career, so she left home and shared a flat with a friend, but had difficulty surviving on her own after her comfortable life at home. She had small parts in two West End plays, toured with a repertory company, did some television work and modeling, and even worked briefly in the post office.

A twenty-two-year-old virgin who had led a rather sheltered life, Zoe was rather bold—and lucky—in her pursuit of Huston: "I read in the newspapers that Huston was casting for the film *Freud*, a subject that fascinated me and in which I was very keen to play a part. I heard that he was in Paris. As a friend of mine knew Jean-Paul Sartre, who was writing the screenplay, I packed my bags and decided on the spur of the moment to leave for Paris. The next day I went to Sartre's house, rang the bell and hoped for the best! He answered the door and invited me in and gave me John's phone number at the Lancaster Hotel. I was astonished at the ease with which this happened. I called the number and, to my surprise, John answered the phone." They met, and John, wearing a tuxedo, canceled a formal engagement, took her to dinner and did not make a pass on their first date. He invited her to Ireland but was leaving the next day, and she made an impulsive decision to go with him. At St. Clerans, she said, "I read the script for the part I felt I could play. I went back to London after a wonderful weekend. Our feelings were still premature and unspoken, and I had no idea at that point where my life would lead."

Zoe wrote that "my first impression of John was of a man with a deep sense of loneliness," which she felt she could assuage. When describing Huston, she tended to exalt and idealize him: "His character was noble-spirited, dignified not only in appearance but also in his very being, with a huge magnanimous heart. . . . I've always been an extremely idealistic person. I thought if I ever made love to anybody—because I never had—the person you made love to was the person you loved. You wait until the great love of your life comes. . . . John did not have to seduce women. His charm, eloquence and exquisite bearing did it for him."

To avoid being typecast as an Indian, Zoe changed her surname from Ismail to Sallis, a variant of Huston's middle name, Marcellus. She got the part of Freud's wife, Martha, but gave it up when she became pregnant. She was innocent and not *au fait* with sexual precautions. John didn't use a contraceptive and "it just happened, it was meant to be." She never had to make a decision about whether to have the baby. She knew that "John and I loved each other and were both very happy that we were going to have a child." Huston introduced Zoe to Eloise and her husband, the writer Hans Habe, then living in Munich, and proudly said, "She's carrying my baby." Eloise thought Zoe was a sweet little innocent who desperately wanted to play a part in Huston's life and films. Another unidentified woman, also pregnant with Huston's child, asked Eloise for advice and help. When Eloise spoke to Huston about her, he said, "Isn't that wonderful!" and she called him a callous "son of a bitch."[5]

Looking for a place where she could discreetly give birth, Zoe went to Rome to see what it was like, felt immediately at home and stayed for twenty years. Their son, Danny, born there in May 1962 (and now a successful actor), forged her lifelong bond with Huston. Danny said he was conceived during *Freud,* born during pre-production on *The Bible* and teethed during *The Night of the Iguana.* More like a grandson than a son, he became John's favorite child, partly because he grew up in Rome, rarely saw his father and never lived with him. Both Zoe and Danny thought that Rome, just after *La Dolce Vita* appeared in 1960, was a delightful place to live. The Italians adored children, and there was great food and a sensuous atmosphere. Danny went to an Italian kindergarten, to British and American grade schools and to Millfield, an English boarding school in Somerset. He then attended the London International Film School, which emphasized practical work and the technical aspects of film. After all this he felt he was more

Italian-Irish-British than, like his parents, Indian and American. John's visits to Rome were rare and wonderful events, when the bearded, piratical figure would suddenly appear with tall tales and exotic gifts acquired on his worldwide travels.

Zoe hoped that Huston would marry her as he'd married Ricki when she got pregnant. "John had been leading a separate life from Ricki for years before I met him," Zoe wrote. "She had many other relationships, as did he. When John wanted a divorce from Ricki so we could get married, Ricki refused. She wanted to keep her position as John's wife. Unless she found another ready-made identity to slip on with someone else who was willing to marry her, I believe she needed to keep the status quo."

In 1962 Tony, aged twelve, and Anjelica, aged eleven, took the recent arrival of their half-brother rather badly. When Tony came to the set of *Freud* in Munich and first met Zoe, he expressed his adolescent confusion and anger about all John's women. The script girl remarked, "The poor kid, he was absolutely trembling. He was quite nervous around his father. Tony was bitterly resentful. It was normal that a child should hate somebody who has supplanted his mother." Zoe admitted that Tony and Anjelica "weren't very keen on the idea of Danny and me. Tony hated the whole situation. Anjelica absolutely went into a crying fit and left the room." Two years later the situation became even more troubling and difficult to accept. Anjelica was confronted with "her father [who] had a child with another woman, and her mother [who] was about to have a baby with a man whose identity she suspected but didn't want to know."[6]

Danny's birth was also the breaking point for Ricki. For years she had run the house at St. Clerans and supervised the children's education, apparently content to be the wife of a powerful but absentee husband. The arrival of Zoe and Danny on the scene provoked her to reexamine her life. She finally burst out of her passive existence, left Ireland, moved with the children to London and got a flat in Maida Vale. She started a new life, as Mrs. John Huston, with a new circle of friends and took several lovers, including the dashing Patrick Leigh Fermor, who'd failed to score with Juliette Gréco in Africa. Celeste recalled a dramatic incident that took place during a dinner with a local Irish priest at St. Clerans. Ricki, whom John had not seen for a year, suddenly appeared, pulled open her cape and revealed that she was pregnant.

Allegra, born in August 1964 (and given the same name as Byron's illegitimate daughter), was Ricki's revenge for Zoe and Danny. Allegra looked like her father, the English viscount and historian John Julius Norwich who, terrified of scandal, didn't acknowledge her until she was in her teens. Despite Ricki's high hopes, Norwich didn't marry her when his own marriage broke up. With typical generosity, John adopted Allegra and gave her his name. They met for the first time when she was four years old, and the pretty little girl charmed and delighted him.

After his separation from Ricki—though they had always lived separately—Huston was more interested in Suzanne Flon than in Zoe. He saw Zoe and Danny in Rome whenever he could, and they came to St. Clerans for the holidays. John supported them, but they were essentially on their own. When they visited Puerto Vallarta in 1963, during the shooting of *The Night of the Iguana*, he was in Las Caletas, accessible only by boat, and Zoe was stranded in town.

Zoe finally got a small part in *The Bible* (1966) as Ava Gardner's Egyptian attendant and sexual substitute with the aged Abraham. She was very photogenic and looks stunning in the movie. Danny's first memory was visiting the set, seeing the ark, the animals and John dressed as Noah, then watching the rough cut with his mother as Hagar. John arranged for Zoe to help publicize the picture in America, which he hoped might also jump-start her acting career. In August 1966 Gladys Hill wrote to Paul Kohner, "John believes Zoe Sallis will be useful to Fox for the premiere in New York and Los Angeles. He thought Zoe might go on tour with Ulla [Bergryd, who played Eve] but we don't yet know about that. . . . Zoe will come to New York with Danny and her Italian maid, probably a week before opening, in order to get outfitted properly. . . . Naturally Zoe and all of us hope that, once she's seen, she'll get work in a film or some films that will keep her busy working as an actress, which of course is what she longs to do." Kohner was going to be her agent and she was being groomed for a big part.

But just as she was about to get everything she'd always desired, she was horrified by the whole tour and realized she didn't want that kind of life for herself or for Danny. Zoe, who really wanted to be a mother, felt she had to get out of Hollywood or be lost forever.

Earlier that year John had tried to help Zoe in another way by instructing his business manager to send her all the money he got for acting in *Casino Royale*. His lawyer told Gladys that "Jess [Morgan] will send John the entire $40,000 to use as a down payment on a house for Zoe. I am hoping that Zoe keeps the cost of the house down considerably because I believe that the acquisition of the furniture and furnishings will cost another $30,000 or $40,000."[7] But Zoe never got this money and never bought the house.

During the filming of *The Kremlin Letter* in Rome in May 1969, John—an often forgetful father who'd missed many important events in Danny's life—came through by renting an entire Italian circus, at the producer Dino De Laurentiis' studio, and putting on a splendid show for Danny's seventh birthday. Danny invited a busload of school friends, had lunch at the swimming pool with ice cream and popcorn, and was entertained by animals and clowns. Zoe and other lovers attended the event, and as Nan Taylor (the wife of Huston's producer and friend) remarked, "only John could pull this off." Zoe said that John was more affectionate with Danny than with his other children, and Danny fully reciprocated his feelings. Anjelica, more aggressive and demanding, constantly complained that John was a "monster" of a father; Danny was much more responsive and loving.

Zoe was perhaps too sweet and too worshipful. She admitted that Huston, a hard-headed rationalist, spent years criticizing her religious and mystical beliefs (accompanied by yoga and vegetarianism), and that there was an unbridgeable intellectual and temperamental gap between them. His Italian lover Valeria Alberti called Zoe "a marvelous girl, beautiful and sensitive, but it was a kind of Oriental sensitivity, born out of politeness and passiveness." Alluding to Zoe's role in *The Bible* as Sarah's maidservant, Celeste more tartly remarked, she was "a handmaiden and a convenience. John got tired of her and didn't want her around any more."[8] John could not sustain interest in a woman for more than a few years. He needed the constant excitement of a new young conquest—and a new lover to listen to his old stories.

When Leonard Gardner, who wrote the novel and screenplay of *Fat City,* visited St. Clerans in 1971, Zoe was the only woman there. But John ignored her and seemed tired of her, and it was clear that they were no longer a couple. Zoe told Gardner that their affair had ended and that John was interested only in Danny. But Zoe was no longer willing to be a mere camp follower and wrote, "We stayed great friends, but our relationship was over. [I] was always part of an entourage and I was a bit fed up with that. I think I just grew up. I wanted to be important to one person. John wasn't capable of that, it just never happened."

When Celeste first arrived in St. Clerans, just after her marriage to John in 1972, she was shocked to find Zoe in residence. John was highly amused that Celeste didn't even know who Zoe was. Always highly competitive with other women, Celeste considered Zoe a serious rival. She took revenge when Zoe was perfectly cast as the Afghan princess in *The Man Who Would Be King* and threatened to leave him if Zoe appeared in the film. Trying hard to salvage his last attempt at marriage, John gave in to his wife and Zoe, for the second time, lost her long-desired part.

In 1983, when Danny was twenty-one years old, Zoe married a German-French banker, very different from John, whom Danny didn't like. The marriage lasted only three years—John's usual time span. Two years later John praised in Danny some of the qualities that he himself had and most admired in other men: "Danny, age 23, is everything one could hope for from a son. He is intelligent, imaginative, inclined to be brave, and gentle, and besides, or rather on top of all that, he's physically quite beautiful, 6 ft. 2 in., and an athlete."[9] Zoe's family had lost a lot of their wealth when they left India and never recaptured their grand style of life. She never married John and, after her divorce from the banker, never remarried. She never realized her ambitions for a film career that first propelled her into John's life. But—still a gentle, charming and attractive woman—Zoe had an idyllic life in Rome, is proud of Danny's success, still adores John and has no regrets.

TWENTY

IGUANA AND THE FLOOD,
1963–1966

· I ·

H uston made a film adaptation of Tennessee Williams' 1961 play *The Night of the Iguana* (1964) partly because he'd be able to shoot it in Mexico. From his experience in Africa, he believed the location would enhance the realism of the picture and work its spell on the actors. In a remote, uncomfortable and even dangerous place, they would gain intensity and commitment, and give superior performances. He gathered a volatile cast in Puerto Vallarta, halfway down the Pacific coast of Mexico, and shot the film at Mismaloya, inaccessible by land, eight miles distant and a rough twenty-five-minute boat ride from town. The small, isolated peninsula has spectacular scenery, with a thick green jungle running right down to the deep blue sea. Huston, acting as cool ringmaster to a combustible set of characters, provoked a few emotional explosions. The Mexican actor Emilio Fernandez had once shot a producer during a quarrel and could no longer get work in the Mexican film industry. This bloodthirsty résumé greatly appealed to Huston, who hired him as assistant director and gave him the role of a bartender to liven things up.

Gladys Hill—with fair hair, large glasses and a wide, flat face— is recognizable as Miss Dexter (an allusion to her job as Huston's "right-hand" girl). She sits just behind Richard Burton as he recklessly drives the tourist bus, filled with Texas schoolmarms, to Ava Gardner's run-down hotel. Both in real life and in the picture, the bus and all its passengers actually did get stuck on a dangerous precipice. In a letter to the producer Ray Stark in October 1963, Gladys described the endless difficulties they had when transporting the materials to construct the badly designed buildings: "A fairly constant parade of heavy laden burros moves up the hill [for one *peso*] through the normal traffic of pigs, dogs, hens and bare-assed kids. But not at Mismaloya. The burros have a very strong union and they wouldn't go up those hills for less than 1.60."

Huston had once planned to build a house in Tarzana that would eventually return to the earth. The flimsy buildings erected for the staff of *Iguana* returned to the earth much sooner than expected. The main casualty was Tom Shaw, Huston's valuable first assistant director since *The Unforgiven*. A tough, strong-jawed, belligerent cross between a pit bull and Popeye, Shaw was adept at dealing with egomaniacs and didn't like to be crossed. When Huston looked at him, Shaw usually knew exactly what he wanted. They worked perfectly together and Shaw performed many difficult tasks that made Huston's work much easier. Shaw was sitting on the balcony of his room when the concrete, mixed with friable beach sand, suddenly disintegrated. Shaw fell eighteen feet, broke his back in two places and had to be flown from Vallarta to a big-city hospital. He survived and would work with Huston through *The Dead* (1987).

Huston's exotic setting and celebrated actors attracted a swarm of journalists to the set. Their dispatches created interest in the picture before its release, and their hyped-up curiosity added to the excitable mood. Richard Burton was accompanied by Elizabeth Taylor and her secretary, cook, chauffeur and children. Because of their scandalous love affair and the disaster-plagued production of *Cleopatra* (1963), the reporters devoured every detail about them. The beautiful and talented, though sometimes drunken and miserable Ava Gardner, as well as the flirtatious seventeen-year-old Sue Lyon, who'd just achieved tremendous fame in *Lolita* (1962), were equally notorious. Michael Wilding, who'd once been Elizabeth Taylor's consort, continued to serve by handling publicity for Burton. Peter Viertel, who—like his old pal Huston—had once shared Gardner's bed, had recently married Deborah Kerr and was on the scene with her. Sue Lyon earned $175,000; Deborah Kerr,

$250,000; Ava Gardner, $400,000 and Burton, $500,000. Though Tennessee Williams felt uneasy with the swaggering Huston, he came to Mexico to help him and Tony Veiller revise the screenplay. *Time* magazine duly reported that Tennessee wore a bathing cap and Elizabeth did not.

Despite the financial rewards and the pleasure of working with Huston, Gardner recalled that "everyone was on edge from the heat and the sickness. Scorpions and iguanas hopping on your bed. You never knew if you were going to be bitten by something or stranded by a storm. . . . Everyone got a bit desperate, everyone wanted to be loved or to love." Huston gathered his stars at a solemn ceremony and presented Burton, Taylor, Gardner, Lyon, Kerr and Ray Stark each with a gold-plated derringer and five bullets. Every bullet had a name on it, as if he expected them all to kill each other by the end of the movie.

Iguana was the first of four films that Huston made with Ray Stark, one of the last movie moguls, known for his Machiavellian maneuvers. Stark and Huston had three great interests in common. Stark was a keen seducer of actresses and inspired the phrase "casting couch." He raised Thoroughbred horses on a three-hundred-acre ranch at Los Olivos, north of Santa Barbara, and he was a major art collector who would bequeath his modern sculptures, valued at $750 million, to the Getty Museum in Malibu. He also bought Bogart's house in Los Angeles, and left an estate worth $2 billion. Stark wrote amusing letters to Huston and made many shrewd suggestions about the rough-cut versions of their movies. He hero-worshipped Huston and later praised him as "the best read and the most knowledgeable man I've ever met, or that's ever been connected with the film industry. He was a Renaissance man, and everything he did was bigger than life."

Stark was nervous about hiring Ava Gardner. He agreed that she'd be great for the part of the earthy keeper of a seedy hotel, but warned Huston that he'd have to control his temper with her. Stark had heard that on her last picture Gardner "was impossible, drunk on the set, started at 11 o'clock every day, had to go through many takes so that they finally had to break up her lines; that she was uncooperative, bitchy and, as Sam Goldwyn would say, 'in two words: impossible.' "

Stark also told Huston that Gardner herself was worried about "whether or not she was actress enough to handle the part. I reassured her that under the 'cloak' (I hope it's only the cloak!) of John Huston she will emerge as a streamlined Sarah Bernhardt."[1]

Ava, occasionally a mean drunk, was sleeping with several of the handsome Mexican beach boys who appeared in the movie as her ardent pursuers—following her, shaking their maracas and dancing around her. The swimming scene, in which she kisses one of the boys as the waves break on the beach, echoes the once-shocking scene of Burt Lancaster and Deborah Kerr kissing as the ocean crashes next to them in *From Here to Eternity* (1953). (Huston borrowed the bit of business in which Burton and Gardner push the rolling drinks cart back and forth across the room from Billy Wilder's *Love in the Afternoon,* 1957.) Immensely grateful for Huston's sensitive treatment in the swimming scene, Gardner recalled, "I was nervous about doing it, and John . . . understood. He stripped down to his shorts and got into the water with me for a rehearsal, showing me exactly how he wanted it to go, then directed the scene soaking wet. That is my kind of director. . . . Working with him gave me the only real joy I've ever had in movies."

Huston had two brilliant choices for the part of Nonno, Kerr's doddering grandfather and the oldest practicing poet in the world. He first chose Carl Sandburg (born in 1878), an effective performer who strummed the guitar as his silky white hair drifted over his eyes. (His rival Robert Frost caustically remarked, "Everything about him is studied—except his poetry.") But Sandburg's poor health prevented him from appearing in the picture. Huston then fixed on Robert Graves (born in 1895), a tall, swaggering, broken-nosed war hero and natural actor, who would also have been perfect for the poet. But in August 1963 Graves, replying by cable from Majorca, said, "Regrets. Playing part of Oxford Professor [of Poetry] October through December."[2] The part eventually went to Cyril Delevanti, who was seventy-six but looked terribly frail and much older. At the end of the movie the aged bard dies just after completing his poem.

The young actor Hampton Fancher, Sue Lyon's fiancé, came to visit. He thought Huston seemed laconically high, strangely detached, in some other world. Like many others, Huston was drinking quantities of bootlegged *raicilla,* a 180-proof firewater, needle sharp, made in the nearby jungle from the maguey cactus. One night at 3 A.M. Fancher, coming up a steep cobblestone street in Vallarta, met Huston in his khaki safari suit, coming down drunk. He stopped and boomed out in a challenging theatrical voice, "Hampton Fancher." Fancher replied in kind by bellowing out "John Huston." They circled each other for five minutes, repeating each other's names about thirty-five times. Huston was taking his measure as Fancher played the pointless but congenial game.

Some journalists compared Huston to a general commanding an army—in absolute control of the twenty-three people in his cast and crew. Others described him as courteous but remote, never losing his temper but resorting to sarcasm when displeased. Burton and Kerr, like Gardner, admired his direction. Burton said, "He holds me back when, as a stage actor, I go too far emotionally." Kerr noted, "Huston is such a good actor that he can always act your part better than you can." Sue Lyon, however, needed much more guidance and encouragement than the more experienced actors. Fancher thought she was completely out of her depth and terribly insecure, and that Huston didn't pay much attention to her or handle her properly.[3] Yet he had his own way of getting what he wanted out of actors, and her performance is surprisingly effective. The best scene takes place when Lyon enters Burton's hotel room to seduce him and he desperately tries to resist her. Extremely agitated, he knocks a bottle of whiskey off the dresser and paces barefoot on the broken glass. Inspired by his pain, which she takes for love, she kicks off her shoes and joins him in masochistically cutting up her feet.

Burton, who'd just played the Archbishop of Canterbury in *Becket* (1964), was ecclesiastically demoted to a defrocked minister in *Iguana.* The film starts, like *Moby Dick,* with a sermon. But, in contrast to Welles' rhetorical tour de force, Burton's is a rambling and confused peroration. Taking his incriminating text from Proverbs 25:28, "He that hath no rule over his own spirit is like a city that is broken down, and without walls," he confesses his failure to control his appetites and drives his bewildered congregation out of the church. In the movie

Burton, trying to run away from excessive drink and sex, encounters three women who represent a nympho, a nymphet and a nun. He has some very good lines—cynical with Gardner, anguished with Lyon and tender with Kerr, playing a refined, déclassé artist who sells her sketches for a precarious living. When Burton and Gardner meet, they have a terse exchange in which he pointedly inquires about her husband: "Where's Fred?" "Dead!" Well aware of his fondness for alcohol, she discreetly asks about his habit and is told, "If I'd been drinking I wouldn't be here. I'd still be drinking." Trussed up in a hammock to prevent another suicide attempt, he remarks, "All women want to see a man in a tied-up situation." Finding it hard to resist the predatory advances of Sue Lyon, he defines statutory rape as "a man seduced by a girl under twenty."

The connection between the characters is strengthened by the witty, allusive script. Burton's relations with the well-bred and ladylike Kerr are like Bogart's with Hepburn in *The African Queen* and Mitchum's with Kerr in *Heaven Knows, Mr. Allison*. Though Kerr supposedly comes from Nantucket, she speaks with a posh English accent. Alluding to the aphorism by the Roman playwright Terence, "Nothing human is alien to me," Kerr tries to win Burton's trust and redeem him by saying, "Nothing human disgusts me, Mr. Shannon, unless it is unkind or violent." Trying, like everyone else, to calm down Burton, she gives him poppyseed tea as a sedative, which recalls the failure of poppy and drowsy syrups to induce sweet sleep in *Othello*. When Kerr sweetly tells him that "love builds its nest in the heart of another," she alludes to the title of a novel by Hemingway's former wife Martha Gellhorn. Bent on self-annihilation, he tells Kerr, who's trying to save him, "Don't rob me of the credit for destroying myself." But he also companionably asks, with faint hope after his disastrous trip to Mexico, "Is it possible to travel together? Just travel?"—and avoid the torments of sexual desire.

The iguana in the movie represents Burton's primeval instincts, just as the Gila monster stood for Bogart's in *Sierra Madre*. But the iguana, again like Burton, loves its bonds and when liberated cannot accept its freedom. As Byron wrote in "The Prisoner of Chillon": "My very chains and I grew friends, / So much a long communion tends / To make us what we are." Kerr later explained that when Burton freed the iguana in the film, "it didn't want freedom in the least! He has been in a comfortable cage eating off the fat of the land for three months, and getting large and gorgeous, and he didn't see why he should rush off into the jungle." (The iguana may also have been a sly allusion to Huston's lovers—released, but still bound to him and unwilling to depart.)

In Williams' play the character played by Burton is destroyed; in the movie, he's kept alive. After Burton rejects Lyon and Kerr rejects Burton, he returns to heavy drinking with his temperamental soul mate, the newly widowed Gardner. He decides to remain in her shabby hotel and she fortifies him by saying, "I'll get you back up, baby . . . I'll always get you back up." *Iguana* portrays a pitiful man at the end of his rope, torn between physical and spiritual longings, searching for God and trying to live beyond despair.

The main fault of *Iguana* is that Huston, ever faithful to the text, stayed too close to the original setting, dialogue and action, and didn't open up Williams' play. The hotel has the same sweltering, remote and claustrophobic atmosphere as the hotel in *Key Largo,* but does not strongly convey the mood of Mexico. Yet Huston was justly proud of overcoming the formidable obstacles, from *raicilla* to wrecked buildings, and eliciting a fine performance from Gardner. As he wrote Anna van der Heide, "It was bedlam the first two weeks. Houses unfinished—not enough beds—toilets not working—swarms of mosquitoes and no netting. No refrigeration, food poisoning. But despite everything the picture itself went smoothly and well. The performances are extraordinary. Dick, Ava and Deborah. It has been a long time since three like these three have come together. Everyone expects Dick and Deborah to be good, but Ava will be a big surprise. Believe me, she isn't second best."[4]

· II ·

Iguana concerns an individual minister's alienation from God; *The Bible* (1966) portrays the Jewish people's blessed connection to God.

Huston rose to the challenge of a titanic adventure and hoped for great financial rewards. But his most ambitious movie was his most notable artistic failure, another striking example of the recurrent theme in his life and work: the grandiose quest that ends in noble disillusionment. The project was cooked up by the Neapolitan-born Dino De Laurentiis, who'd produced the neorealistic *Bitter Rice* (1949) (and married its sensual star Silvana Mangano), as well as Federico Fellini's great film *La Strada* (1954). In the early 1960s he built Dinocittà outside Rome to produce his elephantine epics. *The Bible* was an attempt to surpass De Mille's *The Ten Commandments* (1956), which focused on the story of Moses in Exodus. For this epic De Laurentiis hired Giuseppe Rotunno, the superb cinematographer of *The Leopard* (1963); and he originally planned to have four directors: Welles, Luchino Visconti and Robert Bresson as well as Huston himself. In the end, Huston took responsibility for the entire movie, which was mercifully reduced to the first twenty-two chapters of Genesis: from the Creation of the world to the sacrifice of Isaac before the angel of the Lord stays Abraham's hand.

Huston scouted locations all over Europe and North Africa, and even the efficient Gladys couldn't keep up with his perpetual motion. In January 1964 she wrote to his business manager, who was chasing after him to sign some important papers, "John is still in Rome. He returned from Yugoslavia last Sunday, may be in Sicily today—and will be going to London this weekend. . . . After London he either returns to Sicily or goes on to Egypt." It's amazing that Huston could get so much work done while constantly moving around and living in a series of hotels and rented quarters.

As always, Huston sought the best men in the business. He hired the English playwright Christopher Fry, who'd worked on the script for *Ben-Hur* (1959), to write the screenplay. Huston wanted Igor Stravinsky to compose the music but was turned down; Fry recommended Benjamin Britten, who was also unavailable; Leonard Bernstein refused when his ideas clashed with Huston's; and they finally got Toshiro Mayuzumi. He'd done scores of traditional scores for Japanese movies and somehow seemed just right to make music for the Hebrew epic.

Huston himself, the triple pillar of the picture, not only directed the most demanding work of his career, but also narrated it and played Noah. As he spoke the majestic opening cadences of Genesis—"And the Spirit of God moved upon the face of the waters"—with a deep resonance and theatrical intonation, his voice, lingering on the word *wah-térs*, was in fact . . . divine. But it's not always clear who God is talking to. Sometimes, at the Creation of the world, he seems to be speaking to the movie audience (no one else is there). At other times, Huston as God speaks to Huston playing Noah, and Huston as Noah answers Huston as God. It seems entirely fitting that the godlike director and creator on the set should also play God Almighty in the film.

The Creation scene—with its volcanic lava and raging torrents, its boiling mud and vaporous gases—expresses (more explosively than in Genesis) primordial nature emerging from the dark chaos of nothing. Huston wrote that the photographer Ernst Haas "brought back scenes of waters leaving the dry land; volcanoes rearing up from the sea; lava building itself into smoking mountains; flowers, plants and trees groping up through mists towards the sun. And finally, animals emerging." But the visual equivalent of the beginning of the world looks like an old Walt Disney nature movie, complete with jangling and obtrusive music.

The Italian sculptor Giacomo Manzu ingeniously created the creation of Adam in three stages: first, an abstract mound of earth; then the suggestion of man's proportions and shape; and finally, the nearly finished man, who morphs into the young actor Michael Parks. Ulla Bergryd, a nineteen-year-old Swedish anthropology student at the University of Göteborg, played Eve to his Adam. Parks described her as the first true hippie, wearing huge hats, delightfully eccentric, always laughing and "levitating along." Both actors had trouble keeping their not-so-private parts covered during the nude scenes. Ulla's blond tresses, pasted to her breasts, were blown off by the wind machine. It also parted Michael's fig leaves and left him completely exposed, which caused quite a stir when he was seen in the rushes. He felt he would have given a better performance if he'd been allowed to appear naked. Both actors cracked up when Ulla, looking at the fake snake in the Tree of Knowledge and then at Michael's wind-blown member, asked, "Have you seen the great serpent?"[5] But the temptation by Satan was dramatically unconvincing; and Adam and Eve seemed to commit incest, since she had come from his body, to the strains of a swelling choir.

Ulla spoke with a Swedish accent. Michael had a distinct American accent that seemed to come from a different part of Eden. Huston felt it broke the spell and had to be replaced by the dubbed voice of another actor. He clashed with the young Michael, whom he found too cocky and rebellious. When discussing the stars he wanted to attend the premiere of *The Bible*, Huston angrily told the director of publicity at Fox: "I would suggest you send Michael Parks either to the Matto Grosso [in the Brazilian jungle] or to the Pribilof Islands [in the Aleutians] until after *The Bible* is in general release. Or, better still, simply do him in."

Parks explained the source of their conflict. He felt Huston was emotionally detached, temperamental, insensitive, and when exercising his absolute power, sometimes sadistic. He once told Michael, when facing a real tiger, "Just go and pet him, and walk away. It's all right, kid." When Michael said, "No, you do it," Huston boldly petted the tiger and calmed him with "nice kitty, nice kitty." The tiger then became restive, started to rip things up and scratched his keeper. Huston didn't seem to care if the tiger mauled Michael. On another occasion Huston, contrary to his usual practice, filmed Cain (Richard Harris) killing Abel (Franco Nero) about twenty-four times, until Harris finally shouted, "What the fuck is he doing?" Michael found it difficult "to work for Genghis Khan." He said the other actors, who didn't have the balls to stand up to the oppressive director, disliked him for opposing Huston.[6]

By contrast, Huston loved Ava Gardner and loved working with her. Using his most seductive and irresistible charm, flattering her and promising adventure, he persuaded her to take the part of Abraham's wife Sarah, who waxed old and was stricken in age: "It would be another adventure for us. It's not just that I think you can speak the lines beautifully—but I'd get to see you on the back of a racing camel [in Egypt] all swathed and bedizened. . . . The truth, dear Ava, is simply I want you to be in every picture I ever make." Gardner threw herself into the role and, when drunk, amusingly remarked, "I'm becoming so Jewish these days. I almost believe in circumcision & by God I'm beginning to think that—at 41—I can produce a child. . . . P.S. I really *was* pissed [when I wrote this letter]—not to worry—I'm going to mail it even so! Ava." But Gardner (like all the other actors) had to intone pretentiously solemn and impossibly stilted lines. The close paraphrase of Genesis 16:2 in the 1611 King James translation of the Bible, in which she offers Father Abraham some doctrinal instruction while encouraging him to commit adultery, might be effective as narrative but is far removed from ordinary speech: "Abram, behold now, the Lord hath restrained me from bearing, I pray thee, go in unto my maid according to that law which says, when the wife is barren, her maid servant may bear for her. It may be that I may obtain children by her."

The supposedly Middle Eastern scenery also seemed strangely unreal as they shifted locations from the lush gardens outside Rome to the austerity of the Egyptian wasteland. The Edenic landscape seemed semitropical, became rocky desert beginning with the Tower of Babel and turned to high sand dunes when Abraham wandered in Beersheba. The costumes, yet another drawback, resembled the *schmatas* in the ugly oleograph illustrations of nineteenth-century Bibles.

If Gardner was a delight to work with, George C. Scott, who played Abraham, was sheer torture. Crazy about Ava, Scott sought the Promised Land in her bed. He was drunk most of the time, often quite violent and sometimes berserk. Gardner, who tried to avoid him, recalled, "George, I knew, had been a bit pissed all day, and suddenly he went absolutely bonkers and began ripping his costume off. He literally flung the clothes on the floor and stormed off the set in his underwear."[7] Later on he punched her and bruised her face. Huston admired Scott as an actor, but was outraged by his behavior. In a seriocomic episode, he had to physically restrain him. "I have very little use for Scott as a private person," he wrote. "He was insanely jealous, extremely demanding of Ava's time and attention, and he became violent" with her. "One night Scott got very drunk in the bar and threatened Ava physically when she entered. In the process of trying to slow him down before he hurt someone, I climbed on his back. He's very strong, and he carried me around the room, bumping into things. He couldn't see where he was going because I had my arms wrapped around his head. Ava was persuaded to leave, and we finally got Scott calmed down."

The absurdity of her role and her dangerous encounters with Scott made Gardner hate *The Bible* more than any of her movies. After attending the opening, she angrily stated, "I was up until four A.M. at that goddam premiere of *The Bible*. I will personally kill that John Huston if he ever drags me to another mess like that. There must have been ten thousand people clawing at me." As they were watching the picture, "I kept punching Johnny on the arm and saying, 'Christ, how could you let me do it?' "[8]

· III ·

Christopher Fry said *The Bible*'s spiritual truths had to be conveyed in images. Huston based the appearance of Adam and Eve, their pose around the snaky Tree of Knowledge and their expulsion from the Garden of Eden, on the figures in Masaccio and other Renaissance masters. He gave Eve long, blond tresses to cover her nakedness and satisfy the religious censors. His treatment of the Flood was inspired by Leonardo da Vinci's dynamic drawings of the swirling, foaming, tempestuous waves that nearly destroyed the Ark in which Noah rescued the animals.

Acknowledging that it was difficult to direct and act in the same film, Huston explained how he approached the complex task: "I'd put somebody else in, and direct the scene and get the camera, the shot, and then step in and enact the part. Then I would look for approval to my assistant director and the cameraman, and see whether I'd been all right or not." In his late fifties but looking much older, the tall, gray-haired and pouchy-eyed Huston was excellent as the stooped, slow-moving, subservient-to-God Noah. He's mocked by a shaven-headed pagan crowd (who look like extras from a sci-fi movie) as he follows the divine command, folds his tents and builds the massive Ark for the greatest ecological operation of all time.

Noah's story reverses Ahab's: Ahab kills animals, Noah saves them. This rescue story marks Huston's personal transition from hunting elephants in Africa and tigers in India to portraying heroes who save elephants in *The Roots of Heaven* and conserve every beast on earth in *The Bible*. Wild animals were flown in to Rome from Germany, Libya, Egypt and tropical Africa; semitame beasts from Althoff's European Circus were trucked down through the Alps; and a whole zoo was constructed for two hundred creatures.

A Hollywood axiom states that animals, children and water are the most hazardous risks in movies. But Huston—who would feature a tame bear in *The Life and Times of Judge Roy Bean*—believed, "If you think like an animal, why, you are seldom disappointed." While filming Noah's family on the animal-packed Ark during the Flood, he handled all three elements with consummate imagination and skill. Clearly at ease with all the animals, including the tigers, he splashes gallons of milk down the throat of the hippo. The biggest problem, for the most impressive sequence of the movie, was getting all the brutes up the gangway and into the Ark while preventing them from devouring each other or mauling the crew. To achieve this stately procession, Huston wrote, "First, ditches were dug on either side of the road leading into the Ark. . . . The handlers started by leading individual animals along the road. . . . The next step was to have the handlers walk in the ditches, leading their charges in longer nylon lines."

Accidents, of course, were inevitable, and Huston was lucky that no one was seriously injured or killed. "One water buffalo charged up the gangplank and crashed through the Ark. . . . Huston was knocked down by an elephant. Another tore off the director's robe searching for peanuts, and a camel fell off the ramp into a tankful of water."[9] The last passenger to crawl into the Ark was a sluggish but determined tortoise. Huston wanted a real lion to attack a pagan king, but found this was impossible: the lion was too tame. By making the biblical scenes literal, he sometimes made them absurd. Polar bears marched incongruously alongside giraffes; tigers remained quiescent in their fragile-looking cattle pens; there was no meat for the ravenous carnivores; and no hint of an excremental mess. The Ark tossed about in the Flood was too obviously a boat in a studio tank.

When the picture was released, Richard Burton wrote to De

Laurentiis, "You were inspired to choose John to direct and let him play Noah and to narrate. He does all three with shameless brilliance." But after the Noah sequence, Huston seemed to lose interest and momentum in this three-hour extravaganza. Gardner's biographer noted, "Huston's low threshold of boredom had been reached, his growing disengagement apparent—one morning nearly a thousand people stood around waiting for direction while he sat working on a crossword puzzle." Such apparent unconcern must have been infuriating, but he was not being frivolous or high-handed. He was taking time to think, solve the problem at hand and plan his next move. It took two years to shoot the picture (*The Maltese Falcon,* simpler but infinitely better, took only three months). The entry of the animals on the Ark cost $3 million, and the entire budget swelled by nearly fifty percent, from $13 to $18 million. As Huston wryly confessed, "I don't know how God managed. I'm having a terrible time."[10]

Since the movie had to please a mass audience yet offend no one, Huston—for personal, artistic and commercial reasons—"looked at the Bible as a collection of myths and legends, not from a religious standpoint." In July 1967 an executive at Fox told Gladys that box office returns were frustratingly uneven. The picture was not fundamentalist enough for the Bible Belt and not interesting enough for college students. It did well with children and on Saturday morning shows, and was most successful with churchgoing Blacks, Hispanics and Catholics.

Gene Phillips, a Jesuit priest and film historian, gave it his bland imprimatur in the *Homiletic and Pastoral Review* by stating that it "manages for the most part to be not only entertaining but artistic and religious as well." The sharp-tongued Rex Reed remarked, "At a time when religion needs all the help it can get, John Huston may have set its cause back a couple of thousand years." The distinguished critic Edmund Wilson observed, in a perceptive account of the picture, "Huston's film *The Bible* covers only a few episodes in Genesis. I had heard that parts of it were good, but though it is not so comic as most Biblical films, it is actually not any good—pretentious, inartistic, unimaginative, and three hours long. The animals in the Ark have a circus interest; but . . . there is not the least suggestion that everybody but Noah and his family are being drowned in the Flood."¹¹ Huston's hard work, however, paid off. Though some dud episodes had more extras in the movie than people in the theater, *The Bible* was a popular hit and a great financial success.

· IV ·

The Bible had two notable spin-offs: a new mistress and the chance to direct an opera in Italy. Valeria Alberti was a Roman countess and painter who knew Manzu and many of the Italian artists who worked on the movie. Tall, long-nosed and plain, she was the least attractive of Huston's women and spoke no English. Since Huston did not know Italian, they had to call in an interpreter whenever they got into an argument. But she was a daring glider pilot, which greatly appealed to him.

Curtice Taylor, a lowly assistant on *The Bible*, had to look after Valeria. On location on the Amalfi coast, south of Naples, and speaking to each other in broken English, they impulsively decided to go for a swim. Curtice, in his hippie phase, stripped off his clothes and jumped into the sea. Valeria, then about forty, followed in the nude. When they returned to the hotel Huston, who loved to scare people, told Curtice, "I heard you had a good time with Valeria." His chauffeur had followed them down to the water and taken incriminating photos.

Valeria, who took the erotic Japanese bath with Huston at St. Clerans and whose affair lasted until 1971, remembered him fondly: "John appeared to be a wise man. He understood the human spirit like the great writers and the great artists. . . . Even though we spoke very little, we were in tune. It was a fairy-tale love story." When Valeria tried to prolong his life by getting him to stop drinking and smoking, Eloise Hardt (who knew him better) said, "Leave him alone. He knows what he's doing. He wants to die with his boots on."¹²

As early as February 1961 Rudolf Bing, manager of the Metropolitan Opera in New York, had asked Huston to direct Puccini's *The Girl of the Golden West* (set in America) for the modest fee of $5,000. Though Huston had acted in, written and directed plays in New York, he had less musical experience than most of the ushers at the Met. He refused the offer, but it aroused his interest in opera. Four years later, after he'd completed *The Bible* in Italy and wanted a change from filmmaking, La Scala in Milan offered him Verdi's *La Forza del Destino* and Wagner's *The Flying Dutchman*. He preferred to direct a new work, Richard Rodney Bennett's opera *The Mines of Sulphur*, which did not have a long operatic tradition behind it and gave him a freer hand. He had catholic tastes in music, directed the singers as if they were actors and naturally tried to bring his visual sense to the operatic stage: "I like everything from Louis Armstrong to Gregorian chants. And I can see. This is what opera is all about—listening and seeing. . . . I have tried to amalgamate and enhance the acting and the singing. . . . [The opera] pleases me because it satisfies my atmospheric, cinematic sense." A critic called Huston "eager as a schoolboy and yet somehow remote as a Buddha."

The twelve-tone opera by the English composer (with its libretto translated into Italian) was set in the west of England in the eighteenth century. In this macabre ghost story, a troupe of actors stage a *Hamlet*-like play within a play. They hope to catch the conscience of the Gypsy thieves who've killed the owner of a haunted manor house. The rather static *Mines* did not provide much scope for Huston's talents, and the critics were lukewarm about his work. Claudio Sartori said he remained in the shadows: "The director was none other than John Huston, though no one noticed it." Franco Abbiati focused more on Huston's contribution: "As director, John Huston, aided by Nicola Benois' set design, had no big problems to solve. It goes without saying that while this production can hardly compete with Huston's many achievements in filmmaking, he resolved the dramatic problems in his own way, using the natural realism of the stage."[13] Guardarino Guidi agreed that "his staging went its unobtrusive way, placing the singers as in a chess game." The La Scala audience, notoriously hostile to innovation, was predictably savage. Guidi noted that "cries of '*Vergogna!*' '*basta!*' '*buffoni!*' (For shame! Stop it! Clowns!) echoed across the Teatro alla Scala. . . . Attendance was sparse. 'A squalid success,' said *La Notte.*" But it was not Huston's fault. The music was dissonant and the libretto unappealing.

Huston took Ava and Anjelica to the premiere in Milan on March 1,

1966, and was rather shocked by the loud boos and hisses. He had enjoyed a new artistic challenge, but the opera, he said, pleased neither the modernists nor the traditionalists in the theater. And he didn't much care for it himself: "The first night, half the audience was modern and looked to the future, and the other half was there for the operas of Verdi and Puccini. . . . It was avant-garde but not John Cage. However, I couldn't sing a single bar of the opera. There was no melody whatever."[14]

TWENTY-ONE

LOVE AND DEATH,
1967–1969

· I ·

After the epic extravaganza of *The Bible* Huston returned to a more congenial type of film, an adaptation of a modern literary work. He stayed on in Italy to make *Reflections in a Golden Eye* (1967), based on Carson McCullers' novella of 1941, a typical piece of Southern Gothic writing. The title came from T. S. Eliot's "Lines for an Old Man": "Reflected from my golden eye / The dullard knows that he is mad," and there's plenty of dullness and madness in the book. Edgar Allan Poe created this genre, and William Faulkner and Tennessee Williams perfected it. Gothic tales contain grotesque, tempestuous characters, bizarre and spooky sensuality, overheated emotions and melodramatic violence. The movie uses narcissism and voyeurism to tell the story as characters stare into mirrors and spy through windows. The soldier whom Major Penderton (Marlon Brando) is in love with frequently creeps into the bedroom to stare at Penderton's wife, Leonora (Elizabeth Taylor), and fondle her fetishistic underwear while she sleeps. The sickly colonel's wife, played by Julie Harris, has lost a baby and cut off her nipples—in two surgical slices and with intense pain—with a pair of garden shears. Edmund Wilson defined McCullers' curious blend of styles when he observed that the novella "was dramatic but quite unreal. . . . It did not achieve the validity either of realistic fiction, supposed to take place in the actual world, or of the imaginative poem in prose which is true to psychological experience."

In the novella the characters are portrayed through their dreams and remain paralyzed until the final burst of action. It was difficult to translate this story into a movie, which demands action and movement. The young Francis Ford Coppola (just out of film school) wrote one version of the screenplay and Christopher Isherwood (attracted to the homosexual theme) did another. Gladys Hill did a third version with the obscure Scottish novelist Chapman Mortimer, but their faithful and static adaptation lacked Huston's characteristic pace and interest. Huston also tried to secure three different composers—Benjamin Britten (once again), Samuel Barber and John Cage (who was very cagey)—before falling back on the reliable but uninspired Toshiro Mayuzumi. Huston earned $400,000 and a bonus of $100,000 if he brought the picture in on schedule. Brando and Taylor earned $1 million each.

The movie—shot mostly in Italy—opens with a coolly objective line from the opening paragraph of the novella. It sets the scene, sparks the plot and foreshadows the dramatic conclusion: "There is a fort in the South where a few years ago a murder was committed." Taylor was perfect for the adulterous wife of an impotent husband. She'd also played the sensual wife of a repressed homosexual in *Cat on a Hot Tin Roof* (1958) and a sluttish castrating wife in *Who's Afraid of Virginia Woolf?* (1966). She looks alluring in tight jodhpurs, taunts her incapacitated husband (who cannot have sex with either his wife or the soldier) and seems to express their mutual sadomasochistic fantasies when she asks, "Have you ever been collared and dragged out into the street and thrashed by a naked woman?" She later takes off her capacious bra and flings it in Brando's startled face.

Huston was daring in his choice of subjects, and *Reflections* was the first Hollywood movie to deal openly with homosexuality. Unlike most actors, Brando was willing to play Major Penderton. Deeply disturbed, sweating constantly, hopeless with horses, a repressed homosexual, in conflict with his military image and even with his idea of himself, he moons over a private soldier (even collecting his discarded candy wrappers), and is cuckolded by his superior officer Colonel Langdon (played by Brian Keith). Trying to justify his career, Penderton says, "There's much to be said for a life of a man among men. . . . You're never lonely"—though he himself is desperately alone. *Reflections* dramatizes

Penderton's emotional breakdown and ends when he murders the man whom he loves and who loves his wife.

Brando's Penderton, who gives classroom lectures on tactics in the pre–World War II army, speaks with a plummy, pseudo-southern and sometimes unintelligible accent. Huston said that in the scene where Brando stares at himself in the mirror, "I wanted to show a man who is trying to protect the image he has of himself. And that image doesn't exist, it's a dream. He goes through a variety of feelings and states of mind: ambition, servility, satisfaction. He sees himself decorated, received by a general, promoted to an important position." Tremendously impressed by his performance, Huston remarked, "I don't suppose I addressed myself to Brando more than half a dozen times during the making of the picture. Just stood back and watched this *phenomenon.*"[1]

The important scenes with horses, a test of character and courage, were strongly influenced by D. H. Lawrence's dramatic connection between restive horses and earthy sexuality in *Women in Love* (1920), *St. Mawr* (1925), "The Rocking-Horse Winner" (1926) and especially "The Prussian Officer" (1914), where the officer's sadistic homosexuality also ends in murder and self-destruction. The name of Leonora's horse, Firebird, alludes to the phoenix symbol that Lawrence adopted and had stamped on the covers of his books. Taylor, who'd achieved stardom in her girl-horse picture *National Velvet* (1944), has a fine command of her mount in the movie. The soldier expertly rides bare-assed and bareback to excite and tempt Penderton. The major rides badly, loses control of his runaway horse, and is cut and bloodied by the whiplike branches. Leonora intensifies the fear and pain by slashing him across the face with her riding crop. Brando wrote, "For a long shot in that scene, Huston used a stunt rider, and for the close-up he put me in a saddle mounted on a pickup truck and photographed me with a lot of fright on my face."

The sick character played by Julie Harris recalled the sick author Carson McCullers. The pathetic, severely disturbed aspect of her personality is suggested by a famous painting that hangs on the wall of her bedroom. Andrew Wyeth's *Christina's World* (1948) portrays a scrawny, crippled woman who crawls through a field of brown grass toward an unreachable destination. Harris' devoted servant Anacleto, played by Rosauro (Zorro) David, was a hairdresser at Saks Fifth Avenue in New York when he was cast in the role. Huston wanted Zorro to be flagrantly faggy, but (a friend observed) "couldn't bring himself to tell him what he wanted. It gives you some idea of how old-fashioned, Hemingway-macho Huston was being as a director."[2] Finally, the Filipino understood what was required, asked, "Am I supposed to be gay?" and camped it up as an over-the-top effeminate servant. Anacleto, Penderton's alter ego, acts out the flamboyant queen that the major is trying to repress. Colonel Langdon, with unconscious irony, says Anacleto "wouldn't be happy in the army, but it would make a man of him."

In this innovative film, Huston continued his experiments with color, begun in *Moulin Rouge* and *Moby Dick*, to enhance and soften the mood of the harsh military setting. He achieved a muted, subtle, autumnal quality and what he called "a golden effect—a diffuse amber color—that was quite beautiful and matched the mood of the picture. . . . [The golden hue] served to separate the audience somewhat from the characters, who were in various ways withdrawn from reality, and make their story a bit more remote and erotic."

The film critic Pauline Kael admired Huston's " 'desaturated' [toned down] color process—golden hued, with delicate sepia and pink tones."[3] The "golden eye" effect was also praised by the director William Wyler, who "believed the color print . . . is a most remarkable example of the way to use color for the proper mood of a film." The playwright William Inge agreed that "*Reflections* is one of the most beautiful films I have ever seen." When the Technicolor officials objected to Huston's variations of their process, Huston defended his work: "Audiences must not be denied the right to see *Reflections* at its best: I do not intend to see the content or impact of Carson McCullers' great novel diminished by showing it in old fashioned calendar colors." But the studio executives, as usual, put financial above artistic considerations and had the last word. Despite his personal prestige and fierce defense, Huston lost this fight. The studio's telegram insisted: "Warner distribution organization completely convinced full color more desirable from commercial point of view than desaturated version."⁴ As a "compromise," they used Huston's golden tones for the first two weeks, then released the inferior version.

Both Brando and Taylor, constantly hounded by the paparazzi, refused to publicize *Reflections,* and Warners didn't know how to handle the weird picture. Ray Stark told Huston, "We have a helluva job getting anything into the ads that newspapers will accept." In Stark's view, the whole promotion campaign was misguided: the picture was "delivered to the public prematurely, with no in-depth advance publicity or advertising and no Premiere . . . during Jewish Holy Week and in the middle of the World Series." The serious film reviewer Vernon Young, echoing Edmund Wilson's criticism of the novella, defined the mood that puzzled and disturbed the audience: "an atmosphere of spiritual infirmity and moral caprice . . . of numb tranquility stretching between outbreaks of violence."⁵

· II ·

After Ray Stark rented a movie theater in her hometown, Nyack, New York, to screen *Reflections* for her, McCullers was even more ecstatic about the picture than Traven had been about *Sierra Madre.* She wrote Huston: "The weird power and brilliance quite overcomes me. The [novella] is so faithfully adhered to. . . . The characters are exactly as I saw them. . . . The dialogue, most of which you created, rings completely true to the ear. You have made my original book a new and tremendously powerful creation."

McCullers, who had to be treated gently, had been deeply scarred by an endless series of medical catastrophes that made her feel like Job. Crippled by a stroke when she was only twenty-four, she had lurched around with a cane, drunk heavily and gulped down barbiturates, had tried to kill herself and done time in a psychiatric clinic. She'd also been afflicted by rheumatic heart disease, cardiac failure, breast cancer, paralysis, pneumonia and a shattered hip, and was now confined to her wheelchair or her bed. Remembering his own years in hospitals and always compassionate with sick people, Huston made a grand gesture that gave her a last chance to have a normal life. She recalled him asking, on their first meeting, " 'Why don't you come to Ireland to visit me?' Since I'd been in bed for three years, it seemed a little fantastic, but I said, 'Are you serious?' 'As serious as I can get. You know, there are always airplanes.' So at Christmas John sent Ida and me round trip first class tickets to Ireland via Irish Airlines." (Ida Reeder was her maid and companion.) He hired an ambulance to meet her at Shannon Airport and, to cheer her up, promised to take her trout fishing in his own private stream. He even offered to borrow a helicopter from the Irish Ministry of Defence, which she regretfully refused. Her stretcher would have to be slung underneath it and she would have had to ride *outside* the aircraft. "What a wild one you are!," she exclaimed. "Helicopter indeed! I can see Ida flying over Ireland and landing on your Castle lawn."[6]

Huston was not as forthright as he claimed to be and was rather surprised when she accepted his magnanimous offer: "This wasn't something I meant seriously. It was inconceivable to me that she could make such a trip in her condition." Instead of safely canceling the journey because of all the medical problems—she might well have died en route and been sent home in a coffin—Huston (as always) was excited by the challenge. Though it was a tremendous responsibility to invite and care for a paralyzed invalid who was close to death, he was willing to follow through when she unexpectedly responded to his invitation. He risked her life, but also gave her the joyous hope that prolonged it. McCullers arrived for a seventeen-day visit on April 2, 1967, and Huston found her "so intelligent, so alert, so terribly stricken." After a brief wheelchair tour through the gardens and house, she was confined to her hospital bed, with siderails and raised upper part, and used a bent straw for her silver whiskey cup. The heavy carved figure of a crucified Christ gazed down on her bed, a sconce on the wall held thick wax candles, the fireplace burned heavy logs and a vase of flowers brightened the room. Anticipating her every wish, Huston did everything he could to make her comfortable and happy. He treated her like a celebrity and gave her more than two weeks of pure happiness. They talked at length about foxhunting, politics, art, *Reflections* and James Joyce. A photo in the *Irish Times* showed McCullers—with cropped convict's hair, jagged teeth and spindly arms—clutching Huston, with an uneasy smile, as their heads touch on her pillow.

Huston's Irish doctor, who looked after her, wrote that "Mrs. McCullers has a formidable talent for overcoming physical handicaps," but she still had one terrible decision to make. She'd established such a close rapport with Huston that, after she'd returned to New York, he was the first person she consulted about the amputation of her "dolo-genic member." She wrote, "The visit was one of the happiest times of my life. John was the first person I told about the leg operation and he was the first to advise my following the doctor's orders in respect to the amputation. 'You'll move about so much easier,' he said, 'and it will be a blessing to be rid of all that useless pain.' "[7] Once she agreed to the dreadful operation and gave him the exact date in October, Huston promised to come to New York and be with her before, during and after the surgery. Soon after making the arrangements, she had a stroke. She was five feet eight inches tall, but at the end of her life weighed only seventy-five pounds. After the stroke she was unconscious for five weeks, and died at the age of fifty on September 29, 1967—only five months after returning from Ireland.

· III ·

Sinful Davey (1969), a very different kind of movie, was an attempt to make a popular comedy and capitalize on the success of Tony Richardson's *Tom Jones* (1963) and on the publicity surrounding *Where's Jack?* (1969), about the highwayman and escape artist Jack Sheppard. In Huston's romp, set in nineteenth-century Scotland, Davey is a reckless youth, army deserter and thief, whose father has been hanged by the Crown. He plans to surpass his father's reputation as an outlaw before he's also captured and executed. At the end, after many crimes and adventures, he escapes the gallows and gets the girl. Huston was attracted to the picture because it had a fox hunt and could be shot in Ireland. Seamus Byrne, a lowly assistant on the movie, noted that

Huston rode unconventionally, with his legs out in long stirrups. He saw him as The Leader: a virile commander with great physical presence.

Huston wanted the seventeen-year-old Anjelica to play the female lead, but the producer Walter Mirisch was adamantly opposed and Huston finally gave in. The part was played by the eighteen-year-old Pamela Franklin. Born (like Olivia de Havilland) in Tokyo to British parents, she'd trained as a ballet dancer, given a fine performance as the spooky little girl in *The Innocents* (1961) and gradually evolved from juvenile to ingenue roles. John Hurt, who played Davey, spent a month in Hampshire learning to ride with the man who'd been master of the horse in *Lawrence of Arabia*. Since Huston didn't like makeup on men, he sent Hurt to Ibiza, off the northeast coast of Spain, to get a healthy suntan.

Hurt recalled that Huston was a great teaser, tester and practical joker, especially with horses. He put Hurt on a strong-willed mount during slashing rain in the Irish hills, starting far away and out of sight, riding through the hunt and through the hounds (which is never done), then off into the distance and out of camera range. He made Hurt repeat this maneuver again and again. When Hurt kept control of his horse and survived the taxing ride, Huston complimented him by throwing his hat on the ground, stamping on it and shouting, "Hats off to you, Johnny!" The last shot of the movie was of race day at the Curragh, the course in County Kildare, and Hurt was subjected to a final prank. He had to be underwater in a freezing Irish river, but by the time he came up, he found everyone had disappeared. He was alone, cold and soaking wet. Huston had told the crew to repair to the club and, abandoning Hurt, had joined them there for drinks around the fire. Hurt thought Huston was attracted to this picture, very different from his usual subjects, for personal reasons: It was really about his relations with his father. Like Davey, Sinful John wanted to do everything Walter had ever done, outdo his father and get away—in both senses—with everything.

Seamus Byrne remembered Huston as a gentle and courteous man who spoke very slowly. Hurt found him complicated rather than unpleasant, and completely aware of how to deal with each actor. He'd say "I'll talk to you later about that" or, more caustically, "There's not a great deal we can do for you—apart from plastic surgery." Huston could be impulsive, self-indulgent, even extravagant. When he inspected a huge set, the size of a ballroom, he told the crew, "You've done a great job, boys. Just put the fireplace at the other end of the hall"—a moving job that took three whole days. One morning there was a long scene, with complicated dialogue, between Hurt and Ronald Fraser. As they began to act, Huston opened the *Irish Times*. Without ever lowering the paper or looking at the actors, he repeatedly said, "Okay, we'll go again." It was agonizing never to see his face during the two-hour scene. But he preferred to listen to rather than to watch them, and taught them how to do the scene in their own way. Hurt thought Huston was tough as a director. It was not an easy game working for him, but a struggle you had to get through, a battlefield, a baptism of fire. It was rewarding because you learned a lot, especially that life was a fight for survival and that with Huston you had to be prepared for anything.

The movie had some fatal flaws. Hurt said that Huston could be sophisticated and funny, but was not the right director for that sort of broad comedy and didn't quite know how to make it work. It was too evenly paced, too slow, too arbitrary.[8] Byrne recalled that there was a lot of interference from the studio, that Huston disliked what they did to the picture and that his version was much better. Huston said, "Some of the pictures that I most wish I hadn't made were pretty good pictures at one time. I mean, I wasn't responsible for their being bad." He believed that Walter Mirisch ruined *Sinful Davey*, just as Dore Schary had ruined *The Red Badge of Courage* and John Wayne had ruined *The Barbarian and the Geisha*. He was furious about "the FUCK UP that Walter Mirisch made of it" by adding unnecessary narration and turning the whole story into a flashback. Huston liked the picture and refused to be influenced by the disastrous previews. Defending himself, Mirisch wrote that Paul Kohner told him, " 'I think you must do whatever you need to do.' I then supervised the re-editing of the picture until the previews had improved considerably. But it didn't really help." Mirisch thought Huston was "unprofessional" to abandon the picture after handing in his version and leave the producer to deal with all the problems.[9] After one unsuccessful week in New York, *Sinful Davey* was pulled from the theaters. It's rarely seen on television, didn't make it into tape or disk and is considered one of Huston's major failures.

· IV ·

Between 1968 and 1973 Huston made five poor pictures, including *Sinful Davey—A Walk with Love and Death, The Kremlin Letter, The Life and Times of Judge Roy Bean* and *The Mackintosh Man*. Why were there so many bad movies in these years? The chance to work in attractive locales (Mexico, Africa, Japan, Ireland) or with especially companionable actors occasionally outweighed a poor choice of subject or an ill-prepared script. He sometimes had an obligation to fulfill a contract and a pressing need for money, or wanted to keep working and had nothing better on offer. In the case of *A Walk with Love and Death* (1969), he also wanted to launch his teenaged daughter as an actress. As in a fairy tale, John and Anjelica's wish was granted, but the consequences were unpleasant.

The movie was set in France during the Peasants' Revolt of 1358, and medieval knights, castles and battles were clearly not Huston's forte. He described it as a story of two doomed "young people—children almost—who were in love and trying to escape from a world that was all violence and desolation." The producer Carter De Haven recalled that he sent Huston the script of *Walk,* based on a novel by the Dutch-born Hans Koningsberger. Huston loved it and De Haven flew to Ireland to discuss the project. Huston said, "Let's do it right away," and asked if De Haven was willing to see Anjelica in London on the way home. Though she was very young, Huston assured the producer that she was perfect for the role and he hired her. They originally planned to shoot the movie in France, but after the student revolution of 1968—whose chaos is reflected in the lovers' plight in the picture—that location became impossible. They looked for settings in Italy, couldn't find the right castle and finally settled on Austria.

The script was written by Dale Wasserman, who'd had a tremendous success with *Man of La Mancha* (1965), a musical based on *Don*

Quixote. He was new to screenwriting, very determined to protect this "very literary" material, but no match for Huston. Assuming his most imperious manner when they were revising the script in Ireland, Huston informed him: "Let me tell you how I work. You can accept this or, after a few days' vacation here, go back to New York. I don't want to keep you any longer than necessary. If a bird flew in the window with a seed in its mouth and that was a fortuitous idea that worked, I'd use it." In the end, Wasserman capitulated and agreed to most of Huston's suggestions.

Koningsberger, who was on the scene, noted that Huston never lost his temper or exploded in anger, was always polite, cordial and genial, and seemed to have "boundless patience and gentleness."[10] Curtice Taylor, an assistant on this movie, remarked that Huston was prudish, and disliked kissing and nude scenes. Anjelica and her costar Assaf Dayan (son of Moshe Dayan, the Israeli war hero and minister of defense) couldn't appear naked in the pond scene and (like Adam and Eve in *The Bible*) had to wear flesh-colored body suits. Since Dayan's hair showed through his body suit, Taylor was delegated to mow his extremely hairy legs. But the children of two famous fathers in Romeo and Juliet roles failed to attract a young audience.

Anjelica, who'd led a very sheltered life at St. Clerans, had had a patchy education. She was first taught by private tutors, then by nuns at a convent. After Ricki moved to London, she attended a French lycée and an English school. She had had a tiny part in *Sinful Davey*, but was very tall and skinny, still gawky and awkward, and not especially attractive. Considering Mirisch's forceful opposition and Anjelica's natural reluctance, John was rather disingenuous when he said, "The problem about Anjelica has been to keep her off the screen until now. I never wanted her to be a child actress. But she has been proposed by associates of mine for important roles ever since she was a little girl." In fact, he himself had actively promoted her career.

John's problems with Anjelica began well before the minefield of the movie. She was angry about the way he'd treated Ricki, parading his lovers at St. Clerans and having a child with Zoe Sallis. He disapproved of Anjelica's swinging life in London and what Dale Wasserman called her "curiously intense interest" in drugs. (Later, in 1977, she got into serious trouble and was caught with cocaine when the police were investigating the rape charges against Roman Polanski.) John may have been patient and gentle with the other actors, but was extremely harsh with Anjelica. In an effort to avoid favoritism, he was very hard on her and (Danny Huston said) "she had a terrible time on *Walk.*" Penelope Tree—a friend of Anjelica, a famous model and the daughter of Marietta—spent a few days on the set. She said that John, too critical and demanding, was foul to Anjelica and (despite all her efforts to please him) persecuted her as if she were doing a terrible job. They had lots of rows and she was in tears most of the time.[11] John's fine performance as her uncle Robert the Elder merely emphasized her own ineptitude.

The Mexican actress Lupita Kohner, married to John's agent, thought Anjelica was too young, ill prepared—and scared to death. Anjelica disliked her own appearance and her role, was insecure about her acting ability, felt lost in Austria and was terrified of her father. When she saw the first screening, her biographer wrote, "she laughed to the point of hysteria. Under that laughter lay a lot of pain." The reviews were harsh, and John Simon delivered the unkindest cut of all: "There is a perfectly blank, supremely inept performance . . . by Huston's daughter, Anjelica, who had the face of an exhausted gnu, the voice of an unstrung tennis racket, and a figure of no describable shape." Anjelica was so bruised by the experience that she gave up acting and worked as a fashion model in New York.

Many years later, when she'd become an established star, Anjelica looked back on *Walk* with unqualified horror. She told Sofia Coppola, "I was a sulky teenager and I wasn't ready to be an actress, even though I had illusions about it. . . . When I look at that film—I saw it about five years ago—it's as embarrassing to me now as it was then."[12] In another interview she said, "I didn't really like the character. I wanted to be an exalted creature. I didn't want to be a fourteenth-century French maid who didn't wear any make-up. . . . My father granted me my life wish and here I was reluctant, obstinate and unprepared. I think I was a big disappointment to him on that one. It took fifteen years to right that wrong"—until they made *Prizzi's Honor* together in 1984.

In her most serious and substantial interview, Anjelica recalled:

My father had become rather critical of my looks, my habits, my developing sense of myself, and I felt that he wanted to drag me back to [my innocent] childhood. The last thing I wanted to do was work with my father. I wasted a good deal of his time. I wasn't clear on my lines; he was very dismayed by our relationship.

I was extremely unhappy about not being able to wear make-up, which was my biggest crutch, and of my father being extremely difficult. One day he just let me have it in front of the whole crew and from that moment I just shut down. My father treated me quite harshly, and I think really he was probably very hurt by the fact that I was so non-compliant. . . .

I was on a publicity tour for *A Walk with Love and Death,* which I despised—this was almost worse than making the movie because you had to talk about it. I remember not being comfortable at all and at a certain point actually confessing on the David Frost show how I had loathed every second of making the film.

Shortly before his death, John also regretted the whole episode: "It was a mistake to have pushed Anjelica into it. She was too young, and she had no training. But it was quite curious that during the making of the film, there was a flickering of the real meaning of the character in her—it was not technique, because she didn't have any. It was simply truth."[13] Anjelica thought she had to do the picture to please him; John felt he had to do the picture to please *her.* Anjelica felt she'd disappointed her father and failed to uphold the high artistic standards of the Hustons. John was angry at himself because he'd made a mistake by insisting she play the part, by pushing her into an embarrassing role before she was ready and by failing to get a good performance out of her. For both father and daughter, *Walk* was a personal and professional disaster.

· V ·

On Wednesday, January 29, 1969—between Huston's finishing and releasing *Sinful Davey* and *A Walk with Love and Death*—Ricki and her much younger lover, a black Jamaican musician, were driving in eastern France, about twenty-five miles from Dijon. The local newspaper reported:

> M. Gilles Marcoux, 24 years old, employed by the Motoculture Saônoise company and living in Arc-les-Gray, was driving yesterday, at 3:15 P.M. on Route Nationale 67 between Besançon and Gray, when about 2 kilometers from Gray, an English sports car suddenly appeared in front of him, making several zigzags before hitting the left front of the small truck he was driving. The accident killed Miss Enrica Huston, born on May 9, 1929 in New York, and living at 31 Maida Avenue in London W2.
>
> Miss Huston, the passenger in the sports car, was killed instantly, while the driver, Mr. Brian Anderson, a 29-year-old musician living at 99 Shirland Road in London W9, was seriously wounded in the face, and was taken to the hospital in Gray, where M. Gilles Marcoux, wounded in the leg, is being treated.

When Anderson's sports car hit a pothole, he swerved across the road and crashed head-on into Marcoux's van. Anderson had severe facial lacerations and cracked ribs; Marcoux lost his left leg; and Ricki was smashed by the collision and burned up in the car. One friend remarked that there was nothing much of her to bring back. It would have been more fitting had the driver been killed and more romantic had she died with her great love, the aristocratic Norwich. The lovely thirty-nine-year-old Ricki became doubly martyred: first as a neglected wife, then as a tragic young victim.

On Thursday afternoon in Rome, Huston and his friends were planning to have a picnic in a park. As Carter De Haven was leaving his hotel that morning, a London newspaper called to tell him that Ricki was dead. De Haven had to tell Huston. When they met he said, "I have something to tell you. Can we talk?" "Sure, sure, kid. Let's talk." "It's not good news. Ricki's been killed." "My God, my God." He looked at De Haven quietly, with no tears, and turned away for a few minutes. He then said, "Well, we'd better have our lunch." Huston, as always, held in his emotions and controlled everything he ever did.[14] Ricki's car crash must have reminded him of his own fatal car accident in 1933 and of his mother's death in 1938, except that Ricki's was completely unexpected and more shocking.

Ricki's death had far-reaching consequences for her three children: Tony, now aged eighteen, Anjelica, seventeen, and the four-year-old Allegra. The youngest—still unaware of her real father—was brought up by various friends and relatives: first by the Waddingtons, who were art dealers in London; then by Ricki's father and stepmother in New York; and also by Celeste Huston and her parents in Beverly Hills. Though she had a disrupted and wandering childhood, Allegra suffered less than the others. After losing their mother, Anjelica and Tony had to depend on a difficult and mainly absent father. For Anjelica, the loss came in the same year as her wretched experience in *A Walk with Love and Death*. When Ricki moved the family to London, Tony had gone to the prestigious Westminster School, which pleased John. But Tony had hated the sudden change from a freewheeling Irish childhood to a strict and demanding English school. He spent three years at Westminster, but made no friends. At the time of his mother's death, he was about to enter London University.

John—who had had very little contact with Walter when he was a boy—had a difficult time with the prickly and contentious Tony. He'd praised Tony's work in *The List of Adrian Messenger*, in which the twelve-year-old played a young heir whom the villain is trying to murder, and noted, "He did exactly what I told him to do. He said his lines reasonably and sensibly. He wasn't being an actor or anything. There was one thing I was quite proud of. He was to jump a horse over a gate. . . . And he did it beautifully, without turning a hair."[15] John insisted on obedience and was especially pleased by a dangerous but well-executed feat.

Tony felt that John wanted to be proud of his children, but did not seem to love them for their own sake. In October 1973 the twenty-three-year-old Tony wrote John a rather self-pitying letter, saying that he'd been deeply insecure since Ricki's death and was depressed by his father's gratuitous pep talks. He complained that John didn't find him interesting or appealing, but valued him only as an elder son. Two months later Tony wrote Gladys Hill that he hadn't been able to find his vocation, and that his "head problems" came from trying to please his father and earn his own living. Danny Huston recalled that John was pretty hard on Tony, adopting a tough manner and challenging him with a certain bravado. In contrast, the old man had "mellowed out" when Danny was growing up and treated his younger son more gently.[16]

TWENTY-TWO

SPIES AND BOXING,

1970–1972

· I ·

In 1970 Huston became involved in two projects with Orson Welles. In Huston's *The Kremlin Letter* (1970) the immensely fat and jowly Welles was wasted (as he was in *The Roots of Heaven*) in the clichéd role of Bresnavitch, a high Russian official who's plotting to advance his career by overthrowing the head of Soviet intelligence. Like Harry Lime, Welles' character in *The Third Man*, Ward, the leader of the American spies, is supposedly dead but actually alive. While they were making *The Kremlin Letter,* Welles persuaded Huston to play James Hannaford, a character based on both Hemingway and Huston, in *The Other Side of the Wind* (1970–75). Welles had spent some time with Hemingway in Spain, and the film takes place on July 2, the date Hemingway killed himself. Welles' promising but self-indulgent film dragged on for five years and was never finished.

In Huston and Gladys Hill's convoluted spy movie, a classic product of the Cold War, the Americans have to infiltrate Russia to retrieve the Kremlin Letter, a secret plan between the U.S. and Soviets to attack Communist China. Like Bogart in *Across the Pacific*, the hero is supposedly kicked out of the military at the beginning of the movie. Huston, who plays a smartly dressed admiral, sends him on his mission. Raf Vallone and George Sanders (as a homosexual transvestite) as well as Max von Sydow and Bibi Andersson (refugees from Ingmar Bergman's films) are excellent. But the young leads, Patrick O'Neal and Barbara Parkins, are a wooden and colorless couple.

There's a lot of secret-agent mystification, influenced by the James Bond movies, but the baffling, labyrinthine plot (compounded by confusing cuts from scene to scene) soon exhausts the patience and interest of the audience. It's very talky for an action movie and has more exposition than drama, too much dialogue in Russian (the fur-hat scenes were shot in Finland) and no interesting characters among the Americans or the villains. Huston asked Curtice Taylor, "Tell me what you think of the script, kid." Curtice, who thought it was a piece of crap but could hardly say so, admitted, "I have no idea what is going on." Huston seemed to reassure him with "lots of people say that," but didn't bother to clarify the screenplay. He made the movie for the money and thought the script, with all its weaknesses, was good enough. Huston filmed one scene with a low camera in imitation of *Citizen Kane*. Impressed, the young Curtice enthusiastically told Welles, "I just took a whole course at UCLA on *Citizen Kane* and we watched it every week for thirteen weeks." To which Welles replied, "What a fucking waste of time!" When Welles told Huston, "John, that [scene] will never work," Huston fell back on his reassuring response, "Oh, Orson, it will be fine, just fine."

Though imperfectly realized, the movie had an important theme that reflected Huston's own darkening view of the world: America's complete lack of principle—in contrast to the idealism of World War II—during the Cold War. In the picture an old-fashioned spy, motivated by pure revenge against his Russian antagonist, is brought back into service. The movie followed the bitter, cynical and disillusioned tradition of *The Spy Who Came in From the Cold* and *The Ipcress File* (both 1965), but lacked their tight plots and convincing characters. In a publicity release, Huston emphasized the sensational elements in the plot: "The American and Russian spies 'are not merely double agents,' says Huston, 'but men and women with five and six faces.' Moreover, they include a San Francisco transvestite, and a Harlem lesbian, a nymphomaniac and an agent who poses as a male prostitute, narcotic addicts and their behind-the-curtain connections, plus a host of other unsavory types. 'I was attracted to the story by its depravity,' explains Huston. 'I thought the story shocking, immoral, vicious and cynical.' " With engaging honesty, he later contrasted the films that were ruined by the studios against his will with the failures that were entirely his own fault: "In the case of *Roots* [*of Heaven*], *A Walk with Love and Death,* and *The Kremlin Letter,* I was given every freedom. I chose those stories, helped write them, directed them, and virtually produced them, and they didn't turn out well."[1]

· II ·

In the spring of 1975, with *The Other Side of the Wind* still unfinished, the playwright and critic Kenneth Tynan noted in his diary the connection between Huston and Welles: "John's charm increases with age: the hooded eyes, the rangy, stooping gait, the incredibly winning smile. He shares my passion for Orson, and told us how Orson had talked him into playing the lead in his last movie." Welles said that his central character, like Hemingway and Huston, is a great figure, a great adventurer, a great fascinator and a "super-Satanic intelligence." After a long exile Hannaford, the aging, embattled, doomed director returns to a Hollywood transformed by the self-conscious intellectuality and fashionable hippiedom of the 1970s. Hannaford feels completely alienated from contemporary taste, yet decides to signal his comeback and compete with this new movement. He sets out to go against his grain and "make a modish low-budget film full of nudity, symbolism, and radical-chic violence, but winds up killing himself in a suicidal car crash."

Welles shot the film in Carefree, Arizona, about thirty miles north of Phoenix, and hired midgets to run through the legs of the actors and amuse the audience. David Thomson wrote that Huston "was magnificently unfazed to find that there was no script, only speeches on pieces of paper. But he did not have to learn these, Welles said, it was enough to read them and then come up with talk of his own that approximated them. So Huston, who had been acting like a character most of his life, stood there in the light and did his best, assured by Welles that he was in no way playing anyone who might be deemed to be a version of Huston or Welles." Baffled by Welles' methods and trying to inject some order into the chaos, Huston would occasionally ask, "Orson, what page are we on?" "Well, John, what the hell difference does it make?" And Huston replied, "I want to know how *drunk* I'm supposed to be."[2]

Welles' biographer Joseph McBride said, "Huston was really his peer in a way that nobody else was, someone he respected greatly as a director, and an old friend. He was not the kind of person you could order around or bully. You had to treat him with great tact and diplomacy." When Welles felt Huston was crudely leering at a young girl during a sex scene, he subtly suggested that Huston imitate his father: "Try using Walter's kindly paternal air. No one ever had a higher score with women than Walter."[3] Well pleased with Huston, Welles summoned up some rare modesty when puffing the picture and called his performance "one of the best I've ever seen on the screen. When I get to the Heavenly Gates, if I'm allowed in, it will be because I cast the best part I ever could have played myself with John Huston. He's better than I would have been—and I would have been great!" Though Welles never paid his $75,000 fee, Huston was typically cavalier about the money. He liked collaborating with his old friend, found the theme of the film appealing and told Peter Viertel that "he had enjoyed the experience . . . because the movie was 'such a desperate venture' . . . which made work the kind of perilous undertaking John enjoyed, an adventure shared by desperate men that finally came to nothing."[4]

· III ·

Thinking, no doubt, about the success of *The Maltese Falcon* and the fiasco of *The Bible*, Huston came to believe "the smaller the budget, the better the movie." *Fat City* (1972), made in forty-two days for only $2.6 million, was his one artistic success, amid five potboiling failures, between 1969 and 1973. Ray Stark, once again the producer, was a lively companion on the set. An amusing character, full of energy and excitement, he was also a nonstop talker. His sexy secretary said they always had to take separate planes—not for safety or to prevent sudden pounces—but because Stark never shut up. Huston, an inveterate gambler, would always challenge fate, or whoever challenged him, in any contest. Stark complained that Huston's addiction to backgammon took too much time away from work and threatened to confiscate the game. But every night at Stark's house they had a communal dinner, which bonded the cast, and each actor prepared one course (Stacy Keach's specialty was lemon soufflé).

When they were planning the film, Stark sent Huston a precious pre-Columbian statue and ordered his associate producer, David Dworski, to hold it in his lap on the plane to Ireland. But Dworski got tired of holding the heavy package and put it in the stewardess' closet. He arrived at St. Clerans and presented it to Huston, who ceremoniously unwrapped the gift and found it broken into pieces. He turned to ice and didn't speak to Dworski for the rest of his visit, but relished the thought of Stark's furious reaction when he found out how his emissary had bungled the mission.[5]

Like Huston, Leonard Gardner—author of the *Fat City* novel and screenplay—had had a sickly childhood and been confined to bed for a year. Also like Huston, he'd compensated for his invalidism by becoming an amateur boxer and had fought seven matches as a 145-pound welterweight. Huston loved getting back into the boxing world in Stockton, California, where the film was shot. He and Gardner acted as corner men in a real fight, busily sponging and rubbing down their boxer. But Huston was now at the beginning of his sixteen-year bout with emphysema. He refused to have surgery and had to have a huge oxygen tank, nearly three feet high, near the bed in his rented apartment. He did not keep it on the set during filming, but would sometimes erupt in terrible coughing fits and turn purple while the stagehands crossed their fingers and hoped he'd survive yet another attack.

The title *Fat City*—particularly ironic in working-class, down-and-out Stockton—means not only being "out of condition," but also having the "hopeless dreams" of a loser who's beaten before he even starts. The story counterpoints two boxers: Billy Tully, an alcoholic has-been, and Ernie Munger, a talented young man at the beginning of his career. Huston wrote that the next stop for Tully (played by Keach) is "Skid Row, and his younger counterpart [Jeff Bridges' Munger] is headed in the same direction despite the living lesson before his eyes." After

Munger gets knocked out, his girlfriend gets knocked up—and he has to marry her. Munger doesn't want the wife he has; Tully, stuck for a time with the drunken and sluttish Oma, longs for the wife who's sensed his spiritual defeat and left him.

Gardner had the rare good fortune of adapting his own first-rate novel, remaining the film's only screenwriter from beginning to end and having relatively little interference from Huston, Stark or the studio. But he did encounter a few problems. Just before shooting began, Stark sent him Huston's last-minute rewrites and asked for Gardner's comments. Gardner wrote candid remarks such as "that doesn't sound like what a real person would say" and told Stark, "Please *don't* show them to Huston." Stirring up some mischief, Stark immediately sent them right on to the director. At their next meeting Huston, abandoning his lordly and theatrical accent for the first and only time with Gardner, angrily said, "Leonard, your comments were inappropriate and uncalled for."[6]

Tully says, "The job I'd really like has never been invented." When he's washed up as a boxer and forced to join the deadbeat farm laborers, who use short hoes to pick out the weeds without hurting the onions, the work is painful and backbreaking. After seeing the dailies, the studio complained that the drive-in audience couldn't see the workers' faces as they bent over. So the scene was reshot with long hoes, the dialogue about back pain was left unchanged and the whole point of the episode was pretty well lost.

There's a tremendous contrast between Tim Holt's idealized recollections in *Sierra Madre* of joyously working as a California fruit-picker and the harsh realism (despite the use of long hoes) of working the onion fields in *Fat City*. Holt remembers: "One summer when I was a kid I worked as a picker in a peach harvest in the San Joaquin Valley. . . . Hundreds of people—old and young—whole families working together. After the day's work we used to build big bonfires and sit around 'em and sing to guitar music. . . . Everybody had a wonderful time." But in *Fat City* the exhausted workers of Stockton, instead of singing 'round the bonfire, drag themselves to the nearest bar. One of the onion workers condemns the exploitation and bitterly exclaims, "I worked like hell all day yesterday; after they made the deductions, I had only five bucks left." This parallels the grim scene in which a fight manager pays off the battered and bloodied Tully, takes extortionate deductions and gives him only $100.

Stacy Keach was saddened when they cut a twenty-minute sequence that takes place after Tully has reached his peak as a fighter. In these scenes Tully wins a fight and moves out of his seedy apartment, but begins a downward spiral, can't pay his new rent and is forced to live in a dumpster. The studio felt the sequence was too depressing in an already-too-depressing film. But Keach thought, "What the hell, it wasn't *Rocky*" and wasn't meant to have a sentimental uplift. When Gardner also objected to scenes that were dropped, Huston would put him off with, "Oh, no, we won't go into that." During their final discussion in Huston's apartment, he poured out two huge whiskeys (which he could handle much better than Gardner) and when they'd drunk them he said, "Well, we're all finished; that takes care of it." Gardner called this "the slick maneuver of a great manipulator."

Gardner remembered that Huston used a lot of nonprofessionals in the film and that everyone in the Stockton boxing scene got into the act. Though eager to make a strong impression, the pickup actors naturally needed more guidance than the pros. During the scene in the bowling alley, Huston put the manager at ease by offering him some food—"Would you like a hamburger?" "Oh yes, thanks"—and encouraged him to eat it while speaking his lines. Keach liked the way Huston trusted actors and let them find their own emotions and interpretations. He would ask, "How do you think we should do this scene?," and then tell Keach and Susan Tyrrell (who played Oma) to work up their encounter in her apartment by themselves. When they did the scene, he'd make a few subtle suggestions. His most frequent directions were merely "a little more" or "a little less."[7]

Curtis Cokes, a professional boxer with no acting experience, gives a superb performance as Earl, Oma's black boyfriend. Huston admired his work and said, "There's something in that face, a melancholy and a worldliness, and a [special] cadence in his voice." When Earl is sent to jail, Tully, whose failure as a boxer and a man has been mercilessly pounded into him, moves in with Oma and has some sadly amusing ironic dialogue with her. She tells Tully that her second husband "had unnatural desires," which she undoubtedly did her level best to satisfy. Mentioning in passing that she'd been raped, she high-mindedly asserts, "I've never been ashamed of the act of love." When Tully tries on Earl's hideous and impossibly small clothing, Oma compliments him and he asks, with a touch of vanity, "Have I got flair now?" She gives him a backhanded compliment by stating, "You're the only son of a bitch that's worth a shit in this place," and he gratefully replies, "I appreciate that."

After Earl is released and moves back in with Oma, Tully returns to pick up his own clothes. Their lively speech comes almost verbatim from Gardner's novel:

> EARL: Don't listen to her. She been drinkin'. . . . We been
> out on the town. . . . She just like to blow off steam. Don't
> listen to her. We gets along. I'll handle her. I just don't
> pay her no mind. Thing you got to understand about her,
> she's a juicehead.
> BILLY: I know. She won't eat either.
> EARL: Yeah, thass on account of her unhappy life and all
> that shit. Nothin' I can do about that, so I don't let it
> worry me.

Huston had originally wanted Brando for *Fat City*. When David Dworski expressed doubts about Brando's ability to get into proper shape, Huston put Dworski down by insisting that Brando "could play a babe in arms." The fight scenes, which complement the miserable encounters with women, are the core of the film. Six months before shooting began, Keach went to New York to begin training as a boxer with the Puerto Rican light-heavyweight José Torres. He worked with both the speed and the heavy bags, and did long runs while bending to pick up imaginary stones along the way. Describing Tully as a fighter, Torres told Keach that he had big hands and constantly bobbed and weaved.

The fight scenes between the defiant antagonists are realistic and vivid. They took two days to shoot and were choreographed like a ballet. The professional boxers had to hold back and let Keach and Bridges land some tough punches, and after watching the dailies they redid some of the shots. No one was seriously hurt, but after the last fight scene was finished, Huston said, "Let's have two minutes of real boxing." The pro Sixto Rodriguez (who played the Mexican fighter Lucero) told Keach, "Hit me as hard as you can, it's okay." "You mean it?" "Absolutely." Keach, in good shape, hit him hard and Rodriguez, acting reflexively, knocked him out with a right hook. Keach thought Huston certainly had a devilish side to his nature, but could be extremely kind. When Keach had the title role in a three-and-a-half-hour, sold-out performance of *Hamlet* and couldn't get even one extra ticket, Huston— eager to watch him—sat on the stairs throughout the whole play.[8]

Tully's victory over Lucero is really a stoic defeat. He's so badly beaten up that he doesn't even realize he's won the fight against his tough Mexican opponent. Lucero is alone and without a manager, just as Tully had been all alone when his face was cut by a razor punch in Panama. Though desperately sick and pissing blood from a damaged kidney, Lucero still struggles on, and when Tully consoles him, the two victims embrace each other in mutual pain.

After a nasty and potentially damaging article had appeared in the *Los Angeles Times* before the film was released, Gardner defended the actors in a letter to Ray Stark: "Stacy and Jeff did well in the ring. They didn't look like champs, but they weren't playing champs. . . . Both moved well. Each threw good straight jabs; neither telegraphed his punches; neither threw wild swings. . . . Stacy looks tough and banged around by life; and Jeff has the innocence, vulnerability and robustness of Ernie." The next day Stark, a powerful figure in Hollywood, blasted the journalist in a feisty letter to his editor: "If Nachman had spent as much time with the people he has misquoted as he did with the attractive young stand-ins, you would have had a more accurate story though he would have had a less interesting sojourn in *Fat City*."

Apart from *The Set-Up* (1949) and *The Harder They Fall* (1956), most boxing pictures from *Golden Boy* (1939) to *Rocky* (1976) emphasized the champions. Gardner didn't want to write a typical boxing movie, with gangsters and fixed fights, and *Fat City* focuses on the losers. Though Munger seems to be on the way up and Tully is clearly going down, both are implacably doomed. At the beginning of the movie Tully, exaggerating Munger's ability in order to hide his own decline, calls him a "natural." When they meet at the end, he tries to pull Munger down to his own level by claiming, "There's a guy that is soft at the center"—good for candy, bad for boxers.

The poignant diner scene at the end of *Fat City*, in which the two washed-up and now-hostile boxers find they have nothing more to say to each other, recalls Edward Hopper's *Nighthawks* (1942). This painting, itself influenced by Hemingway's "The Killers," tells a story. The bright, glaring light bounces off the yellow walls and tall metal coffee containers in an all-night diner, and illuminates the dark, empty street, lined with vacant storefronts and red brick tenements. Inside Hopper's cinematic scene, beneath a sign advertising cheap Phillies cigars, a crouching, white-uniformed attendant serves—on a high-stooled, triangular, shiny brown counter—a single man (his back to the window) and a pale, garishly dressed redhead with her dark-suited companion. The late nighters or insomniacs, with nowhere else to go, have found their last refuge. Hopper's portrayal of these isolated, lonely figures in an indifferent or even hostile city is menacing, chilling, even spooky.

The concluding scene in the film is different, and even better, than the novel. Gardner wanted to bring Tully and Munger together in an all-night diner. Tully has hit a brick wall and finally sees that he has no future. He sits down with Munger and they don't speak. Huston was willing to extend their long, bizarre silence to make it more effective. Looking at the wrecked old Chinese man working behind the short-order counter—a figure right out of *Nighthawks*—Tully finally says:

BILLY: How'd you like to wake up in the morning—and be like him? . . . Waste! . . . Before you can get rollin', your life makes a beeline for the drain.
ERNIE: Maybe he's happy.

BILLY: Maybe we're all happy. . . . Right? (*to old man, who nods and smiles hugely, simply in response to Billy's own grin*). . . . Ya think he was ever young once?
ERNIE: Maybe he wasn't.

Their desperate hope for something better has been destroyed. Tully is not yet ready—never really was ready—for a comeback. He can no longer fight and is even more broken down now than he was at the beginning. Though Munger does come back, his fate is foreshadowed in Tully's sad decline.

The camera work and the music enhance the movie. The cinematographer Conrad Hall emphasized the contrast between the dark bar, which hides Tully's despair, and the blazing light, which reveals it when he staggers out into the street. (The studio, missing the point, complained that Hall had overexposed the daylight.) The reprise of the song over the closing credits also leaves the theme echoing in the audience's head: "Yesterday is dead and gone, / And tomorrow's out of sight, / And it's bad to be alone, / Help me make it through the night."

Fat City shows compassion for both winners and losers, and relates the boxers' fights to the farmworkers' struggle to survive. The vivid details and realistic dialogue of Huston's quietly moving film portray deadbeat characters and drifting alcoholics who fall through the cracks of society. The style, mood and theme are remarkably close to those of Hemingway's story, "A Clean, Well-Lighted Place," in which the older waiter, sympathizing with the despair of the old patron, observes: "I am of those who like to stay late at the café. . . . With all those who do not want to go to bed. With all those who need a light for the night."[9]

TWENTY-THREE

CELESTE SHANE AND

A DESERT IDYLL,

1972–1975

· I ·

Like the novelist Saul Bellow, Huston had five wives. Impatient of bourgeois restraints and constricted by monogamy, both men were eminently unsuited for wedlock, yet were always ready to marry, and marry again. But while the solitary Bellow craved a stable and emotionally supportive wife to nourish his spirit and encourage his writing, Huston's work led him to roam the world, making pictures and acquiring art, and he spent very little time with his wives and children. In a frequently quoted statement at the beginning of his autobiography, Huston asserted, "No one of my wives has been remotely like any of the others—and certainly none of them was like my mother. They were a mixed bag: a schoolgirl; a gentlewoman; a motion picture actress; a ballerina; and a crocodile." This description distorts the truth. Dorothy Harvey, hardly a schoolgirl, was twenty-two when they married; Ricki Soma had had only a brief ballet career before she turned to modeling and marriage. Each new wife was about ten years younger than her predecessor, and his fifth bride, the thirty-three-year-old Celeste (Cici) Shane, was exactly half his age when they married in 1972. His first four wives in various ways gave up the struggle to remain with Huston. Dorothy Harvey drank; Lesley Black succumbed to deep depression; Evelyn Keyes resented his impulsive acqustion of the orphan Pablo and the chimpanzee; Ricki Soma endured his neglect and turned to her children.

Despite their youth and comeliness, Huston lost interest in all his wives after a few years and relapsed into compulsive infidelities. He declared, in a mock-solemn statement with a cynical sting in its tail, "Women need to be married. Women need the respect and the commitment of marriage. And frankly, if I am married to that woman, I will be committed and she will have the best of me and the best I can offer in life. And the same with my relationships." He added, "I regret that lack within myself that enables a man to pour all his affections into one individual," but there is little evidence that he ever tried to do so. When in 1949 he received an idealistic award to promote world unity, he turned it down, saying that he couldn't even maintain the unity of his own family. With Betty O'Kelly to run his household and Gladys Hill to deal with the details of his personal life, Huston was so often absent from home and so involved with his current lovers that it didn't make a tremendous difference when one wife departed and another took her place.

Huston told Cici Shane that she reminded him of his mother— a dubious compliment and dangerous sign. Cici, the only one of his wives who fought back, has had a bad press, mainly because of Huston's negative comments about her. But when her side of the story is told, the reasons for their marriage and for the disintegration of their love become more compelling than his mere condemnation of her character.

Cici came from a privileged background. Her mother was said to have been the prettiest girl in Kansas City. Her Jewish father owned a successful car rental and leasing business, as well as a lot of real estate, and had a series of chauffeur-driven Rolls-Royces. Her parents owned a grand house on four acres in Beverly Hills, which had belonged to Greta Garbo in the 1920s, and a good deal of their furniture came from the sale of William Randolph Hearst and Marion Davies' luxurious estate in Santa Monica. In contrast to Ricki, who was young and insecure when she was first married, and to Evelyn Keyes, a Texas girl who was ill at ease with Pauline Potter and New York socialites, Cici felt right at home with celebrities and tycoons. She had no financial worries and knew her father would help her whenever she needed money. She admired Huston for spending more than he had, living in grand style, and generously helping his children and his friends.

The refractory young woman "went to all the good schools and was kicked out of most of them." Cici said, "I didn't want to be a socialite, and I certainly didn't want to be presented. But I had to go through all that stuff. I went to the Debutante Ball, fell down the stairs, dropped the roses, knocked over my date—it was a night of horrors for me" and, whether she was drunk or deliberately subversive, for her parents and friends as well.[1] She briefly attended the University of Mexico (though her Spanish remained rudimentary) and Finch College (a fashionable finishing school in Manhattan) before modeling in New York and living the high life in Beverly Hills, where people played polo and were rich together. Her teenage marriage to a fashionable hairdresser, against her parents' wishes, was a "nine-month catastrophe." Her second marriage, to her childhood sweetheart, the successful screenwriter Wally Green, was the "fulfillment of her dreams" until the arrival in 1966 of her son Collin, who suffered from lack of oxygen during his birth. Severely disabled, he had ataxic cerebral palsy, could not control his muscles and mobility, and eventually had to wear three braces. The marriage ended when Cici would not give up Collin and her husband would not accept the responsibility of caring for him.

Huston's old friend Eloise Hardt introduced John and Cici at a dinner party at her home in Los Angeles, and he was immediately attracted to her youthful exuberance, defiant behavior and luscious sensuality. The tall and athletic, witty and warm-hearted girl was stunning. Allegra wrote that Cici's "hair fell back from her face in waves, like a lion's mane. Her shoulders were bare, and her skin tanned and freckled by the sun." She had a strong personality and was "powerfully beautiful, protective of her own, and able to turn in an instant fierce and unforgiving."

Cici and John hit it off right away. She loved animals and was an expert rider, and they talked about raising wolves and racing horses. She called him the next day and was temporarily blocked by Gladys, who sensed yet another serious rival, but they agreed to meet at a ranch. Cici recalled how she set out to attract him: "One of my girlfriends took over and dressed me in this western outfit: tight leather chaps and a really hot top! When John came, I was bent over cleaning one of the stalls. There was a saddle hanging on the door. John picked it up and said, 'Is there anything I can do for you, ma'am?' "[2] She felt there was an aura around him when he imitated a Gary Cooper cowboy, and her posture was not lost on John. Noting both the way she rode and the nicely rounded shape of her bottom, he thought she had "a marvelous seat."

Though sophisticated, Cici was impressed by John's romantic courtship. They searched for precious black pearls in Mexico, swam in the Mexican Pacific, went fishing and diving, and caught sea turtles. When their captain suddenly ordered her to get out of the water and back into the boat, Huston, well aware that sharks were nearby but curious about what might happen, told her to keep on swimming. "Our first days were magic," she wrote. "And then it just got more magical, mystical and mysterious to where the excitement was always there."

Huston invited her to the Arizona desert near Tucson, where he was shooting *The Life and Times of Judge Roy Bean* (1972), and the film set, as always, was a powerful aphrodisiac. Jacqueline Bisset, acting in the movie, remembered that Cici kept a bottle of vodka in the freezer of their trailer. She thought Cici was very outspoken and liked to shock people, but was a compassionate woman who really cared about John. Always testing friends and actors—from Bogart and Gable to Hurt and Keach—Huston was excited and mightily impressed when Cici rode a real lion in Arizona. Her mane blowing in the wind, she looks cool but determined in the photograph that captured her courage.

In 1971 they celebrated Thanksgiving together and Huston lured squirrels into the trailer with a seductive trail of nuts. "It was incredibly romantic," she said, "alone in the snowy Arizona desert, drinking champagne, eating popcorn and John reading Kipling aloud. That was the beginning of our real relationship!" Though Huston was jealous and possessive, and had puritanical inhibitions about kissing and sex scenes in his films, he was now proud of his latest sexual conquest and wanted to show her off. Just as Billy Pearson had burst into the room when Huston was in bed with Ricki so, Cici said, "John loved to parade our sexual exploits in front of others. He once allowed a flunky to walk in on us, while we were naked and making love! I immediately had latches installed on our bedroom door!"[3]

In a heartfelt tribute Cici exclaimed, "I loved having sex with John—he was the best of my whole life. Honest to God. John was an incredible lover." Huston told Zoe Sallis that Cici also "had sexual tricks—that's all I'm going to say," but Zoe preferred not to think about them. When asked if she'd care to explain what her tricks were and how they excited him, the uninhibited Cici declined to reveal her "trade secrets."[4] Though Cici was always ready for adventure, she could also be rather innocent. When Huston found out that she and a visiting girlfriend had been to see a porn film, "he insisted that we take three hundred dollars and go shopping at the Pleasure Chest—an adult store! We bought every new gadget in the shop! We even bought things that I didn't know what to do with!"

Even in her thirties Cici was still rebelling against her strict upbringing. She wore provocative clothes, used coarse language and had a sexual frankness—outrageous, bawdy and wild—that shocked Huston's older friends. They considered her brash and abrasive, a first-rate mistress but not a suitable wife. The English cameraman Ossie Morris, for example, "never understood how John, who consorted with some of the most beautiful women in the world, could ever have become involved with someone who I thought was rather common." But Victoria Principal, who starred in *Roy Bean,* said—with a touch of envy—that Cici "appeared to me to be a functioning voluptuary." The much-married Billy Pearson, who had a cameo role in the picture, put it more crudely when he told his friend, "I've never seen anyone more incompatible in my life than you two. She must be the greatest fuck in the Western world." And Huston said, "Yes, that's right."[5]

· II ·

Roy Bean, like *The Mackintosh Man, The Man Who Would Be King* and *Prizzi's Honor,* was produced by John Foreman. Born in Idaho in

1925, the witty and literate Foreman taught English in college, served in the navy in World War II and became an executive at MGM and a cofounder of the ICM agency. He was Paul Newman's agent, then his partner, and produced many of Newman's pictures. Foreman asked John Milius, who later coauthored the screenplay of *Apocalypse Now*, to write the script of *Roy Bean*, but when it had to be rewritten, the production was temporarily shut down.

As Cici waited impatiently with the freezing Stolichnaya, Huston's directing was even more distracted than usual. Trying to justify the chaotic plot of a dark comedy that wasn't funny, he remarked (in unusually contorted language) that he used "a 'fragmented' technique, in which all sorts of things can be happening without necessarily justifying them logically." Stacy Keach was closer to the mark when he said the picture had built-in absurdities and none of the actors took it seriously. The setting provided a certain structure, as the town of Vinegaroon, Texas, gradually grows from an isolated saloon to a cluster of buildings and finally burns down, along with the new oil wells, at the end. Newman's biographer, noting its weaknesses, condemned the picture as "stilted by forced goofiness, chockablock plotting, and an indistinct tone, alternately satirical, elegiac, comic, and laconic."[6] Bruno the trained bear, who swilled beer at the bar, was more interesting than any of the actors and stole several scenes. The western spoofs that followed *Roy Bean* in the 1970s—*Rancho Deluxe, The Missouri Breaks* and, most outrageously, *Blazing Saddles*—were all much better films.

Paul Newman, playing the ruthless hanging judge Roy Bean in his first departure from a romantic leading man, had a scruffy beard and a grizzled look. Nervous about his new image, he said, "I hope the public will like it" (they didn't). Intimidated by Huston and feeling very bourgeois when he was with him, Newman confessed, "One always feels a certain sense of uneasiness around a man of genius." Keach, in a brief but striking role as an albino cowboy, had a spirited horse that required expert control. Fortunately, he played polo and knew how to handle his stallion. Keach had to wear tinted contact lenses to give him a lurid, red-eyed look, though the desert sandstorms made his eyes bloodshot and naturally red. When he's shot through the back, a camera trick creates a gory-looking bullet hole.

The elegant Jacqueline Bisset, miscast as Bean's daughter, remembered that the snowy landscape was very cold and Huston, frail and preoccupied, was not at all well. She got no direction from him. He shunted her off to Newman, who was very helpful and directed her well. By contrast, Huston gave the star, Victoria Principal, some useful instruction. He took her aside and asked, "Have you ever seen baby fawns when they are frightened? You know how they become very stiff-legged and they tremble, and you see the whites of their eyes? I want you to do that in this scene." And she gratefully said, "It worked wonderfully." Anthony Perkins appeared as a crackpot preacher. His psychiatrist had tried to solve his personal problems by transforming him from gay to straight. To ensure his "recovery," she gave him electroshock treatments and prescribed an affair with the delightful Victoria. Perkins followed her advice, but his reluctant consummation merely confirmed his taste for men.

Bisset, unaware of Huston's close ties to Ava Gardner, was impressed that the woman she considered the most beautiful star of all would agree to make a brief appearance as the English actress Lily Langtry. Lily's arrival is eagerly awaited throughout the picture, and as she finally emerges from the train, she's greeted by the bearded and bowing Billy Pearson. He "doffed his stationmaster's cap and, with his back to the camera, said, 'Welcome, Miss Langtry. . . . And on behalf of the entire railroad let me jes' say . . . *I would be honored if you would let me eat your pussy!*' "[7]

· III ·

John's union with Cici, the triumph of hope over experience, is the most difficult of all his marriages to understand. Dorothy Harvey was his high school sweetheart; Lesley Black straightened him out and helped him mature; Evelyn Keyes, an impulsive reaction against Marietta's rejection, was in the movie business; Ricki Soma was pregnant and he did the right thing. Cici was young, attractive and sexually exciting, and though not well educated or intellectual, was lively, quick-witted and intuitive about people. But Huston was a very poor prospect for *her*. After four failed marriages, he was a heavy drinker, in poor health and a compulsive satyr. She overestimated her powers by believing he would remain faithful when they were apart. Cici herself, almost young enough to be his granddaughter, was twice divorced and fiercely devoted to her disabled son. Worried about Cici's reputation, her mother insisted, "You're not going to be that Huston man's mistress. You must be married"—and he was the marrying kind.

On July 12, 1972, Gladys Hill, closely involved in the delicate negotiations, reported that Cici was a stubborn hold-out: "Huston was very upset when Cici refused to come to New York saying she was afraid [to commit herself]. However, since then he has talked to her and, while I don't know what was said, I suspect she may come to New York. Meanwhile, John's lawyer is drawing up the necessary papers to be ready by the 25th. So we'll see." Cici's strategy worked. Huston was infatuated and rejuvenated by her, and after considerable hesitation, finally capitulated. She wrote that "we married in a civil ceremony on August 8, 1972—three days after his 66th birthday. I arranged a big reception for 200 guests at my parents' hilltop Beverly Hills mansion." Everyone in the beau monde knew that Huston had once again been captured, if not tamed.

Huston's previous wives were more tolerant and compliant than Cici. Though much younger than John, who was a world-famous figure, she was strong-willed and rebellious. Though he admired these qualities, they made their marriage even more difficult than the others. Cici had spent her twenties in the freewheeling 1960s, and she didn't have John's puritanical streak about revealing clothing and public displays of affection. She was—in dress, speech and behavior—more uninhibited than her predecessors. She recalled that one day, to please her husband, "I went on a very expensive shopping spree for lingerie. After I got home, I began to model for John. I asked him how I looked and he replied, 'You look like a trollop, honey,' " which recalled the time in Mexico that he tore off Evelyn's low-cut halter.[8] "Cici wasn't 'a lady,' as I'd been brought up to conceive of one," wrote Allegra, who loved her as a mother. "She walked around wearing very little, she swore, she cackled when she laughed with her friends. There was nothing proper about her. She wasn't particularly interested in art, didn't read books; she and Dad didn't have intellectual conversations." John was not absolutely certain, but thought Cici had once read a book—*National Velvet* or something like that.

But Cici did appreciate his sometimes crude sense of humor. She described a truly amusing practical joke, beautifully staged by Huston in their house in Pacific Palisades, when she was entertaining four lady friends. Unabashed about nudity, he shocked his captive audience and seemed capable of anything:

> There we were: five naked beauties in the Jacuzzi, when in
> walked John wearing only his ancient pajama bottoms—
> which were littered with holes from his cigars. Leaving them
> behind, he joined us. After a while some of us noticed this
> brown chunk floating in the water. None of us wanted to
> say anything about it, because we couldn't believe our eyes!
> I was horrified and screamed and grabbed it just in time as
> the brown chunk headed straight for the mouth of one of my
> friends! It turned out to be only a piece of orchid bark with a
> remarkable resemblance to a piece of shit—but then, knowing
> John, nothing would have surprised me! John thought the
> whole episode was hysterically funny—although he was angry
> that I had alerted my girlfriend before it reached her mouth.

Eloise called Cici "a fascinating original, but more than John could handle," and Allegra agreed that they brought out the worst in each other. Writing on a TWA letterhead after a flight from New York to Los Angeles, the slightly disillusioned Cici identified a crucial flaw in his character: "It's quite sad and lonely for you, I am sure, to be so feared yet treated with such reverence." She wanted to be an actress as well as a prominent hostess, but he soon crushed her hopes. None of his wives ever made it into his films, even in the role of a harridan. When she asked him about appearing in his movies, "he looked at me as if I were crazy and said, 'Honey, you couldn't be an EXTRA in one of my movies.' And I yelled 'Why can't I?' So he says, 'Well, first of all . . . it's your voice . . . the way you talk. To listen to you, it sounds as though you were born in a stable in Palmdale somewhere.' So, he doesn't want me to be an actress—he just wants me to be a lady. And if I stray from that—I'm sunk!"⁹ But playing a lady, for her, was just as difficult as being an actress.

· IV ·

Cici's honeymoon visit to St. Clerans in August 1972—just after their wedding and accompanied by Collin and his Mexican nursemaid Maricela Hernandez—was a disaster. The rich California girl who grew up in a mansion was not impressed by all the luxury; she hated the isolation, wet weather, heavy drinking and wild fox hunts; and she was horrified when she discovered the seething sexual history of the estate and the rampant theft by the Irish staff. Ricki, burdened by children and exiled to the Little House, had learned to tolerate the residential and visiting mistresses. Cici, the latest bride, was thrust into a weird situation she didn't understand and couldn't accept.

Children, lovers and staff were all jealous of and hostile to the interloper. Willing to do almost anything to defeat her, protect their privileged positions and keep John to themselves, they spread rumors that Cici beat the servants. "I went into what is called 'enemy territory,' " she said. "I had a house of eleven servants, many of them John's old girlfriends." They included the ubiquitous Betty O'Kelly, whom Tony called "Dad's live-in Hot Water Bottle." Cici expressed her rage in letters to her parents from St. Clerans: "John has the women around for amusement. Zoe is back to 'see her boy.' Ha ha. She's here to ask 'Big Daddy' whether she should turn Jewish as her supposed future husband [the English director Michael Winner] wants her to or whether she shouldn't." Cici soon realized that John would never remain faithful, that she would be sacrificed like all the others and thrown into his sexual dustbin: "THANK GOD I'm not madly in love or I would be destroyed by him as he's done to these three I mentioned [Gladys,

Betty and Zoe]. Also, Eloise is another wreck of John's, as well as the Italian countess [Valeria Alberti] and Tony's poor mother! I can see it so clearly! He is the devil!"

Cici was equally savage in her letters to John after she left Ireland. She was fed up not only with hearing about but also becoming personally involved with his old mistresses. She condemned him for egoistically demanding a band of courtiers, and categorically stated that she would not become one of his followers: "It seems Eloise & you have been screwing each other for years & that Eloise feels you are a wonderful 'ball'! I am fucking bored hearing about who you've fucked and especially since you put me with all your 'OLD' Bangs. . . . Have you not finally cooled your 'ardor'— [don't you have] ego enough NOT to need your entourage of jesters, mistresses from year one and court à la JH? . . . You *have* someone who is part of NOW and who is unable to take part in the melodrama of your yesteryear! . . . I am never going to be able to be or become another character in your interwoven cast of many!"

While still in Ireland, their encounters frequently erupted into fierce quarrels and constant combat. The servants always brought John breakfast in his majestic Napoleonic four-poster, and when he had one of his frequent hangovers, Cici would add a shot of Stolichnaya. When their fights got going, he would raise his glass and propose a caustic toast: "This is to all the bitches I've known in my life—and especially to you, Cici." To which she responded, "Do you really like this kind of life?" One day Cici—like Ray Bradbury and Susannah York—surprised herself. When the drunken John threatened her physically, she finally exploded, punched him and escaped to her room. Surprised by her assault, he became abjectly apologetic and, scratching at her locked door, pleaded forgiveness and confessed, "I'm so sorry, so sorry!"[10]

In the midst of their conflict Wally Green suddenly turned up to see Collin, and Cici rather awkwardly asked if her ex-husband could stay at St. Clerans. Ready for a mano a mano, John replied, "Of course, I'll handle him like a Meissen jar." Displaying his treasures for his well-educated guest, he told Tony to bring out the death mask of James Joyce on its black velvet pillow. Determined not to be impressed,

Wally remarked, "Well, at least he died with a smile on his face," but John revered Joyce and didn't much like the joke. He tested Wally's knowledge by showing him some inferior pieces of African art and asking for his opinion: "You've been to Africa?" "Yes." You know about African art?" "Yes." "Then what do you think of these Dogon masks and Ashanti statues?" Put in an awkward position and weary of being tested, Wally found it difficult to criticize the collection and managed to evade the question. His visit marked another stage of Cici's growing unhappiness with John. Wally departed with Collin, and Maricela, spooked by St. Clerans, ran away. A few days later, when John called out, "Send Cici up here!," Tony told her, "You'd better go." She replied, "Fuck him! I'm upset. My kid has gone to my ex-boyfriend's house with my ex-husband. Maricela is gone; I'm all alone; and no one likes me."

Another great cause of contention was the widespread theft at St. Clerans. Cici, who knew all about horses and raised them in California, soon discovered that John's employees were pilfering hay and grain. O'Kelly also threw huge parties when John was away, and spent $10,000 a month both when he was in residence *and* when he was abroad. Cici told her parents, "There is NO way to completely eliminate Betty as she controls the 4 brood mares & John too. It's revolting." The staff's salaries had quadrupled since 1959 and they often didn't appear for work until eleven o'clock in the morning. Ricki, in residence for many years, had been either unaware of the theft or unable to do anything about it. Tony, who planned to take over the management of the estate, was there for months at a time and observed everything that was happening. He saw the staff stealing hay from the barn and petrol from the garage, but he did nothing to stop them.

When Cici told John about all this, he responded by giving O'Kelly a raise and a new car to soothe her wounded feelings. He persuaded her to stay and allowed—even encouraged—her to continue to steal from him. All this, of course, put Cici in an impossible position. John was well aware that he'd been robbed by Billy Pearson, Sam Spiegel and Orson Welles as well as by his Irish mistress and servants, but he always put loyalty before money. When his publicist-friend Bill Gardner heard about the theft from Cici and mentioned it to him, John surprised him by exclaiming, "What are you trying to do, lose all my friends?"[11] Both John and Cici seemed to realize, during the very first months of their marriage, that they had made a terrible mistake.

It was not only a question of money: the whole future of St. Clerans was at stake if John, with his careless ways, could no longer afford to maintain it. His mother had taught him that money was for spending; as a child and an adult, he had been both very poor and very rich. He believed that style was everything and that a man should live, and die, beyond his means. He worked continuously and always made a great deal of money: Six of his films, from *Moby Dick* (1956) to *The Night of the Iguana* (1964), had earned from $4 million to $5.2 million. But he confessed that he often felt guilty about being paid for doing work he loved: "Maybe that's why I always get rid of it so quickly. It was like money you win at the races, not the rewards of honest toil."

His mistake, he admitted (though he did nothing to correct it), was spending money before he made it, acquiring debts instead of savings and—always short of cash—living on future expectations and the advances on forthcoming films. Accumulated money seemed like a burden that tied him down while massive debts, paradoxically, seemed to set him free. He had a craving for luxury and, with Babylonian extravagance, spent large sums on clothes, travel and alimony; on Ricki and their children; on Zoe, Danny and Allegra; on St. Clerans, breeding and racing horses; on collecting art and giving generous gifts to friends. Most wasteful of all were his heavy losses from gambling.

Like sex, drink, practical jokes, hunting foxes, shooting big game, racing camels and other dangerous feats, Huston's addiction to gambling provided momentary excitement and a temporary respite from boredom. Getting free money or carelessly losing it not only strengthened his friendships with men, but also challenged fate and acknowledged the role of chance in life. Michael Fitzgerald, who produced two of Huston's films, played poker with him every Sunday night for several years. Fitzgerald called him both a cunning and a mischievous player, who was amused by the game but didn't take it too seriously. Knowing he had a better hand, Huston would goad Fitzgerald by saying, "Oh, my, don't raise on that." Bill Mauldin, who frequently gambled with

Huston while they were making *The Red Badge of Courage,* recalled that he "was marvelous as a poker player simply because he didn't give a shit. He'd throw his last seven hundred dollars in to make a point. He was a powerful bluffer and he had [Gottfried] Reinhardt pretty heavily in debt to him."[12] His Italian film editor, Roberto Silvi, said Huston didn't bluff very often, but was very good at poker. They played for high stakes and would win or lose as much as $5,000 to $15,000 a night, but Huston didn't care about his losses. He would gamble on horses, cards, backgammon, dice, anything—even the length of a reel, and would eagerly bet on whether it was ten feet or ten and a half. Despite constant setbacks, gambling kept him eternally optimistic and indifferent to defeat. He affirmed, "I've never got up in the morning to a hopeless day, and I've never thrown the dice when I didn't expect to win. The one great lesson in gambling is that money doesn't mean a goddamn thing." Huston was, paradoxically, a man who obsessively collected art and accumulated material possessions and, at the same time, compulsively wasted his wealth.

Huston's business manager in Los Angeles, his lawyers in California and New York, and his producers all over the world tried, in vain, to rein him in. James Woolf, for example, of Romulus Films in London, urged Huston to make the money needed to finance *Moulin Rouge* last as long as possible. Until Woolf completed all the necessary formalities, he could not get the Bank of England to send any more money to France. With paternal advice, but well aware of Huston's dangerous proximity to the track at Chantilly, he added a handwritten postscript: "So eke it out!!! No racing!!!"[13] Huston, by contrast, wanted immediate material rewards for all his hard work. When he failed to get his long-overdue money for *The African Queen,* he warned his manager that he was as restless as a racehorse at the starting gate: "If my state of enforced poverty continues much longer, the day will come when I break out. In other words, you'd better let me buy one horse or something soon."

Peter Viertel told the story of how Huston bought a yearling with money he didn't have, used Viertel's bum check to pay for it and then covered it with a loan from William Wyler, who signed a blank check put before him when he was still in bed and half asleep. This incident shows not only his reckless extravagance, but also his intimate friendship with Wyler, who (like Walter) could always be relied on to bail him out in an emergency. In 1982 Huston was amused by his own television advertisement for a California bank, urging his fellow citizens to save their hard-earned money.[14]

At the end of 1972 Huston finally realized that he could no longer afford to maintain St. Clerans. He had to work to support the house and staff, yet had no time to live there. He told Tony Veiller that one year he had stayed there for only five days, but had paid $50,000 to keep it up. His emphysema now prevented him from foxhunting, and Cici had returned to her house in Pacific Palisades. Collin, a handsome boy for whom Huston had the deepest sympathy, had been having epileptic fits and could not be treated or helped in Ireland. When the Irish doctors told Cici they'd have to put Collin in a home for spastics, she knew he'd have much better care in America and decided to leave for good.[15] She now put Collin before John as she'd previously put him before Wally. Huston sometimes said he'd had to choose between Cici and St. Clerans, as he'd once had to choose between Evelyn and the chimpanzee, and had made the wrong choice. But even if he'd wanted to, he could not have kept the estate. St. Clerans was put up for sale in 1972 with an asking price of $320,000 and finally sold three years later, with the Japanese bath and Napoleonic bed thrown in, for $300,000. Later on, it was bought by the television star and media mogul Merv Griffin, who turned it into a five-star luxury hotel. It closed in 2009.[16]

· V ·

It's clear from the letters John wrote to Cici after she returned to California that he was still passionately in love with her. His letters expressed his sexual desire when they were separated, and he tried, with all his seductive charm, to win her back and save their marriage. In late 1972, when he was shooting *The Mackintosh Man* in Ireland and Malta, he longed for her and wrote, with unusual emotion:

You have such a free, open way. I hear your voice as I read
[your letters]. But those echoes aren't enough. I long, long
for your *presence*—& to feel your touch. I tried to imagine
feeling you last night. It didn't work.

My bed gets emptier & emptier. I hardly realized how much
a habit you'd become. Never a night passes I don't wake up
groping around for your lovely ass.

No talk here of impinging souls, enjoining hearts or
entwining psyches: I mean that instant when our limbs &
our very assholes tangle.

When Huston came home to Los Angeles for the Christmas holidays in 1972, he carefully planned their first encounter—delaying the
exquisite pleasure for as long as possible—to perfect and realize the
sexual newsreels that had been playing for months in his head:

A request: do not meet me at the airport! Be at home & in
bed. Send everyone off so we can be alone. Don't answer the
door when my car drives up. I'll undress in the other room &
come into you. . . .
    Let's not say hardly anything or not say *anything* at all
but just hold each other until we can't bear it any longer
& then make love & then perhaps exchange a few remarks
before making love again. . . .
    I'm thinking—imagining—what it will be like,
having my cock hard against your belly isn't conducive to
slumber. . . . My groin is throbbing.[17]

They were certainly glad to see each other and their passionate
meeting revived their union. John was soon off to Morocco to make
The Man Who Would Be King. Cici saw herself as a rescuer and enabler
who tried to keep their sinking ship afloat. They had a few good years

together, partly sustained by the time they were apart, but she complained in an interview that "our marriage was always filled with his inevitable entourage: the lackeys, hangers-on, secretaries, girlfriends—past and present—the people who sucked the life out of John." Such resentments, which could neither be resolved nor repressed, soon resurfaced in her antagonistic letters.

Starting off affectionately and addressing him as "Darling Love," Cici wrote that she was lonely, missed him and wanted him to be with her. She then addressed him, with heavy-handed irony, as "Your Majesty" and said she would not join his band of flatterers. She criticized his selfishness and mistresses, and demanded recognition as his one and only wife. She was a decent woman—devoted to Collin, Allegra and the twenty-one-year-old Anjelica—but saw that her life, apart from horses, was essentially empty and meaningless. Her nagging and whining letters, filled with dyslexic spelling, made her laments seem childish and absurd. She didn't realize that they made a negative impression, were entirely counterproductive and would neither please John nor make him eager to come back.

Huston complained that when he returned home, expecting to find a loving wife, he found instead a "crocodile" (his favorite word for Cici) constantly *snapping* at him. He expressed his ambivalent feelings, the *odi et amo* of Catullus, when he wrote, "When we're apart I love you completely. When we're together I love you half the time & hate you half." But he didn't want Cici to hate *him:* "Hating me in my absence would lead to [your] unfaithfulness & then there's no hope whatever. Duplicity, then dishonesty, & presently you're caught red-handed in a supermarket lifting a bottle of tomato ketchup." Yet, she later recalled, "John once said to me, 'honey, you'd be a lot more successful if you were a little more deceitful.' And I said, 'what does that mean? I just feel why waste your life away playing games.' " Allegra, who was mainly brought up by Cici, believed she was always faithful to John.[18]

John described a catastrophic holiday in Puerto Vallarta, in striking contrast to their idyllic courtship, as "days and nights devoid of affection." Cici now told her once highly praised lover, "You've got a sex problem. . . . You've been asking me to stroke you for three years.

I never have." He had presumably asked her to pleasure him without receiving pleasure herself. Their difference in ages now began to show. She was in her prime, and his sexual capacity seemed to be waning. Still trying to be positive and rescue the wreck, he wrote from Mexico City, "People will tell you, as they've been telling me these last few days, that it could never possibly have worked & that we're both well out of it. It could have worked & we aren't 'well out of it.' That will take a lot of doing." As their relations continued to deteriorate, Cici compiled "a list of everything about John that I hated and left it [for him]. I mentioned his hangers-on, cigarette smoke, lies, bullshit stories, lies, cigars, false promises, lies, etc. John later read it back to me. He said, 'it seems there are quite a few things you don't quite like about me.' "[19] He tried to disarm her with humor, but refused to alter the habits of a lifetime merely to satisfy the whims of his wife.

The final and most devastating crisis began when John—echoing his reaction when he discovered Monty Clift in bed with a man—said he woke up in the middle of the night and found his wife in bed with another woman: "It's the most shocking thing I ever witnessed in my entire life. At this point I realized that I'd been with spoiled meat." Cici said that John misunderstood what he saw and explained what had really happened. They had quarreled one night and retired to separate beds: "I had a girlfriend who is gay, who was wild about me. John was being a beast one night and I was real upset. She was rubbing my back and then took a beer and poured it down my back and started licking my back, the dyke! He walked in and thought she was doing things to me. That was his big lesbian story about me."

John had been shocked, but took his revenge on Cici in an even more shocking way by seducing her maid Maricela. Trying to break up the marriage and protect his prospects, Tony told Cici that he'd walked in on Maricela and John—sudden intrusions into bedrooms were a family tradition—and "found them naked and wrapped around each other like two pretzels." Cici noticed that Maricela had become unusually withdrawn, and Maricela's sister claimed she had fallen in love with an airline pilot. But Cici didn't realize that John had started a liaison with Maricela "while we were all living together. He was lizarding around with her, giggling all the time. She was my closest friend, the only friend I could really trust."[20] (Cici's mother knew about the affair before Cici did.)

Cici had raised Maricela from the age of fifteen and helped her family come from Tijuana to America. Short, ugly and masculine, with close-cropped hair, always in T-shirts and jeans, Maricela did not seem to like men. A lady-in-waiting in both senses, she had become jealous of Cici's beauty, wealth and social position, and wanted to take her place with John. Pancho Kohner (Paul's son) and several other friends agreed with Cici that John slept with Maricela as revenge and as "a slap in the face to Cici." John seemed to be saying, You don't like my past mistresses? All right, I'll take a new one. Maricela even thought she might be pregnant by John, though it turned out to be a false alarm.[21] He took the nearest woman he could find, and both betrayed Cici and wounded her by wounding Collin, who was deeply attached to Maricela and had to begin again with another nurse. For Cici this was the end. She could never forgive John for what he had done and "dumped him."

Cici was the only woman who ever left Huston, and their break made him furious and bitter. After all his experience with women, he'd badly misjudged her character and, late in life, made a humiliating mistake. He told the actor Burgess Meredith that he was "ashamed of himself" and said, "I couldn't believe that I had married Cici. I really couldn't. I stood back, aghast. . . . I survived. But barely." John maligned her as a "crocodile" and compared their marriage to "putting my finger in a [venomous] sea-snake's mouth." But for all her ferocity, she had a strong moral character. She remained loyal to her son. She tried to protect John's best interests in St. Clerans, stood up to his drunken behavior and dared to attack her sexual rivals. As Elizabeth Bishop observed in her poem, "Florida," alligators, like crocodiles, have "five distinct calls: / friendliness, love, mating, war, and a warning."[22]

TWENTY-FOUR

Morocco and Mexico,

1973–1978

· I ·

Like Erich von Stroheim, Charlie Chaplin, Vittorio De Sica and Orson Welles, Huston not only wrote and directed, but also had an impressive career as an actor, beginning on stage with the Provincetown Playhouse in 1925. With typical insouciance, Huston tended to dismiss his roles in movies: "I don't look on myself as an actor. Just take the money and get a kick out of it. It's so easy. And everyone behaves as though I'm doing a great favor when I agree to take a part. . . . Whether the pictures were good or bad or indifferent was of no consequence, as I don't take that part of my life seriously. Each episode has been a lark—and they actually pay me to do it." But to uphold professional standards, he always gave his best and most immediate performance. With his striking face and larger-than-life personality, he was a vivid screen presence. Bogart, who often saw him in action, believed that "Huston has more color and is more photogenic than 90 per cent of the actors in Hollywood."[1]

Huston loved the high ecclesiastical costume, had the commanding self-assurance needed for the title role in *The Cardinal* (1963) and tactfully concentrated on the job of acting. The authoritarian and difficult Otto Preminger, who'd also directed him in *In Time to Come* on Broadway in 1941, praised his expertise and discretion: "Huston was a joy to direct. He behaved as we both want actors to behave: he came to the set on time knowing his lines. He rehearsed and did the role without the slightest critical comment about the direction or even a hint of professional advice. Perfect."

Huston's most outstanding role, by far, was the evil tycoon, Noah Cross, in Roman Polanski's *Chinatown* (1974). Named for his part as the biblical patriarch (whom it is unwise to cross) and ironically associated with the flood, Noah criminally controls the water supply to Los Angeles. A suave villain with a charming aura of evil, he's murdered his partner and raped his own daughter, who's hidden *her* sister-and-daughter so he can't contaminate her. Jake Gittes (Jack Nicholson), a private detective, helps Cross' daughter, Evelyn Mulwray (Faye Dunaway), solve the mysterious death of her husband. She warns him that her father is a dangerous man. A criminal (Polanski), working for Cross, slits Gittes' nose to deter him from nosing around, but he survives the threats and moves in on the murderer. Huston's Noah, a striking blend of charm and ruthlessness, appears halfway through the film wearing jodhpurs, wide braces, embroidered shirt, colorful cummerbund and Stetson hat. His resonant, courtly voice radiates cunning and power. He invites Nicholson to lunch at the yacht club he owns and self-reflectively tells him, "You've got a nasty reputation. I like that." In a clever in-joke, Huston confronts him by asking, "Are you sleeping with my daughter? Come, come, Mr. Gittes—you don't have to think about that to remember, do you?" At the time Nicholson, in real life, was living with Anjelica.

In the final scene Huston pleads with Dunaway to give him back his daughter-granddaughter. She refuses, shoots and wounds him, tries to drive away and is accidentally killed by the police. Polanski's biographer wrote, "As the villainous Cross walks off into the night, the detective, and by extension the audience, are left as helpless bystanders." With cold authority, Huston speaks the lines that express the savage theme of the film—similar to Conrad's in *Heart of Darkness*—when he tells Nicholson, "You see, Mr. Gittes, most people never have to face the fact that at the right time and the right place they're capable of anything"—even, in his case, incest and murder.[2]

· II ·

As he made the transition from his marriage to Cici to living with Maricela, from living in Ireland to settling in Mexico, Huston completed *The Man Who Would Be King* (1975). He then became seriously ill and didn't make a movie for the next three years. He had planned to make a screen version of Kipling's ironic story of two British adventurers as early as 1953, but could not get the actors he wanted. Bogart was not keen to go to India with the "Monster" and Gable would not commit to the project. In July 1955 he had asked Aeneas MacKenzie, his coauthor on *Juárez*, to meet him in Deauville, on the Channel coast of France, to work on the screenplay and was furious when MacKenzie refused. Reminding MacKenzie of the crucial help he'd once given him, he asked with heavy irony, "Do you have a nervous disorder from shingles, delusions of grandeur through working with Cecil B. De Mille or just have a very short memory for things past?" He also vented his rage, that same day, in a letter to Paul Kohner: "I suggest that you remind Mac who it was got him out of the research department at Warner Brothers and gave him his first opportunity as a writer and saw to it that he had a screen credit—on second thought, fuck that."

In 1955 Huston went to India to look for locations, shot an eight-foot female tiger, and sent his secretary an amusing and obscene little poem:

> The walli of Swat
> Tied his cock in a knot
> And challenged his wives to undo it.
> But the harder they tried
> The harder it got
> Till the eldest and wisest said "Screw it."

He also met a young director, Satyajit Ray. Unlike most men in the movie business, Huston saw his fellow directors as colleagues, not rivals, and helped them whenever he could. He gave generous support to the unknown Ray, even though he didn't know his work nor understand his language. Ray, who was just finishing the innovative *Pather Panchali*, wrote, "Huston had come to Calcutta to set up *The Man Who Would Be King*, at that time with Humphrey Bogart. . . . I went [to his hotel] and said, 'I am making a film Mr. Huston. I know your work.' . . . He said, 'Well, I would like to see what you've done.' . . . He happened to be a friend of Monroe Wheeler, who was with the Museum of Modern Art. . . . I then got a letter from Monroe saying, 'I want your film. If John Huston likes it, his word is good enough for me.' " Five years later, when Huston was shooting *The Unforgiven* in Mexico, he gave vital help to another director. He was so impressed by Luis Buñuel's controversial film *Nazarin* (1958) that "he spent a morning ringing Europe, arranging its showing at the 1959 Cannes Festival."[3]

Twenty years after his first attempt to make the movie, Huston set off again to look for a location. On a budget of $7.7 million, he scouted places in Afghanistan, Pakistan and India before choosing Morocco. North Africa then was almost as rough and bleak as Afghanistan. In 1938 George Orwell, wintering for his health in Morocco, called it "a beastly dull country, no forests and literally no wild animals, and the people anywhere near a big town utterly debauched by the tourist racket and their poverty combined, which turn them into a race of beggars and curio-sellers." His essay "Marrakech" (1939) conveyed a series of vivid impressions: "fly-blown funerals, starving Arabs, squalid Jews, hopeless farmers, agonized porters, brutalized donkeys and wretched soldiers." In 1974, when Huston arrived at the location, a town called Ouarzazate, ten miles outside Marrakech, conditions in the country hadn't changed much in thirty-six years. Michael Caine called the town "a camel stop with a couple of fleapit hotels and bars and amazingly, a discothèque. It was boiling hot in the daytime and freezing cold at night. The place had dirt roads and dirt air, as the wind blew off the desert and whipped up a mixture of dust, sand and dried camel shit."

After their great success in *Butch Cassidy and the Sundance Kid* (1969), Huston tried to get Paul Newman and Robert Redford, but they seemed too American to play Kipling's Victorian soldiers. He also wanted the British actors Richard Burton and Peter O'Toole, but they were not available. He finally chose Sean Connery to play Dan Dravot and Michael Caine for Peachy Carnehan. They were perfectly cast as two wily ex-soldiers who venture into the wilds of Kafiristan to take advantage of gullible tribesmen and make Dan a king.

Kipling's story of two egomaniacs considers the nature of kingship and regal power, and suggests the need for moral authority represented by the law of the British Empire. Dan and Peachy are grimly comic figures whose impetuosity and pride defeat their ambitions. But their bravery and martyrdom show Kipling's sympathy for the roguish and daring aspects of their characters and obscure—almost justify—their imperial bravado and unscrupulous behavior as rulers. As Dan tells his Kafiri soldiers, with unintentional irony, "When we're done with you, you'll be able to stand up and slaughter your enemies like civilized men."

As always, Huston and Gladys Hill remained faithful to the story, which has the same structure as Homer's *Odyssey:* the setting out, the adventurous journey and the return. They quoted some speeches verbatim, and at the beginning Peachy reads the entire "contract" (modeled on the one in Mark Twain's *Huckleberry Finn*) to Kipling, played by Christopher Plummer. The bald, cautious, pink-skinned Plummer is contrasted to Connery and Caine, two hairy, suntanned, wild adventurers dressed in native clothing. The great opening scenes in the exotic Djmaa el Fna square in Marrakech—filled with food sellers, storytellers, letter writers, witch doctors, dentists, mystics, actors, jugglers, acrobats, drummers and dancers—and in Kipling's broiling newspaper office vividly capture the atmosphere of India. At the end of the picture Peachy, like Ishmael in *Moby Dick,* survives to tell the tale. Blinded and alone, he brings Dan's crowned but severed head back to Kipling to prove the veracity of his fantastic tale.

In their travels to Kafiristan in the remote Afghan mountains, Dan and Peachy have to overcome many life-threatening obstacles: marauding thieves, raging rivers and a crevasse fortuitously filled up by an avalanche. When they arrive, they watch a polo match that uses a human head instead of a ball. Huston and Hill created crude and evocative dialogue, a blend of Kipling and their own invention, to contrast the clever and resourceful Peachy with the rough and brutal Dan. Peachy says of the mules they've used in the mountains, "They all died but one—and she died later on." Their faithful and colorful Gurkha companion Billy Fish complains that their enemies are "pissing downstream on our peoples" and gleefully asserts that the women who've captured a rapist "will cut off his bollocks." After Peachy and Dan (adhering, at first, to their contract) refuse the offer of women, Billy helpfully informs them that the tribal chief also "has twenty-two sons if you are liking boys." When Connery becomes king of Kafiristan, through force of arms and Masonic mumbo-jumbo, he graciously tells Caine, "You may kiss my royal arse."

The costumes in *The Man Who Would Be King* came from an obscure source. In his autobiography Huston recalled that "the inspiration for the designs in this instance—the manner of draping the materials, the hair styles, diadems, armlets, pins—were Greek Tanagra figurines."[4] Dating from the third century B.C., these small, delicate, elegantly draped, painted terracotta statues show women in the costumes of daily life. The popular figurines spread from Greece to Afghanistan, the setting of the movie, through the conquests of Alexander the Great. The high priest's temple was vaguely modeled on the Potala Palace, the Dalai Lama's residence in Lhasa, Tibet.

On location, Huston revealed many of his characteristic traits: a relaxed atmosphere, sympathy with animals, benign neglect of actors and perceptive advice about how to play a scene. Unlike most directors, he welcomed everyone to watch the rushes. When Plummer said that a camel was interfering with his acting, Huston insisted that the animal was an essential part of the setting and told the actor to get used to it. Huston shrewdly urged Caine to speak rapidly since Peachy was an honest man, had nothing to hide and didn't need time to calculate. Huston did not get on well with Plummer, who complained that "he was nothing but brusque, terse and downright rude. He clearly resented the fact that I wasn't Burton, whom he obviously wanted around for late-night drinking and good times." But when Plummer needed crucial advice, Huston came through for him: "I was having trouble saying a very important line which I longed to make touching. He finally came up to me and as gently as his gravelly accent allowed, he said, 'Ah—ah—Chris, just take the music out of your voice.' And when at the end of the story Kipling stares in horror at the rotting severed head of his favourite character, Dravot, what to do? . . . 'Don't think at all. Drain yourself of feeling. Empty your head—then look at him.' By God, it worked. Those two bits of direction are the best I've ever received on any movie set."

Huston originally hired Tessa Dahl, the seventeen-year-old daughter of the writer Roald Dahl and the actress Patricia Neal, to play the beautiful Indian princess Roxanne (named after the wife of Alexander the Great). Roxanne does not appear until late in the film and speaks very few words. But when she bites Connery and he bleeds, the Kafirs realize he's human rather than divine, and he and Caine must try to bluff and fight their way out of danger. Huston almost never dropped an actor during shooting, but he finally decided that Tessa was too pale and too European-looking, and that he wanted a real Indian. Zoe, visiting Morocco with Danny, was the obvious choice, but she was vehemently blocked by Cici. Huston then gave the part to Caine's Indian-Guyanian wife, Shakira. In the film, when Caine, playing Peachy, sees Roxanne, he exclaims, "I must say, she really is an eyeful."

Huston had to tell the deeply disappointed Tessa that they could not use her as Roxanne. Instead of having Gladys deliver the bad news, he wrote in his most gracious manner and let Tessa down as gently as possible: "This means, for me, giving up one of the central themes in *The Man Who Would Be King*, as the Kafirs were, indeed, blond and blue-eyed. But as I continue to view the rushes and as I continue to film, I have come to realize that this motif must be relinquished. If there anything I can do for you in any way on your next picture, I do not offer to help—I insist upon it." He also told her parents, "I have just written to Tessa, telling her that North Africa and the features, color, and size of its people, have forced me to depart from my original conception of Roxanne." After Roald and Patricia had stoically accepted his explanation, Gladys told an executive at Columbia Pictures, "Huston and I heaved a sigh of relief when we read your telex saying that his letters to Tessa and her parents had been well received."[5]

The most dramatic moment of the picture occurs when Connery, halfway across a suspension bridge, turns to defy his enemies, who sever the ropes and hurl him to his death in the deep gorge. Instead of using a dummy figure, Huston paid the stuntman Joe Powell an extra $10,000 to fall off the bridge and into the ravine. To achieve this spectacular feat, they filled a wide area under the bridge with scores of large cardboard boxes and covered them with a thick layer of foam rubber.

The stuntman fell about seventy-five feet and—despite a light wind and swaying bridge—landed perfectly and walked away unhurt.

Both in Kipling's story and in the film, "they cut, and old Dan fell, turning round and round and round, twenty thousand miles, for he took half an hour to fall till he struck the water, and I could see his body caught on a rock with his gold crown close beside." Dravot's fantastically long and theatrically slow fall not only marks the dramatic death of the would-be king, but also echoes the momentous fall from heaven of the rebellious Satan in John Milton's *Paradise Lost* (1667):

> from Morn
> To Noon he fell, from Noon to dewy Eve,
> A Summer's day; and with the setting Sun
> Dropd from the Zenith like a falling Starr.

The "gold crown" recalls the lost heavenly status of Satan, the fallen angel.

As if alluding to the crucial waterfall episode that freed him from invalidism in his childhood, Huston defined his characteristic approach to filmmaking when he exclaimed, "The picture has its faults, I suppose—but who gives a damn? It plunges recklessly ahead. It swims toward the cataract." Despite its uncertain oscillation between the serious action and the joking tone, both French and American critics agreed with him. The *Nouvel Observateur* declared, "Here's a beautiful dream, finally realized . . . a sumptuous meditation on power, which goes back to the time of English colonialism and ends with its fall." And John Simon authoritatively called it "Huston's best film in 23 years, or since *The African Queen*."[6]

· III ·

The completion of *The Man Who Would Be King* marked one of the major turning points in Huston's life. It roughly coincided with his break with Cici and the sale of St. Clerans, with his move to Mexico and connection with his unexpected savior, Maricela. After Cici left him, according to Danny Huston, he felt humiliated and drank heavily for several months. Then, during the fallow years, he did some acting, failed to film *Across the River and into the Trees* and other unrealized projects, made a short documentary and some television programs, and began to gather the prizes and awards that come to distinguished artists late in life.

An unusual pattern recurred in his last decades: he would make a series of poor movies, then recover with a spectacular major film. He made *Sinful Davey, A Walk with Love and Death* and *The Kremlin Letter* before *Fat City; Roy Bean* and *The Mackintosh Man* before *The Man Who Would Be King; Phobia, Victory* and *Annie* before ending his career in his eighties with three dazzling films: *Under the Volcano, Prizzi's Honor* and *The Dead*. He always got back on his feet at the last minute, before being counted out, and had an uncanny ability to attract backers after a number of disasters. As his producer Gottfried Reinhardt observed, "John is such a colossal failure" that even his failures seem impressive.

By the mid-1970s Huston had been suffering from lung problems for about twenty years and, at least since *Fat City* in 1972, had needed an oxygen tank to help him breathe. An irreversible degenerative condition caused by heavy smoking, emphysema is characterized by a loss of elasticity in the lung tissue that impedes the flow of air and makes breathing extremely difficult. According to *The Merck Manual*, the medical bible, "about 50% of patients die within 10 years of initial diagnosis." Huston, afflicted for twice that time and smoking till near the end, defiantly gambled and beat the odds. In *White Hunter, Black Heart*, Peter Viertel describes how the actors and crew of *The African Queen* were worried and frightened by his gasping, choking and struggling for air: "[Huston] started to cough, his head hanging down below his thin shoulders, his body doubled up as if he were in extreme pain. . . . It seemed almost that he would choke with coughing, that his lungs would burst, that his throat would ultimately come out of his mouth."[7] During his long, slow fade-out, Huston exchanged the warmth of women for the steely comfort of a green oxygen tank.

In October 1977, at the age of seventy-one, Huston had a life-threatening operation in Los Angeles for an abdominal aneurysm, a weakening and possible rupture of the artery, the same disease that had suddenly killed Walter in 1950. As his doctor explained, the operation for an aneurysm was "very, very serious in a man with mammoth emphysema, because it's a big abdominal incision. . . . John's serious complication was an obstruction and he had to have his gall bladder removed, which was also a difficult operation because of the respiratory problem." He endured three major surgeries of eleven, nine and seven hours, and exaggerating a bit, as if his guts were mobile snakes, remarked, "It's a terrible thing, they put your intestines on a tray and there they lie smoking and writhing while your aorta is being worked on." He spent seven weeks in intensive care and everyone was astounded that he survived. Seven years later, in July 1984, he had eye surgery. It improved his fading vision, but he had to wear "castanets" over his eyes and couldn't see for several weeks. After being treated for "senile" cataracts, he told Charles Elliott, his editor at Knopf, "Maybe it's time to admit my hoary (not whorey) age."[8]

· IV ·

Huston had close and lifelong ties to Mexico. He'd joined the Mexican cavalry in his youth; had *Frankie and Johnny* illustrated by the Mexican artist Miguel Covarrubias; collected, stole and smuggled pre-Columbian statues; adopted a Mexican boy, Pablo Albarran; wrote the script for *Juárez;* and would make four films there: *Sierra Madre, The Unforgiven, Night of the Iguana* and *Under the Volcano.* The move from St. Clerans and Cici to Vallarta and Maricela, from wet gray skies to brilliant tropical sunshine, was not only a radical transformation of climate, culture and companion, but also a change from baronial splendor to ascetic simplicity and a near total renunciation of worldly goods. He'd spent decades passionately acquiring his precious possessions and then quite easily gave them up.

He called Las Caletas (The Coves)—about fifteen miles south of Puerto Vallarta, ten miles south of Mismaloya and thirty minutes away by boat—"the most primitive home I have ever had, with the jungle at my back and the ocean a few steps from my house. No running water."

Las Caletas was a series of palm-thatched buildings, open to the air and ascending the hill. Huston lived at the bottom, next to the beach, in an open living room, with his bedroom and bath behind. It had screens instead of glass windows and walls, and movable canvas to keep out the rain. Next up the hill was a common dining room and kitchen. Gladys' house, slightly smaller than John's, was a bit higher. Up the hill from Gladys' house was a guest house and a place for the servants: a Mexican couple with a baby. Each place had a beautiful view of the bay. Archie, a Filipino and U.S. Navy veteran who owned an Asian restaurant in Puerto Vallarta, came from town every day to cook. In loose white cotton shirts and billowing pants, Huston enjoyed the simple, unpretentious life. He drank, smoked cigars, swam in the clear water, caught fish, walked barefoot on the beach, watched the sunsets, explored the coast, devoured books, worked on scripts, sketched, painted and talked to visitors. At parties in town, he directed the conversation, provoked people with unexpected remarks and liked to be entertained.[9]

Las Caletas allowed Huston to indulge his taste for exotic pets. He had a macaw, a pet pig, two deer, an obscure ant-eating animal, two well-fed boa constrictors and a semi-tame ocelot. His open-handed yet menacing invitations challenged the courage and endurance of his prospective guests. As he wrote to his editor, Charles Elliott, who neglected to come, "The servants have learned the ways of the Gringo and would do their best to defend you against everything from scorpions to tidal waves. . . . No shark has ever taken anyone in our little cove." The producer Michael Fitzgerald described the place as magnificently simple and breathtakingly beautiful. Huston didn't need a grand life and was relieved (in a way) to shake off the heavy burdens of St. Clerans. Though he didn't know any Spanish and was not interested in learning the language, he was blissfully happy in his little domain. The cove had no distractions and was a good place to work.

Jacqueline Bisset, who boldly ventured down to Caletas to discuss the script of *Under the Volcano*, found it a strange and unnerving experience. She flew from Los Angeles to Puerto Vallarta and was taken to the dock. Suddenly overdressed in her neat city clothes, she had to take her boots off and roll up her trousers to board the boat, which bounced heavily on the rough water. The compound of white buildings had a jungly feeling, and she was led to a sparsely furnished whitewashed room. She was greeted by a large black dog and a pet reptile, and was given a tuna sandwich. Maricela, who seemed more like a servant than a mistress, then crept in—small, dark, silent and mysterious. Bisset had been on a diet and was very hungry, but was left alone in the room all afternoon while insects scurried madly around. When Huston finally appeared, they talked about alcoholism in *Volcano,* but he didn't take a drink or offer one to her. She'd heard that Huston was a gourmet, but there were only rows and rows of tinned food in the cold larder: tuna fish, corn and other basic food. A very simple dinner was served at 8 P.M. Finally, she asked for and was given a drink, and Huston disappeared early. The next morning she ate breakfast alone, then swam with him on the beach. Huston always made her feel nervous, both in Caletas and afterward when making *Volcano.*[10]

· V ·

Huston rarely went in for popsies, starlets or one-night stands. He wanted intelligent women who were good companions as well as lovers. He treated them well, kept up with most and usually remained friends with them. Cici and Maricela, who appeared toward the end of his life, were the exceptions. There was a great contrast between the two women: American and Mexican, rich and poor, grand and humble, mistress and servant, glamorous and homely, sexy and drab, courageous and timid, assertive and shy, brash and self-effacing, short-tempered and patient, rebellious and obedient, jealous and tolerant, critical and adoring, talkative and silent.

Maricela Hernandez was born in Mexico City in about 1952 and had a poverty-stricken childhood. According to her profile in *People Weekly,* she was "the fourth of nine children, and said that her father died when she was 5. Her mother moved the family to the border city of Tijuana, where Hernandez eventually crossed into California illegally and began dishwashing, raking leaves and waiting tables to make a living." She was very short and dark, had peasant features, and never wore makeup or feminine clothes. She reminded both John and Danny of a miniature pre-Columbian idol, with slightly slanted eyes and prominent cheekbones. She seemed like a small, quiet animal scurrying around in the dark and (Allegra wrote) "had a way of hiding from people, like a feral cat."

In 1975 Huston, nearly seventy, drinking heavily and seriously ill, was alone and had no one to take care of him. Gladys had to look after her dying mother, Anjelica wouldn't help and he didn't seem to want Zoe. That left Maricela, the last one standing and quite willing to pick up the pieces. She was a good nurse, had taken care of Collin for many years, and was well qualified to look after an aged and ailing man. She came from Mexico and liked his remote hideout. Huston, who always favored the underdog, was used to her, found her amusing and liked having her around as part of his menagerie.[11] Huston had to be cared for even before he became sick, and Maricela now managed his practical as well as his medical needs. He gratefully declared that he couldn't have survived without his new servant-and-mistress: "She dishes out the medication, cooks, puts my contact lens in, cuts my hair, manicures me, puts me to bed, and sometimes when I'm done in, she gives me a massage." She lasted longer than any of his mistresses and wives, stayed the course and saw him out.

Both Cici and Zoe, who also hated Maricela, paid tribute to her devotion to John. Cici admitted that Maricela was wonderful with him and that she herself could not have taken care of the sick man as Maricela did. Zoe also respected Maricela for helping John, but remarked that her behavior was far from selfless and disinterested, and that her family constantly took advantage of him. Maricela came up trumps in his will: "She took care of him. And he generously took care of her and her family. I believe she saw this as an opportunity to be taken care of. I always judged the relationship with a certain scepticism. After Gladys Hill died [in 1981] she started to have a somewhat sinister control over him and I saw him suffer because of it. He seemed to me to be trapped in the relationship as his health deteriorated. My big regret is that I did not step in at this point and take care of him myself. My only justification for not doing so at this most vulnerable time was my desire not to

cause havoc when John was so terribly ill and add anxiety to a potentially explosive situation."[12]

Huston's attraction to Maricela, his intimate companion in Mexico and Los Angeles during the last twelve years of his life, was both
puzzling and irrational, practical and sound. Michael Fitzgerald (who
could not provide specific examples) believed that John liked Maricela's complete unpredictability, the constant surprise in their daily rou-
tine, the complete lack of knowledge about what would happen next.
Guy Gallo thought Huston no longer wanted (or could endure) the
Sturm und Drang of life with a sophisticated and ambitious woman.
He treated Maricela kindly, as an old servant and new mistress, and
gave no indication that he would stay with her until the end of his life.
Eloise Hardt, like many others, found Maricela "creepy." But she was
totally obedient, devoted and adoring, and would sit in the car and
wait patiently while Huston played backgammon till two or three in
the morning.[13] He remarked, "She's not at all jealous when I chase after
whores or come in reeling with two or three women. My last marriage
took all the romance out of me. . . . Five was my absolute limit."

The cameraman Ossie Morris, noting that Maricela had a limited command of English, said, "She had no conversation. And John
liked conversation. I couldn't imagine what those two would talk about
when they were alone together." But after years of constant strife with
women, Huston gradually became less social and more self-absorbed,
and welcomed a more silent and peaceful existence. Jan Lavender, his
art dealer friend in Puerto Vallarta, found Maricela very strange, aso-
cial, unfriendly and "at war with everyone." She was territorial about
John and kept everybody away from him, and he seemed to like (or at
least to accept) a more isolated life with her.[14] The mousy servant used
his total dependence upon her to dominate the master, control his life
and supplant Gladys as gatekeeper to the throne room. When Maricela
once rashly asked Gladys if there was anything about Caletas that she
didn't like, Gladys bluntly answered, "Your presence."

TWENTY-FIVE

FAILURES,

1979–1982

· I ·

Huston's Southern Gothic films—Tennessee Williams' *The Night of the Iguana*, Carson McCullers' *Reflections in a Golden Eye* and *Wise Blood* (1979), based on a 1952 novel by Flannery O'Connor—form a trilogy. Their subjects ranged from a defrocked alcoholic minister and predatory adolescent nymphomaniac, through a repressed homosexual, adulterous wife and voyeuristic murderer, to a masochistic religious maniac. *Wise Blood* shares the sensational southern milieu and grotesque character of *Reflections*. Both pictures have literary roots in the macabre works of E.T.A. Hoffman and Edgar Allan Poe, in Charles Baudelaire's self-mortifications, and in the perverse violence of the impotent Popeye raping Temple Drake in Faulkner's *Sanctuary* (1931). Both are also influenced by the weird cruelty (a razor blade slashing an eyeball) of Surrealist works like Luis Buñuel's *Un Chien Andalou.*

Michael Fitzgerald, the producer, was the elder son of Robert Fitzgerald, the distinguished poet and translator, and his wife Sally, who were O'Connor's close friends and literary executors. O'Connor lived for a time with the Fitzgeralds, and Sally edited her letters. The whole Fitzgerald family genuflected at the altar of Saint Flannery, who died of lupus in 1964, and the movie is a testament to their devotion. Sally designed the sets and costumes, and her younger son, Benedict, wrote the screenplay. Michael, who'd grown up in Italy and gone to boarding school in Ireland, took three years to get the financing and came up with an unusually low budget, variously reported as $900,000 to $2 million. He said he knew nothing about how to make a film and left all the practical details to the gruff assistant director and production manager, Tom Shaw, who'd worked for Huston, Richard Brooks and Burt Lancaster.

There were no major stars, and Huston—who usually got about $400,000, but was eager to try new things and recharge his career—accepted a low fee of only $125,000. He did a fair amount of work on the script and, ever faithful to the author, preferred to use her dialogue whenever possible and squeeze every word out of the text. But the final script was too unrelentingly faithful. Mark Ford has described O'Connor's work as "ferocious stories populated by backwoods prophets and club-footed hoodlums, mass murderers and one-armed con artists, savage saints, drooling idiot boys, tattoo-freaks, wary xenophobes and hick racists." Huston's film, though admired by certain critics, was a box-office failure. It succeeded in translating the bizarre and disturbing events of the novel into film, but its episodes of black comedy failed to lighten the bleak tone or mitigate the hero's absurd tragedy.

As with *Fat City* in Stockton, Huston used real townspeople alongside professional actors when shooting *Wise Blood* in Macon, Georgia. The bums hanging out in an alley were given vodka, which went to their heads and made them genuinely frightened by the scene when the gorilla escaped. At the rehearsals Huston would formally announce, "And now I want the artists." In one scene a minor actor, Dan Shor, was supposed to deliver a shrunken black mummy that he'd stolen from the museum. (In a sly allusion, it was wrapped in layers of newspaper, just like the package that Walter brings to Bogart in *The Maltese Falcon*.) Shor kept getting it wrong till finally, in frustration, he threw down and broke the package, which had to be rewrapped. Huston was furious, yet maintained his habitual self-control. He didn't yell at Shor, but lost all respect for him and dismissed him from his mind. A journalist on the set reported, with a striking comparison, that Huston "seems to be everywhere, tall, slightly hunched, oddly frail, so bony now that his hands seem immense, like drawings by Egon Schiele."[1]

Huston had originally wanted Tommy Lee Jones for the leading role of the self-tormenting fanatic Hazel Motes but eventually hired

Brad Dourif, who'd played one of the mental patients in *One Flew Over the Cuckoo's Nest* (1975) and could project the necessary mad intensity. Huston made a brief but forceful appearance as Hazel's grandfather, a fiery backwoods preacher. Echoing the frequent misspellings on southern fundamentalist billboards, Huston's first name appears three times in the titles as "Jhon." At the beginning of the picture, when Hazel visits his mother's grave, the misleading inscription reads: "Gone to become an angle."

In his burning desire to deny the teaching and divinity of Jesus Christ, Hazel becomes an "atheistic evangelist" whose zealous message is: "The blind *don't* see, the lame *don't* walk, and what's dead stays that way." Devoting himself to his own idea of God and trying to achieve a kind of sainthood, Hazel imitates Christ's crown of thorns by wrapping barbed wire around his bleeding torso. His landlady tries to explain, "It's not natural, Mr. Motes. It's not normal. . . . People have quit . . . boiling in oil or walling up cats"—as in Poe's story "The Black Cat." Motes, who can't see the truth for the mote (or speck) in his own eye, ignores the vital question in Matthew 7:3: "Why beholdest thou the mote that is in thy brother's eye, but considerest not the beam that is in thine own eye?" Like Oedipus the King, who blinds himself because he cannot bear the truth, Hazel, trying to see a deeper truth with an inward light, finally blinds himself with quicklime.

The title of *Wise Blood* suggests the kind of intuitive knowledge that Blaise Pascal defined in the *Pensées* (1670): "The heart has its reasons that reason doesn't know." But the title is ironic, and Hazel's story is actually a kind of Pilgrim's Regress from orthodox religion into a sickening parody of Christianity. Following O'Connor's statement in the preface to a reprint of her work, "It is a comic novel about a Christian *malgré lui*" (in spite of himself), Huston conceived the movie as a black comedy in which "Jesus wins" and Hazel achieves salvation at the end. But the audience did *not* find it terribly funny. He tried to make a serious picture but was defeated by the intractable material: by the strangely disturbing story and the absolutely repulsive characters. The religious message meant nothing to Huston, who was drawn to this material for other reasons. Alluding to the invalidism of his boyhood, he called it "the drama of a young man who is trying to rebel. It is as if someone were recovering from an illness, fighting against something that had afflicted him when he was a child."[2]

Wise Blood is slow, uneventful and repetitive, with long preaching scenes and lots of aimless driving around in an old wreck of a car. Critics were quite negative about its Manichean struggle between good and evil, though the uneasy tone and obscure meaning made it difficult to distinguish between the two extremes. *Films and Filming* called it "wildly uncommercial," but added that "the film's very mordancy is part of its fascination." Andrew Sarris, writing in the *Village Voice*, noted the grim mood and discouraged the potential audience by writing, "Every thoughtful person should see *Wise Blood* once if only to experience a profound and original depression."[3]

· II ·

Huston had had a contract to write his autobiography for many years, but was always too busy to start it. He was prodded into signing up by Swifty Lazar, who'd been Bogart's agent. Swifty swept Huston through the New York publishing houses and extracted a large advance from Knopf. During his fallow period in the late 1970s, when Huston needed the rest of the advance, he finally got down to work. Gladys Hill, obsessed by Huston and involved in every aspect of his life, typed the pages and made suggestions as he dictated his memories. But he needed a responsive audience and soon got bored telling her the stories she'd often heard during their years together. He was then helped by a former navy diver and CIA agent, William Reed, who lived down the coast at Las Animas. Huston, who thanked Reed in the author's note, recalled, "I found out that he loved my stories. So I switched on the tape again and started talking to him. And I got the book done."

Not quite. His editor at Knopf, Charles Elliott, worked with him for a week in Toronto while Huston was unsuccessfully trying to get a government subvention to shoot *Victory* in Canada. He questioned Huston closely, extracted more material and got a third of the book down on paper that week, though Huston's ironically titled *An Open*

Book (1980) left out as much as he put in. Elliott said that Huston didn't want to reveal himself and that he couldn't make him more forthcoming and outspoken. A great raconteur, at once self-absorbed and self-detached, he told a series of lively but mostly impersonal anecdotes and recalled his emotions in tranquillity, without becoming confessional or brooding about the past. He admitted, "The whole story has not been told, of course. I've refrained from making any dark disclosures regarding my secret life. My misdeeds are not sufficiently evil to justify their being put on display." Like everyone else, the sophisticated Elliott came under his spell and said no one he'd ever met quite measured up to charming Johnny.[4] Knopf commissioned an expensive portrait by the famous photographer Irving Penn, very formal and stiff, which Huston hated and wouldn't use. They then sent Eve Arnold to Hungary, where he was shooting *Victory*. She took a picture of Huston with a fur hat and a big grin, which he liked, and they put it on the dust jacket.

Huston was also portrayed in nine novels and one play. The most illuminating, apart from Peter Viertel's *White Hunter, Black Heart*, were Norman Mailer's novel *The Deer Park* (1955) and Arthur Miller's last play, *Finishing the Picture* (2004). Like James Hannaford in Welles' *The Other Side of the Wind*, the director Charles Eitel, in Mailer's novel, uses his courage and integrity to oppose the prevailing trend in the film industry—in this case, the craven acceptance of the Cold War blacklist. Mailer described Eitel's eyes as "bright blue, and when he smiled, they were alive, and his broken nose gave him a humorous look. But only his [seductive] voice gave a hint of his reputation." Eitel also expresses Huston's characteristic inability to remain monogamous: "I've never been the kind of man who can be faithful with any regularity. I've always been the sort of decent chappie who hops from one woman to another in the run of an evening because that's the only prescription which allows me to be fond of both the ladies." Miller's Derek Clemson, the director of a film based on *The Misfits*, is also modeled on Huston. A female character describes him as "very macho and doesn't really relate to women." He loves horses, and has directed the character based on Marilyn Monroe in her first important film (*The Asphalt Jungle*). He courts danger by losing thousands of dollars when gambling all night in Reno and by smuggling pre-Columbian artifacts from Mexico.[5]

In 1980, the year *An Open Book* appeared, Huston's old enemy Ronald Reagan reached the apogee of his political career. This mediocre actor—who'd been anti-Communist, pro–Joseph McCarthy and a friendly HUAC witness—astonished everyone in Hollywood by becoming first the right-wing president of the Screen Actors Guild (1947–52), then governor of California (1967–75) and finally president of the United States (1981–89). Huston, who swore to Cici, "if Reagan becomes president I'm never coming back to America," kept his word and remained in Mexico. In a published interview he vented his spleen and called him "a bore. And a bad actor. Besides he has a low order of intelligence, with a certain cunning. . . . He's inflated, he's egotistical." In a letter of 1982 to Charles Elliott, he frankly expressed his hatred for the new president: "He is a monster of ineptitude. . . . Heel—callused, coarse grained, yellowish and the very lowest part of the human anatomy. One doesn't know whether he is motivated by monumental dullness or malevolence."[6]

· III ·

After Huston had failed to secure funds in Canada, he shot *Victory* (1981) in Budapest on a sixteen-week schedule and a budget of $14 million. Michael Caine got a sizable chunk: $1 million. Max von Sydow, who was Kohner's client and had appeared in *The Kremlin Letter*, played a German officer. The English actor Tim Pigott-Smith, who played one of the British prisoners and later went on to achieve television stardom in *The Jewel in the Crown* (1984), recalled that Hungary wasn't too bad, though they all got bored with the food in what was then a poor country. He once queued for a banana, but the man in front of him grabbed the last one and he never saw another. The cast consoled themselves with the Budapest opera, movies in English with Hungarian subtitles, dinners on the Danube, and baths and massages in the Gellert Hotel.

The plot of *Victory* is a tediously familiar rehash of old movies. As in *Stalag 17* (1953) and numerous prison-escape pictures, the inmates of a German prisoner of war camp excavate a tunnel and crawl through it to escape. (In *We Were Strangers* they also dig extensively to blow up a dictator.) They plan to escape through the sewers, like Welles in *The Third Man* (1949), and the patriotic crowd sings the "Marseillaise," as in *Casablanca* (1942). In World War I soldiers on both sides had walked out of the trenches to play soccer matches in no-man's-land. In *Victory* the German jailors play their Allied captives to achieve a propaganda coup. In *The Bridge on the River Kwai* (1957), Alec Guinness builds a bridge for the Japanese enemy instead of sabotaging it. Similarly, Caine, the gung-ho soccer coach, continues the game to achieve an ironic victory instead of following Sylvester Stallone's plan to escape at halftime.

Tim Pigott-Smith had vivid recollections of the seventy-five-year-old Huston as director. His "vesuvian spasms of coughing" worried everyone. He didn't seem to have much energy for activities after work, and on one very hot afternoon was seen dozing off during a take. But as an old man with a limited supply of time and energy, he was usually very focused. He did not give Pigott-Smith any notes about his character, but would comment on a specific line or make an odd filmic suggestion. He was extremely good at getting the actual feeling of a scene and catching the tone of a speech that didn't seem quite real. "Sounds acted," he'd say. "Do it again."

On two memorable occasions, Huston lost his temper. He insisted that everyone do his job and give a professional performance. When someone driving a car turned the wrong way, he got annoyed and told him, "Do it again." When he messed up the second time, Huston shouted at him, dismissed him and said, "Get someone else." In another horrendous episode, after a break in shooting, the actor Julian Curry forgot to put on a sweater that he had worn in an earlier shot and the continuity people did not spot it until later. Huston was very angry with them, though not with Julian. "Goddamn. God DAMN!," he spat. "Well . . . we'll just have to do it again." Once he'd vented his anger, he just got on with it and they did it again.

When the producer Freddie Fields was wasting time like mad, Huston, with admirable sangfroid, just sat there and allowed people to quarrel and panic all around him. After Fields had invited 150 foreign journalists to a press conference, Huston moved to a tall director's chair and answered questions with affable charm and Irish blarney. Asked why he made films, he paused and said, "Because I like them or to make money." He paused again and added, "Or for both reasons." He was clever, funny and honest, and could not be caught out.[7]

The film editor Roberto Silvi remarked that the star, Stallone, was at the top of his career after *Rocky* (1976). He was also "an arrogant son of a bitch" who thought he was Jesus Christ. Stallone even told a Texas reporter, "Sometimes you're not aware that Huston is even around." He was always late and would make Huston wait half an hour to watch the rushes. Huston didn't seem to care, said to "let it be" and just wanted to finish the picture. No one said anything about Stallone's difficult behavior. When he was late, Huston simply called for another scene, as he did when it rained. Stallone did not always speak to the actors and crew, and had his instructions relayed indirectly. He was quite remote, but not unpleasant; people coped with him and there was no bad feeling. When he became bored toward the end of the shoot, he started writing *Rocky II*.

Huston was much more interested in foxhunting than in soccer games. The day before shooting the match Pigott-Smith talked to him on the pitch and got the feeling that he was not madly concerned about it. He had a limited knowledge of the game, didn't know how to make penalty shots for fouls and needed help when staging the soccer sequence.[8] Silvi agreed that Huston didn't know or care much about soccer, which was "a strange subject" to him. He thought Huston had ended up with a movie that someone else had planned to make and that for him *Victory* was just another job. There is, however, one prescient theme in the picture: the role of rabid nationalism and aggression in modern sports events. As Orwell wrote in "The Sporting Spirit" (1945), "Serious sport . . . is bound up with hatred, jealousy, boastfulness, disregard of all rules and sadistic pleasure in witnessing violence: in other words it is war minus the shooting."

Huston always watched the World Cup finals on television, and had seen the Brazilian superstar Pelé in four of them. Very few people ever impressed Huston, but he *was* impressed by Pelé—the temperamental opposite of Stallone. In his twenty-two years of professional play, Pelé had made only two spectacular somersault goals, but to heighten the drama in *Victory* he made three of them in one game. Pelé's autobiography has a long, revealing passage about his role in the movie:

My best known performance, without doubt, was in John Huston's 1981 film, *Victory*. My participation occurred as an indirect result of my contract with Warner Communications, which owned Warner Bros. The film, which mainly took place in a prisoner of war camp during World War II, revolved around a Nazi propaganda plan to organize a game of soccer between their best players and a team of stars from the prisoner of war camp. The prisoners intended to use the match to disguise their bold plan of escape.

I also acted as technical advisor for the soccer scenes, directed by Luis Fernández, and during the course of the filming I went on to the playing field with the same passion that I had in real games. Huston shouted at me: "Relax, Pelé! It's a film, you have to act properly in each scene and must control your emotions." He was a genius of the cinema and I learned a lot from him. I also learned that the stars are not always democratic. Stallone, for example, didn't allow anyone to sit in his chair on the set and insisted that he must be the one to score the winning goal. As he was the goalkeeper, he could not do this. But they created a scene in which Stallone kicked the goal during a final penalty shot.

Most of the movie was filmed in Hungary because they had a stadium in Budapest that served our purpose. It was big enough for the decisive game and didn't have modern lights. Many other soccer players took part in these scenes: Osvaldo Ardiles, a member of the Argentine team that had recently won the World Cup; the English star Bobby Moore, another winner of the World Cup, who had been on my old Cosmos team and was also a good actor; and a group of players from Ipswich Town who were hired as extras. I shined a little in the final scene. My character, though injured by a German player, limped onto the playing field in order to avoid a draw and made the spectacular Chilean shot![9]

Pigott-Smith remembered Pelé as a charming and likable chap. The actors often had to spend a long time sitting around and doing nothing in the stadium. They once saw Pelé trapped on the soccer pitch when security was lax and the crowd broke down the barriers. Instead of getting agitated, he just calmly stood there and signed hundreds of autographs. He didn't merely scrawl his name, but wrote "From your friend, Pelé." He fully returned Huston's admiration and exclaimed, "I have met popes, presidents, kings, and queens, but I have never been so impressed with a man's charisma as with John Huston's."[10]

· IV ·

Huston always maintained that he was not interested in filming Broadway plays, and in *The Deer Park* Eitel states, "I hate musical comedies." The nauseous sentimentality of *Annie* (1982), with heartwarming songs like "You're Never Fully Dressed Without a Smile," was a striking contrast to the hard-nosed cynicism of his early films. Ray Stark—on his fourth and worst picture with Huston—persuaded him to direct with a million-dollar fee. Huston's adaptation cost $9.5 million for the rights and about $52 million to complete on a shooting schedule that took twenty weeks. He took very little interest in the picture, which certainly shows. But he did have to deal with a number of serious crises: "two heart attacks (one fatal) to key personnel, four different cinematographers, the threat of a directors' strike, the remaking of two multimillion-dollar production numbers." Based on the popular comic strip, radio serial and successful Broadway musical of 1977—instead of literary works by Hammett, Melville, Kipling and Crane—it was his most unfortunate mismatch since Audrey Hepburn was cast as an Indian maiden in *The Unforgiven*. The film's editor Margaret Booth exclaimed, "John did the best he could with it, although he never should have done it—never, never, never. But he was hard up."[11]

Huston was not good with children, either in his own family or on film. The story of a repulsively "cute" little girl who escapes from an orphanage to achieve happiness with her soft-hearted tycoon, Daddy Warbucks, reverses both Dickens' *Oliver Twist* and Huston's unhappy relationship with his adopted son Pablo. The saccharine, screechy-voiced, ten-year-old Aileen Quinn beat out thousands of other nymphettes in a nationwide search. Albert Finney, badly miscast as Warbucks, took singing and dancing lessons, and had a shaved billiard-ball head that clashed with Quinn's flourishing red Afro. Carol Burnett crudely overacted the cruel, alcoholic head of the orphanage. The location used for Warbucks' mansion was at Monmouth College in West Long Branch, New Jersey, a few miles from the Jersey shore. The lavish home, which once belonged to the president of Woolworth's, had been built for $10.5 million in 1930 on the site of Woodrow Wilson's summer White House.

Puzzled by the notices, Huston wrote Charles Elliott that "ANNIE's reception has been the queerest in my experience. The reviewers either denigrate it or go into ecstasies. I guess all that matters is that it is making its money back." Huston got his fee, but the movie actually lost money. The critics were mostly hostile, and *Variety* zeroed in on its blatant lack of subtlety: "Whatever indefinable charm the stage show had is completely lost in this lumbering and largely uninteresting and uninvolving exercise, where the obvious waste reaches almost Pentagonian proportions." Wieland Schulz-Keil, the intellectual German who would produce Huston's next film, had a small part as a bomb-throwing Bolshevik assassin. He's caught by Annie's ubiquitous dog and prevented from blowing up Warbucks and his mansion. Schulz-Keil hung around the set while Huston was making *Annie* and had many long talks with him about their next and infinitely more interesting project, *Under the Volcano*.[12]

TWENTY-SIX

TRIUMPHS,

1983–1985

· I ·

Under the Volcano (1984), based on the powerful English novel by Malcolm Lowry (1947), was the fourth picture Huston shot in Mexico. As early as 1949 Frank Taylor, a publisher before he produced *The Misfits*, wrote Lowry that Huston "is such a Mexican at heart, I'm sure he will be thrilled by it." The novel *did* have a strong personal appeal and was related to Huston's two best Mexican films. Lowry's biographer noted that the writer "would lock himself in his rooms for days with whiskey and sardines and read the novels of B. Traven," author of *Sierra Madre*. Both Reverend Shannon (Richard Burton) in *Iguana* and the ex–British consul Geoffrey Firmin (Albert Finney) in *Volcano*—the titles symbolize the menacing aspects of Mexico—are self-destructive alcoholics who've disgraced themselves in their former professions. They've lost the capacity to love, lost faith in themselves and in the world, and are sustained by self-sacrificial women who cannot save them.

Volcano takes place on November 1, 1938, the Mexican Day of the Dead, between seven in the morning and seven in the evening, when Firmin is killed. The Spanish Civil War is still being fought, and the war in Europe is about to break out, which intensifies Firmin's sense of menace and impending disaster. On this day his divorced wife Yvonne (Jacqueline Bisset) unexpectedly comes back to him. She also finds her former lover, his half-brother Hugh (Anthony Andrews), who's just returned from reporting the Loyalist losses in the Spanish Civil War— the fatal prelude to World War II. Both the characters and the town of

Cuernavaca are overshadowed by Popocatepetl, the extinct volcano of the title, which seems to symbolize Firmin's violent passions and sexual impotence.

Many eminent directors—including Luis Buñuel, Joseph Losey, Jules Dassin and Ken Russell—had tried to get the project off the ground; and as many as sixty-seven writers, including Gabriel García Márquez, had tried to transform the novel into a screenplay. The tangled and complex rights to the book were expensive to sort out, and the producer Michael Fitzgerald eventually gave up trying to acquire them. But Wieland Schulz-Keil persisted over the years, managed to clarify the matter and finally bought the rights. Schulz-Keil knew Paul Kohner and approached Huston through him. Still enthusiastic about the novel, Huston was eager to do it and said, "Let's make the movie."[1] The budget was a modest $4 million.

Through interviews with Fitzgerald, Schulz-Keil and the screenwriter Guy Gallo—and abundant new material provided by Gallo—we now know more about the evolution of this script than about any screenplay Huston filmed. The twenty-eight-year-old Gallo, born in New Orleans and nearly fifty years younger than Huston, had graduated from Harvard and was then studying at the Yale School of Drama. Fitzgerald heard about Gallo's script and showed it to Huston. It was not, like the extremely convoluted novel, metaphysical and mystifying, with a coruscating style and many philosophical digressions. Gallo translated the novel into film by eliminating the interior monologues and emphasizing the external surface of the characters. His most ingenious stroke, which no one had ever thought of, was to intensify the love triangle by combining Firmin's half-brother Hugh and the movie director Laruelle into one character. Everyone agreed this was the best approach.

In a letter to Gallo of June 15, 1982, Huston offered superb criticism of the story, the characters and their motivation:

> I think your script of *Under the Volcano* is very interesting.
> The idea of combining the characters of the Consul's brother
> and Laruelle is good and it certainly works dramatically.

However I feel that it would have been better if you had kept the brother rather than the motion picture director. The relationship between the three would be that much more complicated. I think the Consul would find more difficulty in dealing with his cuckoldry if the lover were his beloved brother.

I'm glad you chose to give importance to the wartime incident. I think even more could be made of it so that we are led to understand it was that deed of the Consul's which is the root cause of his drunkenness. After the [Great] War and his marriage to Yvonne, it came back to haunt him. I would like to know what caused him to commit such a savage act—perhaps the enemy had been shooting defenseless men in the water around the sinking ship. I don't think the device of the Familiar is at all necessary, nor for that matter is the flashback technique you employ sporadically. On the whole it seems to me that the more legitimate you keep the outward form of the story, the better. Your most valuable innovation is with the characters—where it really counts.

Gallo said that Huston, "a sadist and practical joker," gave him a hard time. Huston told him, "Don't worry about revising the first twenty pages. We're using someone else's script for this." They discussed the rest of the script during their backgammon games, and the next day Huston left for his poker game in Puerto Vallarta. Gallo then took up the implicit challenge and rewrote these twenty pages precisely because Huston told him *not* to revise them. Wanting to escape from Huston's domination and avoid "incarcerated writing," Gallo rebelled against his control, left Mexico and went back to New York to work at home. Huston respected him for this decision. The game was played and points scored on both sides. "He was a gamesman in all things," Gallo said. "And this, his opening gambit, was, I am sure, designed to test my pride, my resolve, my resilience." When Gallo returned to Mexico, Huston tried to crush his rebellious spirit.[2] Fitzgerald confirmed that Gallo and Huston did not get along. Arrogant, cocky and self-confident, Gallo was chastened and subdued by Huston, who "increasingly wrung these qualities out of him." Using various coercive techniques, Huston usually got what he wanted from everyone.

Gallo was naturally ecstatic that his script would be made into a major film by John Huston. But, he recorded, "Huston has a way of making me feel so small. Not a word of encouragement. I suppose the fact that Finney, Andrews and Bisset have signed should be encouragement enough. Still, it is hard to be told 'these scenes are not the work of a dramatist.' " Maka Czernichew, with Huston at the time and sympathetic to the young writer, warned him, Gallo said, "to be careful because I could easily leave [Mexico] in anger. Perhaps that's what prompted Huston to open up a bit and try to work with me."[3]

When Gallo tried to enhance the script by adopting Lowry's novelistic techniques, Huston rejected his use of "subtext and symbolism." He challenged Gallo but would not accept his explanations:

"What does rain mean?," John asked me.

"Tone. Ambiance. An amplification of the macabre opening in the cemetery. Dramatic. Visual. The bar is crowded because of it. The awninged booths with rain seeping through. The streets glisten. Foreshadows his end. It rains at the Farolito [bar]. Preparation."

"Yes, but what does it mean?"

Finally, the rain was excised because they had no rain machine.

In *Volcano* Huston observed the classical unities of time, place and action, and insisted on a linear structure that started at the beginning, finished at the end and had no flashbacks that distracted from the main thrust of the story. Gallo wrote that Huston wanted a script that was "lucid, well motivated and motivating, with no loose ends. Not something 'literary,' as he says with a sneer. Not something to be comprehended. But, rather, something to be apprehended immediately— without the mediation of the audience's own mind." Always very concrete and more interested in character than in the innovative aspects of the novel, he was totally focused on Firmin. Though an atheist, he thought the consul's worldview, even his negative, self-destructive qualities, tended toward the superhuman and the divine. When drunk, Firmin's thought was clearer and more in touch with his own reality.[4]

Despite their unremitting conflict, Gallo learned a great deal from Huston. The master would say, "The draft is fine, but it's only writing," and it always had to be more than fine writing. He often praised Tennessee Williams for adding the broken bottle and glass shards when Richard Burton and Sue Lyon are barefoot in Burton's hotel room. He called this the under action that amplifies the main action, provides the visceral twinge and draws the audience into the scene.

Describing the writing process and the gradual evolution of the script, Gallo told an interviewer:

> We met four times, for long stretches, and at each stage, his reaction was geared to what the realities were. When we met in California the first time, the criticisms were very general. When we met in Puerto Vallarta for the first time, again it was a sort of structural question about the clarity of the beginning, primarily. The third time, the criticisms became a little more specific. And then, when we had an actual production date, we met again in Puerto Vallarta for six weeks, with Wieland Schulz-Keil and, for a while, Michael Fitzgerald. That was day-to-day, page-by-page, scene-by-scene. But the major thrust was always the same: to clarify the immediacy.

Gallo found Schulz-Keil an amusing companion and liked working with him during the six weeks in Mexico. Schulz-Keil recalled that he, Gallo and Huston worked on the script practically every minute of the day. They talked about scenes in the morning; then all three went away, wrote separately and met again for lunch. They parted again, met in the late afternoon and read what the others had written. Huston was not competitive about the script and did not insist on having things his own way. He was open to suggestions and always eager to accept what the others had to offer.[5]

Instead of plastering over the defects of the story, Huston would say, "This bothers me," and Gallo, working under pressure, would have to solve a problem in almost every scene. He constantly rewrote and met most of Huston's demands, but Huston did not always exert his power and Gallo persuaded him to change his mind about a few things. There had to be some equality and respect or Gallo would have gone mad. They finished the final draft—when the script was "locked in" and there were supposed to be no more changes—a week before the actors arrived in Mexico. But Schulz-Keil and Fitzgerald then added more scenes to the screenplay. Bisset and Andrews had approved the "final" script, which originally had more material about them, and when it was changed after their agreement, they naturally wanted to recover what they had lost.[6]

· II ·

Huston persuaded almost everyone to indulge his reckless lust for poker and backgammon, another form of domination, and gambling was pandemic both during and after work. Gallo described Huston's strategy: "I played a more modern game of backgammon than Huston. He was all about racing around the board, hitting as many of my checkers as possible, taking large risks. Huston thought of backgammon as a variation on poker. That he could bluff. That he could intimidate and bluster." The competition intensified because Gallo and the slightly older Fitzgerald (both of whom could have been Huston's sons) thought of themselves as his protégés. Fitzgerald invited Gallo to their poker game and gave him a friendly introductory lesson. Without telling him that they were actually playing for money, Fitzgerald immediately won Gallo's entire Mexican per diem.

Though Gallo had received a low fee of only $25,000 for his exceptionally difficult, innovative and important screenplay, Fitzgerald continued to exercise his power as executive producer (who controlled the money) to humiliate him. Before shooting began and with the scripts still warm from the printer, Fitzgerald told Gallo—eager to see his work transformed into a film—that he was no longer needed and could go home. Schulz-Keil then intervened and gave him permission to stay. Gallo wrote that "Fitzgerald's compromise was to kick me out of the Cuernavaca Racquet Club (where most of the cast and crew were staying) and put me with two others in a distant rented house. . . . We had no car to take us to the set. We needed to hitch rides or take taxis everywhere. Another bit of gamesmanship. You can stay. But you aren't part of the club." Two weeks before the film opened at the Cannes Film Festival, Gallo was informed that Universal Studios would not pay his plane fare and expenses. He couldn't afford to pay his own way and still regrets missing that important event.

Huston had mellowed, to some extent, in old age. He now regretted the strenuous tennis match that had led to James Agee's heart attack and could no longer imagine shooting a tiger in India. But he was still quite capable of playing practical jokes. Prompted by Huston, Fitzgerald told Gallo that the coproducer Moritz Borman was claiming script credit, which was absurd since he'd had nothing at all to do with it. Huston then falsely told Borman that Gallo was a black belt in judo and urged Gallo to beat him up. This was his idea of amusement. Huston often used a familiar tactic to get people to work harder: "Piss them off."[7]

Despite his declining health, Huston was still at the top of his form as director and achieved a lot by apparently doing very little. Even if he was reading a book or talking to other people, the actors and crew seemed to know what he wanted. It was almost a mystical process. When he didn't like what they did, he'd jump out of his wheelchair and stretch his oxygen tube to the limit. For insurance purposes Karel Reisz, the Czech who'd directed Finney in *Saturday Night and Sunday Morning* (1960), was on the scene as a substitute. But Huston remained in full control and Reisz wasn't needed.

Though dictatorial and strong-willed, like all directors, Huston was open to suggestions about the script. Gallo recalled, "John called me over and said, 'Albert Finney's objections to this scene are good. I was wrong. I hate to admit it—as you know by now.' Strange, because I really don't think, never did, that John ever had any problem changing his opinion about his own ideas. Quite the contrary." Huston would normally say, "It's not well done. Let's do it properly." Yet on other occasions, when he was crossed, he could become quite angry. Watching the rushes of the scene in the chapel, when Firmin's Mexican friend prays for Yvonne's return, Gallo recalled, "I thought I saw the knee and foot of a technician showing at the side of the church door. I asked John. Dismissed. Then went to the car to ask about the next day's scene. . . . John says: 'Get out of my sight. It was idiotic to see such a scene and then ask about shoes. I love you but get out of my sight!!' And with a disgusted grimace he waved me away." Huston didn't want correction, especially from a novice, and the dramatic effect was always more important to him than a technical flaw. The embarrassed Gallo later realized, "What I thought was a foot and knee is only a curved column base. Fool."

Fitzgerald said most sets are a nightmare, but Huston's were sheer pleasure. It was an easygoing operation, visitors were welcome, and there was always time to talk and entertain. But it did not seem that way to Jacqueline Bisset. Echoing what Lillian Ross had said about Huston's menacing eyes when he was making *Red Badge,* Bisset observed that he was a charming though intimidating and dangerous man, with a big smile on his face but not in his eyes. He was strong, intelligent and ruthless, and she had to be wary of him. He was always the master and no one ever argued with him. All the journalists were male and played a lot of poker. The atmosphere was elitist, very macho, with a touch of self-congratulation among the actors and crew. Everyone wanted to be liked and no one wanted to be left out. Though Huston didn't create drama, there was always the potential for drama around him.[8]

· III ·

Huston had wanted Richard Burton for the leading role in *Volcano.* When Burton, tied up in a play, asked if he could wait, Huston, whose life was precarious, replied: "I might die. I've got to do it now. I don't have time to wait." But he got along well with Finney, another rough-hewn British actor. Finney fell under the spell of Huston's intellectual brilliance and irresistible charm and said, with perhaps heartfelt exaggeration, "When you had to say goodbye there was always this feeling of loss, that terrible sadness that you'd be deprived of his company."

Alcoholism had been the theme of excellent films like *A Star Is Born* (1937 and 1954), *The Lost Weekend* (1945) and *The Country Girl* (1954). José Ferrer in *Moulin Rouge*, Errol Flynn in *The Roots of Heaven* and Burton in *The Night of the Iguana* had played alcoholics; and Firmin is drunk throughout all the degradations and disasters of *Volcano*. The theme of betrayal also recurs in Huston's works. Kirk Douglas, in *The List of Adrian Messenger*, kills off the men he's betrayed in a World War II Burmese prison camp. In *The Roots of Heaven* Errol Flynn played a guilty survivor who's betrayed his fellow British officers to the Nazis. Firmin's guilt comes from World War I, when he was court-martialed for allowing his stokers to throw captured German submarine officers into the furnace of his ship, the ironically named SS *Samaritan*. Huston was also strongly attracted to the dramatic potential of Conrad's dominant theme, especially in *Lord Jim* and *Under Western Eyes*: the quest for self-sacrifice, absolution and redemption after a morally reprehensible act and the loss of personal self-esteem.

Alluding to his forced retirement as consul, Firmin quotes Christopher Marlowe's *Dr. Faustus*, "Cut is the branch that might have grown full straight." And knowing he's doomed, he alludes to Faustus' agonized cry, "Why this is hell, nor am I out of it" by exclaiming, "Hell is my natural habitat." He also refers to the disastrous Hitler–Neville Chamberlain "peace in our time" agreement of September 1938, which delayed the inevitable war by ceding the Sudetenland to Nazi Germany.

Schulz-Keil noted that Firmin is haunted by his horrific memories of war, which is about to break out again, as well as by Yvonne's adultery and his own impotence.[9] At the beginning of the picture Firmin goes into a cinema playing *Las Manos de Orlac* (*The Hands of Orlac*, 1925). In this silent German Expressionist film, the hands of an executed killer, transplanted onto a mutilated pianist, give him an overwhelming urge to kill. Identifying with this murderer, Firmin says, "These very hands. The hands of Firmin. Flung seven German officers into her fiery furnace." This passage clearly alludes to Daniel 3:23, when the furious King Nebuchadnezzar, the enemy of God, casts Daniel's three friends, who refuse to worship his golden image, into a hot oven: "And these three men ... fell down bound into the midst of the burning fiery furnace." In Kierkegaard's *Either/Or* (1843) Phalaris, tyrant of Sicily, roasts his victims alive inside a hollow brazen bull and puts reeds into the bull's nostrils to transmute their horrific cries into ravishing music. This cruel torture also suggests André Malraux's *Man's Fate* (1933), in which the self-sacrificing hero Katov, after giving his cyanide pill to two terror-stricken strangers, is thrown into the boiler of a locomotive and burned alive. Like Kierkegaard and Malraux, Lowry transforms agony into art. It was difficult for the screenwriters to establish sympathy with the bitter and self-pitying Firmin. As one critic noted, he "is an impotent alcoholic who courts destruction, annihilates his marriage, rejects both friendship and his wife's love, and finally manages to get himself killed." But Gallo and Huston portray a man redeemed by his eloquence and wit, his opposition to the forces of evil and his unflinching encounter with his own tragic fate.

Jacqueline Bisset had a demanding, even dangerous role. Yvonne has had a disastrous marriage and returns because she has nowhere else to go. She pleads with Firmin, "I've come crawling back. Let me be your wife," and her character "is always passed through the filter of Firmin's drunkenness." In the film there is a vaporous quality about her, as if she were Firmin's hallucination. Bisset said she "tried to portray Yvonne's solid presence, yet remain somewhat ethereal." Though Yvonne knows Firmin's alcoholism is incurable and that he'll never change, she accepts who he is and what he does. When he dies because he cannot love, she must also die with him.

Gallo remarked that Bisset also had to deal with another difficulty: "Huston's relationship with Albert Finney was paramount. Before shooting a scene they would go off into a mumbling huddle, with thoughtful silences punctuated by nods. Jacqueline Bisset, on the other hand, was directed from afar. 'That's fine, dear,' he would say. And pretty much leave it at that. And I don't think Anthony Andrews got much attention."[10] Bisset confirmed that she had no sense of being directed by Huston, who didn't speak to her for days on end. He closely followed Lowry's story and the camera was always in the right place, but she would have liked to have more guidance. When she was unsure of her performance, he'd merely say, "I'll tell you if it's wrong." When she asked if she could have a close-up, he felt she'd overstepped the mark and ironically asked, "Do you want to direct the picture, too?" She felt she'd been swimming against the tide, but "when John gave you his attention," she recalled, "you felt bestowed." She also felt fortunate in working with the masterful Mexican cinematographer Gabriel Figueroa, who had also shot *Iguana*. He filmed her expertly, neither glossy nor ugly, neither underlit nor overlit. She cried with gratitude when she saw the rushes, and felt Huston and Figueroa had done well with her.

At the climax of the film Firmin, trying to recover Yvonne's letters from the Mexican villain who's stolen them, threatens him with a machete and is shot and killed. A white horse, tied up outside the Farolito, then bolts. Emerging from the shadows, it kicks and kills Yvonne, who's come to rescue Firmin, and gallops away on the wet moonlit cobblestones. Bisset said this scene, when she's kicked by the horse, was the hardest in her entire career. It was very cold and raining heavily, which made the ground slippery and the mud squelching. Though shaking with nerves and fear, she was determined to get it right and land on the exact spot with the horse's hooves perilously close to her head. She refused the offer to quit for the night and wanted to finish the whole scene in one go. Afterward they put her in a hot tub to warm her up, and Huston told Borman, "You can take that girl on a tiger hunt." She was very proud of that comment and felt the praise from Huston had made it all worthwhile. (John Hurt felt exactly the same way, after his dangerous riding scene in *Sinful Davey*, when Huston complimented him by saying, "Hats off to you, Johnny!")

Anthony Andrews, who played Firmin's half-brother and Yvonne's former lover, had a rougher time than anyone. A friend of Finney, Andrews was brought in by him and remained close to him during the shoot. He'd recently achieved fame in the role of the effete and decadent Sebastian Flyte (complete with his childhood teddy bear) in the television adaptation of Evelyn Waugh's *Brideshead Revisited* (1981). But he was completely miscast in *Volcano*. Hugh had to be played by a tough actor, like the young Finney or Richard Harris. (Daniel Day-Lewis or Liam Neeson would be good in this part today.) Andrews also had to show the tender side of Hugh's character, in contrast to Firmin's crudeness, and reveal the sexual spark that suggested his former affair with Yvonne. Handsome, but too delicate and insufficiently masculine, Andrews seems to be wearing makeup and has unnaturally high cuffs on his too-clean jeans. He is weak and unconvincing as a dashing Spanish War journalist, amateur bullfighter, guitarist and singer of Loyalist ballads. Realizing that Franco is going to win the war, he bitterly says that the Fascists have the best army and the Loyalists the best songs. In a café he borrows a guitar and gives a lifeless version of the moving war ballad "Madrid, Your Tears of Sorrow." Huston was not interested in Andrews or in his character. He didn't care how Andrews looked, didn't direct him at all and moved him into the background of the picture. Andrews, neglected and ignored, naturally wanted more attention and more close-ups, which would have made his character stronger and more convincing. He expressed his feelings and whined about his predicament, then got very angry and retreated to sulk in his villa.

Schulz-Keil, making a rather fine distinction, thought the fault was in the script rather than in the casting or character. He felt Hugh was meant to be a spoiled brat and empty shell. He's slightly phony and his guitar singing is a fake. He's been to the Spanish war, then hangs around Cuernavaca to impress his friends. But Andrews does not convey this impression, and there's a very thin line between fake acting and acting a fake character. The problem, as Gallo explained, was not in the script but in the deletions: "The idea—central in the novel—that Hugh and Yvonne are a hairbreadth away from repeating their betrayal, was excised. . . . The fact that they are constantly torn between their loyalty to the consul and their attraction to one another was completely eliminated save for a few glances."

Gallo regretted that Huston deleted the "stone toilet" scene that took place after the bullfight. Yvonne and Hugh, in rented bathing suits that don't quite fit, go swimming in a spring pool. Firmin, moving from tequila to the more potent mescal, retreats into the toilet and hallucinates. Yvonne and Hugh, talking about him and constantly touching each other, are still mutually attracted and capable of betrayal. Always focusing on Firmin, Huston (ignoring his original letter to Gallo) didn't want to portray this sexual tension, which Gallo felt intensified the emotional love triangle and was essential to the story. The erotic connection between Yvonne and Hugh, agonizing to Firmin, would have made him even more hostile and self-destructive. But in the end, it was more Huston's film than Gallo's.[11]

The shooting was problem free except for Andrews' unseemly and dangerous behavior in the bullring. He'd secretly been taking bullfighting lessons and had an exaggerated sense of his own abilities. A box had been specially constructed with a camera set up next to it. Andrews was told to take one step out of the box and one step back into it. Instead he ran out and was knocked down by the bull, which bashed in the box and knocked it over. Both Huston and Tom Shaw were furious with Andrews and shouted, "Get the fuck out of there." He narrowly avoided being hurt or even killed, and the film company would have been legally responsible for the accident. Andrews' attempt to shine made the scene more difficult for everyone else.

By the time a professional matador took over to finish this sequence, their only bull, used eight times, had become both worn out and wise. The father of the young matador, the only real bullfighter on the film, had been knocked down by the bull, and his son felt obliged to fight and kill it. Tom Shaw tried to stop the fight for insurance reasons, but Huston said, "Let it happen." A documentary filmmaker was on the scene but failed to capture the exciting event. Huston shot the scene himself, the matador awarded him the honor of the bull's ear and he bought the young man his first suit of lights.[12]

· IV ·

The twenty-one-year-old Danny Huston, well liked by everyone and still a student in a London film school, was on his summer holiday in Cuernavaca. John, who'd written a marionette play in the 1920s, was not satisfied with the static papier-mâché skeletons and told Danny, "Try your hand with the title sequence." Using a newly invented snorkel camera that could travel through the floating paper skeletons, Danny shot the background scenes in the opening credits and then edited the film so the wires didn't show. Gabriel Figueroa lit it with different colored lights, and Huston was "delighted with Danny's first professional work," which immediately established the morbid mood of the film.

John also used popular folk art in the cemetery on the Day of the Dead, and Figueroa shot the picture in the chiaroscuro style of Goya's lights and shadows. One critic noted that "Figueroa's use of overexposed day scenes adds dry textures, palpable heat, and a feeling of suffocation." In the climactic scene, when Firmin is killed in the whorehouse, the satiric caricatures and fantastic figures—the syphilitic prostitutes, repulsive transvestites and malignant dwarf, the Mexican Nazis, corrupt police and brutal murderers—depict with Goyesque cruelty and horror the modern world propelled toward another apocalyptic war. Always striving for verismo, Huston used real whores in the brothel scene, and one of them even tried to set up shop in the set.

The elemental themes of *Volcano* are love and war. A recurrent motif, as a Mexican friend tells Firmin, is *No se puede vivir sin amar:* You can't live without loving and are not fully alive unless you love. The film suggests that you have to love actively, which is exactly what Firmin, a burnt-out case, cannot do. According to Gallo, "No matter how vicious Firmin is to Yvonne and Hugh, they cannot walk away. It is their penance to stand for his abuse." In the end, all the characters must fail: "Firmin must pursue his demons even into the whore's arms. Hugh must continue to pose as the hero and brother, and still lust after Yvonne. And Yvonne must still want to be forgiven, but remain ambivalent enough to bring on the destruction of this day." Firmin believes that "the world has learned nothing from the Great War and he takes it personally. And on this Day of the Dead in 1938, Yvonne, like Europe, is poised to make the same mistake again."[13]

· V ·

The thirty-nine-year-old Janet Roach, who wrote the screenplay of Huston's next film, *Prizzi's Honor* (1985), got the job in the most circuitous and unusual manner. During her career as a television journalist, she did a program about writers who enjoyed tax-free status in Ireland

and met the novelist Richard Condon, then living there. They became pen pals and he sent her proofs of *Prizzi's Honor* (1982). Roach had an Irish background, and after her work on Bill Moyers' documentary about Huston, he invited her to visit Las Caletas and model for him. She brought him *Prizzi's Honor* and he was interested in the project. Condon wrote the first draft of the screenplay, but had to have heart surgery and couldn't do any more work on it. Huston gave her Condon's draft to read overnight, and asked for her thoughts and ideas about rewriting. He then said, "How would you like to do this?" After finishing her script, she worked with him on it for another four or five weeks. Roach wrote, "There was no pressure on me. I was simply earning my keep as a houseguest by writing for Huston in the mornings, swimming with him in the afternoons and sitting for him in the evenings." It's not clear what went on at night.

Roach added that Huston wanted Jack Nicholson for the leading role of Charley Partanna, called him and began ingratiatingly with "Jack, darling." He spoke most persuasively about all the effort that had gone into the project and all the people who would be out of work if he didn't do it. Used to the perks of big-budget films, Nicholson wanted to have and eventually got his own cook, who made fabulous platters of veal marsala for the whole cast and crew. Roach described Nicholson as a true professional. He was on time and knew his lines, was generous to the other actors and always there when you needed him.[14]

When Marietta Tree visited the set, Huston asked for a longer oxygen tube as a kind of leash, then sat down with her for some reminiscence and flirtation. His increasingly severe emphysema made it difficult for him to work—or even breathe. But he treated Nicholson (born in 1937), another symbolic son and de facto son-in-law (since he was then living with Anjelica), with kid gloves. In a witty and perceptive letter, he explained the character Nicholson would play: "I know, Jack, that you want handles by which to get hold of the character. Making the audience understand at the earliest possible moment that you are playing an entirely different role than the high-flying, liberated one it's used to is extremely important. I'm sure, however, that during rehearsal we will discover a number of ways to bring this about. I'm still of the opinion that Charley [Partanna's] having a wig is a good idea. One of its virtues, by the way, is that it doesn't require dialogue."

Prizzi's Honor was a crucial moment for both Anjelica and John. It was her first film with him since the disastrous *A Walk with Love and Death*. And it was his way of compensating for its personal, artistic and commercial failure, and trying to make things right between them. Praising the personal relations of Anjelica and Nicholson, who would separate in 1989, John remarked, "There is a rare devotion between them. You see it in life and you feel it in their scenes together. Twelve years! That's longer than any of my five marriages lasted!" Anjelica plays the Brooklyn-born Maerose, granddaughter of Don Corrado, *capo di tutti capi,* and winds up with Nicholson after he's killed Kathleen Turner (Irene) in a cowboylike shootout at the end. (He throws a knife into her neck, a stunt that seems improbable and looks fake.) Anjelica remembered "doing this one scene when I say, 'You should have seen him, Papa, he was this big!' and my father saying, 'Make him a little smaller' and the entire crew just cracking up." She won an Oscar for this role.

There are more dons in the family than at Oxford, and *Prizzi's Honor,* a comic parody of Italian gangsters' corrupt lives and violent deaths, is heavily indebted to Francis Ford Coppola's *The Godfather* (1972). It has the same loud clothes; dark rooms with heavy draperies, ornately carved furnishings and stuffed velvet chairs; family feasts and careful preparation of spaghetti; a murder plot during a wedding ceremony; a slick lawyer with business suit and briefcase; secret councils, kissing hands and tributes to Don Corrado; and an attack (this time by fire) during a gathering of the dons. William Hickey, who had an Irish background and played the preacher in *Wise Blood,* is brilliant as the skeletal, horror-movie figure of the godfather Don Corrado, who speaks with a drawling, mannered and not quite Italian accent. When a gangster enters his crepuscular parlor with momentous news, he anxiously but eagerly asks, "Somebody died? Who?" Don Corrado solves his clients' personal problems but cannot solve those of his own troubled family; he sends one son to Las Vegas and has another killed by his own relatives. When Nicholson and Turner (the non-Italian outsider) both have a contract to kill the other, it seems as if *The Godfather*'s Diane Keaton has become a murderer.

Both films have elaborate music and operatic love-death scenes. The choir sings Schubert's *Ave Maria* during the opening wedding mass, when pious Catholics as well as mobsters and cops fill the pews, and Nicholson warns a boy "watch out for dem cannolis." Huston includes overtures from Rossini's *La Cenerentola* and *Il Barbiere di Seviglia*, "*Una furtiva lagrima*" from Donizetti's *L'Elisir d'Amore*, the triumphant march from Verdi's *Aida* and "*Questo o quella*" from his *Rigoletto*, and "*Mio babbino caro*" from Puccini's *Gianni Schicchi*.

There's some very sharp dialogue in the picture, some of it taken from the novel. The dim-witted hit man Charley Partanna, wondering if he should kill Irene as the mob ordered him to do, asks, "Do I ice her or marry her?" He then tells her, "If you was anyone else I'd blow you away." Just before he kills Irene's husband, Marxie Heller, Marxie complains "I think you broke my wrist" and Charley consoles him with "You won't need it." And he casually observes, after dispatching his latest victim, "If Marxie's so fuckin' smart, how come he's so fuckin' dead?" Charley's creepy courtship of Irene, the widow of the man he's killed, parodies high tragedy and recalls the oozing evil of Shakespeare's Richard III, who courts Lady Anne just after he's murdered her husband.

Prizzi's Honor contains Huston's first and only naked sex scene (a vivid contrast to Finney's impotent attempt to sleep with Bisset in *Volcano*), with a momentary glimpse of Turner's bare breast—a shot he refused to give to Marilyn Monroe in *The Misfits*. But he also undercuts their passion with an antiromantic gesture that is rarely seen in movies. As Turner puts on her underwear, Charley casually turns away and washes his sexual parts.

The Mafia creed, in the novel and in the film, is "As we protect you, so you must protect Prizzi's honor." When Nicholson said the film was essentially a story of greed, Huston defined the larger theme: "It's greed all right, but marching under the banner of honor: whatever is good for the family, materially speaking, is morally justifiable according to the Prizzis. This is a trait that might well describe society at large at the present moment."[15]

TWENTY-SEVEN

RAISING *THE DEAD*,

1986–1987

· I ·

Huston's last film, *The Dead* (1987), following *Under the Volcano* and *Prizzi's Honor*, completed his trilogy of dark subjects and provided a triumphant conclusion to his impressive career. Despite its ominous title, which suggested a horror movie, *The Dead* was his kindest, gentlest and most elegiac film. Just as Wieland Schulz-Keil—knowing how much Huston liked coming attractions—had made plans for *Under the Volcano* while the director was shooting *Annie*, so they also discussed the *The Dead* while he was making *Volcano*. They sensed the subtle connection between the setting of Lowry's novel on the Mexican Day of the Dead and Joyce's Irish celebration in *The Dead*—both have a festive atmosphere despite the characters' mournful mood. Like the melancholy feast on a single day in Cuernavaca, the Twelfth Night dinner on January 6, 1904, in Dublin memorializes the dead and keeps them at bay. The screen rights to James Joyce's story cost $60,000, and the budget for the seven-week shooting schedule, at a time when most movies cost between $15 million to $20 million, was a modest $3.5 million.

Joyce had been important to Huston since he was twenty years old. Just after his first marriage, to Dorothy Harvey, he wrote, "Mother went to Europe and, upon her return, smuggled in a copy of Joyce's *Ulysses*, which was banned in the United States. Dorothy read it aloud while I painted. It was probably the greatest experience that any book has ever given me." Joyce's masterpiece of 1922 was connected to Huston's first love, to his creative surge as a painter and to the sound of the lively Irish idiom spoken aloud by his new wife. The title of Huston's *The Mackintosh Man* alluded to an elusive and mysterious figure in *Ulysses*. The man in the mackintosh raincoat appears at Paddy Dignam's funeral and keeps turning up throughout the novel. At the end of the book the "selfinvolved enigma" continues to tease the reader as well as the hero, Leopold Bloom, who asks, "Who was M'Intosh?"[1]

In Joyce's story "The Dead" (1914) Gabriel Conroy's jealousy is aroused and his life embittered when he discovers that his wife, Gretta, feels more passionately about the dead youth, Michael Furey, than about himself. The rather pretentious and vulnerable Gabriel is angered and humiliated to find that Gretta's impalpable lover still has the power to affect their lives. Gretta's final confession in the Gresham Hotel forces Gabriel to reevaluate their marriage. He realizes that he had never aroused her love as intensely as the dying lad who'd called to her in the rain. In the cold bedroom Gabriel seems more dead than his dead rival.

Just as Walter Huston had consistently helped John in his early career, so John, at the end of his life and to compensate for previous neglect, also helped his children advance in Hollywood. In the past, he'd adopted a tough and challenging attitude toward his older son. Tony had begged for attention and had a wretched time when John was making *The Man Who Would Be King* in Morocco. He agreed to let Tony compose the music for the film, but then pitted him against the experienced professional composer Maurice Jarre. Tony often tried to get his father to listen to his music, and finally managed to play it for him when John was trapped in the bathtub. John was furious and angrily rejected Tony's work.

Tony had been raised to be lord of the manor, but lost everything when John had to sell St. Clerans in 1975. Ricki had moved to London, where she enjoyed a smart social life and conceived her daughter Allegra with an English viscount. In a temporary stroke of good fortune, Tony married Lady Margot Cholmondeley, daughter of an English marquess and hereditary lord chamberlain, in 1978. They lived on her great estate in Norfolk, which gave him plenty of time for falcons, horses and country sports, and for playing the grand seigneur. The marriage ended, by her wish, in 1986, and she brought up their three children without him. Tony had recently lost his second grand estate when John rescued him and gave him a chance to work on his current film.

John's artistic credo was "Stick to the text, always stick to the text." He did a faithful adaptation of *The Maltese Falcon* at the beginning of his career and of "The Dead"—both films perfect in different ways— at the end. In Joyce's story the maid Lily, greeting the guests at the door, tells Gabriel, "The men that is now is only all palaver and what they can get out of you."[2] In the film she speaks the almost identical sentence, retains the colloquial "that is now" and drops the word "all" to make the spoken rhythm smoother. (Gretta's chaste and devoted Michael Furey is of course the great exception to her statement.)

In 1986 Huston told his editor Charles Elliott, "My son Tony has written a beautiful script," but the composition of *The Dead* was not quite so simple. Tony wrote the first draft, but John—as he did with all his screenwriters—gave him a great deal of help. Anjelica recalled that "John would show Tony how to organize the important elements of a scene, then send him home to write it. They would meet, discuss the results and move on to the next scene." Worried that there was not enough action in the picture, Tony invented some unnecessary scenes. John and Tony did make a few additions to the story—most notably, the character Mr. Grace reading from Lady Gregory's ballad—but John mainly refined and reduced the script to its dramatic essence.[3]

Zoe Sallis believed that Tony always thought he was right and didn't really want to learn; that he argued with John and was not grate- ful for his help; and that John did much more work than Tony on the script. But with his whole life's work behind him, he wanted to advance Tony's career and gave him sole credit. When the producer Carter De Haven sceptically asked John, "Tony must have come a long way. Weren't you the coauthor?," John smiled and replied, "I'm not quite sure," and De Haven concluded that he'd given Tony a great deal of help. Angela Allen, John's long-serving script girl, categorically stated, "Tony did the first draft of *The Dead*, but John rewrote it to make it great." The masterful screenplay, with its mature wisdom and distillation of a lifetime's experience, bore John's unmistakable imprint. Tony's career as a screenwriter soon fizzled out, and he has had no screen credits in the twenty-three years since *The Dead*.[4]

· II ·

Suffering ever more acutely from emphysema, Huston was a dead man walking, or wheeling, attached to a tall green rocket of oxygen that shot air into his failing lungs and enabled him to breathe. Faced with waning powers and imminent extinction, he was granted a brief reprieve, a period of grace, which gave him just enough time to make his last great work of art. The film had to be shot near Los Angeles because the doctor forbade him to fly to Ireland. "His lungs are like lace," he said, "and he'll drop dead when he steps out of the plane."

With the director Karel Reisz still standing by for emergencies, the interiors were shot in a warehouse in Valencia (part of Santa Clarita), about thirty-five miles north of Los Angeles. The few exteriors—outside the house, the carriage ride along the quay (with the horse's breath steaming in the cold air) and the snowy landscape at the end—were shot later on in Dublin. The second unit had to cover the roofs of the Dublin buildings with fake snow and brought potato flakes from Los Angeles to create the wintry effect. But Irish environmental law wouldn't allow them to be used, and the Irish potato flakes were orange, not white. So white flakes had to be brought in from Belfast (where you'd expect them to be orange). The last shots of snow "general all over Ireland" were of the real thing. The editor had no problem matching the shots made under different conditions in Los Angeles and Dublin, and Huston loved the final unified effect.

As the film progressed, Huston became more and more ill and needed extra care, and the crew treated him like a piece of Waterford crystal. He had bags under his watery eyes, hollow cheeks and drawn features. He abandoned his once-stylish clothes and, bundled up in a warm vest and jacket, wore an old man's zipped-up track suit. The ailing Huston said he could now concentrate fully on the picture since "there were no longer any distractions." Always the gentleman, he never lost his temper or shouted at anyone; he knew exactly what he wanted and achieved it without wasting any time. Making the film was an intensely emotional experience for the Irish actors. They were portraying Joyce's greatest story, celebrating Huston's love of Ireland and fearful about his impending death. Though the theme of the movie was death, the atmosphere was relaxed rather than morbid. The set had, as Yeats wrote in "Lapis Lazuli," "gaiety transfiguring all that dread."[5]

Instead of looking directly at the actors, Huston used a large television monitor—then fairly new and now standard—that allowed him to watch and play back the action, complete with sound. He could look at the earlier takes and see how they appeared on the screen, rather than capturing them on film and waiting for the rushes. Except for Anjelica (playing Gretta Conroy), Huston usually referred to the actors by the names of their characters. Faithful to his lifelong aesthetic principles, he believed that when you've cast the film, you've made the film, and that "you never have difficulties with actors if you select the right ones and nourish them." The actors had to find and discover their own characters by themselves, and "each scene must appear within the emotional framework of the whole picture."

Despite his frailty, he was always well prepared and had impressive self-confidence. Though apparently remote and aloof, he was intently focused, but not, like a theater director, intrusive; he trusted the actors to go their own way, and gave tactful and sensitive direction. He mainly observed, corrected anything that went wrong, and made suggestions about movement and gestures. He always tried to bring out something original and would ask for a little more or a little less. Anjelica recalled him saying to Donal Donnelly, "Now, Donal, remember, Freddy Malins is an alcoholic, he's not on cocaine." Huston worked with Anjelica as an actress, not as a daughter. When she first came down the stairs after hearing the tenor's song that triggers memories of her old love, she didn't perform properly. John called her aside and talked quietly to her. Then, totally relaxed, she did it perfectly.[6]

As the entertainment before dinner begins, the hostesses' young niece plays a virtuoso piece on the piano. Mr. Grace then recites a folk ballad, "The Grief of a Girl's Heart," a lament by a girl who's been disappointed in love, translated from the Irish by Augusta Lady Gregory in 1901. The girl cries: "You have taken the east from me, you have taken the west from me, you have taken what is before me and what is behind me; you have taken the moon, you have taken the sun from me."[7] The ballad shows, early on, that Gretta has been touched by something strange and has dropped into reverie.

Music plays an important role in both story and film. In Huston's *Key Largo,* Edward G. Robinson had forced the alcoholic Claire Trevor, who'd lost her youth, her looks and her voice, to sing one of her old songs in return for a drink. In *The Dead,* Cathleen Delany (Aunt Julia Morkan) also sings with a ruined voice, but the scene that was degrading in *Key Largo* becomes poignant in *The Dead.* Awed by Huston, like all the actors from the Irish theater, Delany explained her attitude to his direction. It would not have occurred to her, she said, to question him: "I would only say yes to his yes, and no to his no." Her sentimental song, "Arrayed for the Bridal," is George Linley's English version of an aria by Elvira in Act I of Vincenzo Bellini's *I Puritani* (1835). In the film, it is ironically and gallantly sung by a maiden aunt who's never been so arrayed:

> Arrayed for the bridal, in beauty behold her,
> A white wreath entwineth a forehead more fair;
> I envy the zephyrs that softly enfold her,
> And play with the locks of her beautiful hair.

The Joyce scholar Clive Hart asserts that in the story "this frail old woman sings beautifully, sings surprisingly well, sings with the voice of a young girl." In the film, he adds, "the producers chose to have Julia sing ill, turning a fine artistic moment into a piece of banal pathos." But Aunt Julia, though she's lost the quality of her youthful voice, still shows great understanding of the music, phrasing and interpretation. Her song, as Huston observed, is "funny, dear and ever so sad."[8]

One of Huston's brilliant but rarely noticed cinematic innovations takes place during Aunt Julia's bridal song. The camera—most unusually—moves away, takes a walk all on its own, goes upstairs to an empty room, focuses on the cherished doll house, embroidery, old photographs, glass slippers, rosary and crucifix, and then returns to the singer. Roberto Silvi (who edited four of Huston's last six films) at first opposed this unmotivated movement and said the camera had to focus on someone in the film. But he discussed this idea with Huston, who said "Let's try it." The camera was like a ghost going through this world, as if another person (not quite Michael Furey), someone present whom the others didn't see, was around and aware of them. This intensely lyrical moment creates subtle tension and gives visual clues to the dominant theme: the enduring influence of the dead on the living.

Huston described his focus on objects as "lacework rather than broadloom" and said the camera movement was "what I do best, yet no critic has ever remarked on it. That's exactly as it should be. If they noticed it, it wouldn't have been any good." Nor has anyone noticed that Huston adopted this technique from James Agee's best work. As Huston wrote in *An Open Book*, "In *Let Us Now Praise Famous Men* [1940] his description of objects in a room is detailed to the point of being an homage to truth. For one fraction of eternity those objects existed in a given arrangement within a circumscribed area; that was truth. Truth was worth telling."[9]

Huston's camera was economical as well as innovative. Directors normally shoot twenty times the amount of film they actually use. Schulz-Keil said that when Huston estimated in the budget the amount of film stock they would need, the studio said nobody could make a picture with so little film. But with limited shots, the editor had only one way to cut Huston's picture. Roberto Silvi refined this statement by noticing that Huston's "editing in camera" was not literally true. He didn't do close, medium and long shots of the same scene, but discussed the scenes before shooting and often used several different angles if he wasn't quite sure what he wanted. The complex dinner scene was shot from every conceivable angle to give a fluid effect. Silvi then had the freedom to cut the film as he wished. Schulz-Keil added that continuity was a nightmare. All the bits of film had to fit together during the elaborate dinner scene. One aunt walks in one direction, the other aunt in the other, some people reach for food, others ladle sauce. But everything eventually found its place, and in the end the choreography was perfect.[10]

When the dinner is over and the guests are leaving, the tenor Bartell D'Arcy is persuaded to sing a traditional air, "The Lass of Aughrim." Like "The Grief of a Girl's Heart" and "Arrayed for the Bridal," the subject of the song is a woman's tragic loss when jilted by her lover. The actual Battle of Aughrim, a major turning point in Irish history, took place on July 20, 1691, near the village of that name in County Galway. On that fateful day King William III's army defeated the Irish-Catholic Jacobites, who suffered ten times more casualties than the English. The defeat devastated the old Gaelic order, ended James II's attempt to regain the English throne and led to the final English victory in Ireland. The poignant and abandoned girl in the ballad, like the defeated Catholic soldiers, is also a victim:

> I am a king's daughter who strayed from Cappaquin
> In search of Lord Gregory, pray God I find him
> The rain beats at my yellow locks, the dew wets my skin
> My babe is cold in my arms, Lord Gregory, let me in.
>
> Lord Gregory is not home my dear, henceforth he can't be seen
> He's gone to bonnie Scotland to bring home a new queen
> So leave you these windows and likewise this hall
> For it's deep in the ocean you must hide your downfall.

The song itself is less important than the effect it has on Gretta. She's deeply moved by the memory of Michael Furey, her first love in Galway (where her family had their roots), who used to sing her that song. In the film, as Huston focuses the camera on Gretta and she lingers at the top of the staircase, we scarcely see the singer and mainly hear his voice. Gretta has blended dreamily into the ensemble during dinner, but at the end, moved by the song, she stands alone. The rain beating on the forlorn lover in the ballad anticipates Gretta's description of Michael Furey when she returns to the hotel room with Gabriel.

Art as well as music enhances the theme of *The Dead*. When Huston was planning this film a friend sent him a copy of *Wisconsin Death*

Trip (1973), a cult book that contains studio photographs taken between
1890 and 1910 (the film also takes place at the turn of the century).
These memorial photographs were meant to be set into tombstones,
and their humble and obscure subjects had the melancholy satisfaction
of knowing they would be immortalized after death. The book includes
portraits of Indians and blacks, and some shocking, grotesque subjects:
maniacs, dwarfs and children in coffins. Many of these photos portray
degeneracy and decline, suicide and murder, morbidity and death, and
suggest the effect of time on human mortality.

At the dinner party that takes place throughout most of *The Dead,*
the camera focuses on and recalls the framed photos, on the dresser
and mantelpiece, of beloved dead members of the family. The guests
at this festive yet strangely tense party are aware—in a similar way—
of their own impending deaths. In the hotel room at the end of the
film, Gabriel imagines the death of his aged Aunt Julia. Huston com-
poses the imaginary death chamber scene exactly like Edvard Munch's
turn-of-the-century *Chamber of Death* (1896). In Munch's painting the
anguished mourners gather, in the spartan room and around the deathbed, in attitudes of supplication, grief and horror.

· III ·

Huston himself, upholding the tradition of Irish hospitality, gave
many grand dinners at St. Clerans. The feast in his film—with absolutely convincing dress, manners, speech, wit and music—recalls the
traditional atmosphere evoked in Yeats' "A Prayer for My Daughter":

> And may her bridegroom bring her to a house
> Where all's accustomed, ceremonious. . . .
> How but in custom and in ceremony
> Are innocence and beauty born?

Yet a disturbing current of social, religious and political hostility,
fueled by alcohol, runs through the festivities. Lily condemns her las-
civious suitors. The drunken Freddy Malins keeps pouring out glasses

of wine for himself, talks too much, behaves foolishly and clashes with his severely censorious mother. Molly Ivors accuses Gabriel of being a West Briton, an Irishman subservient to the culture of the United Kingdom, "instead of depending on ourselves alone" (a reference to the literal meaning of Sinn Fein). She leaves early to hear a speech by James Connolly, an Irish political leader destined to be executed by the British after the Easter Rising of 1916. Aunt Julia is furious that the pope has barred women like the devoted Aunt Kate from participating in church choirs. The only Protestant—the handsome and silver-haired Mr. Browne, who becomes increasingly drunk and disheveled as the evening progresses—questions the Catholic doctrines of monkish flagellation and time off from Purgatory. All this sets up the climactic confrontation between Gretta and Gabriel.

Gabriel is named after the archangel, but Gretta makes the Annunciation about her love for Michael Furey on January 6, the twelfth night after Christmas, the feast of the Epiphany. When Gabriel asks why she's so sad, Gretta replies that she's been thinking of "a young boy I used to know who used to sing that song." He realizes that she was and still is in love with the lad, who had a romantic name but an unromantic job in the gasworks. Gabriel asks, "What did he die of so young?," and she says, "I think he died for me." As she lets down her long dark hair and pours out her deepest, long-suppressed emotions, Gabriel reaches out to her. But she's in a self-enclosed reverie, he cannot bring himself to touch her and she cries herself to sleep like a small child. She's never told him about her first love—"I was great with him at the time"—until her memories are aroused by the tragic fate of the lass of Aughrim. The film ends as Gabriel, shattered by Gretta's revelation, looks away from her and out of the window. He says, "Snow is falling . . . falling in that lonely churchyard where Michael Furey lies buried . . . falling faintly through the universe and faintly falling, like the descent of their last end, upon the living and the dead." As in Joyce's story, the title is echoed in the last two words. Huston said the film was "about a man being revealed to himself, what we think we are and what we really are. This self-discovery is a soul-shaking experience."

The ballads in Joyce's story are women's tragic laments for lost love, yet Gretta's crucial memory focuses on poor Michael Furey, who died before he could marry her and consummate their love. In setting his tale on Twelfth Night, Joyce surely had in mind Shakespeare's comedy, which like his story mingles sadness and satire with love and festivity. Feste's song in *Twelfth Night* is a lament for the wounds of love and suggests the effect Gretta has had on both Michael Furey and Gabriel Conroy:

> Come away, come away, death,
> And in sad cypress let me be laid.
> Fly away, fly away, breath,
> I am slain by a fair cruel maid.[11]

The Dead, Huston's heroic affirmation when he himself was close to death, was released only three months after he died. Everyone involved in the picture was deeply affected when they remembered him. *The Dead* had an enthusiastic reception both in Ireland and abroad, and had a cultural as well as an artistic impact. It reminded people of their family and history, and called many exiles back to their country.

· I ·

At the end of his life, after discarding so many wives and lovers,
Huston wanted to leave his children more than material goods.
Like a magnanimous King Lear (complete with two antagonistic children), Huston divided his movie kingdom into three parts: writing for
Tony, acting for Anjelica, directing for Danny. He had given Tony his
start with his work on *The Dead*. Anjelica, who'd made her career first
with her father's help and then with Jack Nicholson's, had appeared
in John's last two films. To help his youngest child, John made his
final appearance as an actor in Danny's *Mister Corbett's Ghost* (1987), a
one-hour program made for BBC television, and played a "cameo role
as a soul collector, 'an emissary of evil whose job it is to send people
to the devil.' "

Though seriously ill, in 1987 he went to Newport, Rhode Island,
as coauthor, executive producer and actor in Danny's *Mr. North* (1988).
The picture, with Anjelica and Lauren Bacall, was based on Thornton
Wilder's novel *Theophilus North* (1973) and portrayed Newport society
in the 1920s. Huston thought the town would still be like the glitter-
ing days that Scott Fitzgerald had portrayed in *The Great Gatsby*, and
brought along his tuxedo for formal dinners that never took place. He
persuaded Robert Mitchum, his closest actor-friend since Bogart's death,
to substitute for him if he were unable to perform. When Mitchum
was summoned to Newport to replace him, Huston, though dying,
called it the "biggest hoax he ever pulled off." Comparing him to a

vampire, constantly returning from the dead, Mitchum remarked, "He didn't look so bad. I'm telling you, they'll have to drive a stake through his heart."[1]

Since he grew up at a distance from his father, Danny had not suffered as his older siblings did from Huston's sharp-tongued indifference, but when he became an adult, he discovered some drawbacks to being John Huston's son. As a director, he was afraid of letting down his father and the Huston name. Hostile critics naturally said that John had passed the baton to Danny, who took it and fell. Yet, conscious of living under John's shadow, he also felt as if a giant had protected him from the harsh rays of the sun. Danny treasured John's stories and memories, and loved having a godlike Noah-pirate-maverick to inspire his own life. He admired the grand man who maintained his good humor through difficult times, and swept through life with courage, grace and regal elegance.

John moved from the set at Newport to the Charlton Memorial Hospital in Fall River, Massachusetts. He had fought emphysema for twenty years, and the unusually tall and strong man had wasted away to only 140 pounds. Anjelica confessed that when visiting him in the hospital, she was still "nervous and always scared of his disapproval." She also recalled that he retained his wit till the very end. When Mitchum visited him just before his death, "Bob said, 'John, I hear you haven't been eating' and my dad ignored that, so Bob said to the young and pretty nurse, 'Would you roll up your skirt a little?' She happily complied, and then at Bob's request she rolled it even a little higher, and my dad was lying there literally dying—he died two days later—and, finally, he said, 'You're right, Bob. I haven't been eating enough!' "[2] Huston maintained his interest in everything until his final days. When Danny wheeled him around on a gurney, he wanted to stop to look at the art on the hospital walls.

After three weeks in the hospital, Huston was moved to a rented house overlooking Newport harbor, and died there at the age of eighty-one on August 28, 1987. His last, fighting words were "Knock 'em dead, Danny." At the memorial service, Jack Nicholson recalled some of the things Huston disliked: "Any dish that contained chicken, mawkish popular songs, people who strain too hard for social correctness—and women who get drunk." Mourning his friend, Nicholson declared that he'd cry for the rest of his life. Huston had always been close to his father, who sustained him all his adult life, and was emotionally estranged from his mother. But he chose to be buried next to her and, in a kind of Rheabilitation, was finally reconciled with her after death. They are interred in the Hollywood Forever Cemetery, opposite Paramount studios on Santa Monica Boulevard. Their small gravestone, flat on the ground, reads: "John Huston, 1906–1987 ═════ Beloved Mother, Rhea Huston, 1882–1938."[3]

A complicated will divided Huston's estate, worth less than $2 million, between Zoe, Maricela, his four children and his grandchildren. Zoe and Maricela got the largest percentages, and Maricela had also acquired houses in Los Angeles and Puerto Vallarta. Tony received the interest on his share until his three children were twenty-one, when they inherited his money. When John desperately needed help after the break with Cici, Anjelica had refused to come to Mexico, and (according to several sources) "she never did anything for anyone." But Huston thought her career would decline when she reached middle age, and she received her share when she became fifty-seven in 2008. Danny also got his share later in life, when he was in his late forties.

Huston's monetary estate, for someone who had earned so much money, was relatively small. The rest of his belongings, more valuable to posterity, were also squandered. His books, private papers and personal correspondence, his Oscars and honorary degree, some of his own paintings and all his pre-Columbian statues were in the house at Las Caletas, where he lived with Maricela. They were either burned, destroyed, discarded, lost, buried, stolen, stored or hidden, and the many explanations for their mysterious disappearance are unconvincing. Jan Lavender, his friend in Puerto Vallarta, blamed the tragic loss on gross neglect, and on the termites and tropical storms of the Mexican coast. She said Huston's house was deserted when he died in Rhode Island, and his extensive library moldered away in the primitive huts and encroaching jungle. In her view, his papers would have disintegrated and been trashed in a matter of weeks. At the end, there wasn't much left.

Cici believed that "John's papers were lost at sea, floated away. Maricela dumped all the art, which she didn't understand, and sent a bunch of the pre-Columbian things in a 'truck' to Anjelica in Venice, California—which were broken to bits! I heard this direct from Anjelica. Whatever else Maricela scavenged could still be with her. All John's papers, etc." Tony wrote that John's surviving drawings and paintings are now owned by Maricela, Anjelica and himself. "The art books were split between Danny and Allegra; the unimportant rest left over split between Anjelica, Danny and myself." Dad's personal papers were "burnt by Maricela, supposedly under his instruction. Maricela claimed his Oscars were stolen by the garbage men during Dad's lifetime. Then she told another story about burying one in Puerto Vallarta." But Tony, using an expletive, didn't believe her.

Maricela told Lawrence Grobel, the Hustons' biographer, that "she didn't care if the family didn't believe her when she said John's Oscars and awards were accidentally placed in a garbage bag and thrown away, or were put in a box and given to one of the film academies, which lost them."[4] But she did not say *who* put his precious possessions in the garbage or who gave them to which film academy. At various times she has offered many different explanations. After his death Huston's children did not search for or try to recover, with the help of lawyers or the police, the possessions that rightly belonged to them. The self-sacrificial Maricela didn't seem to want anything for herself when Huston was alive, but in her own quiet way she outmaneuvered the family and got more than anyone else after his death.

The fate of other precious documents is equally obscure. Grobel told the scholar Allen Cohen that Huston gave him the correspondence and files since 1980 (the material from the previous years is in the Herrick Library) and that "Grobel turned over what he had to Huston's children, Tony and Anjelica." Tony categorically denied this by asserting, "None of Dad's personal papers came to me, apart from a small folder of material that his mother had written which Larry [Grobel] left for me at the Kohner office."[5] Like the gold dust blown back into the desert in *Sierra Madre*, most of John's possessions have disappeared.

· II ·

Huston shot forty pictures in forty-six years, between 1941 and 1986, and probably made more great films than any other American director. He had a restless and itinerant childhood, and in adult life was constantly on the move, living in hotel rooms or rented houses, and working in chaotic conditions. He often shifted to several different locations for the same film and was accompanied by an entourage of experienced crew and devoted women. He was always pursued by a mass of telegrams from colleagues trying to find out where he was, catch up with him and get him to reply. Huston liked to use the same faithful core of actors, and was especially fond of shooting in Mexico, Africa and Ireland. Three of his worst movies—*The Bible, Casino Royale* and *Annie*—earned him the most money. Despite some notable late failures, he was always resilient and in demand. He tended to ignore critics and sensibly told Danny, "I can't believe the bad, shouldn't believe the good."

A biographer's comment about Orson Welles applies with equal force to Huston—except that Huston was much more professional than Welles, finished all his films and had a far greater number of triumphs: "A lot of great directors do repeat themselves. You knew pretty much what a John Ford film was going to be like, and a Hitchcock film or a Howard Hawks film. There was more consistency in their careers. But not with Welles [or Huston]. He was always trying something totally different every time." Hitchcock made no films during the last five years of his life. At the end of their careers Huston's contemporaries—Ford, Hawks and Billy Wilder—were thought to be over the hill and had considerable difficulty finding work in Hollywood. Huston continued to work full out and created three of his best films—*Under the Volcano, Prizzi's Honor* and *The Dead*—while in extremely poor health at the very end of his life.

Huston, constantly considering new projects, began his next film right after (and sometimes even before) completing the previous one. His never-completed projects fall into two main categories: biopics of titanic historical figures like Judas, Montezuma, Francisco de Goya,

Simón Bolívar and General George Patton; and adaptations of serious literary works by some of his favorite writers: Aristophanes' comedy *Lysistrata* (with Marilyn Monroe), Shakespeare's *Richard III*, Gogol's *Taras Bulba*, Melville's *Typee* and *Benito Cereno*, Crane's *The Blue Hotel*, Joyce's *A Portrait of the Artist as a Young Man*, Jean Giraudoux's *The Madwoman of Chaillot*, Hemingway's "Fifty Grand," "The Undefeated," *A Farewell to Arms* and *Across the River and into the Trees*, Brian Moore's *The Lonely Passion of Judith Hearne* and Brendan Behan's *The Hostage*. Various impediments prevented him from making these films: lack of financing, difficulty in obtaining the rights, poor scripts, inability to secure the best actors. He sometimes had more tempting offers. But all these projects were promising and, under his direction, could have been made into brilliant films.

Huston's best work was enhanced by his painter's eye and inspired by allusions to a wide range of fine arts that gave his films new dimensions of visual richness and complexity: Greek statues, folk art, steel engravings, American photographs, artists' colorful palettes, works by Renaissance masters, da Vinci's drawings, Goya's chiaroscuro, Lautrec's posters and specific paintings by Brouillet, Munch, Hopper and Wyeth. His love of the fine arts shaped his vision of the world and strongly influenced his best films. As Charles Baudelaire wrote in his essay on Eugène Delacroix, "One of the characteristic symptoms of the spiritual condition of our age is that the arts aspire if not to take another's place, at least reciprocally to lend one another new powers." Like the director Josef von Sternberg, Huston could say that actors were "tubes of color which must be used to cover my canvas," and he transformed films, quite literally, into moving pictures.[6] It's entirely fitting that at the end of his life Anjelica got special permission to push the wheelchair-bound invalid through the Metropolitan Museum of Art after closing hours for a final gaze at his beloved masterpieces.

The characteristic theme of Huston's major films is an almost impossible quest, tempered by detachment and irony. In pictures from *The Maltese Falcon* to *The Man Who Would Be King* men sacrifice honor in pursuit of wealth (like Conrad's *Nostromo*), but fail in that quest, are mocked by cruel fate and remain defiant in the face of defeat. His great Conradian subject, from *The Roots of Heaven* to *Under the Volcano*, is a man's fall from grace and heroic attempt to recover his self-esteem. Huston himself said, "I have a tendency to choose stories whose point is the irony of man's pursuit of an impossibly elusive goal." He often portrayed the shifting tensions and allegiances within an isolated group, stranded in a forbidding and desolate landscape.

Christopher Plummer perceived Huston's idealistic beliefs beneath his ironic attitude and wrote that he often displayed "an admiration and a passion for the rugged individual, the loner, the cynical, the disillusioned, who conceals beneath his bitterness a core of heroism that is pure, noble and utterly incorruptible." Huston's most memorable characters and scenes, his most revealing epiphanies and homages to truth, are Kasper Gutman and Joel Cairo discovering the fake black bird in *The Maltese Falcon,* Howard dancing for joy when he finds the gold in *Sierra Madre,* the thieves stealing the jewels in *The Asphalt Jungle,* Charlie and Rose riding the rapids in *The African Queen,* Gay Langland and Perce Howland rounding up the wild mustangs in *The Misfits* and Gretta's confession to Gabriel in *The Dead.*

Most unusually for a foreign artist, Huston left his mark on both Ireland and Mexico. He and his illustrious guests at St. Clerans were often in the newspapers, he was master of the Galway Blazers, he made six films in Ireland and helped start the Irish movie industry. He was also a celebrity in Mexico, shot four films in that country and helped transform Puerto Vallarta from a small, sleepy town into a prosperous tourist resort. After his death, St. Clerans became a luxury hotel, Las Caletas a nature preserve and tropical destination for day trippers.

Remembering the high points of his amazing life in Ceylon, India and the Himalayas, in Nevada and in bed, the great lover wrote: "I've been paddled through the jungles in a pirogue with a Devil Dancer [exorcist] in the bows; seen the Red Fortress of Agra in the moonlight; crossed the boundaries of Bhutan when it was the most secret country in the world; ridden in a camel race . . . and been in and out of love with a number of beautiful and elegant ladies."[7] But Huston would have agreed with Welles, who declared, "I'm awfully tired of old men saying they have no regrets. We're loaded with, burdened with, *staggering* under regrets." In the last paragraph of his autobiography, Huston brooded over his guilty regrets about family, finances, alcohol, tobacco and matrimony. He said that if he had to live his life over again, "I would spend more time with my children. I would make my money before spending it. I would learn the joys of wine instead of hard liquor. I would not smoke cigarettes when I had pneumonia. I would not marry for the fifth time."

Huston could be noble, generous and kind as well as selfish, callous and cruel. But he should be remembered for his intellect, his imagination and his charm, as he was remembered by Pelé and by the historian Arthur Schlesinger, Jr. In 1984 Schlesinger recorded, "He is infinitely beguiling, highly intelligent, elaborately courteous. He had a short gray beard and surrenders periodically to coughing bouts of emphysema. I liked him very much. . . . An enchanting man."[8] As Hamlet said of his dead father, "He was a man, take him for all in all. / [We] shall not look upon his like again."

Huston's most outstanding quality was personal courage: braving the waterfall as a childhood invalid in Arizona, filming under fire in the Aleutians and in Italy, opposing the Communist witch hunt in Washington, shooting *The African Queen* and *The Roots of Heaven* under dangerous conditions in Africa, hunting elephants in Africa and tigers in India, riding recklessly in fox hunts in Ireland, winning a camel race in Nevada, marrying for the fifth time, making *Under the Volcano, Prizzi's Honor* and *The Dead* while confined to a wheelchair, gasping for breath and supported by a tank of oxygen. Yeats composed the appropriate epitaph for the man who loved horses and often portrayed them in his films:

> Cast a cold eye
> On life, on death.
> Horseman, pass by![9]

HUSTON'S FILMS

I. Masterpieces

The Maltese Falcon (1941), *The Treasure of the Sierra Madre* (1948), *The Asphalt Jungle* (1950), *The African Queen* (1951), *The Misfits* (1961), *Fat City* (1972), *Under the Volcano* (1984), *The Dead* (1987)

II. Winners

Across the Pacific (1942), three war documentaries: *Report from the Aleutians* (1943), *The Battle of San Pietro* (1945) and *Let There Be Light* (1946), *Key Largo* (1948), *Beat the Devil* (1953), *Moby Dick* (1956), *The Roots of Heaven* (1958), *Freud: The Secret Passion* (1962), *The Night of the Iguana* (1964), *Reflections in a Golden Eye* (1967), *The Man Who Would Be King* (1975), *Prizzi's Honor* (1985)

III. Worth Seeing

In This Our Life (1942), *We Were Strangers* (1949), *The Red Badge of Courage* (1951), *Moulin Rouge* (1952), *Heaven Knows, Mr. Allison* (1957), *The Barbarian and the Geisha* (1958), *The Unforgiven* (1960), *The List of Adrian Messenger* (1963), *The Kremlin Letter* (1970), *The Life and Times of Judge Roy Bean* (1972), *The Mackintosh Man* (1973), *Wise Blood* (1979), *Victory* (1981)

IV. Duds

The Bible (1966), *Casino Royale* (1967), *Sinful Davey* (1969), *A Walk with Love and Death* (1969), *Phobia* (1980), *Annie* (1982)

PROLOGUE: HUSTON AND HEMINGWAY

1. Andrew Sarris, *Confessions of a Cultist: On the Cinema, 1955–1959* (NY: Simon & Schuster, 1970), p. 174; Norman Mailer, *Marilyn* (NY: Warner, 1975), p. 258; John Huston, *Interviews,* ed. Robert Emmet Long (Jackson: University Press of Mississippi, 2001), p. 122.

2. Letter from Lorrie Sherwood to Russ Lloyd, December 21, 1954, Huston Collection, Herrick Library, Academy of Motion Picture Arts and Sciences, Beverly Hills, Calif.; Cable from Huston to Clark Gable, August 25, 1955, Herrick; William Nolan, *John Huston: King Rebel* (Los Angeles: Sherbourne, 1965), p. 146; Peter Viertel, *White Hunter, Black Heart* (1953; London: W. H. Allen, 1954), p. 153.

3. Peter Viertel, *Dangerous Friends: At Large with Huston and Hemingway in the Fifties* (NY: Doubleday, 1992), p. 35; John Huston, *An Open Book* (1980; NY: Da Capo, 1994), p. 167; Ernest Hemingway, *Green Hills of Africa* (NY: Scribner's, 1935), p. 148.

4. Huston's memo, Herrick; Letter from Huston to Hemingway, November 21, 1954, Hemingway Collection, John F. Kennedy Presidential Library, Boston; Fred Majdalany, *Time and Tide,* November 17, 1956, p. 1397; Letter from Huston to Hemingway, December 31, 1956, Hemingway Collection. These are the only two surviving letters from Huston to Hemingway; Hemingway's letters to Huston, like most of his private correspondence, have disappeared.

5. George Stevens, Jr., ed., *Conversations with Great Moviemakers of Hollywood's Golden Age at the American Film Institute* (NY: Knopf, 2006), pp. 352, 353; Huston, *Interviews,* p. 167.

6. John Huston, "Figures of Fighting Men," *American Mercury*, 23 (May 1931), 114; James Agee, "Undirectable Director," *Agee on Film* (NY: Grosset & Dunlap, 1956), p. 330; Charles Hamblett, *Crazy Kill: A Fantasy*, preface by John Huston (London: Sidgwick & Jackson, 1956), p. 115 and Huston, *Open Book*, p. 167.

7. Interview with Guy Gallo, New York, July 9, 2009; Lawrence Grobel, *The Hustons* (NY: Scribner's, 1989), p. 320.

8. Ernest Hemingway, introduction to *Men at War* (NY: Crown, 1942), p. xvii; Ernest Hemingway, *Short Stories* (1938; NY: Scribner's, 1954), p. 283; Letter from Huston to Paul Kohner, July 5, 1954, Herrick; Hemingway, *Short Stories*, pp. 266, 265.

9. Letter from Huston to Hemingway, November 21, 1954, Hemingway Collection; Letter from Huston to Paul Kohner, July 5, 1954, Herrick; Cable from Harold Mirisch to Huston, May 25, 1954, Herrick.

   In a letter to me of May 5, 2009, Barnaby Conrad explained why the *Matador* film was never made: "Bullfighting was suddenly politically incorrect, said the money men. . . . Huston was also upset that he wouldn't be allowed to show the kill. . . . He kept the rights for some seven years, hoping to make it. Ray Stark then optioned it—and wanted to change it to a boxing film starring Sidney Poitier! Luckily, that fell through after a couple of years. It has been optioned some *ten* times since."

10. Gerald Pratley, *The Cinema of John Huston* (Cranbury, NJ: Barnes, 1977), p. 199; *Memo from David O. Selznick*, ed. Rudy Behlmer (NY: Grove, 1972), pp. 424, 429; Huston, *Open Book*, p. 270.

11. Ronald Haver, *David O. Selznick's Hollywood* (NY: Knopf, 1980), pp. 398, 400; *Memo from Selznick*, pp. 428, 432, 433; Huston, *Open Book*, p. 272.

12. Huston, *Interviews*, p. 58; Jim Walters, "John Huston on Kipling, Hemingway and Jack Daniels," *New York Times*, February 15, 1976, 2:12; Huston, *Interviews*, p. 58.

13. John Huston and Gladys Hill, screenplay of *Across the River and Into the Trees*, 1975, Herrick; Huston, *Interviews*, p. 134.

ONE: BRAVING THE WATERFALL

1. John Weld, *September Song: An Intimate Biography of Walter Huston* (Lanham, Md.: Scarecrow Press, 1998), pp. xiii, 56; Quoted in Grobel, *Hustons,* p. 140; Huston, *Interviews,* p. 164.

2. *Agee on Film,* p. 400; Letter from Patrick Brophy, Curator, Vernon County Historical Society, to Jeffrey Meyers, September 18, 2009; Mark Twain, *The Gilded Age* (1873), *The Oxford Mark Twain* (NY: Oxford University Press, 1996), pp. 29–30 (T. S. Eliot and Marianne Moore were also born in Missouri); Ken Postlethwaite, *Nevada Daily Mail,* n.d., n.p.

3. Huston, *Open Book,* p. 12; Quoted in Axel Madsen, *John Huston: A Biography* (Garden City, NY: Doubleday, 1978), p. 15; Weld, *September Song,* p. 62; Quoted in Grobel, *Hustons,* p. 92.

4. Quoted in Grobel, *Hustons,* pp. 107–108; Quoted in Nolan, *John Huston,* p. 147; Huston, *Open Book,* p. 15 (two quotes).

5. Quoted in Grobel, *Hustons,* pp. 45, 199, 140, 92.

6. Wyndham Lewis, *Tarr* (London: Penguin, 1982), p. 30; Letter from Ray Bradbury to Huston, July 12, 1964, Herrick; Evelyn Keyes, *Scarlett O'Hara's Younger Sister* (Secaucus, NJ: Lyle Stuart, 1977), p. 124.

7. Quoted in Pratley, *Cinema of Huston,* p. 19; John Huston, "Fool," *American Mercury,* 16 (March 1929), 349–350; Quoted in Pratley, *Cinema of Huston,* p. 17.

8. This *Self-Portrait* (1923) is reproduced in Grobel, *Hustons,* after p. 204. The caricature faintly appears in a photo of Gershwin's modernistic living room in Edward Jablonski and Lawrence Stewart, *The Gershwin Years: George and Ira* (1973; NY: Da Capo, 1996), p. 196.

TWO: RESTLESS YOUTH

1. Bernard Drew, Interview with John Huston, Gannett Publications, 1972, pp. 3–4, Herrick; Letter from Walter Wanger, quoting Walter Huston, to John Huston, August 20, 1956, Herrick; Huston, in *Creativity with Bill Moyers,* PBS documentary, 1981; Huston, in *John*

Huston and the Dubliners on the Set of "The Dead," Liffey Films documentary, 1987.

2. Huston, *Open Book,* p. 36. It's worth noting that, in addition to Sam Jaffe, Huston had many Jewish friends: George Gershwin, William Wyler, his agent Paul Kohner, his collaborator Howard Koch, Peter Lorre, David Selznick, his wartime colleague Jules Buck, the director Anatole Litvak, Billy Wilder, Paulette Goddard, Edward G. Robinson, Lauren Bacall, John Garfield, the screenwriter Peter Viertel, Sam Spiegel, Wolfgang and Gottfried Reinhardt, the producer Ray Stark, his lawyer Mark Cohen and his girlfriend Anna van der Heide.

3. Huston, *Open Book,* p. 44; Knud Merrild, *A Poet and Two Painters* (London: Routledge, 1938), p. 292; D. H. Lawrence, *The Plumed Serpent* (1926; London: Penguin, 1971), p. 46.

4. Quoted in Grobel, *Hustons,* p. 115; Huston, *Interviews,* p. 165; Quoted in Lillian Ross, *Picture* (1952; NY: Limelight, 1984), p. 125.

5. Huston, *Open Book,* p. 46; Quoted in Pratley, *Cinema of Huston,* p. 24; Huston, "Fool," p. 351.

6. Huston, "Figures of Fighting Men," pp. 114, 115; Joachim Maass, *Kleist: A Biography,* trans. Ralph Manheim (London: Secker & Warburg, 1983), p. 227; John Huston, *Frankie and Johnny* (NY: Boni, 1930), pp. 111, 19, 23, 37, 58, 78.

7. Edward Jablonski, *Gershwin Remembered* (London: Faber & Faber, 1992), pp. 38–39; Weld, *September Song,* p. 120; Jan Herman, *A Talent for Trouble: The Life of Hollywood's Most Acclaimed Director, William Wyler* (NY: Putnam, 1985), pp. 103–104, 461.

8. *Creativity with Bill Moyers*; Steven Hodel, *Black Dahlia Avenger: A Genius for Murder* (NY: Arcade, 2003), pp. 74, 38, 103, 107.

   In January 1947 Elizabeth Short was murdered and severely mutilated in a sensational, unsolved case. Dr. Hodel's son, a Los Angeles detective, discovered that his late father—Dorothy's second husband—was the murderer and published his findings in 2003.

9. John Houseman, *Run-Through* (NY: Simon & Schuster, 1972), p. 67; George Orwell, *Down and Out in Paris and London, Complete Works,* ed. Peter Davison (1933; London: Secker & Warburg, 1986),

1:206–207; Letter from Huston to B. Traven, December 30, 1946, Herrick; Huston, *Open Book*, p. 69.

10. Robert Hughes, *Things I Didn't Know* (2006; NY: Vintage, 2007), p. 378; Quoted in Ross, *Picture*, p. 48.

THREE: MANY TALENTS

1. Ross, *Picture*, p. 3; Quoted in Stuart Kaminsky, *John Huston: Maker of Magic* (Boston: Houghton Mifflin, 1978), p. 99; Robert Morley, *Robert Morley: A Reluctant Autobiography* (NY: Simon & Schuster, 1967), p. 239.

2. Billy Pearson, with Stephen Longstreet, *Never Look Back: The Autobiography of a Jockey*, introduction by John Huston (NY: Simon & Schuster, 1958), p. 290; Memo from Gladys Hill, October 15, 1964, Herrick; James Goode, *The Making of "The Misfits"* (1963; NY: Limelight, 1986), p. 48.

3. Interview with Eloise "Cherokee" Hardt, Laguna Hills, Calif., August 19, 2009; Huston, Army file, September 21, 1942, p. 24; Interview with Evelyn Keyes, Los Angeles, September 11, 1995.

4. *Agee on Film*, p. 324; Quoted in David Shipman, *Movie Talk* (NY: St. Martin's, 1988), p. 108; Quoted in Ross, *Picture*, pp. 80, 88.

5. Quoted in Lauren Bacall, *By Myself* (NY: Knopf, 1978), p. 173 and in Grobel, *Hustons*, p. xvi; Interview with Danny Huston, Los Angeles, December 15, 2009; Quoted in Martha Harris, *Anjelica Huston: The Lady and the Legacy* (NY: St. Martin's, 1989), p. 111.

6. Quoted in Madsen, *John Huston*, pp. 140–141; Quoted in Grobel, *Hustons*, p. 471; *Agee on Film*, pp. 321, 331; Andrew Sarris, in *Reflections in a Male Eye: John Huston and the American Experience*, ed. Gaylyn Studlar and David Desser (Washington, D.C.: Smithsonian Institution Press, 1993), p. 275.

7. Hamblett, *Crazy Kill*, p. 132; Quoted in Ross, *Picture*, p. 97; Interview with Celeste Huston, Santa Ynez, Calif., July 18, 2009; Interview with Eloise Hardt; Interview with Zoe Sallis, London, April 12, 2009.

8. Quoted in Grobel, *Hustons*, pp. 390, 458; Quoted in Harry Minetree, "In Marrakech, Old Master John Huston Makes His Dream Movie," *People*, April 21, 1975, 65.

9. Interview with Eloise Hardt; Guy Gallo, "Notes from *Under the Volcano,*" 1982–83, p. 28, unpublished memoir, courtesy of Guy Gallo.

10. Huston, *Open Book,* p. 71; Joseph Persico, "An Interview with John Huston, the Dean of American Movie Men," *American Heritage,* 33 (April–May 1982), 10; Howard Koch, *As Time Goes By: Memories of a Writer,* introduction by John Houseman (NY: Harcourt Brace Jovanovich, 1979), pp. 12, 70.

11. Quoted in Grobel, *Hustons,* pp. 199–200.

Four: Return to Hollywood

1. Huston, *Open Book,* p. 72; Koch, *As Time Goes By,* p. 43; Huston, *Interviews,* p. 81.

2. Huston, *Open Book,* p. 70; Houseman, *Run-Through,* p. 390; Houseman, introduction to Koch, *As Time Goes By,* p. xiv.

3. Koch, *As Time Goes By,* p. 66; Jeffrey Meyers, Introduction to Billy Wilder, *Sunset Boulevard* (Berkeley: University of California Press, 1999), pp. viii–ix; Koch, *As Time Goes By,* pp. 67, 69.

4. Thomas Schatz, " 'The Triumph of Bitchery': Warner Bros., Bette Davis and *Jezebel,*" *The Studio System,* ed. Janet Staiger (New Brunswick, NJ: Rutgers University Press, 1995), pp. 85–86; Huston, *Open Book,* pp. 72–73; John Huston, Aeneas MacKenzie and Wolfgang Reinhardt, *Juárez,* ed. Paul Vanderwood (Madison: University of Wisconsin Press, 1983), p. 140; *Graham Greene on Film: Collected Film Criticism, 1935–1940,* ed. John Russell Taylor (NY: Simon & Schuster, 1972), p. 348.

5. Jeffrey Meyers, *Gary Cooper: American Hero* (NY: Morrow, 1998), pp. 152, 151; Rudy Behlmer, *Inside Warner Bros. (1935–1951)* (NY: Simon & Schuster, 1987), p. 126; Memo from John Wexley to Hal Wallis, March 21, 1940, Warner Bros. Archive, University of Southern California; Behlmer, *Inside Warner Bros.,* p. 126; W. R. Burnett, in *Backstory: Interviews with Screenwriters of Hollywood's Golden Age,* ed. Pat McGilligan (Berkeley: University of California Press, 1986), pp. 64, 81.

6. Quoted in Thomas Schatz, *The Genius of the System: Hollywood Filmmaking in the Studio Era* (NY: Pantheon, 1988), p. 305; John Huston

and W. R. Burnett, *High Sierra,* ed. Douglas Gomery (Madison: University of Wisconsin Press, 1979), p. 181; Orwell, *Complete Works,* 12:543–544.

7. Huston, *Open Book,* p. 77; *Agee on Film,* p. 327.

8. Houseman, *Run-Through,* p. 443; Watts, quoted in Burns Mantle, ed., *The Best Plays of 1941–1942* (NY: Dodd, Mead, 1942), p. 35; Koch, *As Time Goes By,* pp. 72–73.

FIVE: BLACK BIRD

1. Robert Warshow, "The Gangster as Tragic Hero," *The Immediate Experience* (1962; Cambridge, Mass.: Harvard University Press, 2001), p. 101; Quoted in Joe Hyams' Hollywood newspaper column on Huston, c. July 9, 1959, in John Huston, FBI file; Dashiell Hammett, introduction to *The Maltese Falcon* (1930; NY: Modern Library, 1934), p. ix; Dashiell Hammett, *The Maltese Falcon* (NY: Vintage, 1957), pp. 110, 124, 128, 183.

2. Rudy Behlmer, *Behind the Scenes* (1989; Hollywood: French, 1990), p. 136; Weld, *September Song,* p. 182; John Huston, *The Maltese Falcon,* ed. Richard Anobile (NY: Avon, 1974), p. 210.

3. Foster Hirsch, *Otto Preminger: The Man Who Would Be King* (NY: Knopf, 2007), p. 237; "Ernest Hemingway, Screenwriter: New Letters on *For Whom the Bell Tolls,*" *Antioch Review,* 53 (Summer 1995), 279; Jim Harrison, *Off to the Side* (NY: Grove, 2002), p. 261.

4. "John Huston," *Interviews with Film Directors,* ed. Andrew Sarris (1967; NY: Avon, 1969), p. 255; Madsen, *John Huston,* p. 51.

5. Howard Koch, "A Playwright Looks at the 'Filmwright,'" *Sight and Sound,* 19 (July 1950), 214; Stephen Youngkin, *The Lost One: A Life of Peter Lorre* (Lexington: University Press of Kentucky, 2005), p. 182.

6. Telegram from Bogart to Huston, October 10, 1953, Herrick; Madsen, *John Huston,* p. 141; Jonah Ruddy and Jonathan Hill, *Bogey: The Man, the Actor, the Legend* (NY: Tower, 1965), p. 156; Howard Thompson, "Humphrey Bogart Speaks Up on *The African Queen* and Future Screen Productions," *New York Times,* March 2, 1952, 2:5.

7. Eric Sherman, ed., *Directing the Film: Film Directors on Their Art*

(Boston: Little, Brown, 1976), p. 75; Behlmer, *Inside Warner Bros.*, pp. 151–152; Interview with Angela Allen, London, July 23, 1996.

8. Huston, *Maltese Falcon,* pp. 108, 79, 118, 92.

9. Viertel, *Dangerous Friends,* p. 21; Huston, *Open Book,* p. 79; Mary Astor, *A Life on Film* (1971; NY: Dell, 1972), p. 163.

10. Astor, *Life on Film,* p. 160; Hammett, *Maltese Falcon,* p. 108; Hal Wallis and Charles Higham, *Starmaker: Autobiography* (NY: Macmillan, 1980), pp. 109–110; Huston, *Maltese Falcon,* p. 132; Meta Carpenter and Orin Borsten, *A Loving Gentleman* (1976; NY: Harcourt Brace Jovanovich, 1977), pp. 262–263.

11. Huston, *Open Book,* p. 79; Jay Leyda, ed., *Voices of Film Experience: 1894 to the Present* (NY: Macmillan, 1977), p. 278; Huston, *Maltese Falcon,* pp. 227, 233, 242, 247; Hammett, *Maltese Falcon,* p. 225; Raymond Chandler, "Casual Notes on the Mystery Novel," *Raymond Chandler Speaking,* ed. Dorothy Gardiner and Kathrine Walker (Berkeley: University of California Press, 1997), p. 70.

12. Huston, *Maltese Falcon,* p. 253; Grobel, *Hustons,* p. 222.

   Most critics who quote this line have missed the allusion to Shakespeare. See, for example, James Naremore, "John Huston and *The Maltese Falcon,*" *Literature/Film Quarterly,* 1 (1973), 249; Jean-Loup Bourget (writing as Jacques Segond), "On the Trail of Dashiell Hammett (The Three Versions of *The Maltese Falcon*)," *Positif,* 171–172 (1975), 18; Virginia Wexman, "*The Maltese Falcon* from Fiction to Film," *Library Quarterly,* 45 (January 1975), 50; Behlmer, *Behind the Scenes,* p. 147; Ilse Bick, "The Beam That Fell and Other Crises in *The Maltese Falcon,*" in *The Maltese Falcon: John Huston, Director,* ed. William Luhr (New Brunswick, NJ: Rutgers University Press, 1995), p. 181; Naremore and Bourget are reprinted, with this error, in Luhr's edition.

13. William Shakespeare, *The Tempest* (1611), *Complete Works,* ed. G. B. Harrison (NY: Harcourt, Brace, 1952), p. 1495; Huston, *Maltese Falcon,* p. 227; Mary Astor, *My Story: An Autobiography* (Garden City, NY: Doubleday, 1959), p. 212; *Agee on Film,* p. 321.

14. Quoted in Goode, *Making of "The Misfits,"* p. 46; Quoted in Grobel, *Hustons,* pp. 682–683; Tom Stempel, *FrameWork: A History*

of *Screenwriting in the American Film* (NY: Continuum, 1988), pp. 184–185.

SIX: THE HUSTON TOUCH

1. *Agee on Film,* pp. 290, 312; John Corry, "John Huston: Musings on *Fat City* and Other Pursuits," *New York Times,* August 5, 1972, p. 52; Letter from Ray Stark to Huston, January 18, 1964, Herrick.

2. Huston, in *Creativity, with Bill Moyers* (two quotes); Huston, *Interviews,* pp. 70, 109; Chabrol, in Jim Shepard, ed., *Writers at the Movies* (NY: HarperCollins, 2000), p. 8.

3. Gideon Bachman, "How I Make Films: An Interview with John Huston," *Film Quarterly,* 19 (1965), 10; Brando, in Leyda, ed., *Voices of Film Experience,* p. 46; Hamblett, *Crazy Kill,* p. 155; Viertel, *White Hunter, Black Heart,* p. 30.

4. Ross, *Picture,* p. 56; Interview with producer Michael Fitzgerald, Taos, NM, July 27 and 28, 2009.

5. Huston, *Open Book,* p. 363; Bachman, "Interview with John Huston," p. 8; Interview with Roberto Silvi, Los Angeles, July 7, 2009.

6. Baldassare Castiglione, *The Book of the Courtier,* trans. Charles Singleton, ed. Daniel Javitch (NY: Norton, 2002), p. 32; Interview with Angela Allen; Keach, in Shipman, *Movie Talk,* p. 108.

7. Huston, *Interviews,* pp. 69, 86.

8. Quoted in Pratley, *Cinema of Huston,* p. 215; Philip Dunne, *Take Two: A Life in Movies and Politics* (NY: Liveright, 1992), p. 47; Viertel, *Dangerous Friends,* p. 128; Quoted in Grobel, *Hustons,* p. 325.

9. John Huston, Army file, October 27, 1942, p. 5; Quoted in Grobel, *Hustons,* p. 235; John Houseman, *Front and Center: A Memoir, 1942–1955* (NY: Simon & Schuster, 1979), p.119.

10. Quoted in Grobel, *Hustons,* p. 225; Nolan, *King Rebel,* p. 18 and quoted in Grobel, *Hustons,* p. 224.

11. Interview with Eloise Hardt; Quoted in Grobel, *Hustons,* pp. 266 (two quotes), 258, 277.

12. Jack Warner, with Dean Jennings, *My First Hundred Years in Hollywood* (NY: Random House, 1965), p. 255; Huston, *Open Book,* p. 81; Lawrence Quirk, *Fasten Your Seat Belts: The Passionate Life of Bette*

Davis (NY: Morrow, 1990), p. 238; Reviewer, in Thomas Doherty, *Projections of War: Hollywood, American Culture and World War II* (NY: Columbia University Press, 1993), p. 217.

13. Dotson Rader, "Rewards and Regrets" [Interview with Olivia de Havilland], *Parade Magazine,* September 7, 1986, 6; Rory Flynn, "Interview with Nora Flynn," 1984, typescript, p. 9, courtesy of Rory Flynn.

14. Huston, *Open Book,* pp. 96–98; Telegram from Errol Flynn to Huston, c. 1954, Herrick; Huston, *Interviews,* p. 122; Nunnally Johnson, *Letters,* ed. Dorris Johnson and Ellen Leventhal (NY: Knopf, 1981), p. 94.

15. Mary Astor, "Bogie Was for Reel," *New York Times,* April 23, 1967, 2:2; Astor, *Life on Film,* p. 168; Huston, *Open Book,* pp. 87–88.

16. Interview with Vincent Sherman, Malibu, Calif., March 7, 1996; Madsen, *John Huston,* p. 60.

SEVEN: INTO BATTLE

1. Pratley, *Cinema of Huston,* pp. 52–53; Irving Howe, *A Margin of Hope* (NY: Harcourt Brace Jovanovich, 1982), p. 92; Richard Layman, *Shadow Man: The Life of Dashiell Hammett* (NY: Harcourt Brace Jovanovich, 1981), p. 188; Diane Johnson, *Dashiell Hammett: A Life* (NY: Random House, 1983), p. 178.

2. Gore Vidal, *Palimpsest: A Memoir* (NY: Random House, 1995), p. 96; Huston, *Open Book,* p. 93; Quoted in Grobel, *Hustons,* p. 532.

3. Huston, Army file, August 14 to December 11, 1942, pp. 47, 24, 30, 29, 2.

4. Michael Haskew, "San Pietro: Capturing the Face of War," *Military History,* 17 (December 2000), 52; and Robert Wagner, "The Battle for San Pietro," *The Texas Army: A History of the 36th Division in the Italian Campaign* (Austin, 1972), p. 63; Martin Blumenson, *Mark Clark* (NY: Congdon & Weed, 1984), p. 151.

5. Haskew, "San Pietro," p. 82; Lance Bertelsen, "*San Pietro* and the 'Art' of War," *Southwest Review,* 74 (Spring 1989), 230, 232, 235; Huston, *Open Book,* pp. 107, 109, 110, 111; Ernie Pyle, *Ernie's War: The Best of Ernie Pyle's World War II Dispatches,* ed. David Nichols (NY: Random House, 1986), pp. 195–196.

6. Eric Ambler, *Here Lies: An Autobiography* (NY: Farrar, Straus & Giroux, 1986), p. 202; Quoted in Grobel, *Hustons*, p. 250; Ambler, *Here Lies*, p. 211; *Agee on Film*, pp. 163, 321.

7. Haskew, "San Pietro," p. 51; Persico, "Interview with Huston," p. 10; Huston, *Open Book*, p. 119 (two quotes).

8. Huston, *Interviews*, p. 117; John Huston, *Let There Be Light*, in *Film: Book 2. Films of Peace and War*, ed. Robert Hughes (NY: Grove, 1962), pp. 206, 207; Huston, *Open Book*, p. 123.

9. Krin and Glen Gabbard, *Psychiatry and the Cinema* (Chicago: University of Chicago Press, 1987), p. 73; Pratley, *Cinema of Huston*, p. 53.

EIGHT: WOMEN IN LOVE

1. Quoted in Grobel, *Hustons*, p. 271; Viertel, *Dangerous Friends*, p. 207; Interview with Celeste Huston.

2. Quoted in Grobel, *Hustons*, p. 363; Lee Server, *Ava Gardner: "Love Is Nothing"* (NY: St. Martin's, 2006), p. 136; Interview with Eloise Hardt; Quoted in Grobel, *Hustons*, pp. 44, 270.

3. Interview with Frances FitzGerald, New York, May 19, 2009; Porter McKeever, *Adlai Stevenson: His Life and Legacy* (NY: Morrow, 1989), p. 272; Keyes, *Scarlett O'Hara's Younger Sister*, p. 95; Arthur Schlesinger, Jr., *Journals, 1952–2000*, ed. Andrew and Stephen Schlesinger (NY: Penguin, 2007), p. 713.

4. Quoted in Grobel, *Hustons*, pp. 259, 238, 282; Server, *Ava Gardner*, p. 136.

5. Roy Jenkins, *Churchill: A Biography* (NY: Farrar, Straus & Giroux, 2001), p. 639; Quoted in Grobel, *Hustons*, p. 276; Interview with Frances FitzGerald; Caroline Seebohm, *No Regrets: The Life of Marietta Tree* (NY: Simon & Schuster, 1997), pp. 138, 156.

6. Letter from Huston to Marietta Tree, January 1948, Schlesinger Library, Radcliffe Institute, Harvard University; Schlesinger, *Journals*, p. 435; Quoted in Grobel, *Hustons*, pp. 491–492.

7. Letters from Huston to Marietta Tree, January 12, 1966 and January 9, 1977, Radcliffe; Quoted in Grobel, *Hustons*, p. 267; Interview with Eloise Hardt.

8. Huston, *Open Book*, pp. 120–121; Seebohm, *No Regrets*, p. 390;

W. B. Yeats, "The Tower" (1926), *Collected Poems* (NY: Macmillan, 1956), p. 195; Robert Lowell, *Letters,* ed. Saskia Hamilton (NY: Farrar, Straus & Giroux, 2005), p. 289.

9. Keyes, *Younger Sister,* p. 81; Interview with Eloise Hardt; Keyes, *Younger Sister,* pp. 109, 148.

10. Bacall, *By Myself,* p. 172; Keyes, *Younger Sister,* p. 112; Quoted in Grobel, *Hustons,* p. 293; Keyes, *Younger Sister,* p. 114.

11. Quoted in Grobel, *Hustons,* pp. 340, 460, 552–553; Huston, *Open Book,* p. 171; Viertel, *Dangerous Friends,* p. 56.

12. Minetree, "In Marrakech," p. 64; Madsen, *John Huston,* p. 94.

13. Keyes, *Younger Sister,* pp. 96, 102; Gerald Clarke, *Capote: A Biography* (1988; NY: Ballantine, 1989), pp. 95–96; Quoted in Grobel, *Hustons,* pp. 255, 264, 260.

14. Interview with Eloise Hardt; Quoted in Grobel, *Hustons,* pp. 266–267; 606; Interview with Eloise Hardt.

NINE: WITCH HUNTS

1. Stephen Ambrose, *Nixon: The Education of a Politician* (NY: Simon & Schuster, 1987), p. 150; Warner, *First Hundred Years,* p. 290; Houseman, *Front and Center,* pp. 252–253; Keyes, *Younger Sister,* p. 116.

2. Dunne, *Take Two,* p. 196; Persico, "Interview with Huston," p. 12; Huston, *Open Book,* p. 131; Dalton Trumbo, *The Time of the Toad: A Study of Inquisition in America* (NY: Harper & Row, 1972), p. 140.

3. Huston, statement of October 20, 1947, FBI file; Larry Ceplair and Steven Englund, *The Inquisition in Hollywood: Politics in the Film Community, 1930–1960* (Garden City, NY: Doubleday, 1980), pp. 275–276 (two quotes); Alvin Yudkoff, *Gene Kelly: A Life of Dance and Dreams* (NY: Back Stage Books, 1999), p. 172.

4. Robert Carr, "The Hollywood Hearings," *The House Committee on Un-American Activities, 1945–1950* (Ithaca: Cornell University Press, 1952), p. 55; Ceplair and Englund, *Inquisition in Hollywood,* p. 281.

5. Nancy Lynn Schwartz, *The Hollywood Writers' Wars* (NY: Knopf, 1982), p. 254; Behlmer, *Inside Warner Bros.,* p. 288; Ceplair and Englund, *Inquisition in Hollywood,* p. 280; Huston, *Open Book,* pp. 130–131.

6. Dunne, *Take Two,* p. 199; Ian Hamilton, *Writers in Hollywood,*

1915–1951 (NY: Harper & Row, 1990), p. 293; Victor Navasky, *Naming Names* (1980; NY: Penguin, 1981), p. 83; Hamilton, *Writers in Hollywood*, p. 290.

7. Carr, *House Committee*, p. 55; Madsen, *John Huston*, p. 92; Paul Henreid, *Ladies' Man* (NY: St. Martin's, 1984), p. 183; Navasky, *Naming Names*, p. 83.

8. Huston, "General Background Information," p. 8, FBI file; Ceplair and Englund, *Inquisition in Hollywood*, p. 289; Huston, "General Background Information," p. 10, FBI file.

9. Hamilton, *Writers in Hollywood*, p. 293; Navasky, *Naming Names*, p. 153; Huston, enclosure to letter of January 29, 1953, p. 9, FBI file; David Caute, *The Great Fear* (NY: Simon & Schuster, 1978), p. 497.

10. Quoted in Grobel, *Hustons*, p. 361; Ed Sikov, *On Sunset Boulevard: The Life and Times of Billy Wilder* (NY: Hyperion, 1998), p. 332; Huston, "General Background Information," pp. 2–3, FBI file.

11. Huston, *Interviews*, p. 95; Huston, letter of January 23, 1953, pp. 4, 5, 1, 6, FBI file; Nora Johnson, *Flashback: On Nunnally Johnson* (Garden City, NY: Doubleday, 1979), p. 156.

Ten: Gold in Mexico

1. Nat Moss, "The Jockey and the Showman," VanityFair.com, January 15, 2009, pp. 2–3; Quoted in Grobel, *Hustons*, p. 384; Huston, *Open Book*, p. 154.

2. Interview with Jan Lavender, Puerto Vallarta, Mexico, August 23, 2009; Interview with Bill Gardner, Palm Springs, August 1, 2009; Viertel, *White Hunter*, p. 271; *From a Darkened Room: The Inman Diary*, ed. Daniel Aaron (Cambridge, Mass.: Harvard University Press, 1996), p. 85.

3. B. Traven, *The Treasure of the Sierra Madre* (1927; NY: Pocket Books, 1961), pp. 70, 81; John Huston, *The Treasure of the Sierra Madre*, ed. James Naremore (Madison: University of Wisconsin Press, 1979), pp. 63, 62, 86; Letter of June 6, 1949, FBI file; Robert Ginna, "In Search of *The Treasure of the Sierra Madre*," *American Scholar*, 71 (Autumn 2002), 84 (first and third quotes); Letter from B. Traven to Huston, September 2, 1946, Herrick (second quote).

4. Keyes, *Younger Sister*, p. 104; Nolan, *King Rebel*, p. 64; Huston, *Open Book*, p. 142.

5. Schlesinger, *Journals*, p. 580; Letter from Huston to Dwight Whitney, February 25, 1948, Herrick; Keyes, *Younger Sister*, p. 107; William Meyer, "John Huston," *Warner Brothers Directors* (New Rochelle, N.Y.: Arlington House, 1978), p. 179.

6. Letter from "Charlie" to Henry Blanke, May 2, 1947, *Sierra Madre* file, Warner Archive, USC; Interview with the actor Michael Parks, Los Angeles, August 19, 2009; Lauren Bacall, *Now* (NY: Knopf, 1994), p. 187; Bacall, *By Myself*, p. 172.

7. William Hawkins, "Bogart Makes Possible Director's Venture," no citation, [1948], Herrick; Jonathan Coe, *Humphrey Bogart: Take It and Like It* (NY: Grove Weidenfeld, 1991), p. 121; Humphrey Bogart, "Locationing in Mexico" (September 1947), *Hollywood Reporter: The Golden Years,* ed. Tichi Wilkerson and Marcia Borie (NY: Coward-McCann, 1984), p. 206; Huston, publicity release, *Sierra Madre* file, Warner Archive.

8. Huston, *Open Book*, p. 147; Huston, *Sierra Madre*, pp. 54–55; *Discovering Treasure: The Story of "The Treasure of the Sierra Madre,"* DVD documentary, 2003, with reissue of film; *Agee on Film*, p. 329.

9. Quoted in Grobel, *Hustons*, p. 290; Huston, *Sierra Madre*, pp. 170, 193–194; Ross, *Picture*, p. 153; and Huston, *Open Book*, p. 184.

10. Pauline Kael, *5001 Nights at the Movies* (NY: Holt, 1991), p. 788; Warner, in *Discovering Treasure*; Virginia Graham, *Spectator*, February 25, 1949, 253.

11. Peter Ericsson, "*The Treasure of the Sierra Madre* and *Key Largo*," *Sequence*, Spring 1949, 34; *Agee on Film*, pp. 291–293; Weld, *September Song*, p. 194.

ELEVEN: CRIME AND THE CITY

1. Stevens, ed., *Conversations with Moviemakers*, p. 535; Quoted in Grobel, *Hustons*, pp. 305–306; Ernest Hemingway, "Who Murdered the Vets?," *New Masses*, 16 (September 17, 1935), 10.

2. John Brosnan, *Movie Magic: The Story of Special Effects in the Cinema* (1974; New American Library, 1976), p. 108; Letter from Collier

Young to Jerry Wald, *Key Largo* file, Warner Archive; Huston, *Open Book*, p. 151.

3. Jon Tuska, "John Huston," *Close-Up: The Hollywood Director,* ed. Jon Tuska (Metuchen, NJ: Scarecrow, 1978), p. 270; Huston, statement about *Key Largo,* July 29, 1948, Warner Archive; *Time,* 52 (August 2, 1948), 74.

4. *Agee on Film,* p. 328; Huston, Letter of August 2, 1948, Herrick.

5. Huston, *Interviews,* p. 6; Letter from Huston to Lindsay Anderson, January 8, 1950, Herrick; *Hollywood Reporter,* April 22, 1949, in "General Background," p. 14, FBI file.

6. José Iglesias, *Daily Worker,* April 28, 1949, 13; *Daily News,* January 29, 1953; Letter from J. Edgar Hoover, August 2, 1949, FBI file.

7. Letter from Huston to Screen Writers Guild, January 9, 1950, Herrick; Ben Maddow and John Huston, *The Asphalt Jungle* (Carbondale: Southern Illinois University Press, 1980), pp. 3, 142; W. R. Burnett, Afterword to Maddow and Huston, *Asphalt Jungle,* p. 145.

8. Maddow and Huston, *Asphalt Jungle,* pp. 19, 77, 127; Sterling Hayden, *Wanderer: An Autobiography* (1963; NY: Bantam, 1964), p. 343; Letter from Hayden to Huston, December 26, 1949, Herrick; W. R. Burnett, *The Asphalt Jungle* (NY: Knopf, 1949), pp. 56–57.

9. Maddow and Huston, *Asphalt Jungle,* pp. 32, 117, 113, [116: this line is in the film but not in the printed script]; Letter from Budd Schulberg to Huston, August 30, 1950, Herrick.

10. Maddow and Huston, *Asphalt Jungle,* p. 30; Letters from Joseph Breen to Louis Mayer, October 6 and September 26, 1949, Herrick.

11. Pratley, *Cinema of Huston,* pp. 78–79; Huston, *Open Book,* p. 22; Maddow and Huston, *Asphalt Jungle,* p. 66.

12. "*Asphalt Jungle,*" *Newsweek,* June 12, 1950, 90; Letter from José Ferrer to Huston, July 21, 1950, Herrick; Letter from Dudley Nichols to Huston, July 5, 1950, Herrick.

Twelve: Sultanate of St. Clerans

1. Quoted in Grobel, *Hustons,* p. 329; Letter from Huston to Celeste Huston, n.d., courtesy of Celeste Huston; Keyes, *Younger Sister,* p. 150.

2. Moss, "Jockey and Showman," p. 11; Tony Tracy, Interview with

Anjelica Huston, in *John Huston: Essays on a Restless Director,* ed. Tony Tracy and Roddy Flynn (Jefferson, NC: McFarland, 2010), typescript p. 13 (I'm most grateful to Tony Tracy for generously allowing me to quote from this interview before publication); Interview with Bayard Veiller (Tony Veiller's son), Pasadena, Calif., May 17, 2009; Quoted in Grobel, *Hustons,* p. 345; James Joyce, "Ecce Puer," *Collected Poems* (NY: Viking, 1957), p. 63.

3. Huston, *Open Book,* p. 134; Viertel, *Dangerous Friends,* pp. 199–200; Huston, *Open Book,* pp. 227, 229–230; Alexander Walker, *Double Takes* (London: Elm Tree, 1977), p. 32.

4. Richard Buckle, *Jacob Epstein, Sculptor* (Cleveland: World, 1963), p. 200, has a photograph of the head of Flaherty; Douglas Cooper, *Nicolas de Staël* (NY: Norton, 1961), p. 88.

    Daniel Wildenstein, *Claude Monet: Biographie et Catalogue Raisonné* (Lausanne: La Bibliothèque des Arts, 1985), tome IV, pages 252–253, and Douglas Cooper, *Juan Gris: Catalogue Raisonné* (Paris: Berggruen, 1977), tome II, page 348, reproduce the paintings. The Monet, sold to a London dealer in 1970, is now in the Legion of Honor Museum in San Francisco.

5. Letter from Gladys Hill to the producer and art collector Ray Stark, April 26, 1967, Herrick.

    The portrait of Pablo appears in the background of a photo of John, Pablo and Evelyn Keyes in Grobel, *Hustons*; the portrait of Anjelica is in Lawrence Grobel, "John Huston: Mercurial Director of *The Maltese Falcon* and *The Dead* at St. Clerans," *Architectural Digest,* 49 (April 1992), 204; *The Spirit of St. Clerans* is in Karl French, *Art by Film Directors* (London: Mitchell Beazley, 2004), p. 101.

6. Huston, *Interviews,* p. 64; Seamus Kelly, "John Huston's Home in the West," *Irish Times,* January 12, 1960, 6; Letter from Huston to Marietta Tree, September [1959–60], Radcliffe.

7. Interview with Carter De Haven III, Beverly Hills, August 7, 2009; Ernie Anderson, "Huston in Ireland: John Huston's Galway Years," *An Gael* [Irish Arts Center, NY], 3 (Winter 1987), 20–21; Interview with Thom Steinbeck, Montecito, Calif., May 1, 2009; Alexander Cockburn, introduction to *Beat the Devil* (1953; London: Chatto &

Windus, 1985), n.p.; Interview with John Hurt, London, August 26, 2009.

8. Viertel, *Dangerous Friends,* pp. 200, 201, 204; Interview with Celeste Huston; Letter of October 31, 1972, Herrick.

9. Citation for Honorary Litt.D., Trinity College, Dublin, Herrick and my translation of the Latin; Letter from Huston to Chancellor F. H. Boland, July 11, 1970, Herrick.

10. Quoted in Grobel, *Hustons,* pp. 360, 485; Madsen, *John Huston,* p. 216; Interview with Eloise Hardt and Grobel, *Hustons,* pp. 384–385.

11. Quoted in Grobel, *Hustons,* pp. 526, 586–587 and Tony Huston, "Family Ties," *American Film,* 12 (September 1987), 16; Interview with Thom Steinbeck.

12. Quoted in Grobel, *Hustons,* p. 484; Madsen, *John Huston,* p. 192; Quoted in Grobel, *Hustons,* p. 481; Harris, *Anjelica Huston,* p. 94; Graham Fuller, Interview with Anjelica Huston, *Interview* (February 2000).

13. Interview with Eloise Hardt; Quoted in Grobel, *Hustons,* pp. 708, 670; Interview with Thom Steinbeck.

14. Quoted in Grobel, *Architectural Digest,* 205; Interview with Penelope Tree, London, October 27, 2009; Afdera Fonda, with Clifford Thurlow, *Never Before Noon: An Autobiography* (NY: Weidenfeld & Nicolson, 1987), pp. 23–24; John Milton, "On His Blindness," *Poetical Works,* ed. Helen Darbishire (London: Oxford University Press, 1958), p. 437.

Thirteen: Heart of Darkness

1. John McCarty, *The Complete Films of John Huston* (Secaucus, NJ: Citadel, 1987), p. 82; Charles Whiting, *Hero: The Life and Death of Audie Murphy* (Chelsea, Mich.: Scarborough House, 1990), p. 196; Dore Schary, *Heyday* (Boston: Little, Brown, 1979), p. 208.

2. Ross, *Picture,* p. 55; Huston, *Interviews,* pp. 27, 88; Alan Trachtenberg, *Reading American Photographs: Images as History, Mathew Brady to Walker Evans* (NY: Hill & Wang, 1980), pp. 78, 73; Mary Panzer, *Mathew Brady and the Image of History* (Washington, DC: Smithsonian Institution, 1997), pp. 108–109.

3. Ross, *Picture,* p. 92; Bergreen, *Agee,* p. 332; Todd DePastino, *Bill Mauldin: A Life Up Front* (NY: Norton, 2008), p. 245.

4. Huston, *Let There Be Light,* p. 212 and Murphy in Ross, *Picture,* p. 26; Christopher Isherwood, *Lost Years: A Memoir, 1945–1951,* ed. and intro. Katherine Bucknell (NY: HarperCollins, 2000), p. 268 (two quotations).

5. Huston, *Interviews,* p. xi; Ross, *Picture,* p. 190.

6. John Huston, foreword to *Agee on Film* (NY: Grosset & Dunlap, 1967), 2:ix; x; Isherwood, *Lost Years,* p. 270.

7. James Agee, *Letters to Father Flye* (London: Peter Owen, 1964), p. 183; Bergreen, *Agee,* p. 346; Ross, *Picture,* p. 125; Letter from Peter Viertel to Rudy Behlmer, August 13, 1976, courtesy of Rudy Behlmer.

8. Viertel, *Dangerous Friends,* pp. 127 (two quotes), 125; Natasha Fraser-Cavassoni, *Sam Spiegel* (NY: Simon & Schuster, 2003), p. 124.

9. Quoted in Grobel, *Hustons,* p. 308; Viertel, *White Hunter,* p. 53; Viertel, *Dangerous Friends,* p. 127; Joseph Losey, *Conversations with Losey,* ed. Michel Ciment (London: Methuen, 1985), p. 102.

10. Jeffrey Meyers, *Joseph Conrad: A Biography* (NY: Scribner's, 1991), p. 104; Katharine Hepburn, *The Making of "The African Queen"* (NY: Knopf, 1987), p. 23; John Huston, "*The African Queen*: Behind-the-Scenes Story," *Theatre Arts,* 36 (Fall 1952), 92; Ross, *Picture,* p. 185.

11. Huston, *Open Book,* p. 204; Jack Cardiff, *Magic Hour: The Life of a Cameraman* (London: Faber, 1996), p. 154; Viertel, *White Hunter,* pp. 282, 72, 65.

12. Ross, *Picture,* p. 181; Huston, *Open Book,* p. 198; *Agee on Film,* 2:200; 197. This volume, with Huston's foreword, misleadingly states that the script was written by Agee "with the assistance and cooperation of John Huston" (151). In fact, Huston was the main author and Agee, the novice, assisted him.

13. Huston, *Open Book,* p. 203; Hepburn, *Making of "African Queen,"* p. 59; Cardiff, *Magic Hour,* p. 153.

14. Letter from Viertel to Behlmer, August 13, 1976, courtesy of Rudy Behlmer (there is no marriage ceremony in the printed screenplay);

Letter from John Woolf to Behlmer, July 5, 1976, courtesy of Rudy Behlmer; Behlmer, *Behind the Scenes,* p. 251; Quoted in Grobel, *Hustons,* p. 377.

15. Letter from Huston to Morgan Maree, February 17, 1952, Herrick; Viertel, *Dangerous Friends,* p. 25; Interview with Michael Fitzgerald; Letter from Huston to Stephen Grimes, n.d. [1961], Herrick.

Fourteen: Paris and Italy

1. Walter Mirisch, *I Thought We Were Making Movies, Not History* (Madison: University of Wisconsin Press, 2008), p. 50; Letter from Huston [1952], Herrick; Letter from Huston to Katharine Hepburn, January 8, 1952, Herrick; Interview with Danny Huston.

2. Interview with Bayard Veiller; Letter from Joseph Breen to Huston, May 15, 1952, Herrick; Quoted in Grobel, *Hustons,* p. 389; Huston, *Interviews,* p. 9; Letter from Ossie Morris to Eliot Elisofon, May 14, 1953, Herrick.

3. Corry, "John Huston: Musing on *Fat City,*" p. 52; Thomas Quinn Curtiss, *Herald Tribune* (Paris edition), [1953], 7, Herrick; Johnson, *Letters,* p. 102; Huston, *Interviews,* p. 175.

4. Kirk Douglas, *The Ragman's Son: An Autobiography* (Boston: G.K. Hall, 1989), p. 224; Huston, *Interviews,* pp. 168, 166; Huston, *Open Book,* p. 372; Huston, "Suzanne Flon," *Paris Vogue,* décembre 1981– janvier 1982, 173 (my translation).

5. Patrick O'Higgins, *Madame: An Intimate Biography of Helena Rubinstein* (NY: Viking, 1971), p. 128; Interview with Thom Steinbeck; *Steinbeck: A Life in Letters,* ed. Elaine Steinbeck and Robert Wallsten (1975; NY: Penguin, 1976), p. 812.

6. Letter from Bogart to Huston, September 28, 1951, Herrick; Ross, *Picture,* p. 127; Huston, *Open Book,* p. 246; Joe Hyams, *Bogie: The Biography of Humphrey Bogart* (NY: Signet, 1966), p. 134.

7. Viertel, *Dangerous Friends,* p. 175; *Memo from Selznick,* p. 400; George Plimpton, "Truman Capote, Screenwriter: *Beat the Devil,*" *Paris Review,* 138 (Spring 1996), 126, 129.

8. Bacall, *By Myself,* p. 231; Truman Capote, *Too Brief a Treat: The Letters of Truman Capote,* ed. Gerald Clarke (NY: Random House,

2004), p. 213; Truman Capote, "John Huston," *Portraits and Observations* (NY: Random House, 2007), pp. 215–216.

9. Capote, in Youngkin, *Peter Lorre*, p. 368 and Clarke, *Capote*, p. 239; "Truman Capote," *Writers at Work: The "Paris Review" Interviews*, ed. Malcolm Cowley (1959; NY: Viking, 1964), p. 294.

10. Claud Cockburn, *Beat the Devil* (1953; London: Chatto & Windus, 1985), p. 255; Burnett, in McGilligan, ed., *Backstory*, p. 65; Letters from Huston to Morgan Maree, May 1 and June 10, 1953, Herrick; David Thomson, *Showman: The Life of David O. Selznick* (NY: Knopf, 1992), p. 588.

11. Viertel, *Dangerous Friends*, p. 176; Ted Sennett, *The Masters of Menace: Greenstreet and Lorre* (NY: Dutton, 1979), p. 177.

12. Huston, *Open Book*, p. 248 and Pratley, *Cinema of Huston*, p. 101; Ezra Goodman, *Bogey: The Good Bad Guy* (NY: Lyle Stuart, 1965), p. 111.

13. Quoted in Grobel, *Hustons*, p. 444; John Huston, "A Friend Pays His Tribute to a Unique and Beloved Man," *Photoplay*, April 1957, 24, 26.

FIFTEEN: WHITE WHALE

1. Quoted in Scott Hammen, *John Huston* (Boston: Twayne, 1985), p. 78; Viertel, *Dangerous Friends*, p. 206; Ray Bradbury, *Green Shadows, White Whale* (NY: Knopf, 1992), p. 205—a fictional account of working with Huston. Bradbury's title echoes Peter Viertel's *White Hunter, Black Heart* (1953).

2. Bergreen, *Agee*, p. 379; Letter from Ray Bradbury to Huston, January 20, 1953, Herrick; Thomas Atkins, "An Interview with Ray Bradbury," *The Classic American Novel and the Movies*, ed. Gerald Peary and Roger Schatzkin (NY: Ungar, 1977), p. 44.

Bradbury was still publicly making this claim at the Santa Barbara Writers' Conference in June 2004.

3. Interview with Celeste Huston; Bradbury, *Green Shadows*, pp. 23, 266, 206–207; Letter from Huston to Paul Kohner, August 24, 1955, Herrick.

4. Letter from John Kilbracken to Huston's assistant, April 13, 1954,

Herrick; John Raymond Kilbracken, *Living Like a Lord* (Boston: Houghton Mifflin, 1956), pp. 223, 216.

5. Huston, *Open Book,* p. 344; Letter from Harold Mirisch to Huston, May 17, 1954, Herrick; Huston, passage on Welles omitted from *Open Book,* typescript, chapter 20, pp. 10–11, Herrick; Letter from Huston to Peter Noble, December 20, 1955, Herrick.

6. Madsen, *John Huston,* p. 150; Letter from Huston to Robert Rossen, December 29, 1954, Herrick; Ivan Moffat, *The Moffat File,* ed. Gavin Lambert (NY: Pantheon, 2004), pp. 115, 23.

7. Letter from Jeanie Sims to Friedrich von Ledebur, [1954], Herrick; Letter from Ledebur to Huston, February 16, 1955, Herrick; Letter from Ledebur to *Newsweek,* March 19, 1956, 2.

8. Huston, *Interviews,* p. 15; Interview with Walter Mirisch, Los Angeles, May 18, 2009; Letter from Huston to Harold Mirisch, November 20, 1953, Herrick; Walter Mirisch, *I Thought We Were Making Movies,* p. 76.

9. Letter from Huston to Harold Mirisch, November 20, 1953, Herrick; Letter from Ossie Morris to art director Ralph Brinton, September 14, 1954, Herrick; Oswald Morris, with Geoffrey Bull, " 'How's My Boy?': John Huston," *Huston, We Have a Problem: A Kaleidoscope of Filmmaking Memories* (Lanham, Md.: Scarecrow, 2006), p. 87.

10. Letter from Gladys Hill to Lee Katz of Elstree Pictures, London, December 21, 1952, Herrick; Huston, in *Creativity with Bill Moyers*; Peck, in Tuska, ed., *Close Up,* p. 283; Huston, *Interviews,* p. 112.

11. Note from Gregory Peck to Huston, September 1954, Herrick; Huston, variant passage from *Open Book,* typescript, chapter 20, pp. 26–28, Herrick.

12. Persico, "Interview with Huston," p. 13; and Pratley, *Cinema of Huston,* p. 105; Letter from Walter Wanger to Huston, August 20, 1956, Herrick; Letter from Carl Sandburg to Huston, March 21, 1961, Herrick.

Sixteen: Tobago, Japan and Africa

1. Quoted in Grobel, *Hustons,* p. 440; David Jampel, Interview with Huston for unnamed English-language newspaper in Japan, May 1957, Herrick.

2. Letter from Huston to Buddy Adler, [1956], Herrick; Lee Server, *Robert Mitchum: "Baby, I don't care"* (NY: St. Martin's, 2001), p. 308; Quoted in Grobel, *Hustons,* p. 439.

3. Morris, *Huston,* p. 100; Nathaniel Peffer, *The Far East* (Ann Arbor: University of Michigan Press, 1958), pp. 94–95; Richard Storry, *A History of Modern Japan* (London: Penguin, 1960), pp. 92–93.

4. Jampel, Interview with Huston, Herrick; Nolan, *King Rebel,* p. 158; Tuska, ed., *Close Up,* p. 286.

5. Allen Rivkin, with Laura Kerr, eds., *Hello, Hollywood!* (NY: Doubleday, 1962), pp. 309, 308; Letter from So Yamamura to Twentieth Century-Fox, December 17, 1957, Herrick; Letter from Eugene Frenke to Huston, March 14, 1958, Herrick.

6. Telegram from Huston to Buddy Adler, March 30, 1958, Herrick; Letter from Buddy Adler to Huston, April 5, 1958, Herrick; Huston, *Interviews,* p. xi; Huston, *Open Book,* pp. 266–267.

7. See Bertrand Dicale, *"Les Racines du Ciel," Juliette Gréco: Les vies d'une chanteuse* (Paris: Lattes, 2001), pp. 354–371; Huston, *Open Book,* p. 276; *Letters of Evelyn Waugh and Diana Cooper,* ed. Artemis Cooper (NY: Ticknor & Fields, 1992), p. 248.

8. *In Tearing Haste: Letters Between Deborah Devonshire and Patrick Leigh Fermor,* ed. Charlotte Mosley (London: John Murray, 2008), p. 42 (two quotations); Letter from Patrick Leigh Fermor to Jeffrey Meyers, May 5, 2000; *In Tearing Haste,* p. 43; Letter from Fermor to Meyers, May 5, 2000 (two quotations).

9. Huston, in Mel Gussow, "Roots of Hell," *Don't Say Yes Until I Finish Talking: A Biography of Darryl F. Zanuck* (1971; NY: Pocket, 1972), p. 187; *In Tearing Haste,* pp. 43–44.

10. Huston, in Tony Thomas, *The Films of Errol Flynn* (NY: Citadel, 1969), p. 219; Interview with Oswald Morris, near Shaftesbury, England, June 20, 2000; Nolan, *King Rebel,* p. 172.

11. Huston, *Open Book,* p. 276; *In Tearing Haste,* p. 44 (two quotations); Leonard Mosley, *Zanuck: The Rise and Fall of Hollywood's Last Tycoon* (NY: McGraw-Hill, 1984), p. 311.

12. Errol Flynn, "Italian Diary," Rome, February 1953, courtesy of Rory Flynn; Errol Flynn, *My Wicked, Wicked Ways,* introduction

by Jeffrey Meyers (1959; NY: Cooper Square, 2003), p. 430; Huston, *Open Book,* p. 277.

13. *In Tearing Haste,* p. 44; Flynn, *My Wicked,* p. 5.

14. Viertel, *White Hunter,* p. 261; Huston, *Interviews,* p. 32; Johnson, *Letters,* p. 177.

Seventeen: Mustangs and Misfits

1. Huston, *Open Book,* p. 283; Gary Fishgall, *Against Type: The Biography of Burt Lancaster* (NY: Scribner, 1995), pp. 184–185; Arthur Miller, *Timebends* (NY: Grove, 1987), pp. 494–495; Dwight Macdonald, *On Movies* (Englewood Cliffs, NJ: Prentice-Hall, 1969), p. 313; Huston, *Open Book,* p. 284.

2. Letters from Guy Gallo to Jeffrey Meyers, August 30 and 31, 2009; Quoted in Grobel, *Hustons,* pp. 466–468, 471–472; Letters from Gallo to Meyers, August 30 and 31, 2009.

3. Arthur Miller and Serge Toubiana, *"The Misfits": Story of a Shoot* (London: Phaidon, 2000), p. 60 and Letter from Arthur Miller to Huston, July 14, 1958, Herrick; "Arthur Miller Chez John Huston en Irlande," p. 36 (no author or source), Herrick (my translation).

4. Arthur Miller, *The Misfits* (NY: Dell, 1961), pp. 64, 58; Hollis Alpert, "Arthur Miller: Screenwriter," *Saturday Review of Literature,* 44 (February 4, 1961), 47; Miller, *The Misfits,* pp. 133, 185. The word *shit* is left out of the film.

5. Goode, *Making "Misfits,"* pp. 206, 45; Huston, *Open Book,* p. 293; Miller and Toubiana, *Story of a Shoot,* pp. 26–27.

6. Miller, *Timebends,* p. 465; Eve Arnold, *Marilyn Monroe: An Appreciation* (NY: Knopf, 1987), p. 87; Huston, passage omitted from *Open Book,* typescript, chapter 23, p. 6, Herrick.

7. Goode, *Making "Misfits,"* p. 182; Interview with Curtice Taylor, Walnut Creek, Calif., August 2, 2009.

  In a macabre coincidence that took place one month after Huston's fatal car accident, Gable, while driving drunk on Sunset Boulevard in October 1933, had also killed a pedestrian.

8. Goode, *Making "Misfits,"* p. 241; Arnold, *Marilyn Monroe,* p. 92; Goode, *Making "Misfits,"* p. 151; Huston, *Interviews,* pp. 172, 118.

9. Goode, *Making "Misfits,"* p. 123; Alice McIntyre, "Making *The Misfits,* or Waiting for Monroe or Notes from Olympus," *Esquire,* 55 (March 1961), 79; Interview with Angela Allen.

10. Fred Lawrence Guiles, *Legend: The Life and Death of Marilyn Monroe* (Chelsea, Mich.: Scarborough House, 1991), p. 387; Huston, negative passage softened in *Open Book,* typescript, chapter 23, p. 5a, Herrick; and Stevens, ed., *Conversations with Moviemakers,* p. 351.

11. Huston, *Interviews,* p. 110 and Huston, *Open Book,* p. 288; Guus Luitjers, ed., *Marilyn Monroe: A Never-Ending Dream* (London: Plexus, 1986), p. 18.

12. Marjorie Meaker, "Marilyn and Norma Jeane," *Sudden Endings* (Garden City, NY: Doubleday, 1964), p. 42n; Huston, *Interviews,* pp. 109, 111.

13. Letter from Huston to Marietta Tree, January 9, 1977, Radcliffe; Pratley, *Cinema of Huston,* p. 137.

EIGHTEEN: MYSTERIES OF THE MIND

1. Huston, *Open Book,* p. 120; Huston, Interview in *Daily Express* (London), December 7, 1961; *Conversations with Paul Bowles,* ed. Gena Caproni (Jackson: University Press of Mississippi, 1993), pp. 99–100.

2. Paul Bowles, *Without Stopping: An Autobiography* (London: Peter Owen, 1972), p. 269; Huston, *Interviews,* p. 94; Brooks Atkinson, *Broadway,* revised edition (NY: Liveright, 1990), p. 414.

3. Huston, *Open Book,* p. 295; Annie Cohen-Solal, *Sartre: A Life,* trans. Anna Cancogni (NY: Pantheon, 1987), p. 387; Huston, *Interviews,* p. 148 and Huston, *Open Book,* p. 295; Pratley, *Cinema of Huston,* pp. 132–133.

4. Cohen-Solal, *Sartre,* p. 386; Quoted in Alexander Cockburn, introduction to *Beat the Devil,* n.p.; Quoted in Jean-Paul Sartre, *The Freud Scenario,* ed. J.-B. Pontalis, trans. Quentin Hoare (London: Verso, 1985), p. viii (two quotes); Cohen-Solal, *Sartre,* p. 386. The title of Sartre's *Lettres au Castor* was a trilingual pun: Beauvoir = beaver = *castor* in Latin.

5. Telegram from Jean-Paul Sartre to Huston, August 24, 1961, Herrick;

Letter from Sartre to Huston, August 26, 1961, Herrick; Telegram from Huston to Wolfgang Reinhardt, August 24, 1961, Herrick.

6. Kenneth Tynan, *Tynan Right and Left: Films, Plays, People, Places* (London: Longmans, 1967), pp. 308–309; Huston, *Open Book,* p. 298.

7. Anna Freud, in Judith Kass, *The Films of Montgomery Clift* (Secaucus, NJ: Citadel, 1979), p. 208; Letter from Marilyn Monroe to Huston, November 5, 1960, Herrick.

8. Robert LaGuardia, *Monty: A Biography of Montgomery Clift* (NY: Arbor House, 1977), p. 234; Patricia Bosworth, *Montgomery Clift: A Biography* (NY: Harcourt Brace Jovanovich, 1978), p. 326 (LaGuardia is quite hostile to Huston, Bosworth more sympathetic); Tuska, ed., *Close Up,* p. 290.

9. Bosworth, *Clift,* p. 324; LaGuardia, *Monty,* p. 235; Huston, *Interviews,* p. 97; Bosworth, *Clift,* p. 331.

10. Clift, in Nolan, *King Rebel,* p. 196; Reinhardt, in LaGuardia, *Monty,* p. 241; Bosworth, *Clift,* p. 329; Huston, *Open Book,* p. 302.

11. Huston, *Interviews,* pp. 118, 173; Bosworth, *Clift,* p. 331; Huston, *Open Book,* p. 302 and Huston, *Interviews,* p. 119.

12. LaGuardia, *Monty,* pp. 248, 250, 229, 257.

13. Interview with Susannah York, London, July 4, 2009; York, in LaGuardia, *Monty,* p. 240; Huston, *Open Book,* p. 301; Interview with Susannah York.

14. York, in LaGuardia, *Monty,* p. 244; Interview with Susannah York.

15. Huston, in *Creativity with Bill Moyers*; Michael Shortland, "Screen Memories: Toward a History of Psychiatry and Psychoanalysis in the Movies," *British Journal for the History of Science,* 20 (October 1987), 444; Eric Lax, *Conversations with Woody Allen* (NY: Knopf), p. 175.

16. York, in Leyda, ed., *Voices of Film Experience,* p. 517; Huston, *Open Book,* p. 303.

17. Slocombe, in Leyda, ed., *Voices of Film Experience,* p. 436; Roger Scruton, *On Beauty* (NY: Oxford University Press, 2009), p. 104.

18. Letter from Geoffrey Shurlock to Universal International, September 22, 1961, Herrick; John Simon, *Private Screenings* (NY: Macmillan, 1967), p. 46; *Newsweek,* December 24, 1962, 63; Richard Whitehall, *Films and Filming,* 10 (October 1963), 22–23.

NINETEEN: LOVERS

1. Quoted in Grobel, *Hustons*, pp. 450, 463, 466; William Hamilton, *The Love of Rich Women* (Boston: Houghton Mifflin, 1981), pp. 59, 11; Quoted in Grobel, *Hustons*, p. 480.

2. Allegra Huston, *Love Child: A Memoir of Family Lost and Found* (NY: Simon & Schuster, 2009), p. 84; Interview with Stacy Keach, Los Angeles, August 20, 2009; Interview with Celeste Huston; Interview with John Hurt, London, August 26, 2009.

3. Interview with Eloise Hardt; Interview with Walter Mirisch; Interview with Bayard Veiller; Huston, *Interviews*, pp. 76–77.

4. Letters from Anna van der Heide to Jeffrey Meyers, July and December 2009; Letter from Anna van der Heide to Huston, January 14, 1962, Herrick; Anna van der Heide Freeman, "John Huston: A Personal Reminiscence," *Reel News* (Waterville, Maine), November 1987, pp. 1–2, 4; Letters from Huston to Anna van der Heide, 1964–65 and 1987, courtesy of Anna van der Heide. Permission must be granted for any and all reproduction.

5. Letters from Zoe Sallis to Jeffrey Meyers, July 2009; Interview with Zoe Sallis, London, December 16, 2009; Quoted in Grobel, *Hustons*, p. 505; Interview with Eloise Hardt.

6. Interview with Danny Huston; Letters from Zoe Sallis to Jeffrey Meyers, July 2009; Interview with Zoe Sallis, April 29, 2009; Quoted in Grobel, *Hustons*, pp. 508, 550, 554.

7. Letter from Gladys Hill to Paul Kohner, August 14, 1966, Herrick; Letter from Mark Cohen to Gladys Hill, June 27, 1966, Herrick.

8. Interview with Curtice Taylor; Interviews with Zoe Sallis; Alberti, quoted in Grobel, *Hustons*, p. 559; Interview with Celeste Huston.

9. Interview with Leonard Gardner, Berkeley, California, June 30, 2009; Quoted in Grobel, *Hustons*, p. 558; Letter from Zoe Sallis to Jeffrey Meyers, July 2009; Quoted in Grobel, *Hustons*, p. 765.

TWENTY: IGUANA AND THE FLOOD

1. Letter from Gladys Hill to Ray Stark, October 30, 1963, Herrick; Server, *Ava Gardner*, p. 422; Quoted in Grobel, *Hustons*, p. 529;

Letters from Ray Stark to Huston, July 22 and August 28, 1963, Herrick.

2. Ava Gardner, *Ava: My Story* (NY: Bantam, 1990), p. 251; Jeffrey Meyers, *Robert Frost: A Biography* (Boston: Houghton Mifflin, 1996), p. 175; Telegram from Robert Graves to Huston, August 8, 1963, Herrick.

3. Interview with Hampton Fancher III, New York, May 20, 2009; "Huston's Gamble," documentary with *The Night of the Iguana* (DVD, 2006); Interview with Hampton Fancher.

4. Lord Byron, "The Prisoner of Chillon" (1816), *Poetical Works* (London: Oxford University Press, 1939), p. 330; Deborah Kerr, "The Days and Nights of the Iguana—A Journal by Deborah Kerr," *Esquire*, 61 (May 1964), 140; Letter from Huston to Anna van der Heide, 1963.

5. Letter from Gladys Hill to Jess Morgan, January 15, 1964, Herrick; Huston, *Open Book*, p. 320; Interview with Michael Parks.

6. Letter from Huston to Jonas Rosenfeld, July 27, 1966, Herrick; Interview with Michael Parks.

7. Server, *Ava Gardner*, p. 439; Letter from Ava Gardner to Gladys Hill, [1963], Herrick; Gardner, *Ava*, pp. 253, 255.

8. Huston, *Open Book*, p. 328; Rex Reed, "Ava Gardner," *Do You Sleep in the Nude?* (NY: New American Library, 1968), pp. 67, 68.

9. Pratley, *Cinema of Huston*, pp. 149–150, 122; Huston, *Open Book*, p. 319; Kaminsky, *John Huston*, p. 165.

10. Letter from Richard Burton to Dino De Laurentiis, May 8, 1966, Herrick; Server, *Ava Gardner*, p. 443; Huston, *Open Book*, p. 320.

11. Huston, *Interviews*, p. 76; Gene Phillips, S. J., *Homiletic and Pastoral Review*, [c. Summer 1967], p. 582; Rex Reed, *Big Screen, Little Screen* (NY: Macmillan, 1971), p. 370; Edmund Wilson, *The Sixties*, ed. Lewis Dabney (NY: Farrar, Straus & Giroux, 1994), p. 551.

12. Interview with Curtice Taylor; Quoted in Grobel, *Hustons*, p. 559; Interview with Eloise Hardt.

13. Huston, in Derek Prouse, "Maestro Huston," *Newsweek*, March 7, 1966, 89; Derek Prouse, "Huston at La Scala," *Sunday Times* (London), February 20, 1966, 30; Claudio Sartori, "Italy," *Opera*

News, 17 (May 1966), 391; Franco Abbiati, "*Le Miniere di Zolfo* di Bennett alla Scala," *Corriere della Sera*, febbraio 26, 1966, 13 (my translation).

14. Guardarino Guidi, "Milan," *Opera News*, 17 (May 1966), 25—26; Quoted in Grobel, *Hustons*, pp. 571–572.

TWENTY-ONE: LOVE AND DEATH

1. T. S. Eliot, *Complete Poems and Plays, 1909–1950* (NY: Harcourt, Brace, 1952), p. 95; Edmund Wilson, "Books That Leave You Blank," *New Yorker*, 22 (March 30, 1946), 80; Huston, "Encounter with Rui Nogueira and Bertrand Tavernier," in Studlar, ed., *Reflections in a Male Eye*, p. 236; David Robinson, "The Innocent Bystander," *Sight and Sound*, 42 (Winter 1972), 21.

2. Marlon Brando, with Robert Lindsay, *Songs My Mother Taught Me* (NY: Random House, 1994), p. 256; Quoted in Grobel, *Hustons*, p. 579.

3. Huston, *Open Book*, p. 332 and Huston, *Interviews*, p. 42; Kael, *5001 Nights at the Movies*, p. 622.

4. Wyler, quoted in letter from Ray Stark to Kenneth Hyman, August 9, 1967, Herrick; Letter from William Inge to Huston, October 18, 1967, Herrick; Letter from Huston to the executive Eliot Hyman of Seven Arts–Warner, September 15, 1967; Telegram from Eliot Hyman to Huston, September 20, 1967, Herrick.

5. Letters from Ray Stark to Huston, October 19 and October 16, 1967, Herrick; Vernon Young, *On Film* (NY: Quadrangle, 1972), pp. 13–14.

6. Letter from Carson McCullers to Huston, October 11, 1966, Herrick; Carson McCullers, *Illumination and Night Glare: The Unfinished Autobiography*, ed. Carlos Dews (Madison: University of Wisconsin Press, 1999), p. 66; Letter from McCullers to Huston, March 24, 1967, Herrick.

7. Huston, *Open Book*, p. 331 (two quotes); Letter from Dr. Martyn Dyar to Gladys Hill, May 24, 1967, Herrick; McCullers, *Illumination and Night Glare*, p. 48.

8. Interview with Seamus Byrne, Dublin, July 29, 2009; Interview with John Hurt.

9. Huston, *Interviews,* p. 102; Curtice Taylor and Glenn O'Brien, "Huston!" *Interview,* September 1972, 44; Mirisch, *I Thought We Were Making Movies,* p. 281.

10. Huston, *Open Book,* p. 337; Interview with Carter De Haven; Hans Koningsberger, "From Book to Film—via John Huston," *Film Quarterly,* 22 (Spring 1969), 2.

11. Interview with Curtice Taylor; Huston, *Interviews,* p. 19; Interview with Danny Huston; Interview with Penelope Tree.

12. Harris, *Anjelica Huston,* p. 116; John Simon, *Movies into Film: Film Criticism, 1967–1970* (NY: Dial, 1971), p. 361; Sofia Coppola, Interview with Anjelica Huston, *Interview,* October 1994, n.p.

13. *Lovefilm,* Interview with Anjelica Huston, n.d., n.p. (online); Anjelica Huston, in *John Huston,* typescript pp. 4, 6, courtesy of Tony Tracy; Christine Sutherland, "John Huston Remembers," *Ladies Home Journal,* 103 (April 1986), 172.

14. "Une américaine trouve la mort en auto près de Gray," (An American is killed in a car near Gray), *Le Bien Public* (Dijon), janvier 30, 1969, 5 (my translation); Interview with Carter De Haven.

   In May 1980 Anjelica had a serious car accident in Coldwater Canyon in Los Angeles when she collided with a drunk and speeding teenager. She was not wearing a seatbelt, crashed into the windshield and broke her nose in four places.

15. Interview with Celeste Huston; Allegra Huston, *Love Child,* p. 28; Quoted in Grobel, *Hustons,* p. 525.

16. Letters from Tony Huston to John Huston, October 9, 1973, and to Gladys Hill, December 3, 1973, courtesy of Celeste Huston; Interview with Danny Huston.

TWENTY-TWO: SPIES AND BOXING

1. Interview with Curtice Taylor; "Huston vs. the Russians," publicity release for *The Kremlin Letter,* 1970, Herrick; Huston, *Interviews,* p. 97.

2. Kenneth Tynan, *Diaries,* ed. John Lahr (London: Bloomsbury, 2001), p. 239; Madsen, *John Huston,* p. 242; David Thomson, *Rosebud: The Story of Orson Welles* (London: Little, Brown, 1996), p. 403; Joseph McBride, *What Ever Happened to Orson Welles?* (Lexington: University Press of Kentucky, 2006), p. 201.

3. Damien Love, "Inherit the Wind" [interviews with Joseph McBride and Peter Bogdanovich], *Bright Lights,* 55 (February 2007), 6 (online); Interview with Joseph McBride, Berkeley, Calif., November 28, 2009.

4. Quoted in Grobel, *Hustons,* p. 677; McBride, *What Ever Happened to Welles?,* p. 199.

5. Interviews with Leonard Gardner and Stacy Keach.

6. Interview with Leonard Gardner; Huston, *Open Book,* p. 338; Interview with Leonard Gardner.

7. Huston, *Treasure of Sierra Madre,* p. 97; Interviews with Stacy Keach and Leonard Gardner.

8. Huston, *Interviews,* p. 35; Quoted in Richard Jameson, "John Huston," *Perspectives on John Huston,* ed. Stephen Cooper (NY: G.K. Hall, 1984), pp. 83–84 (see Leonard Gardner, *Fat City,* 1969; NY: Vintage, 1986, p. 155); Interview with Stacy Keach.

9. Letter from Leonard Gardner to Ray Stark, August 4, 1971, Herrick; Letter from Ray Stark to Charles Champlin, entertainment editor of the *Los Angeles Times,* August 5, 1971; Quoted in Jameson, "John Huston," pp. 86–87; Hemingway, "A Clean, Well-Lighted Place" (1933), *Short Stories,* p. 382.

TWENTY-THREE: CELESTE SHANE AND A DESERT IDYLL

1. Huston, *Open Book,* p. 5; Quoted in Grobel, *Hustons,* pp. 241, 408; "Interview with Celeste Huston," p. 6, unpublished typescript, no author, no date, courtesy of Celeste Huston.

2. Meyers, Interview with Celeste Huston; Allegra Huston, *Love Child,* pp. 67, 106; "Cici: The Last Mrs. John Huston," p. 3, unpublished typescript, no author, no date, courtesy of Celeste Huston.

3. Meyers, Interview with Cici Huston; "Interview with Celeste Huston," p. 3; "Cici: Last Mrs. Huston," p. 3 (two quotes).

4. Quoted in Grobel, *Hustons*, p. 660; Interview with Zoe Sallis, London, May 20, 2009; Letter from Celeste Huston to Jeffrey Meyers, December 28, 2009.

5. "Cici: Last Mrs. Huston," p. 4; Morris, *Huston, We Have a Problem*, p. 126; Quoted in Grobel, *Hustons*, p. 642 (two quotes).

6. Interview with Pancho Kohner, Los Angeles, July 31, 2009; Pratley, *Cinema of Huston*, p. 179; Interview with Stacy Keach; Shawn Levy, *Paul Newman: A Life* (NY: Harmony, 2009), p. 268.

7. Interview with Stacy Keach; Quoted in Grobel, *Hustons*, p. 643 (two quotes); Interview with Jacqueline Bisset, Beverly Hills, July 26, 2009; Server, *Ava Gardner*, p. 467.

8. Meyers, Interview with Celeste Huston; Letter from Gladys Hill to Ed and Barbara Meran; "Cici: Last Mrs. Huston," pp. 9, 5.

9. Allegra Huston, *Love Child*, p. 113; "Cici: Last Mrs. Huston," p. 5 and Meyers, Interview with Celeste Huston; Letter from Celeste to Huston, n.d., all letters courtesy of Celeste Huston; "Interview with Celeste Huston," p. 13.

10. "Interview with Celeste Huston," p. 11; Letters from Celeste Huston to her parents from St. Clerans [Summer–Fall 1972]; Meyers, Interview with Celeste Huston.

11. Meyers, Interview with Celeste Huston; "Cici: Last Mrs. Huston," p. 18; Letter from Celeste Huston to her parents; Interview with Bill Gardner.

12. Quoted in Grobel, *Hustons*, p. 738; Interview with Michael Fitzgerald; Quoted in Grobel, *Hustons*, p. 357.

13. Interview with Robert Silvi; Goode, *Making "Misfits,"* p. 109; Letter from John Woolf to Huston, December 12, 1951, Herrick.

14. Letter from Huston to Morgan Maree, May 1, 1953, Herrick.
    In the early 1970s Huston (selling products, like Orson Welles) endorsed Aer Lingus, which mentioned him as the director of *Fat City*, and did an ad for Jim Beam bourbon with the frequently stoned Dennis Hopper.

15. Interview with Celeste Huston. Despite his extremely difficult childhood, Collin has had a successful adult life. He married, had a son and held a steady job.

16. In his letter to Gladys Hill, December 3, 1973, Tony Huston wrote that some of his father's property was being auctioned at Sotheby's in London that afternoon.

17. Letters from Huston to Celeste, November 3 and 10, 1972. The "tangle" may have been literal. Celeste said she had to have a hemorrhoid operation in "one of John's favorite places" (quoted in Grobel, *Hustons*, p. 668); Letter from Huston to Celeste, Malta, December 13, 1972.

18. Meyers, Interview with Celeste Huston; "Cici: Last Mrs. Huston," p. 11; Letter from Huston to Celeste, Morocco, November–December [1974?]; "Interview with Celeste Huston," p. 13; Interview with Allegra Huston, Berkeley, April 9, 2009.

19. Letters from Huston to Celeste, Morocco, November–December [1974?]; Letter from Huston to Celeste, Mexico City, no date; "Memoir by Celeste Huston," p. 4, no date, courtesy of Celeste Huston.

20. Quoted in Grobel, *Hustons*, pp. 691; 689; Meyers, Interview with Celeste Huston; Ron Arias, "Master moviemaker John Huston finds unwedded bliss as mentor to his caretaker, Maricela Hernandez," *People Weekly*, 25 (March 10, 1986), 45.

21. Meyers, Interview with Celeste Huston; Interview with Pancho Kohner; Meyers, Interview with Celeste Huston.

22. Burgess Meredith, *So Far, So Good: A Memoir* (Boston: Little, Brown, 1994), p. 242 and Harris, *Anjelica Huston*, p. 126; Huston, *Open Book*, p. 372; Elizabeth Bishop, "Florida," *Complete Poems, 1927–1979* (NY: Farrar, Straus & Giroux, 1983), p. 33.

Twenty-four: Morocco and Mexico

1. Persico, "Interview with Huston," p. 14 and Huston, *Open Book*, p. 368; Bogart, in *Newsweek*, January 9, 1956, 67.

   Huston not only acted for other directors, but also took mostly minor (and sometimes uncredited) roles in his own films. He played the man in the white suit in *Sierra Madre*, a bank clerk in *We Were Strangers*, the huntsman Lord Acton in *The List of Adrian Messenger*, Noah (a major role) in *The Bible*, McTarry in *Casino Royale*, Robert the Elder in *A Walk with Love and Death*, the Admiral in *The Kremlin Letter*, Grizzly Adams in *The Life and Times of Judge Roy*

Bean and Hazel's preacher-grandfather in *Wise Blood*. He narrated *The Battle of San Pietro* and *The Bible*, but his scene was cut from *The Red Badge of Courage*.

2. Otto Preminger, *Preminger: An Autobiography* (1977; NY: Bantam, 1978), pp. 194–195; Christopher Sandford, *Polanski: A Biography* (NY: Palgrave, 2008), p. 200. In real life, the woman Nicholson thought was his sister was in fact his mother.

3. Letters from Huston to Aeneas MacKenzie and to Paul Kohner, July 31, 1955, Herrick; Poem in letter from Huston to Lorrie Sherwood, January 29, 1960, Herrick; Ray, in Stevens, ed., *Conversations with Moviemakers*, p. 669; John Baxter, *Buñuel* (London: Fourth Estate, 1994), p. 249.

4. Jeffrey Meyers, *Orwell: Wintry Conscience of a Generation* (NY: Norton, 2000), pp. 185–186; Michael Caine, *What's It All About?* (NY: Turtle Bay, 1992), p. 375; Huston, *Open Book*, pp. 356–357.

5. Christopher Plummer, *In Spite of Myself: A Memoir* (NY: Knopf, 2008), pp. 556, 558–559; Letters from Huston to Tessa Dahl, and to Roald Dahl and Patricia Neal, February 6, 1975, Herrick; Letter from Gladys Hill to "Boaty" Boatwright, February 24, 1975, Herrick.

6. "The Man Who Would Be King," *Best Short Stories of Kipling*, ed. Jeffrey Meyers (NY: Signet, 1987), p. 113; Milton, *Paradise Lost, Poetical Works*, p. 24; Huston, *Open Book*, p. 360; *Nouvel Observateur*, avril 23, 1976, 34 (my translation); John Simon, *New York*, January 12, 1976, 58.

7. Interview with Danny Huston; Reinhardt, in Whiting, *Audie Murphy*, p. 200; *Merck Manual*, 18th ed. (Whitehouse Station, NJ, 2006), p. 400; Viertel, *White Hunter, Black Heart*, pp. 174, 239.

8. Quoted in Grobel, *Hustons*, p. 704; Huston, *Interviews*, p. 84; Letter from Huston to Charles Elliott, July 17, 1984, courtesy of Charles Elliott.

9. Huston, *Interviews*, p. 154; Interview with Janet Roach, Shelter Island, NY, September 8, 2009; Interview with Jan Lavender.

10. Letters from Huston to Charles Elliott, June 29 and September 14, 1983, courtesy of Charles Elliott; Interview with Michael Fitzgerald; Interview with Jacqueline Bisset.

11. Arias, *People Weekly*, 46; Allegra Huston, *Love Child*, p. 124; Interview with Danny Huston.

12. Quoted in Grobel, *Hustons*, p. 765; Interview with Celeste Huston; Letter from Zoe Sallis to Jeffrey Meyers, July 1, 2009, p. 3.

13. Interviews with Michael Fitzgerald; Guy Gallo; and Eloise Hardt.

14. Huston, in Arias, *People Weekly*, 46, 45; Quoted in Grobel, *Hustons*, p. 687; Interview with Jan Lavender.

TWENTY-FIVE: FAILURES

1. Interview with Michael Fitzgerald; Mark Ford, Review of Brad Gooch's *Flannery: A Life of Flannery O'Connor, London Review of Books*, July 23, 2009, 24; Pete Hamill, "Against All Odds," *American Film*, July–1984, 24.

2. Interview with Michael Fitzgerald; Flannery O'Connor, preface to *Wise Blood*, in *Three* (1952; NY: Signet, 1962), p. 8; Huston, *Interviews*, p. 138.

3. Julian Fox, *Films and Filming*, December 1979; Andrew Sarris, "Of Blood and Thunder and Despair," *Village Voice*, February 25, 1980.

4. Madsen, *John Huston*, p. 252; Huston, *Open Book*, p. 373; Interview with Charles Elliott, London, July 29, 2009.

5. Norman Mailer, *The Deer Park* (1955; NY: Signet, 1957), pp. 29, 35. See also: Peter Viertel, *White Hunter, Black Heart* (1953); Niven Busch, *The Actor* (1955); Charles Hamblett, *Crazy Kill* (1956); William Hamilton, *The Love of Rich Women* (1981); Nancy Holmes, *The Big Girl* (1982); David Thomson, *Suspects* (1985); Theodore Roszak, *Flicker* (1991); and Ray Bradbury, *Green Shadows, White Whale* (1992).

6. Interview with Celeste Huston; Huston, *Interviews*, p. 109; Letter from Huston to Charles Elliott, July 27, 1982, courtesy of Charles Elliott.

7. Interview with Tim Pigott-Smith, London, August 28, 2009; Letter from Tim Pigott-Smith to Jeffrey Meyers, September 1, 2009.

8. Interview with Roberto Silvi; Bert Mills, "Huston's *Victory*," *Houston Post*, August 2, 1981, 12AA; Interview with Tim Pigott-Smith.

9. Interview with Roberto Silvi; Orwell, "The Sporting Spirit" (1945), *Complete Works*, 17:442; Pelé, speech at the American Film Institute's *Salute to John Huston*, March 23, 1983; Pelé, *Memorias del Mejor*

Futbolista de Todos Los Tiempos (Memories of the Greatest Soccer Player of All Time), (Madrid: Temas de Hoy, 2007), pp. 251–252 (my translation).

10. Interview with Tim Piggott-Smith; Quoted in Grobel, *Hustons,* p. 720.

11. Mailer, *Deer Park,* p. 37; Kenneth Turan, "Hollywood Puts Its Money on *Annie*: Ray Stark & John Huston Comment," *New York Times Magazine,* May 2, 1982, 43; Quoted in Grobel, *Hustons,* p. 729.

12. Letter from Huston to Charles Elliott, July 27, 1982, courtesy of Charles Elliott; *Variety* review in *Halliwell's Film Guide,* 7th ed. (NY: Harper & Row, 1989), p. 43; Interview with Wieland Schulz-Keil, Berlin, July 6, 2009.

TWENTY-SIX: TRIUMPHS

1. Gordon Bowker, *Pursued by Furies: A Life of Malcolm Lowry* (1993; NY: St. Martin's, 1995), pp. 456, 116; Interview with Michael Fitzgerald; Interview with Wieland Schulz-Keil.

2. Guy Gallo, "Notes from *Under the Volcano,*" 1982–83, p. 4; Interview with Guy Gallo; Guy Gallo, "Gambling with Huston," 1982–83, p. 6, both memoirs courtesy of Guy Gallo. I am most grateful to him for allowing me to use this unpublished material.

3. Interview with Michael Fitzgerald; Gallo, "Notes from *Volcano,*" p. 12; Letter from Guy Gallo to Jeffrey Meyers, August 31, 2009.

4. Gallo, "Gambling with Huston," pp. 10–11; Gallo, Notes from *Volcano,*" p. 18; Interview with Michael Fitzgerald.

5. Interview with Guy Gallo; Todd McCarthy, "Cracking the Volcano," *Film Comment,* 20 (July–August 1984), 63; Interview with Wieland Schulz-Keil.

6. Interview with Guy Gallo.

7. Gallo, "Gambling with Huston," pp. 1, 14; Interview with Wieland Schulz-Keil; Interview with Guy Gallo; Gallo, "Notes from *Volcano,*" p. 5.

8. Gallo, "Notes from *Volcano,*" pp. 34, 30, 35; Interview with Michael Fitzgerald; Interview with Jacqueline Bisset.

9. Melvyn Bragg, *Rich: The Life of Richard Burton* (London: Hodder & Stoughton, 1988), p. 477; Shipman, *Movie Talk*, p. 108; Christopher Marlowe, *Dr. Faustus*, in *The Complete Plays*, ed. Mark Burnett (London: Everyman, 1999), pp. 389, 352; Wieland Schulz-Keil, "The 67th Reading: *Under the Volcano* and Its Screenplays," in *Apparently Incongruous Parts: The Worlds of Malcolm Lowry*, ed. Paul Tiessen and Gordon Bowker (Metuchen, NJ: Scarecrow, 1990), p. 130.

    The name Cuernavaca, Spanish for "cow horn," may also suggest Firmin's cuckoldry. His surname is ironic: a "firman" is an authoritative Ottoman decree, and he's anything but a "firm man."

10. Herbert Gold, "Huston Films a Cult Classic," *New York Times Magazine*, December 11, 1983, 68; Interview with Jacqueline Bisset; Gallo, "Gambling with Huston," p. 20.

11. Interviews with Jacqueline Bisset, Michael Fitzgerald, Guy Gallo, and Wieland Schulz-Keil; Gallo, "Gambling with Huston," pp. 8, 17; Interview with Guy Gallo.

12. Interviews with Michael Fitzgerald; Jacqueline Bisset; and Guy Gallo.

13. Interview with Danny Huston; Christian Viviani, pamphlet with Criterion films DVD of *Under the Volcano*, 2007; pp. 10–11; Gallo, "Notes from *Volcano*," pp. 23; 11; 13.

14. Interview with Janet Roach and Letter from Janet Roach to Jeffrey Meyers, September 9, 2009.

15. Quoted in Patrick McGilligan, *Jack's Life: A Biography of Jack Nicholson* (NY: Norton, 1994), pp. 336, 338; Tracy, Interview with Anjelica Huston, in *Essays on John Huston*, typescript, p. 9; McGilligan, *Jack's Life*, p. 336.

TWENTY-SEVEN: RAISING *THE DEAD*

1. Interview with Wieland Schulz-Keil; Huston, *Open Book*, p. 48; James Joyce, *Ulysses*, ed. Hans Gabler (NY: Vintage, 1986), p. 600.

2. Interview (about Tony) with Celeste Huston; Interview with Wieland Schulz-Keil; James Joyce, "The Dead," *Dubliners* (1914; London: Penguin, 1962), p. 176.

3. Letter from Huston to Charles Elliott, December 7, 1986, courtesy of Charles Elliott; Harris, *Anjelica Huston,* p. 181; Interview with Wieland Schulz-Keil.

4. Interviews with Zoe Sallis; Carter De Haven; Angela Allen; and Leonard Gardner.

5. Interview with Wieland Schulz-Keil; Interview with Danny Huston; W. B. Yeats, "Lapis Lazuli" (1938), *Collected Poems,* p. 292.

6. Interview with Seamus Byrne; *John Huston and the Dubliners on the Set of "The Dead"*; Tracy, Anjelica Huston, in *John Huston,* typescript, p. 11, courtesy of Tony Tracy; Interview with Roberto Silvi.

7. Quoted in Clive Hart, *Joyce, Huston, and the Making of "The Dead"* (Gerrards Cross, Bucks.: Colin Smythe, 1988), p. 38.

   For similar laments, see Isaiah 13:10 — "the sun shall be darkened in his going forth, and the moon shall not cause her light to shine" and W. H. Auden, "Funeral Song," *Collected Shorter Poems, 1927–1957* (NY: Random House, 1975), p. 92: "The stars are not wanted now: put out every one; / Pack up the moon and dismantle the sun."

8. *Huston and the Dubliners* documentary; Quoted in Don Gifford, *Notes for Joyce* (NY: Dutton, 1967), p. 78; Hart, *Joyce, Huston and "The Dead,"* p. 11.

9. Interviews with Roberto Silvi and Wieland Schulz-Keil; *Huston and the Dubliners* documentary; Quoted in Tony Huston, "Family Ties," p. 16; Huston, *Open Book,* p. 190.

10. Interviews with Wieland Schulz-Keil and Roberto Silvi.

11. Yeats, "A Prayer for My Daughter"(1919), *Collected Poems,* p. 187; Quoted in Kevin Barry, *The Dead* (Cork: Cork University Press, 2001), p. 70; *Huston and the Dubliners* documentary; Shakespeare, *Twelfth Night* (1601), *Complete Works,* p. 861.

   See the Joycean conclusion to J. F. Powers' great story, "Lions, Harts, Leaping Does," in *Prince of Darkness* (1947; NY: Vintage, 1979), p. 56: "The snowflakes whirled at the window, for a moment for all their bright blue beauty as though struck still by lightning . . . darkly falling."

Notes to pages 411–417

EPILOGUE

1. Arias, *People Weekly*, 45; Interview with Janet Roach; Interview with Danny Huston; Server, *Robert Mitchum*, p. 513.

2. Interview with Danny Huston; Anjelica Huston, in *John Huston*, typescript pp. 14, 15, courtesy of Tony Tracy.

3. Interview with Janet Roach; Harris, *Anjelica Huston*, p. 176. Several actors who appeared in his films—Peter Lorre, Edward G. Robinson and Louis Calhern—are also buried there.

4. Interview with Jan Lavender; Letter from Celeste Huston to Jeffrey Meyers, September 16, 2009; Letter from Tony Huston to Jeffrey Meyers, September 17, 2009; Quoted in Grobel, *Hustons*, p. 787.

5. Allen Cohen and Harry Lawton, *John Huston: A Guide to References and Resources* (NY: G.K. Hall, 1997), p. 661; Letter from Tony Huston to Jeffrey Meyers, May 15, 2009. When I questioned Grobel about this, he did not respond to my letter.

6. Interview with Danny Huston; Love, "Inherit the Wind," p. 13; Charles Baudelaire, "The Life and Work of Eugène Delacroix" (1863), *The Mirror of Art*, trans. and ed. Jonathan Mayne (Garden City, NY: Doubleday, 1956), p. 309; Josef von Sternberg, *Fun in a Chinese Laundry* (1965; San Francisco: Mercury House, 1988), p. 147.

7. Huston, *Open Book*, p. 336; Plummer, *In Spite of Myself*, p. 558; Letter from Huston to Polly Devlin, editor of British *Vogue*, October 12, 1964, Herrick.

8. McBride, *What Ever Happened to Welles?*, p. 87; Huston, *Open Book*, p. 373; Schlesinger, *Journals*, pp. 580–581.

9. Shakespeare, *Hamlet* (1601), *Complete Works*, p. 890; Yeats, "Under Ben Bulben" (1938), *Collected Poems*, p. 344.

Agee, James. "Undirectable Director" (1950). *Agee on Film.* Vol. 1. New York: Grosset & Dunlap, 1967. Pp. 320–331. See also pp. 163–164, 186, 193, 200, 236–237, 290–293, 312, 385, 398–401.

————. *"The African Queen"* (1952). *Agee on Film.* Vol. 2. New York: Grosset & Dunlap, 1967. Pp. 151–269.

Ambler, Eric. *Here Lies Eric Ambler: An Autobiography.* New York: Farrar, Straus & Giroux, 1986. Pp. 190–194, 199–211.

Barry, Kevin. *The Dead.* Cork: Cork University Press, 2001.

Behlmer, Rudy, ed. *Behind the Scenes.* 1989; Hollywood: French, 1990. Pp. 135–153, 234–252.

Bosworth, Patricia. *Montgomery Clift: A Biography.* New York: Harcourt Brace Jovanovich, 1978. Pp. 314–315, 318–321, 324–333, 360, 366.

Bradbury, Ray. *Green Shadows, White Whale.* New York: Knopf, 1992.

Brill, Lesley. *John Huston's Filmmaking.* New York: Cambridge University Press, 1997.

Caine, Michael. *What's It All About?* New York: Turtle Bay, 1992. Pp. 365–381, 423–428.

Cardiff, Jack. *Magic Hour: The Life of a Cameraman.* London: Faber, 1996. Pp. 147–162.

Cohen, Allen and Harry Lawton. *John Huston: A Guide to References and Resources.* New York: G.K. Hall, 1997.

Cohen-Solal, Annie. *Sartre: A Life.* Trans. Anna Cancogni. New York: Pantheon, 1987. Pp. 384–387.

Cooper, Stephen, ed. *Perspectives on John Huston.* New York: G.K. Hall, 1994.

Dicale, Bertrand. *"Les Racines du Ciel." Juliette Gréco: Les vies d'une chanteuse.* Paris: Lattes, 2001. Pp. 354–371.

Donoghue, Denis. *"The Dead." New York Review of Books,* 35 (March 3, 1988), 18–19.

Fermor, Patrick Leigh. *In Tearing Haste: Letters Between Deborah Devonshire and Patrick Leigh Fermor.* Ed. Charlotte Mosley. London: John Murray, 2008. Pp. 41–45, 56.

Fraser-Cavassoni, Natasha. *Sam Spiegel.* New York: Simon & Schuster, 2003. Pp. 121–135.

Ginna, Robert. "In Search of *The Treasure of the Sierra Madre,*" *American Scholar,* 71 (Autumn 2002), 75–89.

Goode, James. *The Making of "The Misfits."* 1963; New York: Limelight, 1986.

Grobel, Lawrence. *The Hustons.* New York: Scribner's, 1989.

Hammen, Scott. *John Huston.* Boston: Twayne, 1985.

Hart, Clive. *Joyce, Huston, and the Making of "The Dead."* Gerrards Cross: Colin Smythe, 1988.

Hepburn, Katharine. *The Making of "The African Queen."* New York: Knopf, 1987.

Huston, Allegra. *Love Child: A Memoir of Family Lost and Found.* New York: Simon & Schuster, 2009.

Huston, John. "*The African Queen*: Behind-the-Scenes Story," *Theatre Arts,* 36 (Fall 1952), 48–49, 92.

_____. "The Courage of Men: Interview" (1960) and *Let There Be Light* (screenplay, 1946). *Film: Book 2. Films of Peace and War.* Edited by Robert Hughes. New York: Grove, 1962. Pp. 22–35, 205–233.

_____. "Dialogue on Film." *American Film,* 9 (January–February 1984), 19, 22, 70–71.

_____. "Eugene O'Neill, Playwright," *Action,* 5 (May–June 1970), 32–34.

_____. "Figures of Fighting Men," *American Mercury,* 16 (March 1929), 347–351.

_____. "Focus on *Freud*: Huston Analyzes His Own Motivations in Making a Psychiatric Biography," *New York Times,* December 24, 1962.

_____. "Fool." *American Mercury,* 23 (May 1931), 113–115.

_____. Foreword to *Agee on Film*. Vol. 2. New York: Grosset & Dunlap, 1967. Pp. ix–x.

_____. *Frankie and Johnny*. New York: Boni, 1930.

_____. "A Friend Pays Tribute to a Unique and Beloved Man" [Bogart], *Photoplay*, April 1957, 24, 26.

_____. "Harpoons Away!: The Director of *Moby Dick* Finds the Great Tradition of New England Whalemen Still Alive Among the Courageous Men of Madeira." *Sports Illustrated*, June 6, 1955, 66, 69–70.

_____. *Interviews*. Edited by Robert Emmet Long. Jackson: University Press of Mississippi, 2001.

_____. "I See Him . . ." (1960). *Remembering James Agee*. Baton Rouge: Louisiana State University Press, 1974. Pp. 145–147.

_____. *The Maltese Falcon*. Edited by William Luhr. New Brunswick, NJ: Rutgers University Press, 1995.

_____. "*Moulin Rouge*: An Appreciation of Toulouse Lautrec," *Esquire*, 38 (December 1952), 103–107, 215.

_____. *An Open Book*. 1980; New York: Da Capo, 1994.

_____. "Picture Partners" (1941). *Hollywood Directors, 1941–1976*. Edited by Richard Koszarski. New York: Oxford University Press, 1977. Pp. 40–46.

_____. Preface to Charles Hamblett. *The Crazy Kill: A Fantasy*. London: Sidgwick & Jackson, 1956. Pp. 9–10.

_____. "Regarding Flaherty," *Sequence*, 14 (1952), 17–18.

_____. *The Treasure of the Sierra Madre* (1948). Edited by James Naremore. Madison: University of Wisconsin Press, 1979.

_____ and W. R. Burnett. *High Sierra* (1941). Edited by Douglas Gomery. Madison: University of Wisconsin Press, 1979.

_____ and Howard Koch. *"In Time to Come." Best Plays of 1941–1942*. Edited by Burns Mantle. New York: Dodd, Mead, 1942. Pp. 34–71.

_____, Aeneas MacKenzie and Wolfgang Reinhardt. *Juárez* (1939). Edited by Paul Vanderwood. Madison: University of Wisconsin Press, 1983.

_____ and Ben Maddow. *The Asphalt Jungle: A Screenplay* (1950). Afterword by W. R. Burnett. Carbondale: Southern Illinois University Press, 1980.

Huston, Tony. "Family Ties," *American Film*, 12 (September 1987), 16–19, 49.

Isherwood, Christopher. *Diaries. Volume One, 1939–1960*. Edited and introduced by Katherine Bucknell. New York: HarperCollins, 1996. Pp. 423, 425, 468&n, 585, 649, 693n.

_____. *Lost Years: A Memoir, 1945–1951*. Edited and introduced by Katherine Bucknell. New York: HarperCollins, 2000. pp. 126n, 154n, 229, 242, 268–271.

Kaminsky, Stuart. *John Huston: Maker of Magic*. Boston: Houghton Mifflin, 1978.

Keyes, Evelyn. *Scarlett O'Hara's Younger Sister*. Secaucus, NJ: Lyle Stuart, 1977.

Kilbracken, John Raymond. *Living Like a Lord*. Boston: Houghton Mifflin, 1956. Pp. 182–224.

Koch, Howard. *As Time Goes By: Memoirs of a Writer*. Introduction by John Houseman. New York: Harcourt Brace Jovanovich, 1979. Pp. 11–12, 15, 42, 47, 66–74, 86–88, 166–167.

LaGuardia, Robert. "*Freud.*" *Monty: A Biography of Montgomery Clift*. New York: Arbor House, 1977. Pp. 211–216, 229–260, 272.

Madsen, Axel. *John Huston: A Biography*. Garden City, NY: Doubleday, 1978.

McCarty, John. *The Complete Films of John Huston*. Secaucus, NJ: Citadel, 1987.

Meyers, Jeffrey. "John Huston and Hemingway," *Antioch Review*, 68 (Winter 2010), 54–66.

_____. "John Huston: Fine Arts and Films." *London Magazine*, October–November 2010, pp. 8–18.

_____. "The Making of John Huston's *Freud: The Secret Passion*," *Kenyon Review*, 33 (Winter 2011), 178–199.

_____. "Writing Film Biography: John Huston," *Antioch Review*, 69 (Winter 2011), 86–100.

Miller, Arthur. "*The Misfits*" (1960). *Film Scripts Three*. Edited by George Garrett, O. B. Hardison and Jane Gelfman. 1972; New York: Irvington, 1989. Pp. 202–382.

_____. *Timebends*. New York: Grove, 1987.

_____ and Serge Toubiana. *"The Misfits": Story of a Shoot.* London: Phaidon, 2000.

Morris, Oswald, with Geoffrey Bull. " 'How's My Boy?': John Huston." *Huston, We Have a Problem: A Kaleidoscope of Filmmaking Memories.* Lanham, Md.: Scarecrow Press, 2006. Pp. 65–130.

Nolan, William. *John Huston: King Rebel.* Los Angeles: Sherbourne, 1965.

Pearson, Billy, with Stephen Longstreet. "John Huston." *Never Look Back: The Autobiography of a Jockey.* Introduction by John Huston. New York: Simon & Schuster, 1958. Pp. ix-xi, 286–303.

Plimpton, George, "Truman Capote, Screenwriter: *Beat the Devil,*" *Paris Review,* 138 (Spring 1996), 125–131.

Pratley, Gerald. *The Cinema of John Huston.* Cranbury, NJ: Barnes, 1977.

Ross, Lillian. *Picture.* 1952; New York: Limelight, 1984.

Sartre, Jean-Paul. *The Freud Scenario.* Edited by J.-B. Pontalis. Translated by Quintin Hoare. London: Verso, 1985.

Schulz-Keil, Wieland. "The 67th Reading: *Under the Volcano* and Its Screenplays." *Apparently Incongruous Parts: The Worlds of Malcolm Lowry.* Edited by Paul Tiessen and Gordon Bowker. Metuchen, NJ: Scarecrow, 1960. Pp. 129–145.

Seebohm, Caroline. *No Regrets: The Life of Marietta Tree.* New York: Simon & Schuster, 1997.

Server, Lee. *Ava Gardner: "Love is Nothing."* New York: St. Martin's, 2006.

Stevens, George, Jr., ed. *Conversations with Great Moviemakers of Hollywood's Golden Age at the American Film Institute.* New York: Knopf, 2006. Pp. 335–362.

Studlar, Gaylyn and David Desser, eds. *Reflections in a Male Eye: John Huston and the American Experience.* Washington, DC: Smithsonian, 1993.

Viertel, Peter. *Dangerous Friends: At Large with Huston and Hemingway in the Fifties.* New York: Doubleday, 1992.

_____. *White Hunter, Black Heart.* London: Allen, 1954.

INDEX

Index compiled by Valerie Meyers

ABOUT THE AUTHOR

JEFFREY MEYERS, a fellow of the Royal Society of Literature, has recently been given an Award in Literature by the American Academy of Arts and Letters. Thirty of his books have been translated into fourteen languages and seven alphabets, and published on six continents. He lives in Berkeley, California.